The World's Military Aircraft

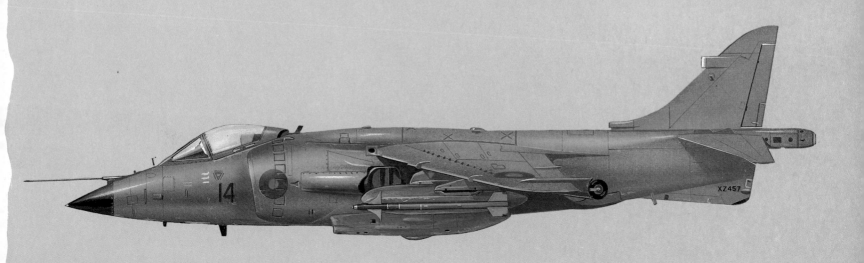

The World's Military Aircraft

Bill Gunston

CRESCENT BOOKS

New York

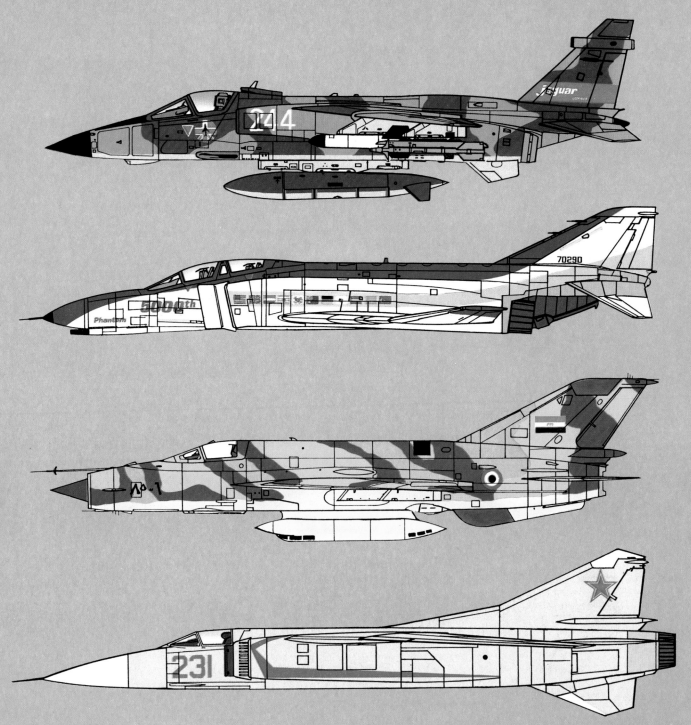

First published in 1983
By Octopus Books Limited,
59 Grosvenor Street,
London W1

© 1983 Octopus Books Limited

**First published 1983 in the United States of
America by Crescent Books, Distributed
by Crown Publishers, Inc. One Park
Avenue, New York, New York 10016.**

Printed in Hong Kong

Library of Congress Catalog Card No:
82-74417

ISBN 0-517-40477X

Front endpapers Left: Rockwell
International B-1, Grumman F-14A Tomcat,
SEPECAT Jaguar GR.1. Right: Lockheed
S-3A Viking, McDonnell Douglas F/A-18A
Hornet, McDonnell Douglas F-4J Phantom
II. **Page 1** British Aerospace Sea Harrier
FRS.1. **Page 2** Lockheed SR-71A. **Page 3**
McDonnell Douglas F/A-18A Hornet.
Page 4 SEPECAT Jaguar International,
McDonnell Douglas F-4E Phantom II,
Mikoyan/Guryevich MiG-21RF,
Mikoyan/Guryevich MiG-23 prototype.
Page 5 Lockheed S-3A Viking.

Rear endpapers Left: Mikoyan/Guryevich
MiG-25, Yakovlev Yak-28P, Yakovlev
Yak-36MP. Right: Mikoyan/Guryevich
MiG-21bis, Sukhoi Su-15, Tupolev Tu-22M.

Five-view illustrations Terry Hadler, Mike
Trim, James Goulding, Tudor Art Studios
Ltd: Janos Marffy and Greg Jones, Mike
Roffe, Peter Endsleigh Castle and Derek
Bunce. **Profile illustrations** Stephen
Seymour, Frank Kennard, Janos Marffy
and Tudor Art Studios Ltd: Greg Jones.

Contents

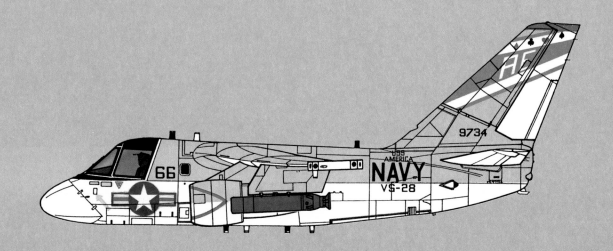

Introduction

Since aircraft have to obey all the world's natural laws, and since certain aerodynamic, structural or engine installational shapes are more efficient than all the others, one might be forgiven for thinking at first that all aircraft would come out looking alike. At the very least, one might suppose that all aircraft designed for the same task would be of similar appearance.

But a glance through this book makes it evident that this is no more true today than it has ever been. To some degree this is because the onward march of technological discovery has opened up fresh options. One obvious example is the speed at which aircraft fly. In 1918 the designer of a high-flying reconnaissance aircraft would hope to achieve a speed of 200km/h (124mph), and would be delighted to manage 225km/h (140mph), but he would have almost no chance of exceeding this upper limit. In 1942 he might set his sights on 600km/h (373mph) and recognize the futility of aiming to exceed 700km/h (435mph). But in this book there appear two Lockheed reconnaissance aircraft whose startlingly different shapes stem from the fact that one flies at 800km/h (500mph), while the other can achieve

a speed of 3500km/h (2,200mph).

Back in the 1950s it was taken for granted that speeds of around 3500km/h would soon become common for almost all fighters and bombers. As far back as January 1951 the Republic Aviation Corporation was designing a very large turbo-ramjet propelled interceptor, the XF-103, that was to fly at Mach 3·7, or 3950km/h (2,450mph). The B-58, a Mach-2 bomber, was succeeded by the B-70 flying at Mach 3 which in turn was planned to give way to a later bomber, for the 1970s, able to cruise at Mach 4 (4250km/h, 2,650mph). How surprised the planners of the 1950s would be to find us in the 1980s making our combat aircraft fly slower and slower!

In the West we have just one new strategic bomber, the B-1B. The original B-1 was thought retrograde because it could hardly exceed Mach 2. To develop it into the B-1B one of the main aims was to make it unable to exceed about Mach 1·6. The latest fighter in the West is the McDonnell Douglas F/A-18A Hornet, which without external bombs or tanks, and at full throttle at the best altitude, can just about work up to Mach 1·8. As for tactical attack aircraft, Vought took the F-8, a Mach-2 fighter of the

1950s, and turned it into the A-7 attack machine of the 1970s that cannot reach Mach 1. In its turn the A-7 has given way in several US Air Force Tactical Fighter Wings to the A-10A Thunderbolt II which would be hard-pressed to catch a World War 2 Mustang or Spitfire!

Why do designers care so little about maximum speed? To a considerable degree the answer is that speed no longer offers much protection against being shot down. The one situation in which it could be important is when the only defending weapons are those carried by the enemy interceptors, which—unless they had long warning time—might be unable to get close enough to a very fast intruder to get within their own effective firing range. Where the intruder enters hostile airspace above defending ships or land forces, speed offers no protection at all. The faster an aircraft flies, the less is its power of manoeuvre and the greater must be its height above the ground, especially when the terrain is hilly. It does not need much thought to see that, with an instantly reacting SAM (surface-to-air missile) system, it is easy to shoot down an intruder flying at twice the speed of sound at a height a little above

A Chinese Nanzhang Q-5 shown in a camouflage scheme first seen during the war with Vietnam in 1979. This attack aircraft, derived from the Chinese-built MiG-19PF, has an internal bomb bay and is shown carrying drop tanks.

the level of the hilltops, but rather difficult to get one flying at 1000km/h (620mph) 15m (50ft) above the ground.

In general, and Falklands experience notwithstanding, any aircraft of any type that comes near modern army or navy SAM systems is as good as dead. Only in exceptional circumstances can such systems be overwhelmed by numbers. But there is one area which sprang to the forefront with the operations of RAF Bomber Command as early as January 1942, rapidly came to dominate the technology and techniques of that command in World War 2, was then largely forgotten again (but not by the Russians, who forget nothing), and then in the 1960s and 1970s increasingly became once more recognized as the dominant factor in modern warfare on land, sea and in the air. It is gathered together under the title of EW, for electronic warfare.

EW embraces a host of techniques, such as Elint (electronic intelligence, finding out about the enemy's emitters of radio signals), ECM (electronic countermeasures, trying to interfere with the enemy's signals) and even the basic design of aircraft to make them as invisible as possible to enemy radars.

Everyone knows that aircraft can be built with what is called a large radar cross-section, or signature, which means that they show up boldly on enemy radar displays and can be seen from 300km (186 miles) away. A B-52, for example, not only shows up like a barn door but can even be positively identified for what it is, unless it leaves half its bombs behind and instead loads up with literally tons of what are called offensive and defensive avionics to try and mask, bluff, confuse or smother the enemy radar networks. But it is also possible to make aircraft whose signature is very small indeed.

It is rather like the process of streamlining. In 1926 the Fleet Air Arm's Blackburn Trainer had the same drag (wind resistance) as a perfect cylinder of 60cm (24in) diameter extending from wingtip to wingtip. In 1955 the DC-7C piston-engined airliner had the same drag as a cylinder of only 2·5cm (1in) diameter, while the most streamlined modern sailplanes get the figure down to below 1cm (0·4in). In the same way the radar signature of modern bombers is being whittled down by factors of ten or even 100. It takes a trained eye to see how the subtle blends of shapes, the

acutely inclined skin surfaces and the absence of any kind of pocket or so-called corner reflector (of the kind used in the small reflectors we fix on gateposts or bicycle mudguards) combine to leave a shape that reflects hardly any radar energy back in the direction whence it came. When RAM (radar-absorbent materials) are also brought into play, the result is almost a bomber that isn't there. It then becomes an easier task for its own cunning avionic systems to pretend it is somewhere else, or to decoy or divert any missile fired at it.

Finally, all technically advanced countries are to some degree crippled in their defence spending by inflation. Whereas in the past each new generation of aircraft meant higher speed, more weapons or some other new capability, today the emphasis is strongly on long life, high reliability and what has become known as the lowest 'total cost of ownership'; this is a generalized figure for amortized first cost, the price of fuel and spare parts over a period, the labour costs and even costs of training. Mach number is taking a poor second place behind money; but this does not mean that we will go back to the Sopwith Camel.

A Northrop F-5E Tiger II serving with the 64th Fighter Interception Squadron at Nellis AFB, outside Las Vegas, Nevada. These F-5Es simulate Warsaw Pact forces in exercises and are painted in a scheme loosely resembling their aircraft.

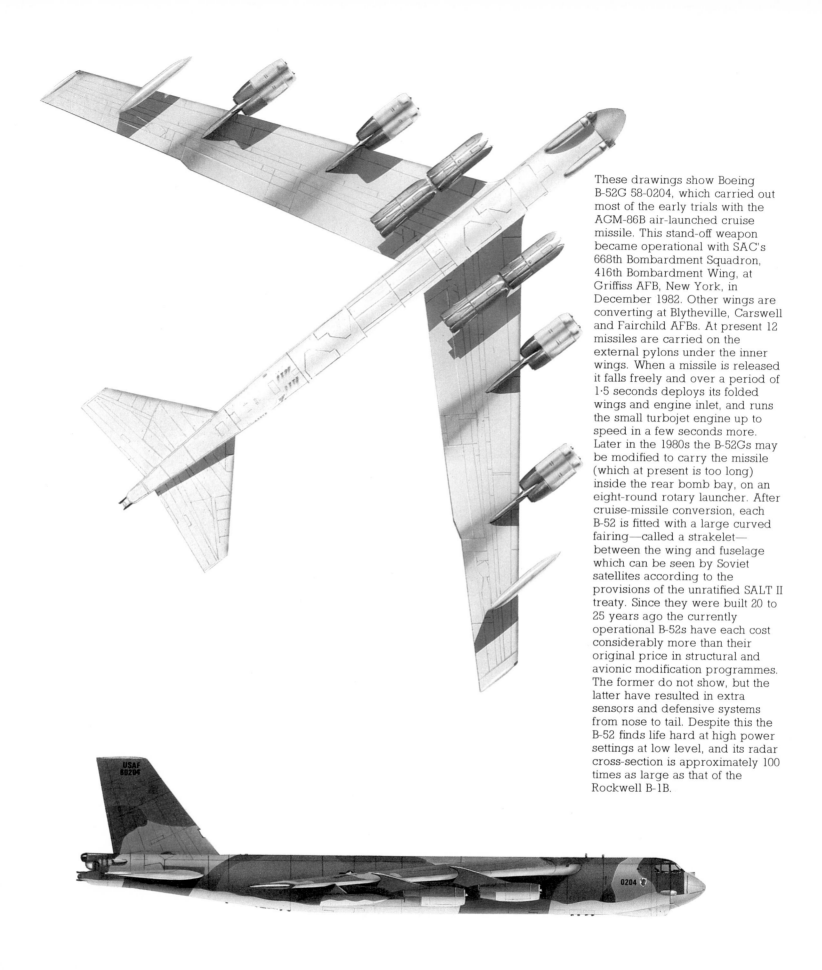

These drawings show Boeing B-52G 58-0204, which carried out most of the early trials with the AGM-86B air-launched cruise missile. This stand-off weapon became operational with SAC's 668th Bombardment Squadron, 416th Bombardment Wing, at Griffiss AFB, New York, in December 1982. Other wings are converting at Blytheville, Carswell and Fairchild AFBs. At present 12 missiles are carried on the external pylons under the inner wings. When a missile is released it falls freely and over a period of 1·5 seconds deploys its folded wings and engine inlet, and runs the small turbojet engine up to speed in a few seconds more. Later in the 1980s the B-52Gs may be modified to carry the missile (which at present is too long) inside the rear bomb bay, on an eight-round rotary launcher. After cruise-missile conversion, each B-52 is fitted with a large curved fairing—called a strakelet—between the wing and fuselage which can be seen by Soviet satellites according to the provisions of the unratified SALT II treaty. Since they were built 20 to 25 years ago the currently operational B-52s have each cost considerably more than their original price in structural and avionic modification programmes. The former do not show, but the latter have resulted in extra sensors and defensive systems from nose to tail. Despite this the B-52 finds life hard at high power settings at low level, and its radar cross-section is approximately 100 times as large as that of the Rockwell B-1B.

Boeing B-52G
Stratofortress

0 4m

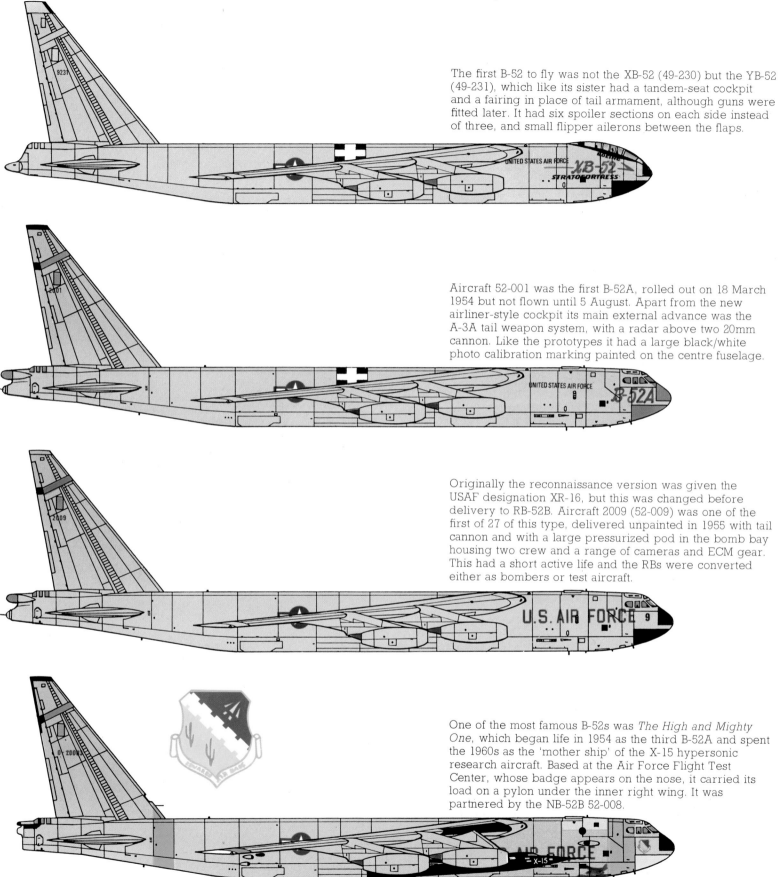

The first B-52 to fly was not the XB-52 (49-230) but the YB-52 (49-231), which like its sister had a tandem-seat cockpit and a fairing in place of tail armament, although guns were fitted later. It had six spoiler sections on each side instead of three, and small flipper ailerons between the flaps.

Aircraft 52-001 was the first B-52A, rolled out on 18 March 1954 but not flown until 5 August. Apart from the new airliner-style cockpit its main external advance was the A-3A tail weapon system, with a radar above two 20mm cannon. Like the prototypes it had a large black/white photo calibration marking painted on the centre fuselage.

Originally the reconnaissance version was given the USAF designation XR-16, but this was changed before delivery to RB-52B. Aircraft 2009 (52-009) was one of the first of 27 of this type, delivered unpainted in 1955 with tail cannon and with a large pressurized pod in the bomb bay housing two crew and a range of cameras and ECM gear. This had a short active life and the RBs were converted either as bombers or test aircraft.

One of the most famous B-52s was *The High and Mighty One*, which began life in 1954 as the third B-52A and spent the 1960s as the 'mother ship' of the X-15 hypersonic research aircraft. Based at the Air Force Flight Test Center, whose badge appears on the nose, it carried its load on a pylon under the inner right wing. It was partnered by the NB-52B 52-008.

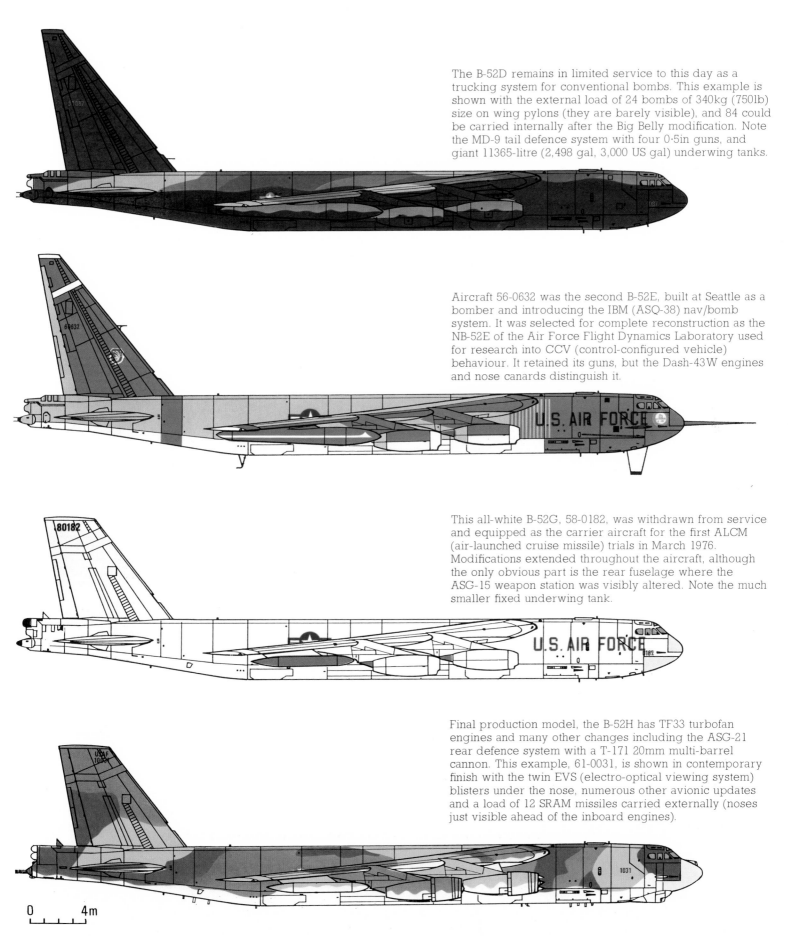

The B-52D remains in limited service to this day as a trucking system for conventional bombs. This example is shown with the external load of 24 bombs of 340kg (750lb) size on wing pylons (they are barely visible), and 84 could be carried internally after the Big Belly modification. Note the MD-9 tail defence system with four 0·5in guns, and giant 11365-litre (2,498 gal, 3,000 US gal) underwing tanks.

Aircraft 56-0632 was the second B-52E, built at Seattle as a bomber and introducing the IBM (ASQ-38) nav/bomb system. It was selected for complete reconstruction as the NB-52E of the Air Force Flight Dynamics Laboratory used for research into CCV (control-configured vehicle) behaviour. It retained its guns, but the Dash-43W engines and nose canards distinguish it.

This all-white B-52G, 58-0182, was withdrawn from service and equipped as the carrier aircraft for the first ALCM (air-launched cruise missile) trials in March 1976. Modifications extended throughout the aircraft, although the only obvious part is the rear fuselage where the ASG-15 weapon station was visibly altered. Note the much smaller fixed underwing tank.

Final production model, the B-52H has TF33 turbofan engines and many other changes including the ASG-21 rear defence system with a T-171 20mm multi-barrel cannon. This example, 61-0031, is shown in contemporary finish with the twin EVS (electro-optical viewing system) blisters under the nose, numerous other avionic updates and a load of 12 SRAM missiles carried externally (noses just visible ahead of the inboard engines).

0   4m

Boeing B-52 Stratofortress

Perhaps the greatest military aircraft in history, this intercontinental bomber began life in June 1946 as a turboprop. In October 1948 a team of Boeing design engineers worked non-stop from Friday to Monday in a hotel bedroom in Ohio turning the proposal into a jet, with four twin-engine pods hung on a swept wing, and eventually the YB-52 made its maiden flight on 15 April 1952.

After the cockpit had been changed to seat the pilots side by side the first B-52A flew on 5 August 1954, and the further-developed B-52B entered service with US Air Force Strategic Air Command's 93rd Bomb Wing at Castle Air Force Base on 29 June 1955. It had a crew of six, the rear gunner riding in the tail to oversee the twin radar-aimed 20mm cannon (soon changed for four 0·5in machine guns). Any pattern of nuclear bomb could be carried, or 27 HE bombs of nominal 454kg (1,000lb) size, and flexible cells in the wing housed 35,000 US gal (29,143 gal, 132487 litres) of fuel, plus 2,000 in underwing external tanks. The landing gear comprised four twin-wheel trucks folding into the front and rear fuselage (these could be steered to facilitate cross-wind landings), with small tip-protection gears to keep the wingtips off the ground. An unusual engineering feature was that hydraulic and electric power was generated in different parts of the aircraft by turbines spun at 100,000rpm by 'red-hot' air bled from the main engines.

Following 50 B-52Bs the Seattle plant delivered 35 B-52Cs with giant 3,000 US gal external tanks. The B-52D was made by Boeing's Wichita factory as well, to speed delivery of the 170 of this very similar type. The two plants then made 100 of the E model which had a new nav/bomb electronic system, and 89 of the F in which the auxiliary power was generated in the normal way by shaft drives from the engines. An almost complete redesign resulted in the B-52G, whose new airframe incorporated a shorter fin and an integral-tank 'wet wing' housing 46,575 US gal in the same space as in earlier models (so the external tanks shrank to only 700 US gal).

The gunner was moved up front with the rest of the crew, the whole compartment being rationalized; the avionics were again rethought; the flight-control system was redesigned with powered tail surfaces and with spoilers alone for roll control; and large pylons were added under the inner wing to carry first Hound Dog cruise missiles and later the SRAM (short-range attack missile) or ALCM (air-launched cruise missile). The two last-named missiles can also be dispensed from an eight-round rotary drum in the bomb bay. No fewer than 193 Gs were built, all at Wichita. Unexpectedly, a further 102 of a still later model were then delivered, with the more powerful and much more efficient TF33 fan engine, and with a very large increase in electric power and a 20mm multi-barrel cannon in the tail. Thus, the total programme numbered 744, including two prototypes and three B-52As.

In the Vietnam war the B-52D and F were modified for the unplanned task of very long (10-hour) missions with ordinary HE bombs, the D being rebuilt to haul not only 24 extra bombs on long rails on inner-wing pylons but also 84 bombs internally! This was on top of prolonged and costly structural rework caused both by intensive flying for many times the originally planned service life, and a switch to missions in the thick turbulent air at low level in an effort to escape detection by hostile radars.

In 1982 the faithful D-models were at last withdrawn (the B, C, E and F having gone earlier), leaving a SAC force of some 240 B-52Gs and Hs to soldier on until at least 1989. For a start just the G is being equipped to carry the ALCM, on the external pylons only, but all the B-52s have received many costly updates in avionics which culminate in the OAS (offensive avionics system) costing $1·662 billion. No aircraft in history have been designed under greater pressure, or built with greater urgency; and certainly no aircraft have ever been so extensively modified, refurbished and re-equipped over so long a period in order to keep them in the front line for 35 years.

COUNTRY OF ORIGIN USA.

CREW 6.

TOTAL PRODUCED 744.

DIMENSIONS Wingspan 56·39m (185ft 0in); length, **D**: 47·72m (156ft 7in), **G, H**: 49·04m (160ft 11in); wing area 371·6m² (4,000ft²)

WEIGHTS Empty (typical) 87090kg (192,000lb); maximum loaded, **G**: 221350kg (488,000lb), **H**: 229060kg (505,000lb), **H** after inflight refuel: 256730kg (566,000lb).

ENGINES **D**: eight 5443kg (12,000lb) Pratt & Whitney J57-19W or -29W turbojets; **G**: eight 6237kg (13,750lb) J57-43W or -43WB; **H**: eight 7711kg (17,000lb) Pratt & Whitney TF33-1 or -3 turbofans.

MAXIMUM SPEED **D**: 982km/h (610mph), **G**: 1019km/h (633mph), **H**: 1009km/h (627mph).

SERVICE CEILING **D**: 13·7km (45,000ft), **G**: 14km (46,000ft), **H**: 14·3km (47,000ft).

RANGE **D**: 11861km (7,370 miles), **G**: 13528km (8,406 miles), **H**: 16303km (10,130 miles).

MILITARY LOAD **D**: 108 HE or 4 nuclear bombs, four 0·5in guns; **G**: 27 HE or 8 nuclear bombs or 20 SRAM or ALCM missiles, four 0·5in guns; **H**: as G but one 20mm cannon.

USER USA (AF).

Boeing KC-135

Seldom in the news, the Boeing KC-135 family is a colossal force of large aircraft built with amazing speed for a unit price less than one-twentieth as great as that of modern fighters such as the Mirage 2000 and F-18. No other group of aircraft in history has been modified into so many different versions.

In the post-1945 era Britain was building the Comet jetliner, but US companies were reluctant to offer competition. Boeing gave long thought to the problem, but the airlines were cautious. A possible way to launch a programme was to sell a jet tanker to the USAF, whose new jet bombers had to descend to uneconomic low altitudes and speeds to take on fuel from the piston-engined KC-97 tankers. In 1952 Boeing risked more than the company was worth in building a prototype, the Model 367-80, from which could be developed both a military tanker/transport and a civil jetliner. The 'Dash-80' flew on 15 July 1954. From it was derived the KC-135 tanker and also, by fitting a longer fuselage of increased diameter, the famous 707 civil transport.

A key to the KC-135 was the same J57 engine as used in the B-52 bomber, but they were installed in four single (instead of double) pods. Although quite primitive by modern standards the KC-135 was able, with a great deal of noise and smoke and using a long runway, to lift prodigious amounts of fuel or other payload and fly as fast and as high as other jet transports or bombers. Its capabilities transformed Strategic Air Command, and it was built in such great numbers that, even though it was soon being used to refuel fighter and attack aircraft as well as SAC's large bombers, many KC-135s became available for conversion.

The basic KC-135A carries 118100 litres (25,979 gal, 31,200 US gal) of fuel in tanks extending from tip to tip in the wing, along the lower portion of the fuselage and in a tank above the floor at the tail. Almost all fuel can be transferred via a Boeing pivoted Flying Boom under the rear fuselage, which can be lowered obliquely down and 'flown' by powered control surfaces by a boom operator lying in the rear fuselage. Receiver aircraft open a receptacle for the boom and formate on the tanker guided by rows of lights under the latter's forward fuselage. The boom operator then fires the telescopic fuel pipe into the receptacle, which seals when the boom is withdrawn.

The first KC-135A flew on 31 August 1956, and altogether 732 were delivered. A further 88 were built to the same basic design: 12 C-135Fs for the French Armée de l'Air, 17 KC-135Bs with TF33 fan engines, 15 C-135A Stratolifter transports, 30 C-135B transports with fan engines, and the first 14 RC-135 photomapping aircraft. At a price of $2 million each this vast force was value for money; today many times that sum per aircraft is being spent in extending the structure life and, in the case of 100 and possibly 300 of the basic tankers, fitting wingtip winglets and completely new CFM56 fan engines to keep them effective to at least 2010.

Meanwhile numerous rebuilds have resulted in sub-types that have used up almost the entire alphabet in suffix letters as far as W! This is because the basic C-135 is so capable, adaptable and reliable; but some of the variants carry so much electronic and other new equipment that they are among the strangest aircraft in the sky. The original KC-135A gave rise to 19 new models, while others were rebuilt C-135 transports or RC-135s, some having the original J57 turbojets and others the TF33 turbofans. The most numerous sub-family is the EC-135; most of these are airborne command posts although some are radio relay platforms and the EC-135N series are spacecraft trackers. The RC-135 special reconnaissance models are largely secret, but about ten variants serve SAC all over the world with SLAR (side-looking airborne radar) in large cheek panels and many other installations. The NKC-135s include versions for laser research, satellite communications and ECM (electronic countermeasures). WC-135s are weather reconnaissance aircraft, and VC-135s are VIP government transports.

COUNTRY OF ORIGIN USA.

CREW Basic KC-135 or VC-135 flight crew 4; special versions up to 22.

TOTAL PRODUCED 820 including 732 KC-135A (since rebuilt into other versions).

DIMENSIONS Wingspan 39·88m (130ft 10in); length (original nose to tips of tailplane) 40·99m (134ft 6in); wing area 226·03m² (2,433ft²).

WEIGHTS Empty (original KC-135A) 48220kg (106,306lb); maximum loaded 143338kg (316,000lb).

ENGINES (As built) four 6237kg (13,750lb) Pratt & Whitney J57–59W turbojets; (suffix B and derived versions) four 8165kg (18,000lb) Pratt & Whitney TF33–5 turbofans; (suffix RE) four 9979kg (22,000lb) CFM56-1B1 turbofans.

MAXIMUM SPEED Typically 958km/h (595mph); cruising speed 856km/h (532mph).

SERVICE CEILING Typically 11·28km (37,000ft).

RANGE Up to 14800km (9,200 miles); can transfer 54432kg (120,000lb) of fuel at radius of 1609km (1,000 miles).

MILITARY LOAD Fuel, troops, cargo and special equipment of many kinds.

USERS France, USA (AF, Navy).

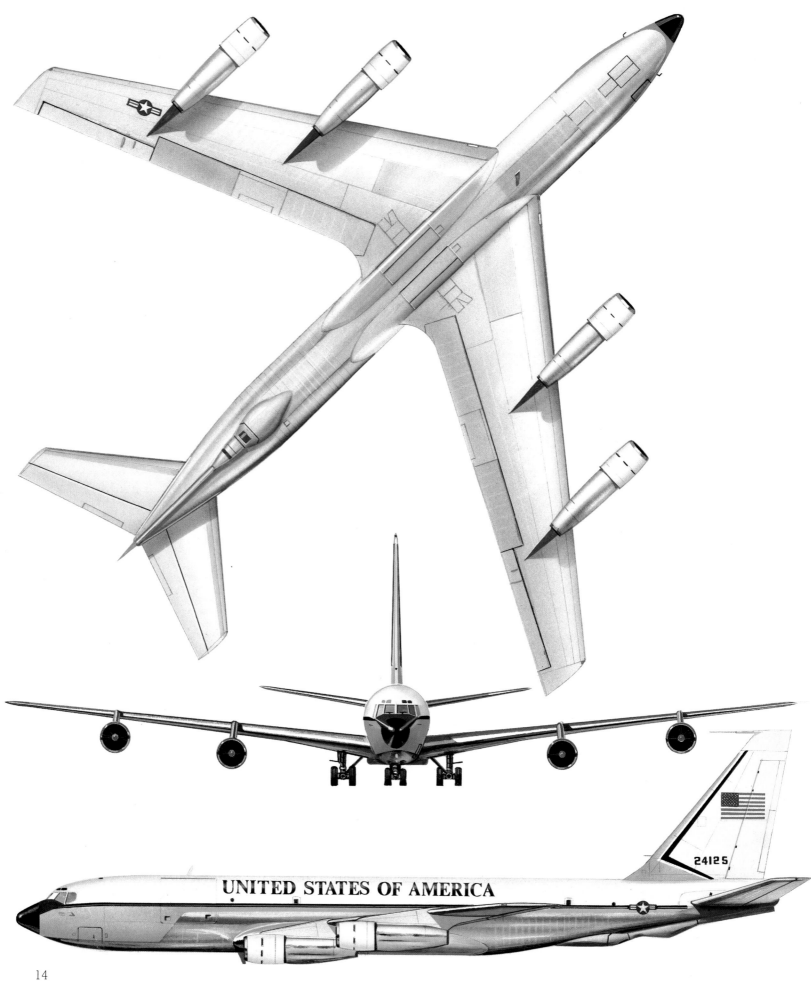

24125

UNITED STATES OF AMERICA

24125

14

Boeing VC-135B

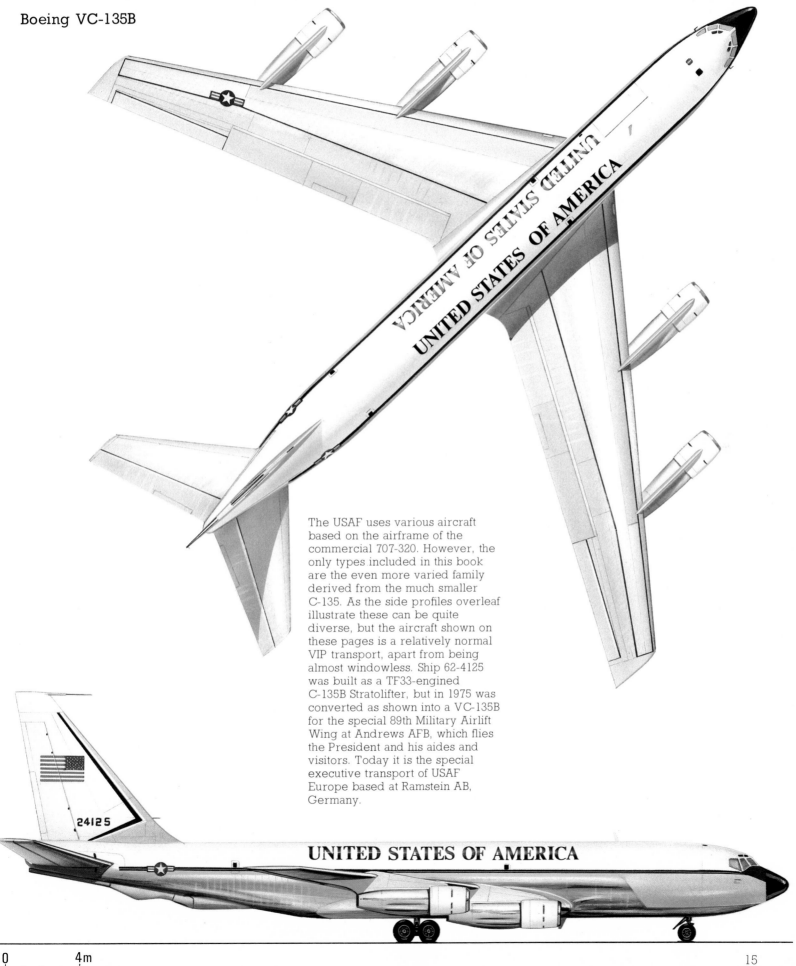

The USAF uses various aircraft based on the airframe of the commercial 707-320. However, the only types included in this book are the even more varied family derived from the much smaller C-135. As the side profiles overleaf illustrate these can be quite diverse, but the aircraft shown on these pages is a relatively normal VIP transport, apart from being almost windowless. Ship 62-4125 was built as a TF33-engined C-135B Stratolifter, but in 1975 was converted as shown into a VC-135B for the special 89th Military Airlift Wing at Andrews AFB, which flies the President and his aides and visitors. Today it is the special executive transport of USAF Europe based at Ramstein AB, Germany.

UNITED STATES OF AMERICA

24125

0   4m

15

Boeing KC-135

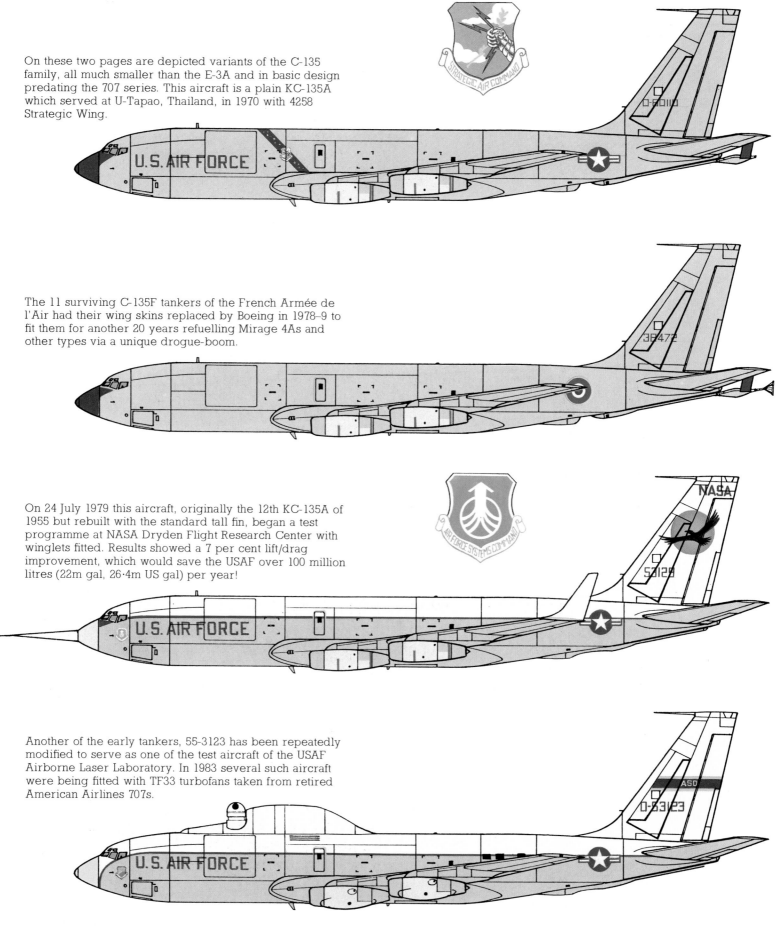

On these two pages are depicted variants of the C-135 family, all much smaller than the E-3A and in basic design predating the 707 series. This aircraft is a plain KC-135A which served at U-Tapao, Thailand, in 1970 with 4258 Strategic Wing.

The 11 surviving C-135F tankers of the French Armée de l'Air had their wing skins replaced by Boeing in 1978–9 to fit them for another 20 years refuelling Mirage 4As and other types via a unique drogue-boom.

On 24 July 1979 this aircraft, originally the 12th KC-135A of 1955 but rebuilt with the standard tall fin, began a test programme at NASA Dryden Flight Research Center with winglets fitted. Results showed a 7 per cent lift/drag improvement, which would save the USAF over 100 million litres (22m gal, 26·4m US gal) per year!

Another of the early tankers, 55-3123 has been repeatedly modified to serve as one of the test aircraft of the USAF Airborne Laser Laboratory. In 1983 several such aircraft were being fitted with TF33 turbofans taken from retired American Airlines 707s.

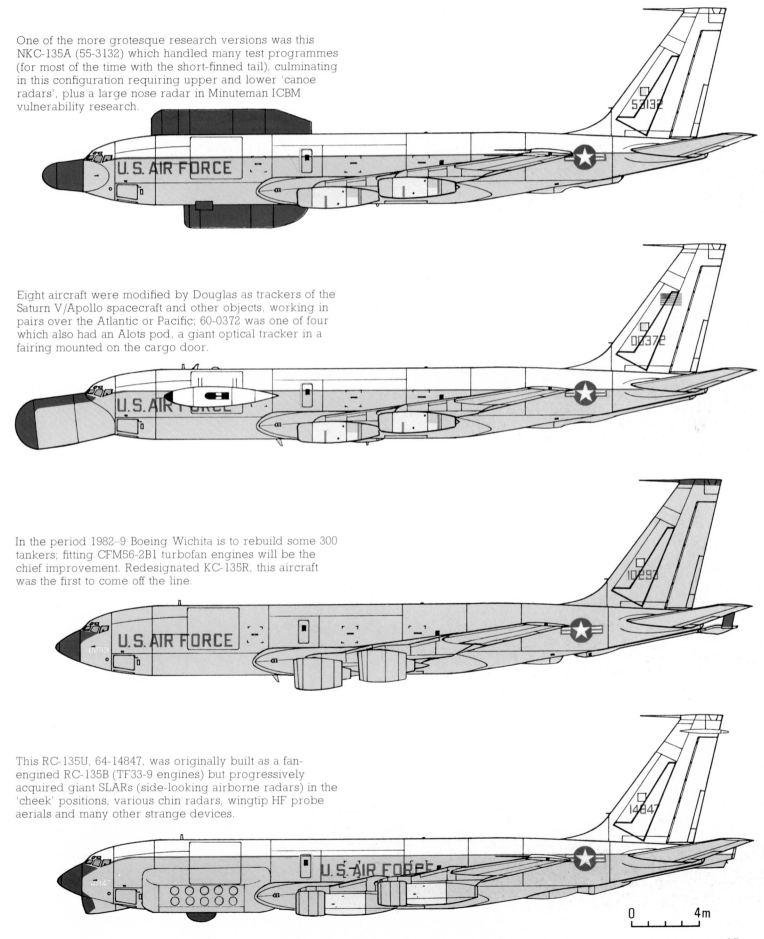

One of the more grotesque research versions was this
NKC-135A (55-3132) which handled many test programmes
(for most of the time with the short-finned tail), culminating
in this configuration requiring upper and lower 'canoe
radars', plus a large nose radar in Minuteman ICBM
vulnerability research.

Eight aircraft were modified by Douglas as trackers of the
Saturn V/Apollo spacecraft and other objects, working in
pairs over the Atlantic or Pacific; 60-0372 was one of four
which also had an Alots pod, a giant optical tracker in a
fairing mounted on the cargo door.

In the period 1982–9 Boeing Wichita is to rebuild some 300
tankers; fitting CFM56-2B1 turbofan engines will be the
chief improvement. Redesignated KC-135R, this aircraft
was the first to come off the line.

This RC-135U, 64-14847, was originally built as a fan-
engined RC-135B (TF33-9 engines) but progressively
acquired giant SLARs (side-looking airborne radars) in the
'cheek' positions, various chin radars, wingtip HF probe
aerials and many other strange devices.

0   4m

British Aerospace Sea Harrier FRS.1

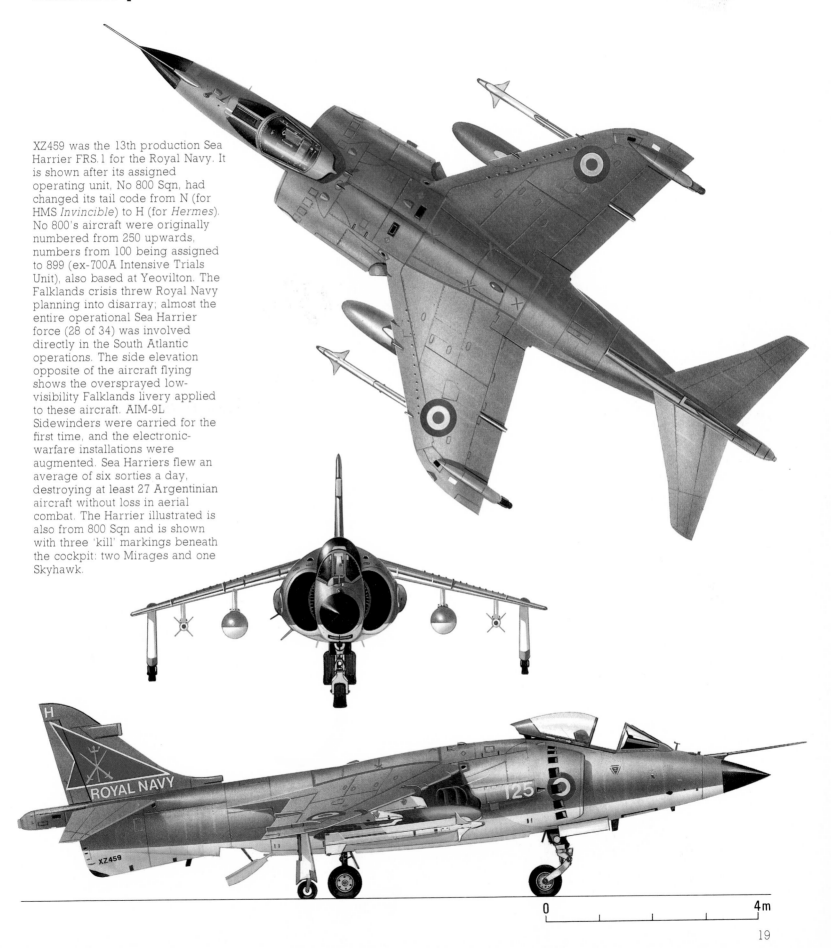

XZ459 was the 13th production Sea Harrier FRS.1 for the Royal Navy. It is shown after its assigned operating unit, No 800 Sqn, had changed its tail code from N (for HMS *Invincible*) to H (for *Hermes*). No 800's aircraft were originally numbered from 250 upwards, numbers from 100 being assigned to 899 (ex-700A Intensive Trials Unit), also based at Yeovilton. The Falklands crisis threw Royal Navy planning into disarray; almost the entire operational Sea Harrier force (28 of 34) was involved directly in the South Atlantic operations. The side elevation opposite of the aircraft flying shows the oversprayed low-visibility Falklands livery applied to these aircraft. AIM-9L Sidewinders were carried for the first time, and the electronic-warfare installations were augmented. Sea Harriers flew an average of six sorties a day, destroying at least 27 Argentinian aircraft without loss in aerial combat. The Harrier illustrated is also from 800 Sqn and is shown with three 'kill' markings beneath the cockpit: two Mirages and one Skyhawk.

0   4m

British Aerospace Harrier

The first prototype Hawker P.1127, pictured in the form in which it began its full flight programme. The first hovering tests took place with various items (such as landing-gear fairings) removed to save weight.

A BAe Harrier GR.3 single-seat attack aircraft of No 233 Operational Conversion Unit, RAF. This Wittering-based unit has used aircraft tail letters as well as individual numbers (as here).

US Marine Corps AV-8A No 158966 serving with VMA-513, the pioneer US Harrier unit originally based at MCAS Beaufort, South Carolina. Aden guns are carried, and the tall aerial mast is for tactical air/ground VHF.

VA-1 Matador single-seater of Essa 008, Spanish Navy (aircraft No 3). When first delivered the rear fuselage carried the legend ARMADA; some aircraft have the unit badge on the nose. Note the extra VHF blade aerial.

No less than 17·07m (56ft 0¼in) long, the two-seat Harrier T.4 has an appreciably higher empty weight. This is XZ147 of RAF Germany's No 4 Sqn, normally based at Gutersloh.

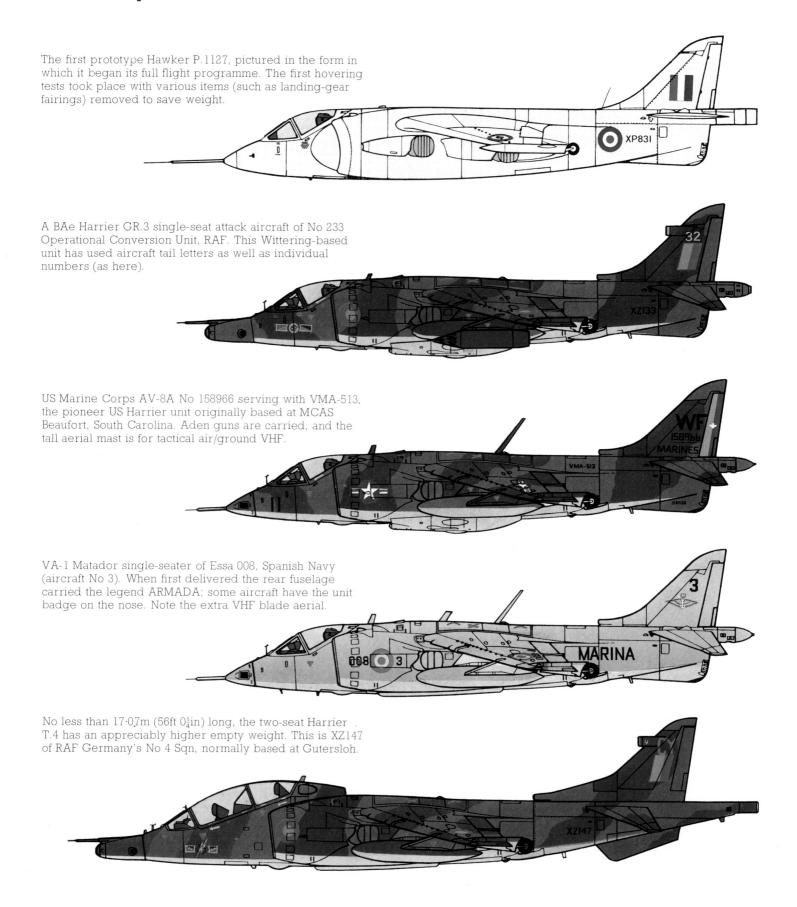

AV-8C No 158395 (CG-7) of US Marine Corps squadron VMA-231, usually based at Cherry Point, North Carolina. This particular aircraft serves with Detachment B.

Built with British Aerospace funds, greatly assisted by the free supply of thousands of bought-out components from supplier companies, G-VTOL is a civil demonstrator equipped with full Airways navigation aids.

Latest operator of Harriers is the Indian Navy, one of whose Sea Harrier Mk 51 single-seat multi-role aircraft is depicted here serving with No 300 Sqn. Eventually No 300 will embark in INS Vikrant.

XW927 was built as a T.4 for the RAF but was transferred to the Royal Navy and is depicted serving with 700A (now renumbered 899) Sqn at RNAS Yeovilton.

The second of the Full-Scale Development AV-8B Harrier II aircraft, complete with LERX wing-root extensions and the new 25mm gun pod. Several FSD aircraft have different shades of camouflage.

0   4m

British Aerospace Harrier

Unique in many respects, the Harrier and its derivatives could be the only combat aircraft left in Western countries a few minutes after the onset of a nuclear war. Yet not many have been built, because air forces have been strangely reluctant to recognize the utter futility of basing costly aircraft on fixed airfields.

The concept of the jet V/STOL (vertical or short take-off and landing) aircraft was all the rage around 1960, when numerous prototypes were flown. Of these only the Hawker P.1127, a predecessor of the Harrier, used a single engine for both lift and cruise propulsion. The unique Rolls-Royce Pegasus is a turbofan with four nozzles, two for the fan air and two for the core jet. These nozzles are rotated together to direct the power down, for lift, or to the rear, for thrust; they can also be pointed obliquely forwards for powerful in-flight braking. Thus the cockpit is normal in all respects except for a nozzle control lever. The normal operating method is actually STOVL (short take-off, vertical landing), because STO enables heavier loads to be carried.

The P.1127 was severely limited in engine thrust, but it was developed into today's Harrier, which is a most capable aircraft. The basic Harrier entered service with No 1 Sqn RAF in April 1969, and since then the RAF has received 114 single-seat Harrier GR.3s and 21 two-seat T.4s and 4As. These are basically close-support attack and reconnaissance aircraft, with two 30mm Aden guns in detachable pods, a normal weapon load of 2268kg (5,000lb) on five pylons, a reconnaissance camera on the left of the nose and a laser nose for target location and ranging. An inertial navigation system and HUD (head-up display) are fitted for all-weather attack.

Close relatives include the US Marine Corps AV-8C (originally built as AV-8A with simpler avionics) and two-seat TAV-8C, and the Spanish Navy VA-1 and two-seat VAE-1 Matadors. These are simpler attack aircraft with neither inertial navigation nor laser nose, but with launch shoes for Sidewinder AAMs (air/air missiles). The US Marines investigated VIFF (vectoring in forward flight) as a method of performing 'impossible' manoeuvres, and discovered the Harrier can act as a dogfighter of unrivalled capability. The Marines received 102 AV-8As, of which 61 are being remanufactured by McDonnell to AV-8C standard, plus eight two-seaters. The Spanish Navy received 11 VA-1s and two two-seaters.

Prolonged study of advanced versions by Britain and the USA in the 1970s came to nothing when the British government announced there was not enough common ground to proceed to a new-generation joint aircraft. As a result the RAF in 1981 was forced to adopt the US McDonnell-developed AV-8B, which was tailored to the needs of the Marines for a better attack version. It has almost the same engine, although with improved nozzles, but a totally new long-span supercritical wing made largely of carbon-fibre composite as well as detailed improvements to increase lift and weapon carriage. Internal fuel is increased from 2268kg (5,000lb) to 3402kg (7,500lb), and maximum weapon load to almost 7711kg (17,000lb). Although slower than earlier versions the AV-8B has approximately double the payload/range, and the USMC is expecting to order 336 to a standard derived from that of the pre-production aircraft flown on 5 November 1981. The RAF will get 60 with different nav/attack systems, designated Harrier GR.5 – these to be assembled in Britain as part of a joint programme.

A third family is the Sea Harrier, which uses almost the original airframe but with a new nose that places the pilot at a higher level, with all-round view. This provides space for additional avionics and instruments, and the nose houses a Blue Fox multi-mode radar. The Royal Navy received 34 Sea Harrier FRS.1s (the designation means 'fighter, reconnaissance, strike') for operation from surface ships with short flight decks without arrester gear or catapults. A ski-jump ramp enables payload to be greatly increased for any given deck run or wind condition. Research is now being directed towards supersonic derivatives.

COUNTRY OF ORIGIN Great Britain (**AV-8B**, USA).

CREW One; trainers: two.

TOTAL PRODUCED 313, excluding P.1127, Kestrel, AV-8B and Harrier GR.5.

DIMENSIONS Wingspan 7·70m (25ft 3in), with ferry tips: 9·04m (29ft 8in), **AV-8B:** 9·22m (30ft 4in); length, **Harrier:** 14·27m (46ft 10in), **AV-8C:** 13·89m (45ft 7in), **Sea Harrier:** 14·5m (47ft 7in), **two-seat:** 17·0m (55ft 9½in), **AV-8B:** 14·12m (46ft 4in); wing area, **Harrier, Sea Harrier, AV-8C**, no ferry tips: 18·68m² (201·1ft²), **AV-8B:** 21·37m² (230ft²).

WEIGHTS Empty 5489kg (12,100lb), **AV-8B:** 5783kg (12,750lb); maximum loaded 11340kg (25,000lb), **AV-8B:** 13494kg (29,750lb).

ENGINE One 9752kg (21,500lb) Rolls-Royce Pegasus turbofan (**Harrier** Mk 103, **Sea Harrier** Mk 104, **AV-8C** F402–402, **AV-8B** F402–404).

MAXIMUM SPEED Over 1186km/h (737mph, Mach 1·3), **AV-8B:** Mach 0·91.

SERVICE CEILING Over 15·24km (50,000ft).

RANGE **Harrier**, with one inflight refuel: over 5560km (3,455 miles); **AV-8B**, no inflight refuel: 4633km (2,879 miles).

MILITARY LOAD Two 30mm Aden guns in detachable pods; cleared for operations with maximum load of 2268kg (5,000lb) carried on five external pylons, but has flown with 3630kg (8,000lb). **AV-8A:** always equipped to fire Sidewinder and in 1982 this missile added to RAF Harriers. **Sea Harrier:** as Harrier with addition of Sea Eagle or Harpoon stand-off missiles. **AV-8B:** 25mm gun and much greater weapon load on nine pylons.

USERS Great Britain (RAF, RN), India, Spain, USA (Marine Corps).

British Aerospace Nimrod

Following several years of studying possible derivatives of aircraft such as the Trident, Andover, VC10 and Vanguard, the decision was taken to use the Comet 4C as the structural basis for a new maritime reconnaissance aircraft to replace the Shackleton in RAF service.

Comets had previously been used by the RAF for many purposes, beginning with the standard C.2 transport in 1955 and more recently including 19 modified Mk 2, 3 and 4 Comets for special trials and research, almost forming a British counterpart to the variants of the KC-135. The last two Comet 4Cs were used to assist development of the Nimrod. The first of 43 Nimrod MR.1s flew at Woodford on 28 June 1968.

With the withdrawal of a unit from Malta the Nimrod now equips Nos 120, 201 and 206 Sqns of the RAF at Kinloss, Scotland, and 42 Sqn at St Mawgan, Cornwall. They have given outstanding service and, despite numerous missions under the most dangerous winter blizzard conditions, often involving sustained flight just over the wavetops, there has been no serious incident or aircraft loss. The 31 aircraft with the least flying time are being remanufactured to extend airframe life and provide a completely updated set of sensors, with designation Nimrod MR.2.

Nimrod MR.2 has the new EMI Searchwater radar, with its own digital computer tied to a totally new central tactical system with enormously enhanced speed, storage and rapid-recall memory. This links the MAD (magnetic anomaly detector) at the tip of the tailboom, and the acoustics processing sub-system which is compatible with all main British, US, Canadian and Australian sonobuoys including the new Cambs (command active multibeam sonobuoy). Communications updates include twin HF and a teletype and encoding system, while the original ESM (electronic surveillance measures) pod on the fin is supplemented by new US Loral EWSM (early-warning support measures) pods on the wingtips. The appearance is also changed by the introduction of a sandy colour scheme, called hemp, and Type B (red/blue) insignia. In May 1982 they were given flight refuelling probes for coverage of the Falklands area.

The original Nimrod purchase was for 46 aircraft, three of which were diverted as development aircraft for a later model, the AEW.3. A further three were also ordered as R.1 aircraft for Elint (electronic intelligence) missions, with appearance slightly altered by the absence of MAD tailbooms and with an electronic installation in the left wing pod. These aircraft operate with 51 Sqn based at Wyton.

The third, and very different, mark is the AEW (airborne early warning) Mk 3. This was delayed while NATO pondered on the acquisition of the Boeing E-3A, but went ahead in 1977 in view of the urgent need to replace the Shackleton in this role. The key to this aircraft is its airborne surveillance radar; built by a team led by Marconi Avionics, it is probably the most advanced yet produced anywhere. A unique feature is the use of two scanners, one at each end of the aircraft and each providing 180° of the 360° coverage. The pulse-doppler radar can be adjusted for ideal performance over any terrain or sea state and also has extremely sophisticated anti-jam features. The same scanners serve the Cossor IFF (identification friend/foe) system. This mark again has ESM in the fin-tip fairing and EWSM in the wingtip pods, as well as exceptionally comprehensive communications systems.

The nose radar installation was flown in a Comet 4C in June 1977 and the first of three development AEW.3 aircraft flew on 16 July 1980. Electronic performance has been even better than predicted, and the general performance and handling of the aircraft is only marginally affected, a reduction in yaw stability being countered by a 0.91m (3ft) increase in the height of the fin. The RAF force of 11 of this mark will have unrivalled capability in the British environment, while being fully compatible with the E-3As of the USAF and NATO. They are manned by crews from various NATO nations but form RAF No 8 Sqn at Waddington.

COUNTRY OF ORIGIN Great Britain.

CREW Flight crew four; tactical crew, **MR:** eight, **AEW:** six.

TOTAL PRODUCED 60.

DIMENSIONS Wingspan, **MR.2**, **AEW.3:** 35·08m (115ft 1in), **Comet, MR.1, R.1:** 35·00m (114ft 10in); length 38·63m (126ft 9in), **AEW.3:** 41·97m (137ft 8½in); wing area 197·0m² (2,121ft²).

WEIGHTS Empty, **MR.1:** 39000kg (86,000lb); maximum loaded, **MR.1** normal: 80510kg (177,500lb), maximum loaded: 87090kg (192,000lb).

ENGINES Four 5516kg (12,160lb) Rolls-Royce Spey 250 turbofans.

MAXIMUM SPEED Normally restricted to 925km/h (575mph).

SERVICE CEILING Normally 13.04km (42,800ft).

RANGE Normally 9262km (5,755 miles).

MILITARY LOAD **MR** versions carry six lateral rows of stores in internal weapon bay including various bombs and nine torpedoes; built with hardpoints under wings for missile pylons or other loads (not normally fitted in RAF service). Sidewinder AAMs added in Falklands theatre.

USER Great Britain

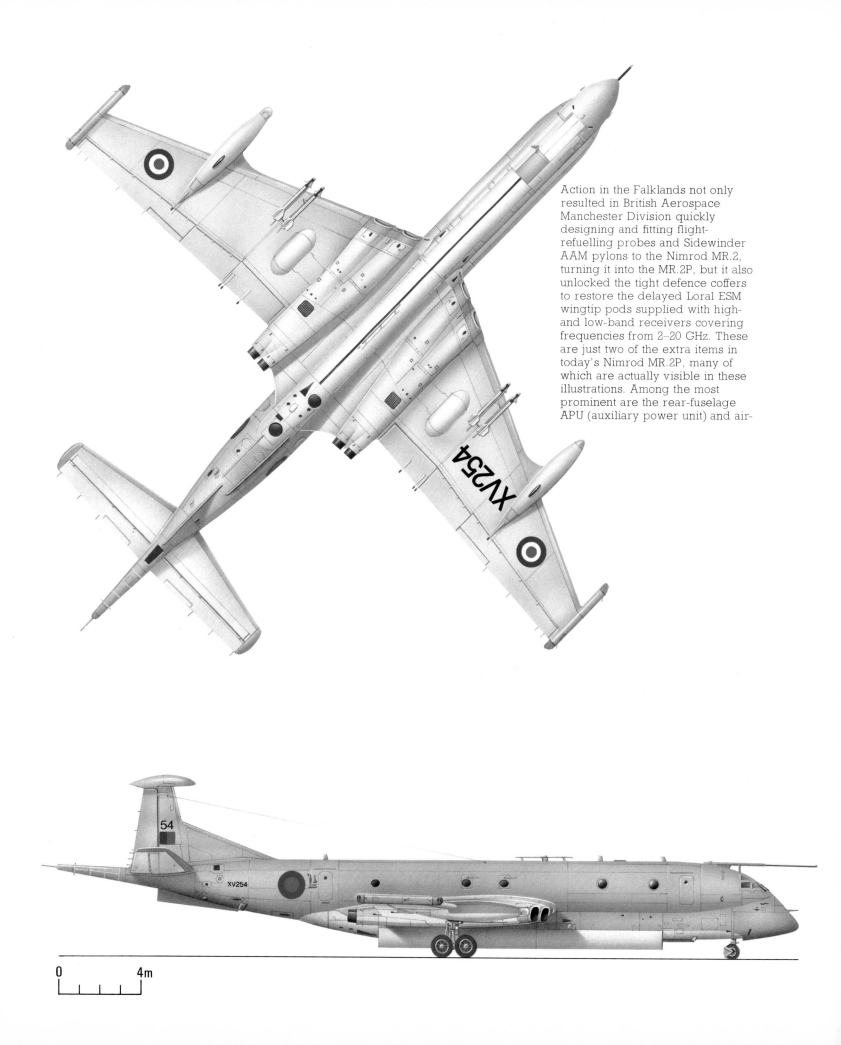

Action in the Falklands not only resulted in British Aerospace Manchester Division quickly designing and fitting flight-refuelling probes and Sidewinder AAM pylons to the Nimrod MR.2, turning it into the MR.2P, but it also unlocked the tight defence coffers to restore the delayed Loral ESM wingtip pods supplied with high- and low-band receivers covering frequencies from 2–20 GHz. These are just two of the extra items in today's Nimrod MR.2P, many of which are actually visible in these illustrations. Among the most prominent are the rear-fuselage APU (auxiliary power unit) and air-

0   4m

British Aerospace Nimrod MR.2P

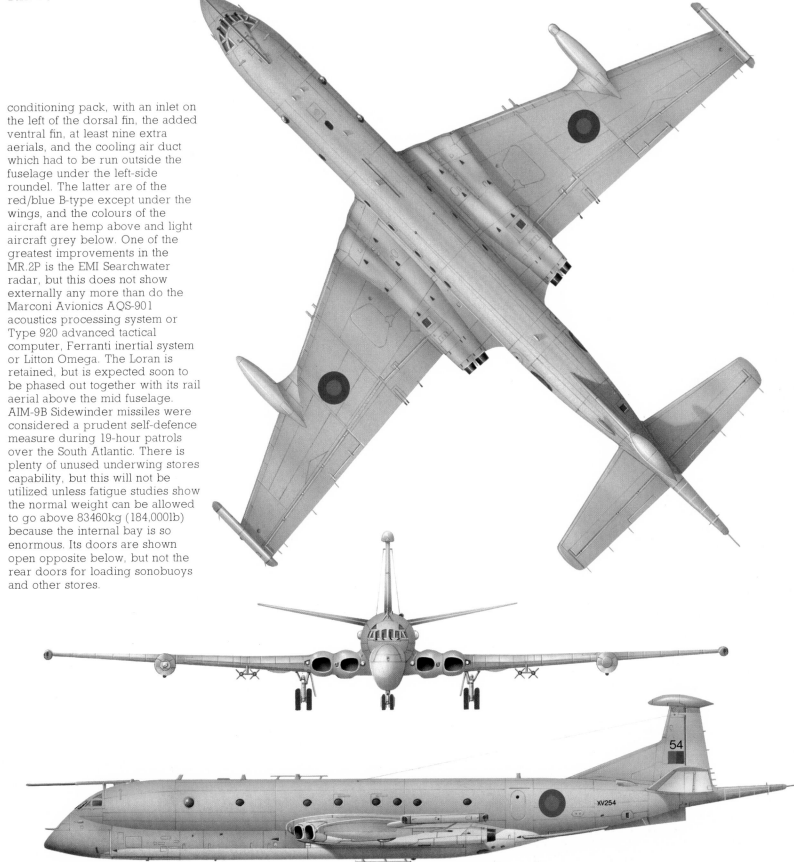

conditioning pack, with an inlet on the left of the dorsal fin, the added ventral fin, at least nine extra aerials, and the cooling air duct which had to be run outside the fuselage under the left-side roundel. The latter are of the red/blue B-type except under the wings, and the colours of the aircraft are hemp above and light aircraft grey below. One of the greatest improvements in the MR.2P is the EMI Searchwater radar, but this does not show externally any more than do the Marconi Avionics AQS-901 acoustics processing system or Type 920 advanced tactical computer, Ferranti inertial system or Litton Omega. The Loran is retained, but is expected soon to be phased out together with its rail aerial above the mid fuselage. AIM-9B Sidewinder missiles were considered a prudent self-defence measure during 19-hour patrols over the South Atlantic. There is plenty of unused underwing stores capability, but this will not be utilized unless fatigue studies show the normal weight can be allowed to go above 83460kg (184,000lb) because the internal bay is so enormous. Its doors are shown open opposite below, but not the rear doors for loading sonobuoys and other stores.

de Havilland Comet/British Aerospace Nimrod

The RAF and MoD have operated 30 Comets, including
five regular C.4C transports used by 216 Sqn to
supplement its original C.2s. Most of the others have been
special research, trials and hack machines, some used for
fascinating tasks over many years. This unique Comet was
flown on 19 July 1954 as the Comet 3, G-ANLO; it became a
3B, then a 4B, and then did 12 years with the Blind Landing
Experimental Unit at the RAE Bedford as XP915.

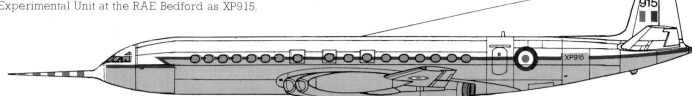

XV814 (Comet 4 No 06407) flew on 11 December 1958 as
G-APDF of BOAC, and was much later leased to Air
Ceylon. In 1967 it went to the RAE Farnborough and spent
ten years doing more research into long-range navigation
than any other aircraft, with a Nimrod fin countering a
large sensor compartment under the forward fuselage.
Today it has been restored as shown.

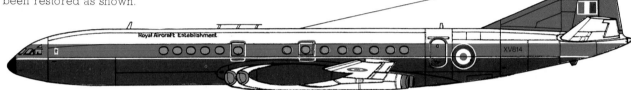

The Nimrod maritime patrol aircraft was preceded by two
Comet 4s, XV147 and 148, which were completed with
Nimrod aerodynamics and most of the systems (147
retained Avon engines). Production Nimrod MR.1s were
numbered from XV226, so this aircraft of No 42 Sqn at St
Mawgan, Cornwall, was the tenth off the line of the 43 built.
The all-white livery began to be obscured by the current
colours in late 1979, squadron badges being removed.

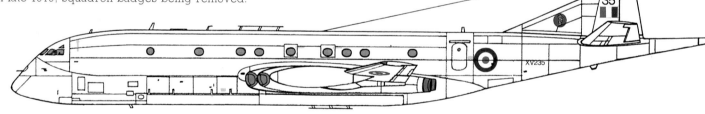

Three Nimrods, XW664–666, were completed as R.1
electronic warfare platforms, with three special radar
receivers, probably conical spirals, on the fronts of the
wing tanks and at the tail of the fuselage (in place of the
MAD boom). They are used by No 51 Sqn on Elint
(electronic intelligence) duties.

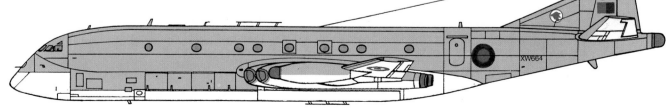

Of 46 Nimrod MR.1s ordered, 43 were built as such, and one was lost in late 1980 in a multiple birdstrike on take-off. Eleven are being rebuilt as AEW.3s, leaving 31 in squadron service for progressive updating to MR.2 standard. XV261 is one of the current fleet of MR.1s, now painted in the standard camouflage of 'hemp' and light aircraft grey.

Rivalling the more curious C-135 variants, this Comet 4C, XW626, was originally a harmless Comet 4, G-APDS of BOAC, first flown on 6 August 1959. After being leased to Air Ceylon and Kuwait Airways in the stretched 4C form, it was taken on charge by the MoD at Boscombe Down on 30 January 1969 and finally found itself on 28 June 1977 taking off with the front 180° sector of the AEW.3 radar on special communications trials.

Most important current part of the programme is the Nimrod AEW.3, whose presence over the Falklands would have been no small help to the Task Force. In almost every way the best high-altitude surveillance and control aircraft in the world, with a perfect view for each 180° scanner and ideal over-water performance, the 11 AEW.3s were joining No 8 Sqn at Waddington as this book went to press.

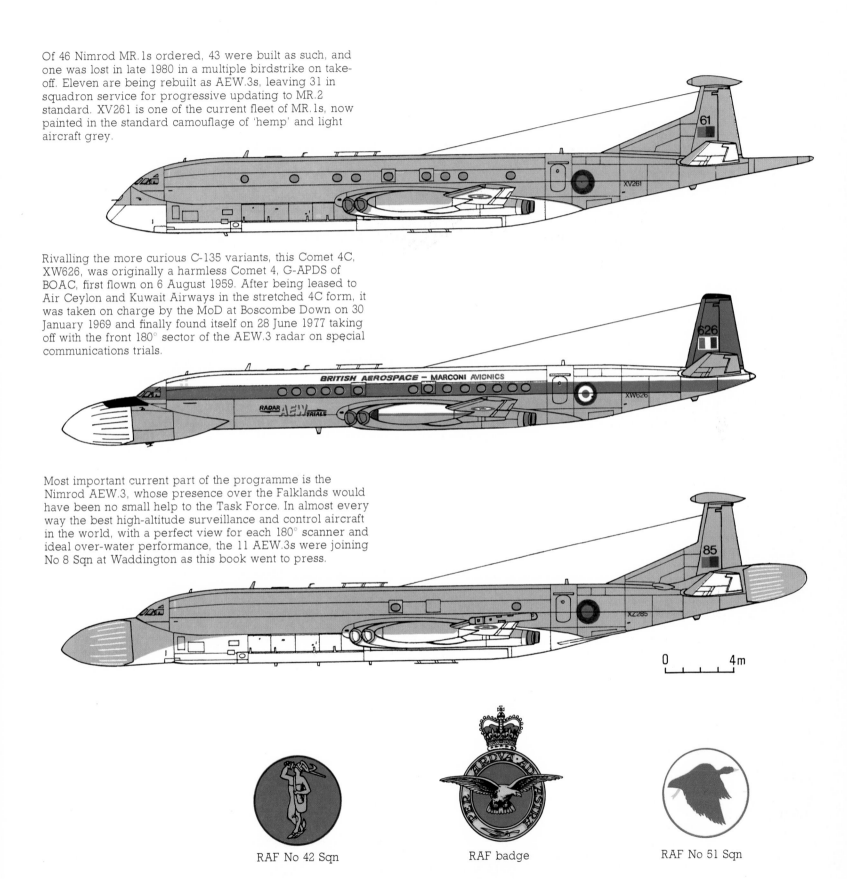

RAF No 42 Sqn

RAF badge

RAF No 51 Sqn

Development of the French Mirage 2000 has been delayed, but the first production aircraft had just appeared when this book went to press in early 1983. These drawings are based on the camouflaged fourth (04) prototype, but with the first production machine at upper right (without the badge of EC 1/2 La Cicogne, the first recipient of the production aircraft). The engine is the M53-5 and the radar the RDM (radar doppler multifunction), both of which are interim features and due to be replaced eventually by equipment more representative of the 1980s. The engine, in particular, is clearly not optimized to the aircraft or the mission, for not only was it designed for twin-engined aircraft (where thrust demands are not so great), but also it has a very low pressure-ratio matched to Mach 2·5, so for

more than 95 per cent of each mission the fuel burn is higher than in more efficient engines such as the F404 and RB.199. The latter engines are also dramatically lighter because of their multi-shaft layout. SNECMA is now developing a new-technology high-pressure engine, the M88, but this is even less powerful than the M53 and thus not suited to the Mirage 2000. From 1985–6 the Mirage 2000 is intended to be powered by the M53-P2, giving slightly more power and with fractionally higher pressure-ratio, but as this book went to press the P2 had not been ordered.

The view upper right shows a basic air-defence configuration with a single 1700-litre (375 gal, 450 US gal) tank and two Magic close-range AAMs under the wings. The side elevation below shows a short-range attack configuration with eight 250kg (551lb) bombs and two Magics and with the fixed flight-refuelling probe attached. The head-on view opposite shows two tanks, two Magics and eight 250kg bombs, the maximum load for EC 2 at Dijon in late 1983.

0   4m

Dassault-Breguet Mirage 2000

Dassault-Breguet Mirage deltas

The Mirage III-001 prototype was produced amazingly quickly, flying on 18 November 1956 only eight months after work started on designing a new fighter which, instead of twin Gabizo engines, would have the 4500kg (9,900lb) Atar 101G. On 30 January 1957, with a booster rocket fitted (not shown), this aircraft reached Mach 1·8.

Dassault then built ten Mirage IIIAs, one of which reached Mach 2 with the new Atar 9B engine (without booster rocket) on 24 October 1958, before finalizing on the production IIIC. The latter first flew on 9 October 1960, and large orders were placed by l'Armée de l'Air, Israel and South Africa. This IIIC serves with the French EC3/10 fighter squadron.

Another of the first customers was Australia, whose RAAF could have had the much more powerful version with an Avon engine, but instead settled for the ordinary Atar aircraft. Designated Mirage IIIO, the RAAF aircraft is basically a IIIE with longer fuselage (note inlets behind canopy) housing more fuel, and with the improved Atar 9C (note multi-flap nozzle). Missiles are Sidewinders and a Matra R 530, and the unit is 75 Sqn.

South Africa uses sub-types of all five major Mirage III families; the IIICZ, EZ and RZ are supplemented by the BZ and DZ two-seaters. This is a BZ of SAAF No 2 Sqn based at Waterkloof. To preserve balance the radar is deleted from all two-seat Mirage III versions. Note the old Atar 9B engine with twin-eyelid nozzle.

Much more modern, Pakistan's IIIRP reconnaissance aircraft have the IIIE airframe, Atar 9C engine, nose filled with OMERA Types 33 and 40 cameras and a doppler navigation radar in the bulge behind the camera bay. A total of 13 is used, gradually being converted to R2P standard with the more powerful Atar 9K50 engine and Cyclope IR linescan in a modified nose.

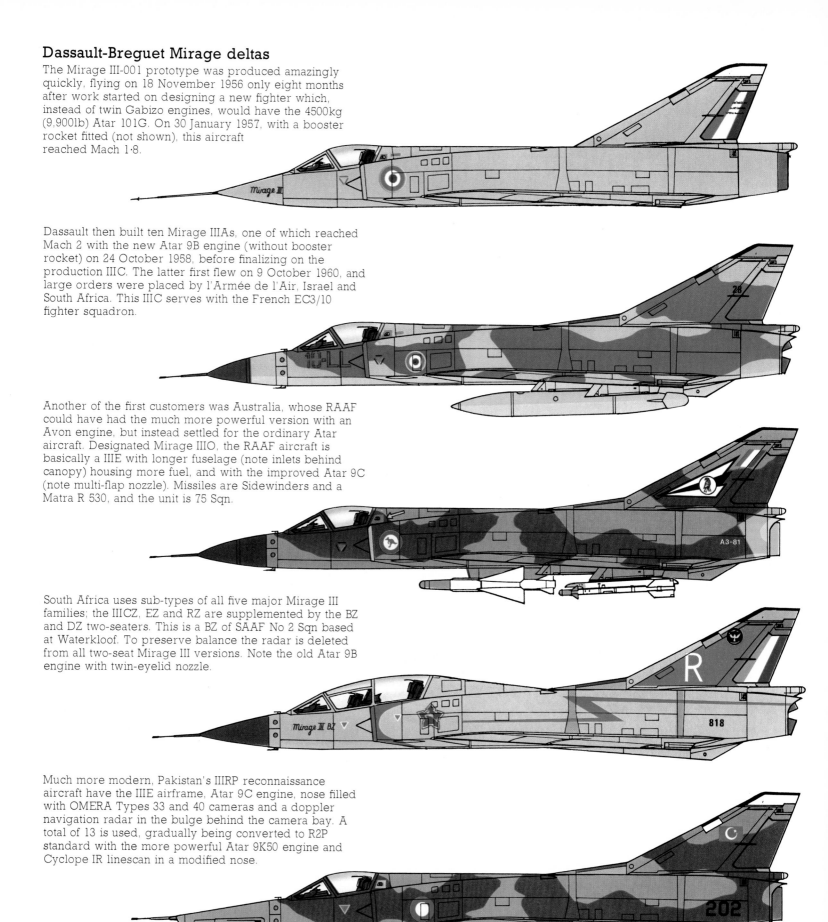

The Fuerza Aérea Argentina used the Mirage IIIEA for home defence, equipping the VIII Brigada Aérea at Morón AB, Buenos Aires, although several participated in the Falklands war on detachment to bases further south. This is one of the first batch (I-003/012); the second batch was I-013/019. More numerous were the slim-nosed IAI Daggers, of which about 20 were shot down, out of 27 Mirage/Dagger types in all.

With a slim nose like the IAI Dagger, the Mirage 5 was at first built without radar, except for an Aïda II radar-ranging gunsight, and with only simple avionics for visual attack missions. This 5COA is one of 12 of this model which, with four trainer/recon aircraft, equip a squadron of the air force of Colombia.

Egypt has a complete regiment equipped with 46 Mirage 5SDEs identical to the SDEs used by Saudi Arabia, which funded the whole purchase. Deliveries were beginning in 1983 of a further 16 5E2 attack aircraft with the same nav/attack system as Egypt's Alpha Jet MS2s. Egypt also uses the two-seat 5SDD and camera-equipped 5SDR.

By 1983 Dassault had secured one customer for the Mirage 50: Chile. This has the powerful Atar 9K50 engine, which is also used by South African and Pakistani R2Z and R2P aircraft and the new canard-equipped IIING (Nouvelle Génération), which first flew on 21 December 1982. As this profile shows, Chilean markings were not applied before delivery of the 16 Mirage 50C aircraft.
Note the Magic AAM.

Israel's IAI-developed Kfir-C2 has been severely handicapped in international marketing by US embargoes imposed because of its J79 engine, but it is so far in advance of regular Atar-powered Mirage deltas that Dassault has developed the IIING to try to compete with it. This example with 400kg (882lb) bombs and Shafrir AAMs is painted in the new all-grey scheme.

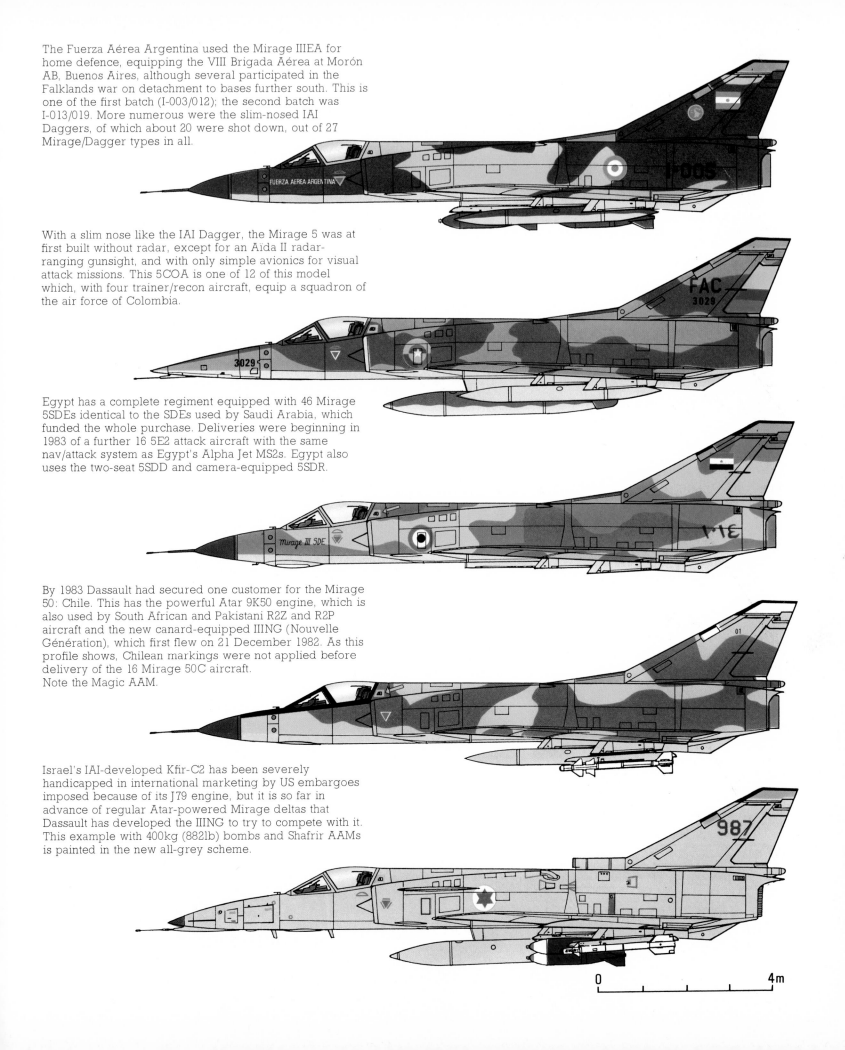

0   4m

Dassault-Breguet Mirage deltas

Today the name Mirage encompasses a large family of supersonic combat aircraft, some of them strategic bombers and some with a high wing and conventional tail. But the name instantly conjures up a vision of small, tailless delta fighters, pleasing in appearance and sold in great numbers to 22 countries all over the world.

Before the Mirage, the dynamic Dassault (today Dassault-Breguet) firm had already begun to carve out an export market for jet fighters by a combination of technical adequacy, low price and early availability without political strings. But the first Mirage, the MD.550 Mirage I flown on 25 June 1955, was a diminutive short-range interceptor designed to defend point targets. With a booster rocket it reached Mach 1·3 in level flight, but Dassault was convinced the concept was faulty and designed a larger aircraft powered by an improved afterburning version of the Atar turbojet. The prototype Mirage III flew on 17 November 1956, and after a great deal of further development the Mirage IIIC interceptor flew in October 1960 and entered service with the Armée de l'Air in 1961.

The IIIC was a simple fighter with a Cyrano I radar and primitive AAMs, but with a high all-round performance that was greatly augmented by a liquid rocket package in the underside of the rear fuselage. With the rocket removed its tankage space could be used for ammunition for two 30mm guns, and these were the armament of the IIICJ Mirages which caught the attention of the world during the brilliant Six-Day War in the Middle East in 1967. Israel's outstanding success with the Mirage practically caused customers to queue.

Israel devised a further simplified version, the Mirage 5, in which for day use in the clear Middle East weather some of the avionics, including the bulky radar, could be removed and the space and weight devoted to extra fuel and weapons. While this was in the design stage Dassault broadened the range with the IIIE attack version with slightly increased fuselage length for extra fuel and augmented avionics; the IIIR reconnaissance model with five cameras in place of the main radar (but often with doppler radar for navigation in a blister under the nose); and the IIIB and IIID dual-control trainers.

The first Mirage 5 flew on 19 May 1967, by which time Israel had paid for the first 50 of this clear-weather attack version. The French, however, refused to deliver to Israel and instead sold this model to numerous Arab countries. This switch in allegiance greatly accelerated Israel's progress to self-sufficiency in fighters, and after years of toil Israel Aircraft Industries perfected a home-grown multi-role fighter derived from the Mirage but with an American engine of greater power and locally produced avionics, the Kfir-C2. This is visually distinguished by jagged dogtooth leading edges, strakes along the nose, foreplanes on the inlets and a cutback rear fuselage cooled by a ram inlet at the front of the dorsal fin. The Kfir-TC2 is a two-seat version, deliveries of which may have brought the total Israeli production to 250.

One of the first Mirage export customers, South Africa, fitted the more powerful Atar 9K-50 engine to enhance the performance of some of its versions, and since 1975 Dassault-Breguet has sold (initially to Chile) the Mirage 50 series with this engine. The redesigned Mirage F1 is described opposite.

In the 1960s Dassault spent vast sums on the Mirage III-V jet-lift V/STOL version and on the equally large Mirage IIIT and F2 from which were derived the swing-wing Mirage G family, some with twin main propulsion engines. These were dropped in favour of the fixed-wing ACF (Avion de Combat Futur), which in turn was abandoned in 1975 to be replaced by a new small delta with a variable-camber wing with leading-edge flaps. This aircraft, the Mirage 2000, first flew on 10 March 1978. It has since been developed as the principal future combat type of the Armée de l'Air, initially as a fighter and by 1985 with better radar and a strengthened structure as the 2000N attack version. The main problem is the price, some US$50 million.

COUNTRY OF ORIGIN France.

CREW 1; trainers: 2.

TOTAL PRODUCED All **III**, **5** and **50**: 1,380.

DIMENSIONS Wingspan 8·22m (26ft 11½in); **2000**: 9·0m (29ft 6in); length, **IIIC**: 14·73m (48ft 4in), **IIIE**: 15·03m (49ft 3½in), **IIIB**, **IIID**: 15·4m (50ft 6¼in), **IIIR**: 15·5m (50ft 10¼in), **5**, **50**: 15·56m (51ft 0½in), **2000**: 14·35m (47ft 1in); wing area 34·85m² (375ft²), **2000**: 41m² (441ft²).

WEIGHTS Empty, **C**: 6155kg (13,570lb), **E**: 7050kg (15,540lb), **5**: 6600kg (14,550lb), **50**: 7150kg (15,765lb), **2000**: 7400kg (16,315lb); maximum loaded, **C**: 12600kg (27,777lb), **E**, **R**, **5**, **50**: 13700kg (30,200lb), **2000**: 16500kg (36,375lb).

ENGINE One SNECMA Atar afterburning turbojet, **C**: 6000kg (13,230lb) Atar 9B3, **E**, **R**, **5**: 6200kg (13,670lb) Atar 9C, **50**: 7200kg (15,873lb) Atar 9K-50, **2000**: 9000kg (19,840lb) SNECMA M53.

MAXIMUM SPEED Clean, at high altitude: 2350km/h (1,460mph, Mach 2·2).

SERVICE CEILING Typically 17km (55,775ft), **2000**: 20km (65,600ft).

RANGE Combat radius at high altitude with four 250kg (551lb) bombs, **5**: 1300km (808 miles), **2000**: 1480km (920 miles).

MILITARY LOAD Most have two 30mm DEFA guns; **IIIE**: three 454kg (1,000lb) bombs, **5**: up to 4000kg (8,820lb) bombload, **2000**: when developed in attack version, 6000kg (13,228lb) weapon load including up to 18 bombs of 250kg (551lb); in interception role all can carry two Magic or Sidewinder AAMs plus Matra R530 or Super 530 AAM.

USERS Abu Dhabi, Argentina, Australia, Belgium, Brazil, Chile, Colombia, Egypt, France, Gabon, India, Israel, Lebanon, Libya, Pakistan, Peru, South Africa, Spain, Switzerland, Sudan, Venezuela, Zaïre.

Dassault-Breguet Mirage F1

By 1963 it appeared that the tailless Mirage delta was becoming obsolescent in the face of competition from more efficient tailed and swing-wing machines, and after prolonged studies in that year Dassault received a contract in January 1964 for the design of a Mirage III replacement. The choice was a large aircraft named Mirage F2, with a conventional wing mounted in the high position, and a normal tail. Powered by a TF306 afterburning turbofan, it flew on 12 June 1966. At the same time Dassault privately developed a smaller aircraft with identical configuration, sized to the existing Atar engine. This, the Mirage F1, flew on 23 December 1966.

In May 1969 an order came for 35 F1-C fighter-bombers for the Armée de l'Air. It was still not certain what the final choice of the Armée de l'Air for a Mirage III successor would be, and additional funds were committed to the large variable-geometry Mirage G series from which stemmed the ACF (Avion de Combat Futur) programme. None of these came to anything, and even the F1 proved to be not a replacement but an addition to the Mirage deltas.

Unlike today's Mirage 2000, the original Mirage III/5/50 family share a wing which is optimized to supersonic flight, with severe penalties at low speeds. It has no high-lift devices, and even at light weights these aircraft must approach at 340km/h (210mph) and land at 290km/h (180mph). A tailed aircraft can be fitted with powerful leading-edge slats and trailing-edge flaps, and thus the Mirage F1—even though it has a much smaller wing than the deltas—can approach at only 260km/h (160mph) and land at 230km/h (140mph). Moreover, improved design and packaging enabled the internal fuel capacity to be increased by 50 per cent.

The original production model, the F1-C, was intended primarily as an interceptor, using the Cyrano radar updated to Mk IV standard and existing weapons. The engine is an uprated model of the Atar, and in almost all respects even this first sub-type is markedly superior to any of the original delta Mirages. Only in the matter of maximum level speed are the two families similar.

No fewer than 225 F1s have been ordered for the Armée de l'Air, including 20 tandem dual-control F1-B trainers and 30 F1-R reconnaissance aircraft to replace the Mirage IIIR. The F1-R is expected to become operational during 1983. The F1-C equips the 30e Escadre at Rheims, 5e Escadre at Orange and 12e Escadre at Cambrai, plus a squadron in the 10e at Creil. In 1979 a batch of 25 F1-Cs were modified to F1-C-200 standard by adding a removable inflight-refuelling probe.

Dassault-Breguet has also sold more than 400 F1s of various kinds to air forces all over the world. The F1-A is a simplified attack version with extra fuel in place of the radar and some other all-weather avionics. In contrast the F1-E is an all-weather attack model with a proper blind first-pass navigation and weapon-delivery system which is absent from the F1-C. A wide range of missiles can be carried for air/air and air/surface use, as well as a reconnaissance pod containing EMI side-looking radar and a Cyclope infra-red linescan system, which builds up line-by-line thermal pictures.

In an unsuccessful effort to get Belgium to buy the F1 instead of the American F-16, two Belgian companies (one part-owned by Dassault) were given the task of making major parts of all F1s. Dassault-Breguet also concluded a technical and licensing agreement with the South African Armaments Development and Production Corporation which includes the right to manufacture the complete F1 aircraft. Atlas Aircraft in the Transvaal has been sub-licensed to produce major F1 parts, but production of complete F1-AZ and F1-CZ aircraft (the South African versions previously supplied from France) has not yet begun.

Although it did not achieve the so-called sale of the century to Belgium, the Netherlands, Denmark and Norway on 7 June 1975, the F1 is a most attractive and successful aircraft. Seven are being built each month until at least January 1985.

COUNTRY OF ORIGIN France.

CREW Fighters: 1; trainers: 2.

TOTAL PRODUCED About 560 by early 1983.

DIMENSIONS Wingspan (excluding missiles) 8·4m (27ft 6¾in); length (all versions) 15·0m (49ft 2½in); wing area 25·0m² (269·1ft²).

WEIGHTS Empty, **F1-C:** 7400kg (16,314lb), **F1-E:** 7620kg (16,799lb); loaded (clean) 10900kg (24,030lb); maximum loaded 15200kg (33,510lb).

ENGINE One SNECMA Atar 9K-50 turbojet rated at 7200kg (15,873lb) with maximum afterburner.

MAXIMUM SPEED Potential limit at high altitude of 2350km/h (1,460mph, Mach 2·2); limit at sea level (clean) of 1480km/h (920mph, Mach 1·21).

SERVICE CEILING 20km (65,600ft).

RANGE Radius of action in attack mission (unstated external fuel) 1200km (745 miles).

MILITARY LOAD Two 30mm DEFA guns, centreline and underwing pylons for maximum combat load of 4000kg (8,820lb) including various bombs, tanks or missiles such as AS.30, AS.37 or Super 530; tip shoes for Magic or Sidewinder close-range AAMs.

USERS Ecuador, France, Greece, Iraq, Jordan, Kuwait, Libya, Morocco, Qatar, South Africa, Spain.

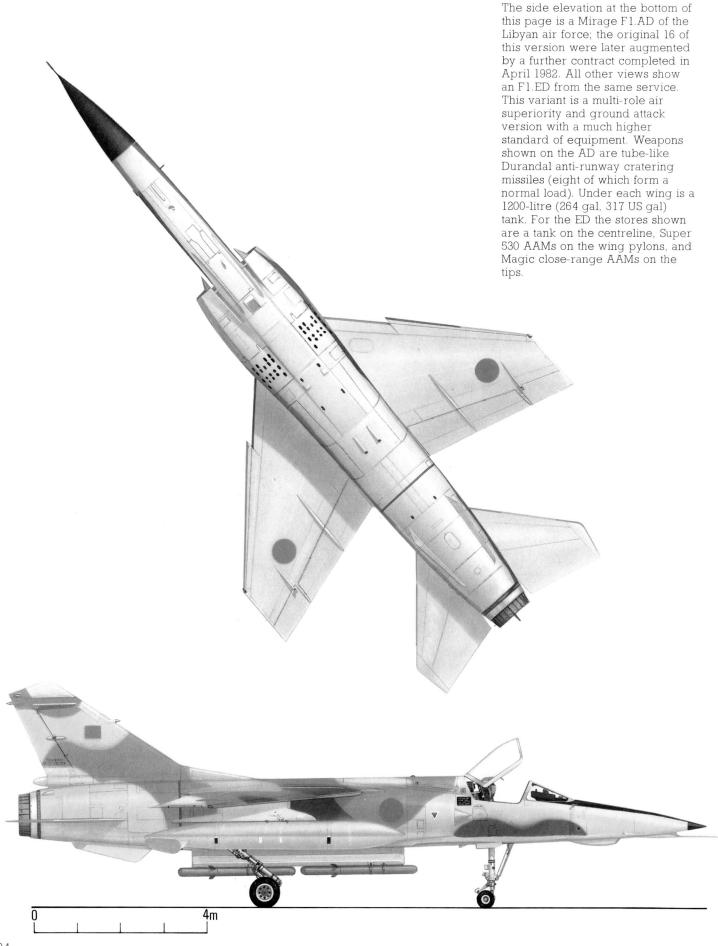

The side elevation at the bottom of this page is a Mirage F1.AD of the Libyan air force; the original 16 of this version were later augmented by a further contract completed in April 1982. All other views show an F1.ED from the same service. This variant is a multi-role air superiority and ground attack version with a much higher standard of equipment. Weapons shown on the AD are tube-like Durandal anti-runway cratering missiles (eight of which form a normal load). Under each wing is a 1200-litre (264 gal, 317 US gal) tank. For the ED the stores shown are a tank on the centreline, Super 530 AAMs on the wing pylons, and Magic close-range AAMs on the tips.

0   4m

Dassault-Breguet Mirage
F1.AD and F1.ED

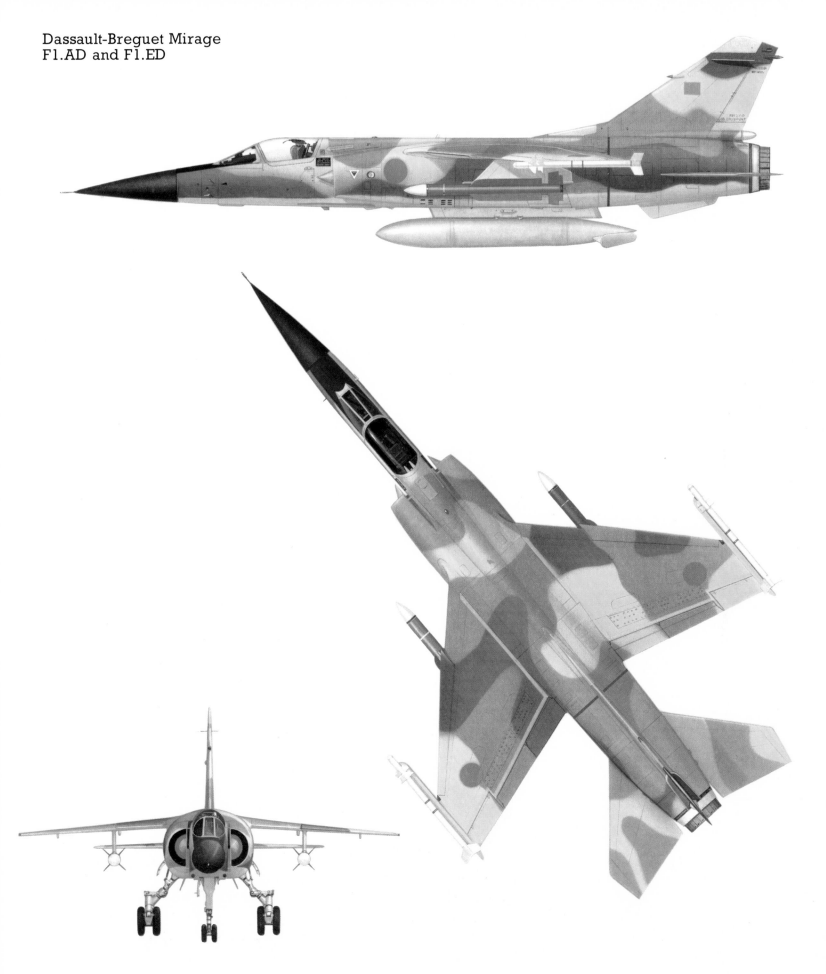

Dassault-Breguet Mirage F1

The first sub-type of F1 to enter inventory service was the F1-C of l'Armée de l'Air. One of the first units to receive the type was EC I/12 Cambrésis (12e Escadre de Chasse) based at Cambrai. The missile is the new Super 530.

Following a large force of delta Mirages the South African Air Force selected the F1-AZ as its chief air-combat aircraft for the period 1970–90, supported by various parts licence-made by Atlas Aircraft. This AZ of 1 Sqn (Waterkloof) is depicted with 1700-litre (374 gal, 449 US gal) tanks. Note absence of radar.

Spain's Ejército del Aire (air force) Mando de la Defensa Aerea (air defence command) has a squadron of F1-CE Mirages as well as two of delta Mirages and two of Phantoms. Esc 141, one of whose CEs is depicted with Magics and 400kg (882lb) bombs, is based at Los Llanos, near Spain's east coast.

When an inflight-refuelling probe is fitted the French Armée de l'Air aircraft are redesignated F1-C-200. Using C-135F tankers, missions have been flown as far as Djibouti. The Dash-200 serves with EC I/5 Vendée at Orange, specializing in low-level interception (note Matra Super 530 and Magic).

Kuwait will probably have replaced the ineffective R.530 missile, seen here on the centreline pylon, by the Super 530 before this book appears. The KuAF originally had 18 of the F1-CK single-seater and two BK trainers, all based at Kuwait City.

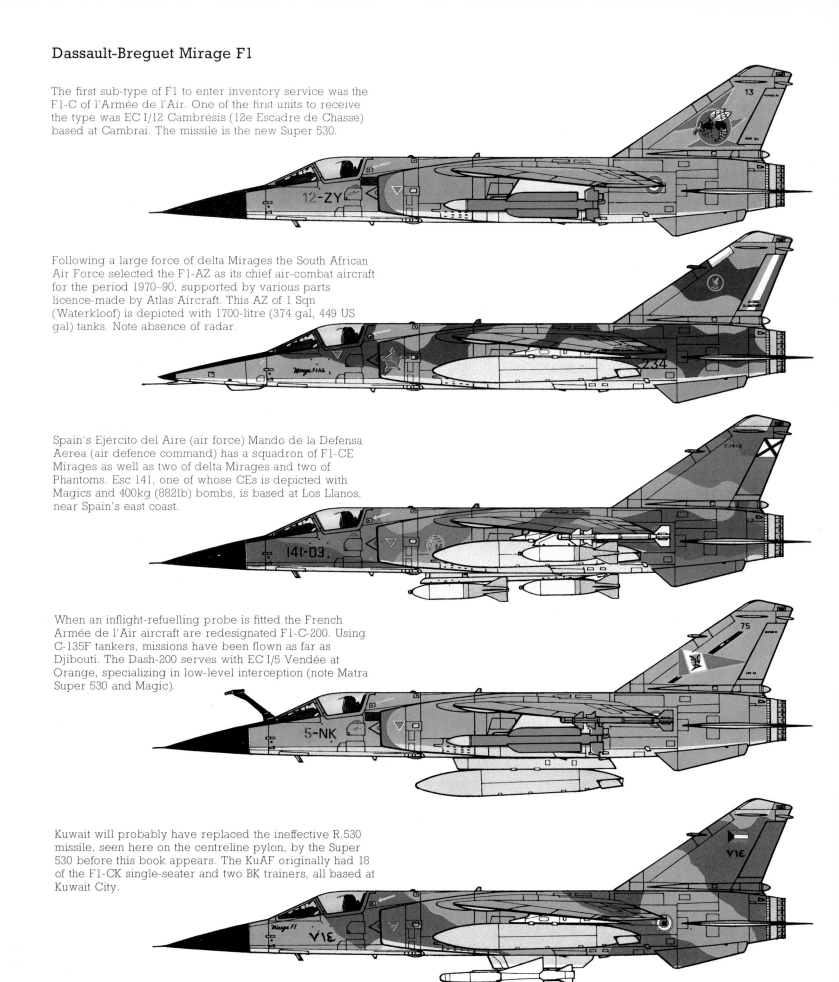

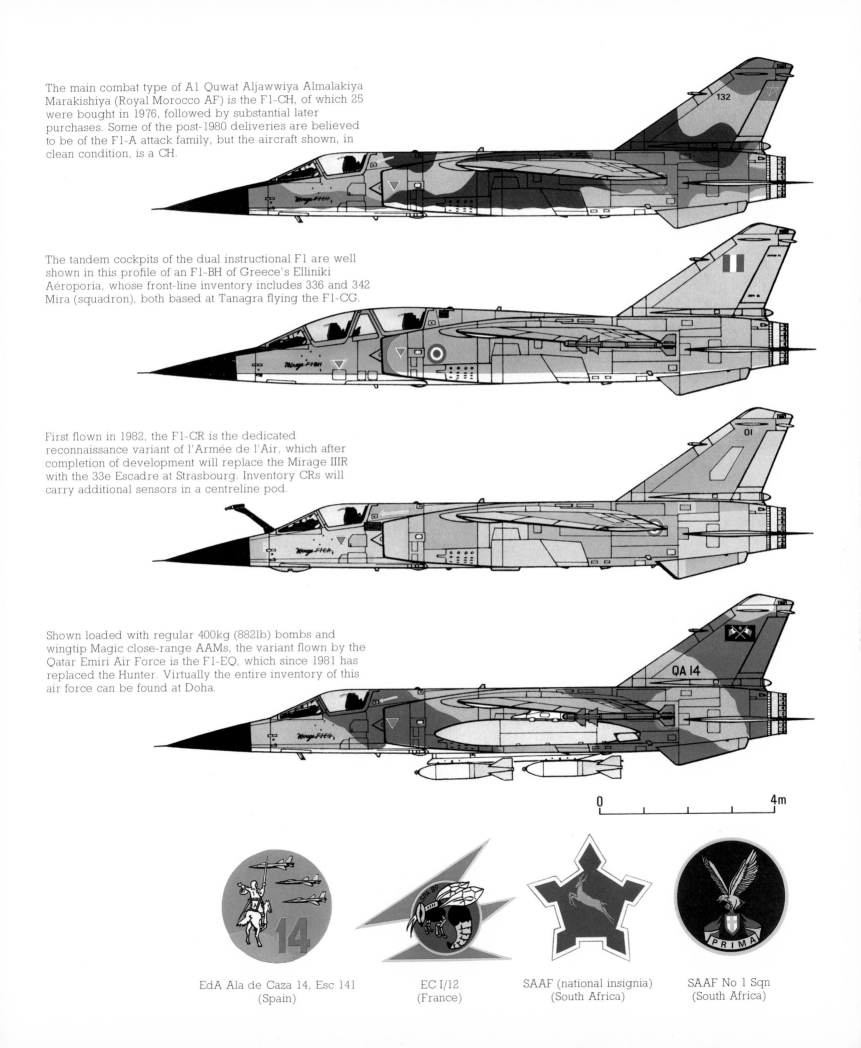

The main combat type of A1 Quwat Aljawwiya Almalakiya Marakishiya (Royal Morocco AF) is the F1-CH, of which 25 were bought in 1976, followed by substantial later purchases. Some of the post-1980 deliveries are believed to be of the F1-A attack family, but the aircraft shown, in clean condition, is a CH.

The tandem cockpits of the dual instructional F1 are well shown in this profile of an F1-BH of Greece's Elliniki Aéroporia, whose front-line inventory includes 336 and 342 Mira (squadron), both based at Tanagra flying the F1-CG.

First flown in 1982, the F1-CR is the dedicated reconnaissance variant of l'Armée de l'Air, which after completion of development will replace the Mirage IIIR with the 33e Escadre at Strasbourg. Inventory CRs will carry additional sensors in a centreline pod.

Shown loaded with regular 400kg (882lb) bombs and wingtip Magic close-range AAMs, the variant flown by the Qatar Emiri Air Force is the F1-EQ, which since 1981 has replaced the Hunter. Virtually the entire inventory of this air force can be found at Doha.

0   4m

EdA Ala de Caza 14, Esc 141   EC I/12   SAAF (national insignia)   SAAF No 1 Sqn
(Spain)   (France)   (South Africa)   (South Africa)

Fairchild Republic A-10A Thunderbolt II

Much attention has been paid to colour schemes for combat aircraft, but such considerations (although still important in the dogfight) will fade in importance as the human eye is replaced by radars and other sensors. This A-10A is painted in the standard scheme of dark green, dark (charcoal) grey and olive drab, the USAF camouflage for aircraft likely to fly at extremely low level over wooded or cultivated terrain. Its unit is the 81st TFW, which has four 18-aircraft squadrons based at RAF Bentwaters and Woodbridge and rotated through four FOLs (forward operating locations) in West Germany. Tail code is that of Wildenrath, WR. It is shown with the Pave Penny laser target designation pod under the right side of the nose and an ALQ-119 ECM pod on Station 11. Missiles are AGM-65A Mavericks. Note the pilot boarding ladder in the view below.

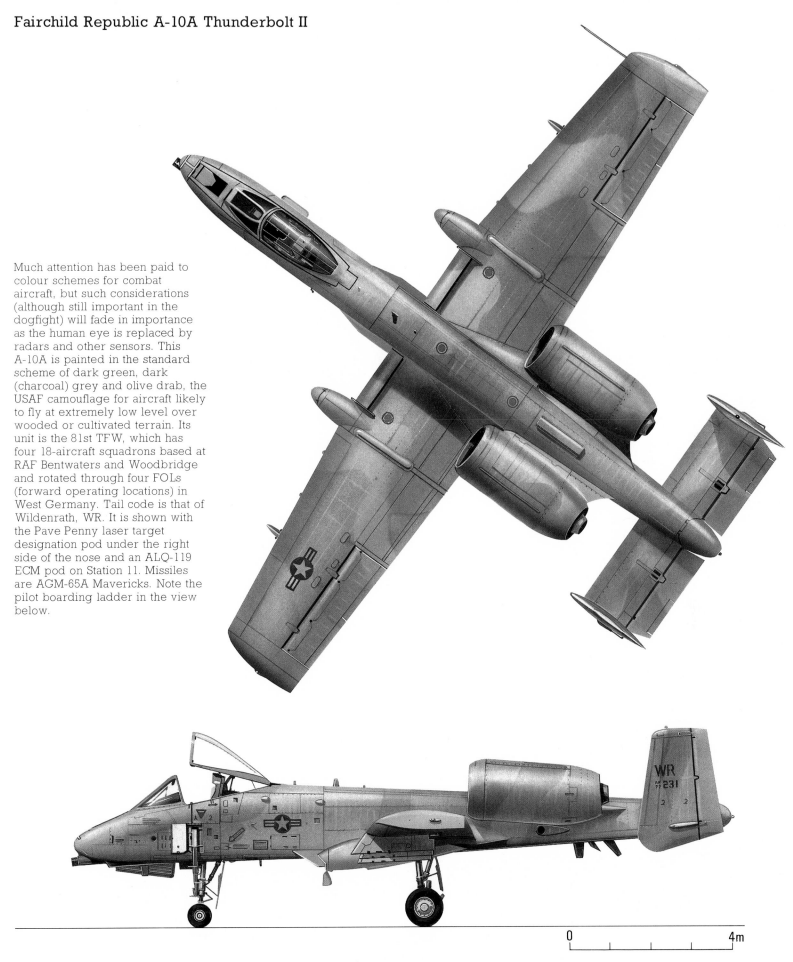

0   4m

Fairchild Republic A-10A Thunderbolt II

Standard camouflage for the A-10A is Lizard/European 1, comprising grey-blue, dark olive-green, and dark blue-green, with national insignia and almost all other stencilling in matt black. This is the wing commander's aircraft (three-squadron tail band) of 23TFW at England AFB, Louisiana.

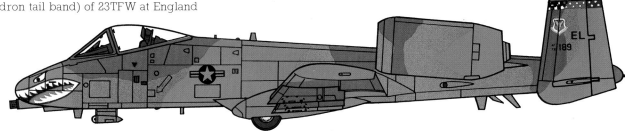

Triple AGM-65A Maverick missiles are seen on this aircraft from 174TFW of the Air National Guard, New York State. Base is denoted by the reference to *The Boys From Syracuse* in black Palace script; aircraft number is 78-607.

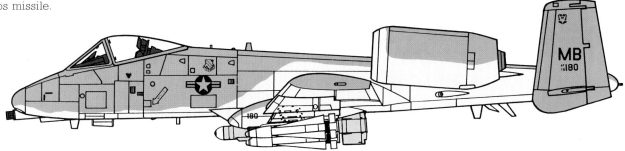

Unusual low visibility for air combat colours of two shades of grey are seen on this aircraft serving with 354TFW, the first user, at Myrtle Beach, South Carolina. Inboard of the Mavericks is a Hobos missile.

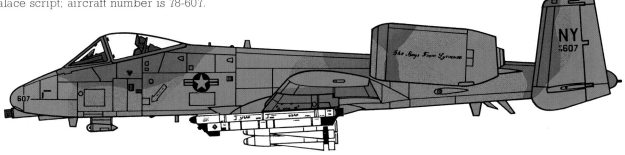

Another low-visibility air-combat scheme is this mix of light grey and blue-grey. The 2273-litre (500 gal, 600 US gal) tanks match the under surfaces, and a dark-grey false canopy is painted on the underside of the nose of this aircraft from 355TFW at Davis-Monthan AFB, Arizona.

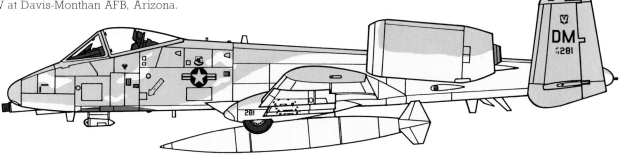

The experimental JAWS II scheme is seen here on an
A-10A from 66FWS of the Fighter Weapons Wing at Nellis,
outside Las Vegas, Nevada. TAC shield on fin and 57FWW
badge on body are both black. Bombs are Mk 82s in dark
olive.

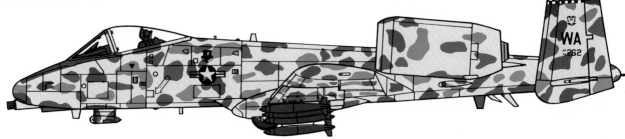

The Air National Guard badge adorns the engine pods of
the aircraft of No 103 Tactical Fighter Group, State of
Connecticut, based at Bradley Field, outside Windsor
Locks. Small pod under the forward fuselage is in all cases
the Pave Penny laser designator.

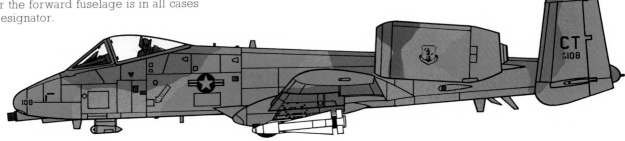

On this A-10A, from Air National Guard No 128TFG, State
of Wisconsin, based at Truax Field, pylon station 11 is
occupied by an ECM pod. The pod in this case is the
Westinghouse ALQ-131 but several others are available, as
well as various payload dispensers.

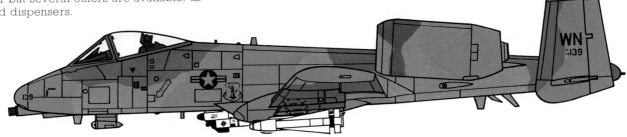

The company-funded Night/Adverse Weather two-seater is
painted light grey all over with red ejection-seat triangles
and yellow UHF/Tacan blade. The external pods include
FLIR (forward-looking infra-red) systems, but these will not
be fitted to the current production two-seat combat-ready
trainer version (which had not appeared as this book went
to press).

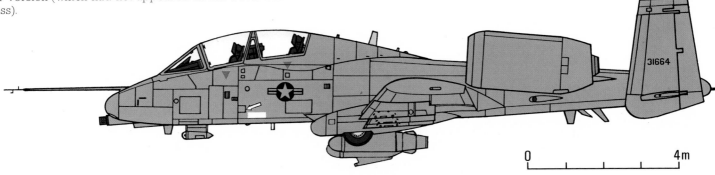

Fairchild Republic A-10A Thunderbolt II

In the 1960s the RAF disdainfully resisted buying the Buccaneer attack aircraft because it was not supersonic, and gave in with an ill grace. At that time the common idea of an attack aircraft was the F-111, which can exceed twice the speed of sound. It took the US Navy to show that it was possible to do at least as good a job by flying lower and slower. The USN took the supersonic F-8 and turned it into the subsonic A-7, which was so successful it was bought in large numbers for the US Air Force as well. Today the main close-support aircraft of the USAF is the A-10, with a speed little over half that of the A-7!

Behind the concept of this unique machine lay many years of studies of aircraft to fly Co-In (counter-insurgent) missions, in what were called 'brush-fire' wars. These were mainly quite light, propeller-driven aircraft, designed to operate from any short jungle airstrip carrying guns, rockets and other stores against minimally equipped troops. Such aircraft might even be useful in a sophisticated war if they had modern defence avionics, but in 1967 the USAF launched its AX programme for a close-support aircraft in a larger and basically new category. Jet-propelled, the AX was to carry a gun of devastating power to pierce the armour of the newest tanks, as well as every kind of tactical munition. Quite slow, it was to rely on flying very low, its ability to make rapid manoeuvres, and an unprecedented degree of survivability.

Fairchild Republic's YA-10A prototype flew on 10 May 1972 and, after evaluation against a Northrop rival, was chosen as a standard type of USAF Tactical Air Command in a 747-aircraft programme. It has yet to be proved how well such a large and rather ponderous machine can actually survive in a battlefield covered by modern radars and SAMs, but the Thunderbolt II itself is lethal enough. The basic weapon, around which the aircraft was designed, is the most powerful gun ever flown (there have been many with larger calibre, but nothing remotely approaching such muzzle horsepower). It fills the left side of the fuselage under the cockpit, together with a car-sized drum of 1,174 rounds of ammunition. Up to 7257kg (16,000lb) of weapons can be hung on 11 pylons from tip to tip under the unswept high-lift wings.

The two turbofan engines, basically the same as those of the S-3A Viking, are hung high on the rear fuselage where they offer minimum infra-red signature to ground-launched missiles and where flight is simple with either engine knocked out. Major parts of the twin-finned tail, landing gear and other items are left/right interchangeable, and the A-10 is designed to get home with any one set shot clean off the aircraft. The pilot sits in a large 'bathtub' of thick titanium armour designed to resist shells of 23mm calibre, and protective measures throughout the aircraft are exceptional. Avionics were originally called 'austere', with no advanced navigation system or radar. But defensive electronics are comprehensive, as are weapon-aiming sub-systems including a Pave Penny laser tracker to assist the pilot in locking on to targets designated (illuminated) by friendly lasers. Laser-guided bombs and the basic TV-guided Maverick are among the 'smart' missiles normally carried.

The first A-10A squadron became operational in October 1977, and by late 1982 all but the last 100 USAF aircraft had been delivered. Included in the 1981 batch were 30 two-seat combat-ready trainer versions, and these have full weapons capability.

For the European theatre the night/adverse weather (N/AW) capability has been recognized as limited. In May 1979 Fairchild Republic flew a company-funded two-seat N/AW version with enhanced avionics. There are no plans to build more, but the existing force are expected to be updated by fitting a Lantirn (low-altitude navigation targeting infra-red for night) pod. This will make possible terrain-hugging operations at night or in bad weather, and facilitate target recognition and the delivery of precision-guided missiles. Tacit acceptance of the worth of such an aircraft is demonstrated by an apparent copy in the Soviet Union.

COUNTRY OF ORIGIN USA.

CREW 1, trainer: 2.

TOTAL PRODUCED About 650 of a total of 747.

DIMENSIONS Wingspan 17·53m (57ft 6in); length 16·26m (53ft 4in); wing area 47·01m² (506ft²).

WEIGHTS Empty 9771kg (21,541lb); forward airstrip weight with reduced fuel and weapons 14865kg (32,771lb); maximum loaded 22680kg (50,000lb).

ENGINES Two 4112kg (9,065lb) General Electric TF34-100 turbofans.

MAXIMUM SPEED At sea level, in clean (unladen) condition 706km/h (439mph).

SERVICE CEILING Not published; would seldom fly higher than 5km (16,400ft).

RANGE Operational radius on deep strike mission 1000km (621 miles); ferry range 3949km (2,454 miles).

MILITARY LOAD One 30mm GAU-8/A gun with 1,174 rounds, firing at 2,100 or 4,200 shots/min; all tactical weapons and other stores, including ECM pods, can be carried on 11 external pylons, with limit of 6505kg (14,341lb) with full internal fuel and 7257kg (16,000lb) with reduced fuel.

USER USA (AF).

General Dynamics F-16 Fighting Falcon

In the author's opinion the most cost-effective warplane in the world today, the F-16 is an all-weather multi-role 'fighter' which, like the F-4 of a previous generation, can do almost everything better than any other aircraft. Yet instead of being designed for the job it evolved by a natural process from a mere LWF (lightweight fighter) project launched by the US Air Force in 1972 as a demonstration exercise in building a simple day fighter smaller and cheaper than the F-15.

The winner of the LWF competition, the GD Model 401, flew on 2 February 1974. There was no thought of buying it for inventory service, but the emergence of a large foreign market spurred a major change in plan. General Dynamics developed the Model 401 (YF-16) into a slightly larger aircraft with very comprehensive and up-to-date avionics which on 13 January 1975 was ordered into full-scale development. By this time a sales battle had developed; on 7 June 1975 Belgium, Denmark, the Netherlands and Norway announced the joint selection of the F-16 and a large-scale collaborative manufacturing programme for the aircraft and its engine (which is virtually identical to the engines of the much larger F-15).

Of classic tailed configuration, with large forebody strakes leading into an unswept wing blended into the body, the F-16 has a relatively conventional structure but very advanced engineering features. The basic flight system is all-digital, with fly-by-wire flight controls governing leading-edge flaps, trailing-edge flaperons (surfaces acting as flaps and ailerons), slab tailplanes and rudder. The wing variable camber is novel. At take-off the flaperons are at 20° and the leading edge at −2°. After lift-off the leading edge goes to −15°. In maximum afterburner, despite the use of a plain fixed belly inlet, Mach 2 can be reached with the leading and trailing flaps all at −2°; for pulling 9g manoeuvres the trailing edge is at 0° and the leading edge fully down at −25°. Like all future fighters the F-16 has relaxed static stability, to the extent that without the high-authority autopilot it would be almost unstable, in order to gain very large improvements in agility and sustained power of manoeuvre (which also needs a relatively powerful engine).

Seated almost lying on his back to resist acceleration loads, the pilot flies the F-16 by a sidestick controller on the right console, with an armrest, which, while scarcely moving, senses the pilot's input force and feeds the required signal to the control system. Outstanding all-round view is provided by a one-piece canopy without separate windscreen. Westinghouse supplies the multi-mode pulse-doppler radar, while other equipment includes an inertial navigation system and internal radar warning.

ECM pods are carried externally, as part of the maximum possible stores load of 9276kg (20,450lb) hung on seven pylons plus the wingtips. The latter locations are reserved for close-range AAMs, usually the AIM-9L. The large radar-guided Sparrow and Sky Flash have been fired, but are not yet carried. Every kind of tactical weapon can be used, except for some very large dispenser pods, up to a unit mass of 2041kg (4,500lb).

Parts for the F-16 and its engine are made in many countries, duplicating US sources, and European customer aircraft are assembled in Belgium and the Netherlands. The total USAF programme is 1,388, including 204 F-16B two-seaters with less fuselage fuel but full weapons capability. The first production F-16A flew in August 1978, and deliveries to the 388th Tactical Fighter Wing began on 6 January 1979. By late 1982 some 700 had flown.

Among a wealth of planned versions, prototypes have flown of the F-16/79, with the cheap J79 engine for export, and the F-16/101 with the GE F101-DFE engine of 12700kg (28,000lb) thrust. One F-16 was tested with direct-force control canard fins and could lead to a new-generation flight-control system. The F-16E has a longer body and very large cranked delta wing, with no separate tailplane; this has twice the weapon load or range.

COUNTRY OF ORIGIN USA.

CREW 1, **F-16B:** 2.

TOTAL PRODUCED Over 700 by 1983 of planned 2,000-plus.

DIMENSIONS Wingspan (without AAMs) 9·45m (31ft 0in); length 15·09m (49ft 6in); wing area 27·87m² (300·0ft²).

WEIGHTS Empty, **F-16A:** 7070kg (15,586lb), **F-16B:** 7374kg (16,258lb); take-off weight in air/air mission 10800kg (23,810lb), same as sea-level engine thrust; maximum loaded 16057kg (35,400lb) early production, 17010kg (37,500lb) later aircraft.

ENGINE One 10800kg (23,810lb) Pratt & Whitney F100-PW-200 afterburning turbofan.

MAXIMUM SPEED Clean at 12·2km (40,000ft) 2124km/h (1,320mph, Mach 2).

SERVICE CEILING Higher than 15·24km (50,000ft).

RANGE Maximum with external fuel more than 3890km (2,415 miles).

MILITARY LOAD One 20mm M61A-1 gun with 515 rounds; total of 9276kg (20,450lb) of external stores carried on centreline (stressed at 5g for 1000kg, 2,205lb), inboard wing pylons (5g limit 2041kg, 4,500lb each), centre underwing pylons (each 1588kg, 3,500lb), outboard underwing (each 318kg, 700lb) and AAM shoes on wingtips (each 193kg, 425lb). For 9g combat manoeuvres most loads are reduced by 45 per cent.

USERS Belgium, Denmark, Egypt, Israel, Netherlands, Norway, Pakistan, South Korea, USA (AF), Venezuela.

This Block-1 Fighting Falcon was assigned to the 8th Tactical Fighter Wing, USAF, at Kunsam AB, Okinawa, where over 70 F-16s were in use by 1983, all in combat squadrons. This is the famed 'Wolf Pack' unit whose insignia is seen on the fuselage aft of the cockpit. The finish is standard three-tone grey, with the new range of stencil colours much less strident than those used before low visibility was an objective. Block-1 aircraft were delivered with black radomes but later had the grey elastomer-coated radomes substituted. The long ALQ-119 ECM (electronic countermeasures) pod was used for a time in 1979–80 before the standard ALQ-131 became readily available. Other weapons shown include the AIM-9L Sidewinder (9J and J1 are also common) and Mk 84 bombs; the MRASM (medium-range air/surface missile), which is on test on F-16s, will later form part of the Falcon's armament. An inset shows the enlarged tailplane fitted to post-1981 F-16s.

General Dynamics F-16A-1-GD Fighting Falcon

General Dynamics F-16 Fighting Falcon

The first unit of the FAB/BL (Belgian air force) to convert to the F-16 was No 349 Sqn, based at Beauvechain. On 1 January 1981 this squadron was declared fully operational to NATO after its re-equipment, the first F-16 unit in any European air force. This aircraft was the third F-16A completed in Belgium.

The Koninklijke Luchtmacht (Netherlands air force) has been progressively changing over from F-104s to F-16s at about the same rate as the Belgians, and Nos 322 and 323 Sqns at Leeuwarden began the process as early as 7 June 1979. This F-16B, J-259, was the first F-16 assembled in the Netherlands by Fokker; it went to 322 Sqn.

Denmark's Flyvevåbnet has F-104s and F-35 Drakens, and used its first deliveries of F-16s to replace the ageing F-100s. This F-16A was assigned to No 727 Sqn at Skrydstrup, where 727 and 730 Sqns deploy 46 single-seat F-16As and 12 F-16B two-seaters in both the interception and training roles.

Norway's KNL not only paints its F-16 aircraft in a non-standard grey colour scheme but also insists on the optional extension under the rudder housing a braking parachute. Belgium's F-16s will later have the same compartment but for ECM (Loral Rapport III) which is being installed from early 1984.

Israel's Heyl Ha'Avir is the only operator of the F-16 to use standard desert camouflage, which is the more surprising as many Kfir fighters are now painted in low-visibility grey. By the time this book appears deliveries may have started of Israel's second batch of 75, making that country the largest foreign customer.

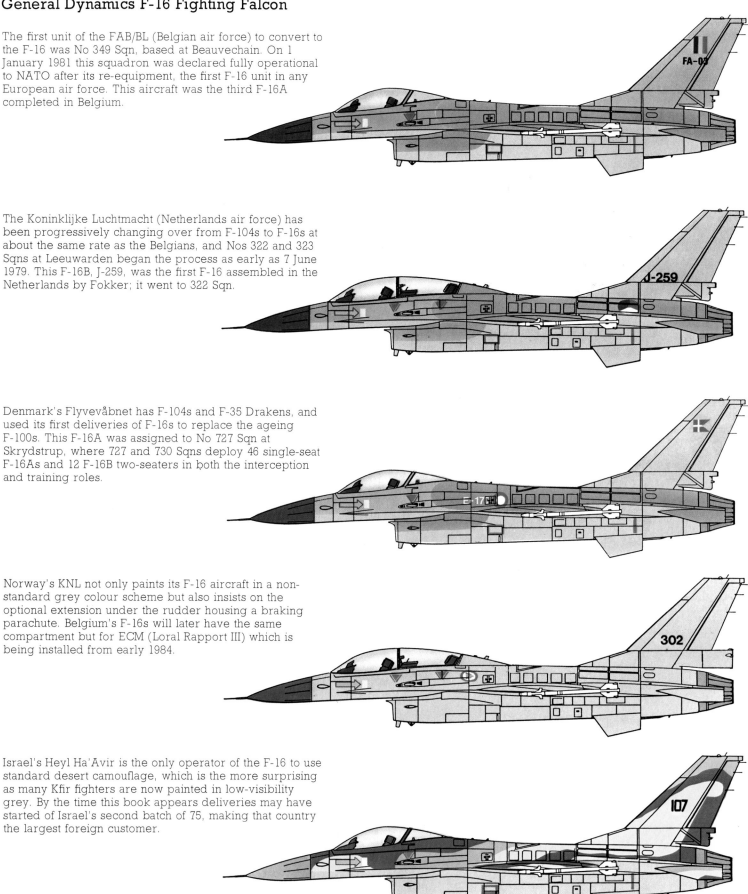

Egypt has bought 40 F-16s almost identical in construction standard and camouflage finish to the USAF choice, and plans to acquire a further batch of 40. Other foreign customers include South Korea, Pakistan and Venezuela, and most of the NATO customers have further big purchases in the pipeline.

The F-16/79, which first flew in this rebuilt two-seat form as the F-16/79B on 29 October 1980, is offered to foreign customers who are not cleared by the State Department to receive the F100 engine, or who already use the J79 turbojet and are prepared to accept its greater weight and poorer thrust and fuel consumption in return for low cost.

In contrast the F-16/101, first flown on 19 December 1980, has an engine offering significant gains over the F100 in several respects, one of which is sheer power. The outstandingly suitable General Electric F110 (previously F101DFE) augmented turbofan could later become the standard F-16 engine.

The AFTI/F-16 is the Advanced Fighter Technology Integration research aircraft. Preceded by the YF-16 No 1 rebuilt in a CCV (control-configured vehicle) layout in March 1976, the AFTI has a totally new flight control system giving incredible manoeuvrability, including direct lateral and vertical movements.

The F-16XL, also known as the F-16E, is virtually a new aircraft, using a large-area cranked-arrow wing which was one of those rejected at the start of the F-16 programme in 1972. Much longer, and with no horizontal tail, it has a shorter take-off, can carry 82 per cent more internal fuel, much greater weapon load on 17 pylons, and fly faster and attack at higher speed. This is the No 1 XL; No 2 is a two-seater with the F110 engine.

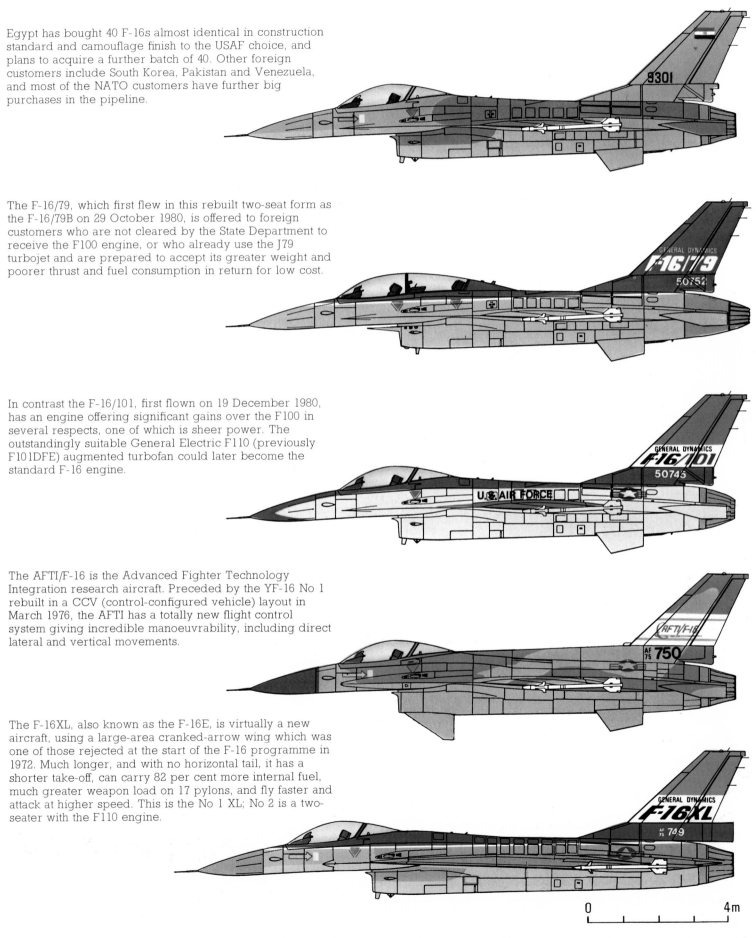

0   4m

0
4m

General Dynamics F-111F

The best and final model of F-111 tactical bomber was the F-111F, notable both for its greatly improved avionic systems (which combined most of the capability of the F-111D systems at a cost little greater than that for the A and E models) and for its very much more powerful Dash-100 engine, which at last conquered the ponderous mass of the fully laden aircraft and gave performance close to what the designers had in mind. Aircraft 70-373 serves with the 48th Tactical Fighter Wing at RAF Lakenheath, England, but accompanied the unit on various overseas detachments, including Pakistan in December 1978. On this page the wings are shown spread at the minimum sweep of 16°, with the four wing pylons carrying 2271-litre (500 gal, 600 US gal) drop tanks; below is a clean aircraft with wings swept at 72·5° and carrying only an ALQ-119(V-12) ECM pod under the rear fuselage. The views on the left show the wings at the maximum 72·5° setting, and the front view below shows tanks fitted with wings spread. The underside view shows the rear warning aerials as small spikes projecting aft of the tailplanes; the rear-facing ECM aerials occupy the blunt pods beside the engine nozzles. In the side elevation, below, the weapon-bay doors, airbrake and tail bumper are all extended, and the wing is shown at 16° sweep with slats and flaps in action and the glove rotated.

General Dynamics F-111

The first YF-111A prototype, USAF No 63-9768, is shown here as it looked at first flight on 21 December 1974. Internally hardly anything was as on today's aircraft, but the outside looks remarkably similar. Later the pointed fairings were cut off the rear ECM and ALR-41 at the tail.

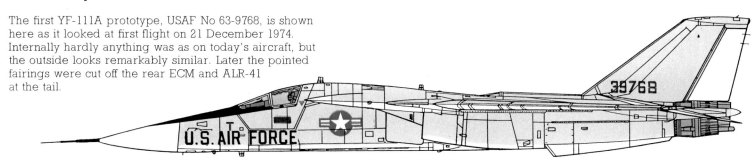

Shorter and in many ways more attractive, the Navy F-111B was primarily an air-defence interceptor, with the capacious electronics bay moved from ahead of the cockpit to behind it. Four XAIM-54A Phoenix long-range missiles are shown carried by the second F-111B.

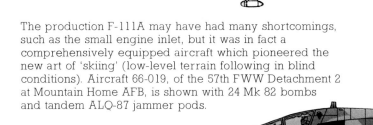

The production F-111A may have had many shortcomings, such as the small engine inlet, but it was in fact a comprehensively equipped aircraft which pioneered the new art of 'skiing' (low-level terrain following in blind conditions). Aircraft 66-019, of the 57th FWW Detachment 2 at Mountain Home AFB, is shown with 24 Mk 82 bombs and tandem ALQ-87 jammer pods.

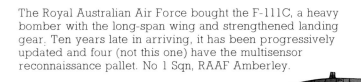

The Royal Australian Air Force bought the F-111C, a heavy bomber with the long-span wing and strengthened landing gear. Ten years late in arriving, it has been progressively updated and four (not this one) have the multisensor reconnaissance pallet. No 1 Sqn, RAAF Amberley.

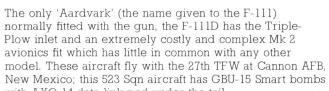

The only 'Aardvark' (the name given to the F-111) normally fitted with the gun, the F-111D has the Triple-Plow inlet and an extremely costly and complex Mk 2 avionics fit which has little in common with any other model. These aircraft fly with the 27th TFW at Cannon AFB, New Mexico; this 523 Sqn aircraft has GBU-15 Smart bombs with AXQ-14 data-link pod under the tail.

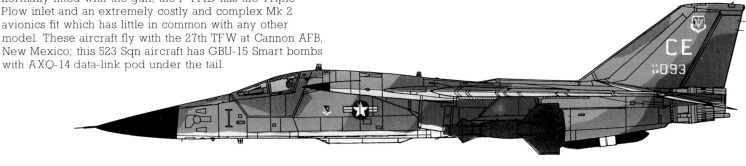

First to introduce the Triple-Plow inlet, the F-111E serves
with the 20th TFW at RAF Upper Heyford, England.
Aircraft 68–060 is shown clean except for 2273-litre (500
gal, 600 US gal) tanks.

There were intended to be 210 FB-111A bombers for SAC,
but inflation cut the number to just 76, of which about 56
are in the inventory. Aircraft 68–247 is shown with SRAM
missiles under its long-span wings. An aircraft with the
509th BW, its tail was painted for a Tiger Meet (NATO
international exercise).

Grumman is rebuilding 41 F-111As into EF-111A 'Electric
Fox' tactical jamming and electronic-warfare aircraft, each
costing more than three times as much as an F-111A.
Aircraft 66-041 is shown after reassignment to the 366th
TFW. As well as the ALQ-99E system, with ventral canoe
and fin-top aerials, an ALQ-131 ECM pod may be hung
under each wing.

NASA, the US National Aeronautics and Space
Administration, used one of the 17 pre-production aircraft,
63-9778, as a basis on which to test a 'natural laminar flow'
wing at various sweep angles. The wing has marked
washout (reduction of incidence) towards the tip.

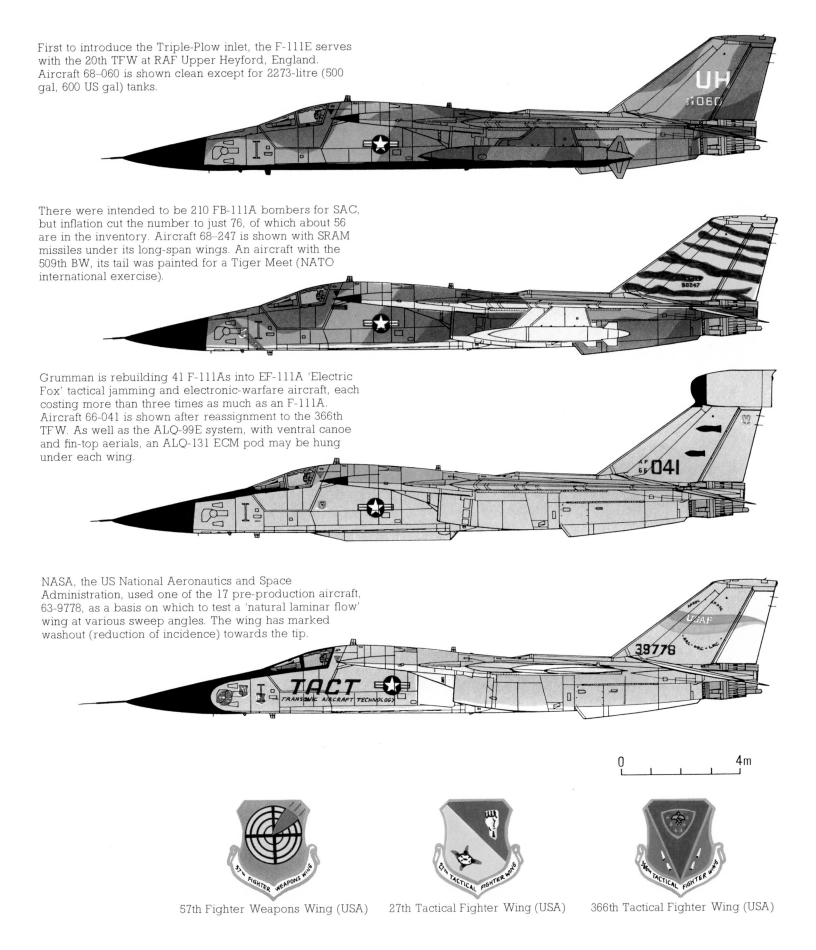

0   4m

57th Fighter Weapons Wing (USA)   27th Tactical Fighter Wing (USA)   366th Tactical Fighter Wing (USA)

General Dynamics F-111

In the early 1960s the US Air Force planned the F-111 as the next standard fighter, to be sold in thousands to many countries. In the event few were built, and not as fighters but as the first of the new breed of blind first-pass attack precision bombers! No aircraft of modern times has been the subject of so many problems and such acrimonious argument, to the extent that its immense capability became almost overlooked.

There were two roots to the problems. The first was that the USAF Tactical Air Command set its sights too high, especially in the matter of mission and ferry range. The second was that the Secretary of Defense of the day tried to save money by combining the USAF requirement with a seemingly similar one for the Navy, in the first and most notorious 'commonality' exercise.

In the original planning of 1959 TAC wished merely to find a replacement for the F-105 as a fighter/bomber, with an internal bay for at least one nuclear bomb. Throughout the 1950s aircraft design had galloped ahead almost daily, and in drawing up Specific Operational Requirement 183 of 14 June 1960 the USAF was determined to capitalize on every advantage it could gain from such new advances as variable geometry (so-called swing wings), afterburning turbofan engines, titanium structure, variable inlets and all-weather electronics. It demanded a fighter that could fly at Mach 2·5, operate from short rough airstrips in forward areas, carry heavy loads of all types of weapons and fly between any two airfields in the world in one day.

After prolonged rounds of bidding, the contract was awarded on 24 November 1962 to General Dynamics, and the first F-111A development aircraft flew on 21 December 1964. The Navy F-111B flew in May 1965. After three years the F-111B ground to a halt, and was replaced by the F-14A.

Meanwhile the F-111A investigated flight with wings spread at 16°, with full-span slats and flaps open, and also folded back at 72° 30' for transonic low-level attack using terrain-following radar. Pilot and navigator sit side by side in a sealed capsule which can be jettisoned complete and used on land or sea as a survival shelter. Despite almost crippling problems with increasing weight, engine/airframe mismatch, severe aerodynamic drag, systems difficulties and catastrophic structural failure, work was pressed ahead and the first TAC unit began to form in June 1967.

GD Fort Worth delivered 141 of the basic F-111A version, despite the fact these were deficient in several respects. Then came 94 F-111Es with improved inlets and slightly better engines, followed by 24 F-111Cs for the Royal Australian Air Force with the original engines but long-span wings and stronger main landing gears (the design of which in all versions prohibits carriage of heavy external loads under the fuselage). Then followed 96 F-111Ds with completely different avionic systems of great complexity and cost. Last of the basic tactical versions was the F-111F, often called 'the aircraft the F-111 should have been from the start', with much more powerful TF30 engines and avionics providing most of the features of the D but at much-reduced cost. The 106th F was the last F-111 to be delivered, in 1976, rising costs cutting off the programme early. For the same reason a planned purchase of 210 FB-111A bombers for Strategic Air Command was cut back to 76. This model has the long-span wing and stronger landing gear, and normally carries several SRAM missiles. All models have an inflight-refuelling receptacle.

Today the USAF has two squadrons (called wings) of FB-111As in the USA, two wings in England (F-111Es at Upper Heyford and Fs at Lakenheath) and a wing of Ds in New Mexico. Pave Tack multi-sensor pods are being added. Since 1979 Grumman has been rebuilding 42 F-111As as EF-111A ECM tactical jamming platforms, with the same ALQ-99E jamming installation as the EA-6B but without the two extra operators. Used in the stand-off, close-support and penetration roles, these costly but vital additions to the TAC attack force entered service in 1982.

COUNTRY OF ORIGIN USA.

CREW 2.

TOTAL PRODUCED 562.

DIMENSIONS Wingspan, 16°, **A**, **D**, **E**, **F**, **EF**: 19·2m (63ft 0in), **C**, **FB**: 21·34m (70ft 0in); 72·5°, **A**, **D**, **E**, **F**, **EF**: 9·74m (31ft 11½in), **C**, **FB**: 10·34m (33ft 11in); length 23·02m (75ft 6¼in), except **EF**: 23·16m (76ft 0in); wing area, 16°, **A**, **D**, **E**, **F**, **EF**: 48·77m² (525ft²), **C**, **FB**: 51·1m² (550ft²).

WEIGHTS Empty, **A**: 20943kg (46,172lb), **C**: 21455kg (47,300lb), **D**: 22226kg (49,000lb), **E**: 22015kg (48,534lb), **F**: 21398kg (47,175lb), **FB**: 22680kg (50,000lb), **EF**: 25072kg (55,275lb); maximum loaded, **A**: 41503kg (91,500lb), **C**: 51845kg (114,300lb), **D**, **E**: 44905kg (99,000lb), **F**: 45359kg (100,000lb), **FB**: 53977kg (119,000lb), **EF**: 40346kg (88,948lb).

ENGINES **A**, **C**: two 8390kg (18,500lb) Pratt & Whitney TF30-3, **D**, **E**: 8890kg (19,600lb) TF30-9, **F**: 11385kg (25,100lb) TF30-100, **FB**: 9230kg (20,350lb) TF30-7.

MAXIMUM SPEED All, clean, high altitude: 2334km/h (1,450mph, Mach 2·2).

SERVICE CEILING **A**, **EF**: 13·7km (45,000ft), **F**: 18·3km (60,000ft).

RANGE Low-altitude combat radius typically 500km (310 miles), ferry range typically 3747km (2,328 miles).

MILITARY LOAD Originally provision for one 20mm M61 gun in weapon bay; weapon bay for B-43 or similar bomb or (**FB**) one SRAM; three hardpoints under each wing (outer two fixed and usable only at 16° sweep) for bombs, missiles or tanks, maximum bombload typically 13154kg (29,000lb).

USERS Australia, USA (AF).

Grumman A-6 Intruder

Until the 1960s little attention had been paid in the USA to the need to hit point targets in bad weather or at night, even though this was the recurrent demand in the Korean war. The one exception was a Navy/Marines requirement of May 1957, won on 31 December 1957 by the Grumman G-128 submission. Ordered as the A2F-1, the first prototype flew on 19 April 1960. Redesignated A-6A and named Intruder it has since been the only aircraft in the US services to rival the F-111 for blind first-pass attacks. Like the F-111 it has also been developed into an ECM platform.

For a low-level transonic bomber a remarkably long-span wing was chosen, with no supercirculation system but with full-span leading-edge drooping flaps and single-slotted trailing-edge flaps. Roll control is by flaperons (spoilers), the outer trailing-edge surfaces being split upper/lower speed brakes. Pilot and navigator sit side by side behind the vast nose radar, computer and nav/attack avionics. The two turbojets (which in the prototype had tilting nozzles) are hung on the fuselage flanks under the wing, with the main gears pivoting forwards under the roots. Weapons are hung externally.

The crew climb aboard up ladders pivoted down from the wall of the inlet duct, and sit in Martin-Baker GRU-5B or -7 seats under a wide canopy which slides hydraulically to the rear. Up to 7230kg (15,940lb) of fuel are housed in fuselage cells and the integral-tank wings, with inflight refuelling by a removable probe ahead of the windscreen. In the production A-6A the jetpipes were given a fixed modest downward tilt, but the perforated door-type airbrakes on the fuselage downstream were retained. Great efforts were made to perfect the complex nav/attack system; the contract was the first ever negotiated by the Navy of the cost plus incentive fee type.

Squadron VA-42 was the first to deploy this extremely effective aircraft, in February 1963, and every Navy and Marines squadron to receive the A-6A saw impressive active duty in Vietnam, the Marines operating from shore bases. At this time small numbers were built, or converted, of the A-6B carrying Standard ARM anti-radar missiles and A-6C with extra sensors, but these had limited service. From 1966 Grumman rebuilt 62 A-6As as KA-6D air refuelling tankers, able to transfer up to 9525kg (21,000lb) of fuel through a hosereel and drogue installation in the rear fuselage. The KA-6D can also act as a day bomber or as an air/sea rescue control aircraft.

In 1963 Grumman flew an A-6A converted to EA-6A standard with more than 30 aerials for detecting, locating, classifying, recording and jamming enemy radars and other signals, while retaining some attack capability. The Marines received 27 of this model, but from it was evolved the fully purpose-built EA-6B Prowler which first flew on 25 May 1968 and has since been the Navy's EW (electronic warfare) aircraft. Heavier and more powerful than other A-6s, the Prowler has a longer forward fuselage accommodating two extra crew to manage the ALQ-99 ECM installation. This has a battery of aerials in a fin-top pod to receive signals, a computer to process them and manage jamming power, and up to five external pods each powered by a nose turbine and covering one of eight frequency bands. Deliveries began in 1971 and are expected to reach a total of 102 in 1986.

On 27 February 1970 Grumman flew the first A-6E, the standard advanced attack version with a strengthened airframe (without fuselage speed brakes) and completely modernized avionics, including a Norden APQ-148 multi-mode radar and Kaiser AVA-1 cockpit display. The IBM computer is related to that in the EA-6B. The first A-6E squadron was deployed in September 1972, and over 320 have now been delivered, more than half the total of all A-6 models to date. Recent updates include the TRAM (target recognition attack multisensor) pod under the nose, with infra-red and laser sensors and also providing automatic carrier landing in bad weather, and the ability to launch up to six Harpoon cruise missiles from wing pylons. About 12 A-6Es are expected to be built annually until 1986.

COUNTRY OF ORIGIN USA.

CREW 2, **EA-6B:** 4.

TOTAL PRODUCED About 630 by 1983.

DIMENSIONS Wingspan 16·15m (53ft 0in); length, **A-6A:** 16·64m (54ft 7in), **EA-6A:** 16·84m (55ft 3in), **EA-6B:** 18·11m (59ft 5in), **A-6E:** 16·69m (54ft 9in); wing area 49.1m² (528·9ft²).

WEIGHTS Empty, **A-6A:** 11650kg (25,684lb), **EA-6A:** 12596kg (27,769lb), **EA-6B:** 14588kg (32,162lb), **A-6E:** 12000kg (26,456lb); maximum loaded, **A-6A:** 27500kg (60,626lb), **EA-6A:** 25628kg (56,500lb), **EA-6B:** 29483kg (65,000lb), **A-6E:** 27397kg (60,400lb).

ENGINES Two 4218kg (9,300lb) Pratt & Whitney J52-8A turbojets, **A-6E:** J52-8B, same thrust; **EA-6B:** 5080kg (11,200lb) J52–408 turbojets.

MAXIMUM SPEED **A-6E**, clean, sea level: 1036km/h (644mph), **EA-6B**, clean: 1048km/h (651mph), **EA-6B**, five pods: 987km/h (613mph).

SERVICE CEILING **A-6E:** 12·95km (42,500ft).

RANGE **A-6E**, max bombload: 1631km (1,013 miles), **A-6E**, max external fuel: 5230km (3,250 miles).

MILITARY LOAD Five weapon hardpoints, each rated at 1633kg (3,600lb), with total limit of 8165kg (18,000lb); typical load 30 bombs of 227kg (500lb) or three 907kg (2,000lb), plus two 1135 litre (250 gal, 300 US gal) drop tanks.

USERS USA (Navy and Marines).

The US Navy's standard EW (electronic warfare) aircraft, the EA-6B is, together with the Lockheed S-3, the most complex aircraft ever to be made compatible with aircraft carriers. It has much of its airframe in common with that of the A-6E attack aircraft, although the engines are more powerful, the wings are stronger and the nose is lengthened to house a new four-seat cockpit. The pilot occupies the left front Martin-Baker Mk 7 seat, with an ECMO (electronic countermeasures officer) on his right responsible for navigation, communications, defensive ECM and chaff dispensing. The two ECMOs in the back manage the ALQ-99 tactical jamming system which receives enemy emissions at a battery of aerials in the fin pod, analyses each signal and then counters selected threats by powerful jamming from up to five underwing pods, each with its own windmill generator and each covering seven frequency bands. This EA-6B of US Navy squadron VAQ-135 (Carrier Air Wing 1 embarked aboard the *America*) is depicted with only two pods, plus two 1136-litre (250 gal, 300 US gal) tanks. In the side elevation below the wings are folded, canopies open, A-frame hook down and boarding ladder unfolded.

0   4m

Grumman EA-6B Prowler

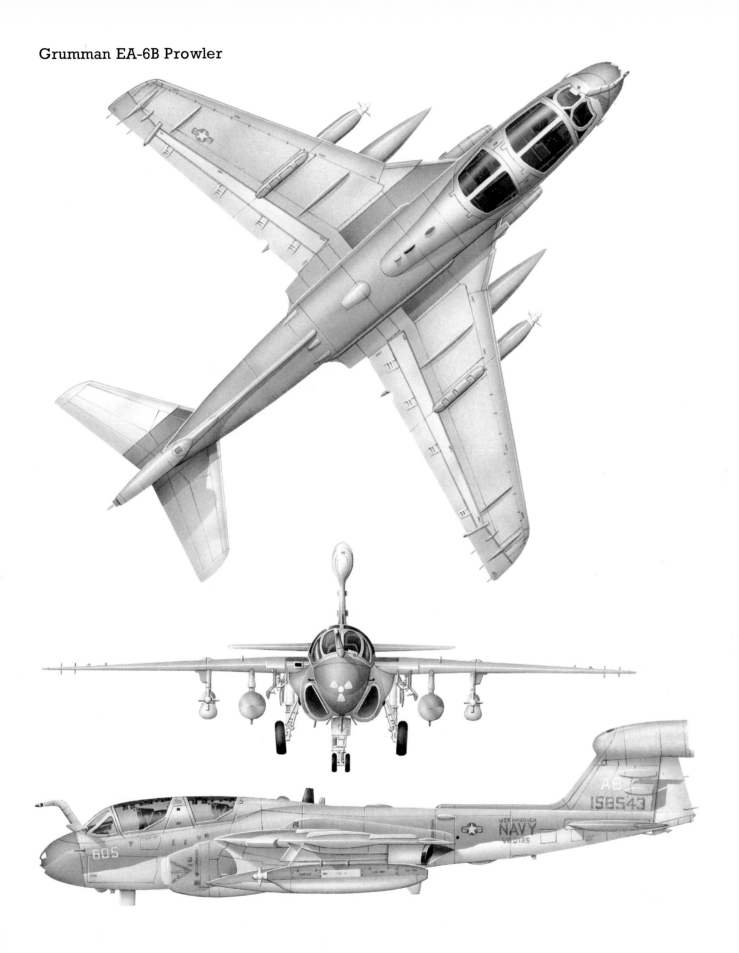

Grumman A-6 Intruder

The first A2F-1 prototype, US Navy BuAer No 147864, was closely similar to the production A-6A. Differences included absence of radar, tilting jetpipes and a smaller vertical tail.

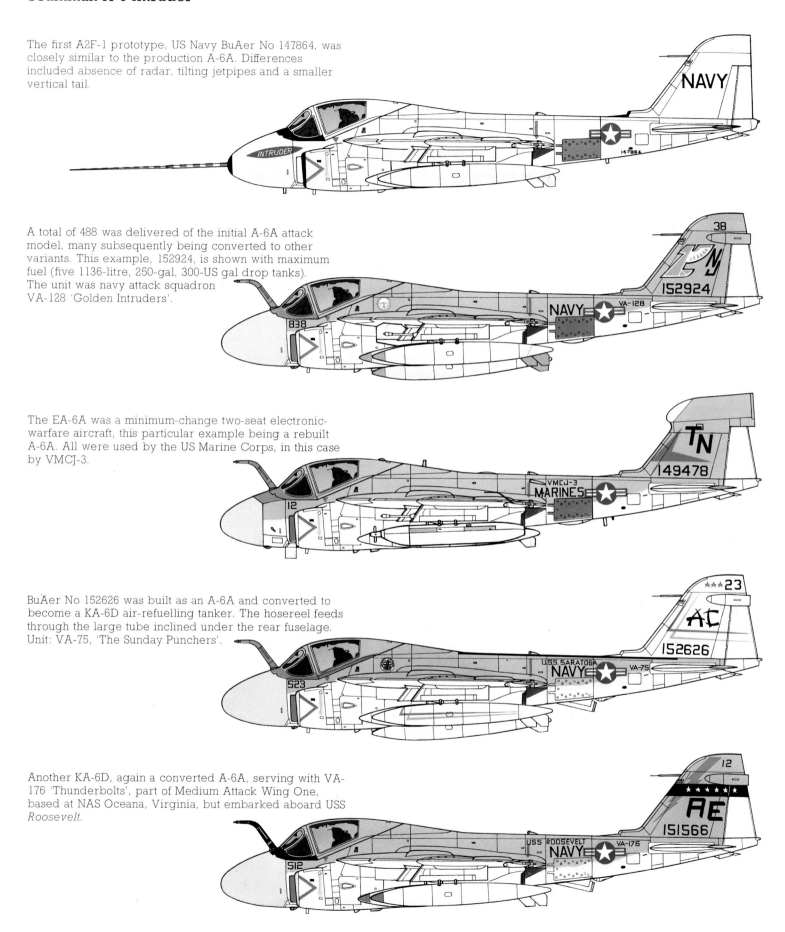

A total of 488 was delivered of the initial A-6A attack model, many subsequently being converted to other variants. This example, 152924, is shown with maximum fuel (five 1136-litre, 250-gal, 300-US gal drop tanks). The unit was navy attack squadron VA-128 'Golden Intruders'.

The EA-6A was a minimum-change two-seat electronic-warfare aircraft, this particular example being a rebuilt A-6A. All were used by the US Marine Corps, in this case by VMCJ-3.

BuÄer No 152626 was built as an A-6A and converted to become a KA-6D air-refuelling tanker. The hosereel feeds through the large tube inclined under the rear fuselage. Unit: VA-75, 'The Sunday Punchers'.

Another KA-6D, again a converted A-6A, serving with VA-176 'Thunderbolts', part of Medium Attack Wing One, based at NAS Oceana, Virginia, but embarked aboard USS *Roosevelt*.

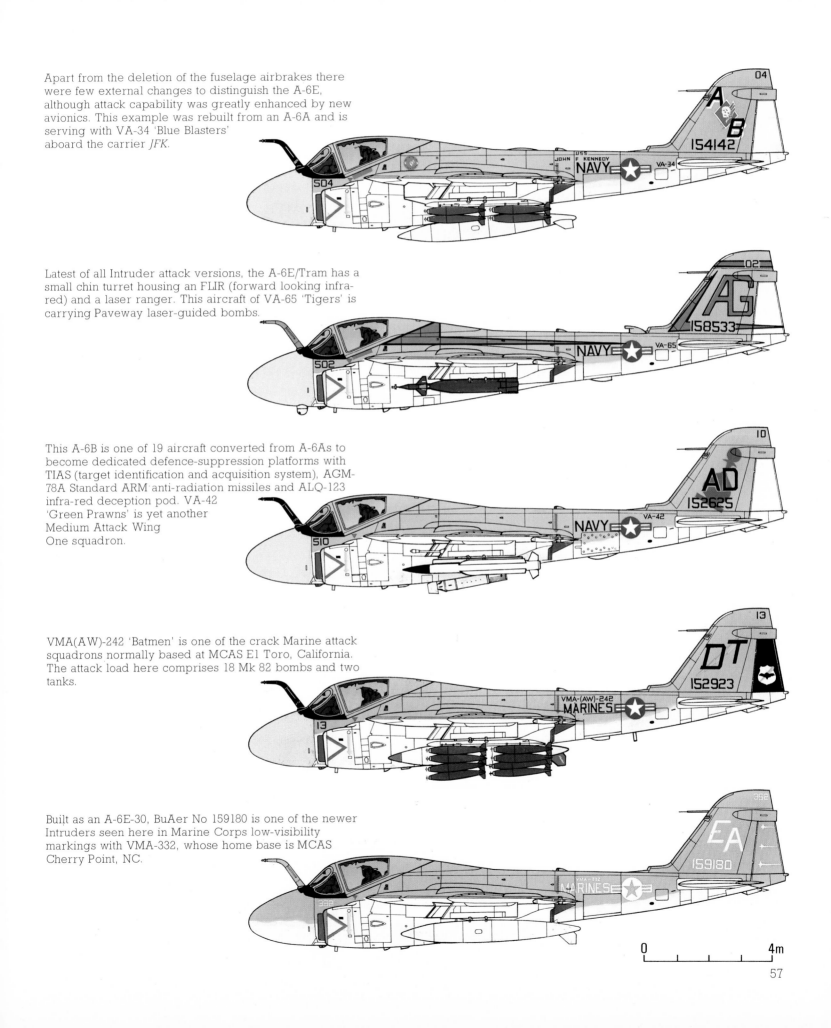

Apart from the deletion of the fuselage airbrakes there were few external changes to distinguish the A-6E, although attack capability was greatly enhanced by new avionics. This example was rebuilt from an A-6A and is serving with VA-34 'Blue Blasters' aboard the carrier *JFK*.

Latest of all Intruder attack versions, the A-6E/Tram has a small chin turret housing an FLIR (forward looking infra-red) and a laser ranger. This aircraft of VA-65 'Tigers' is carrying Paveway laser-guided bombs.

This A-6B is one of 19 aircraft converted from A-6As to become dedicated defence-suppression platforms with TIAS (target identification and acquisition system), AGM-78A Standard ARM anti-radiation missiles and ALQ-123 infra-red deception pod. VA-42 'Green Prawns' is yet another Medium Attack Wing One squadron.

VMA(AW)-242 'Batmen' is one of the crack Marine attack squadrons normally based at MCAS El Toro, California. The attack load here comprises 18 Mk 82 bombs and two tanks.

Built as an A-6E-30, BuAer No 159180 is one of the newer Intruders seen here in Marine Corps low-visibility markings with VMA-332, whose home base is MCAS Cherry Point, NC.

0   4m

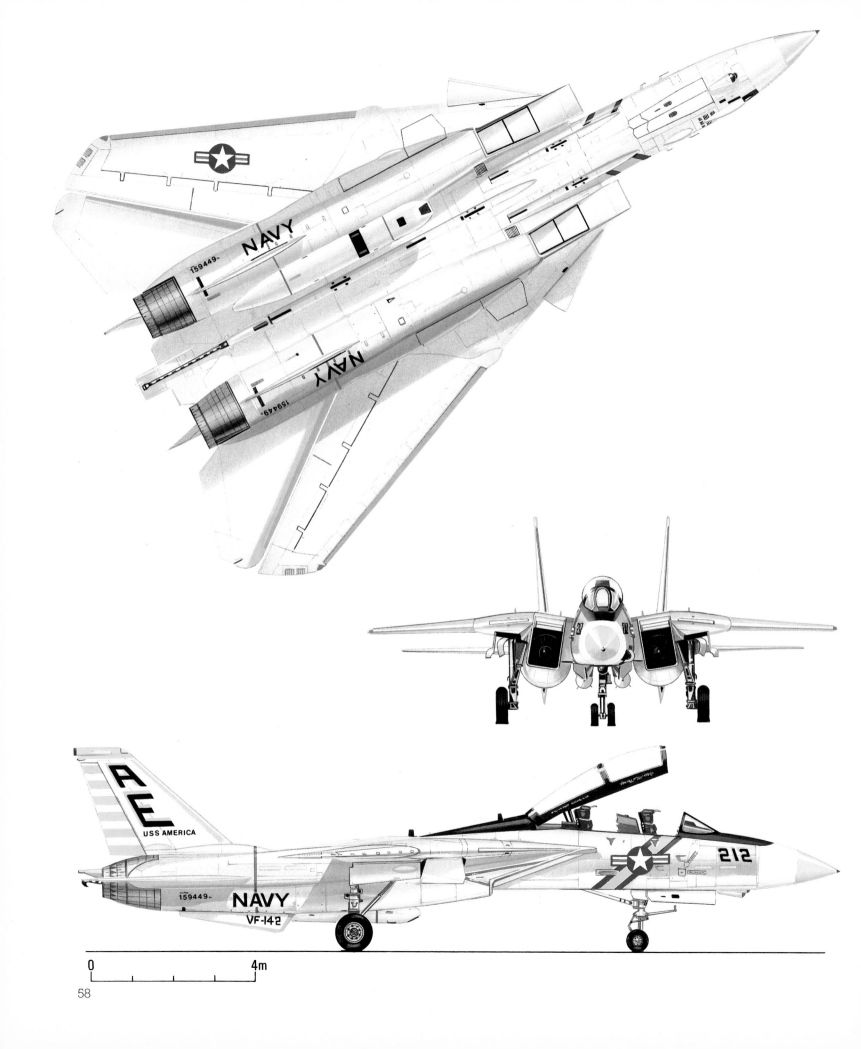

NAVY
159449

NAVY
159449

AE
USS AMERICA

NAVY
VF-142
159449

212

0   4m

Grumman F-14A Tomcat

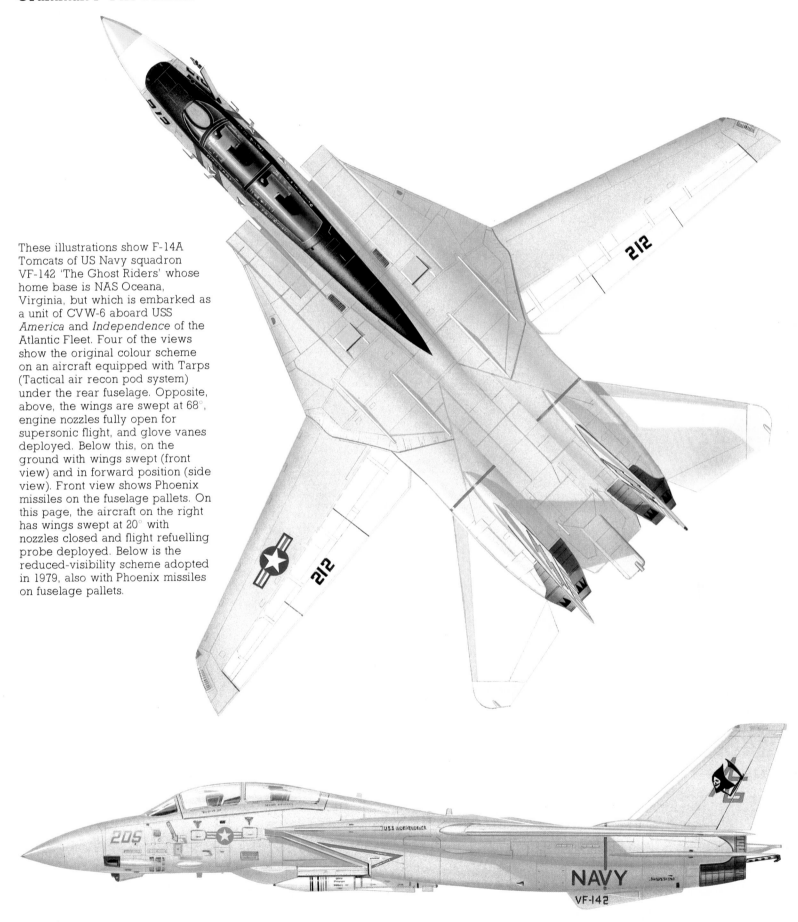

These illustrations show F-14A Tomcats of US Navy squadron VF-142 'The Ghost Riders' whose home base is NAS Oceana, Virginia, but which is embarked as a unit of CVW-6 aboard USS *America* and *Independence* of the Atlantic Fleet. Four of the views show the original colour scheme on an aircraft equipped with Tarps (Tactical air recon pod system) under the rear fuselage. Opposite, above, the wings are swept at 68°, engine nozzles fully open for supersonic flight, and glove vanes deployed. Below this, on the ground with wings swept (front view) and in forward position (side view). Front view shows Phoenix missiles on the fuselage pallets. On this page, the aircraft on the right has wings swept at 20° with nozzles closed and flight refuelling probe deployed. Below is the reduced-visibility scheme adopted in 1979, also with Phoenix missiles on fuselage pallets.

Grumman F-14 Tomcat

Resplendent in one of the experimental alternative paint schemes tested for combat effectiveness in 1976 (actually the Ferris Geometric scheme), this F-14A serves with VF-1, premier fighter squadron of the US Navy. The blister under the nose is the ALQ-100 ECM aerial, which often has an anti-collision beacon beneath it.

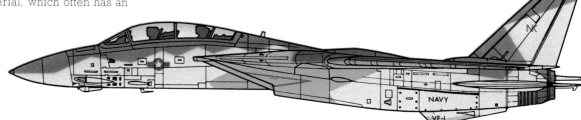

This F-14A of US Navy fighter squadron VF-14 'The Tophatters' is depicted with the ventral missile pallets in place and loaded with pairs of Phoenix missiles (two more are hidden at the rear). On the wings are two Sparrows and two Sidewinders.

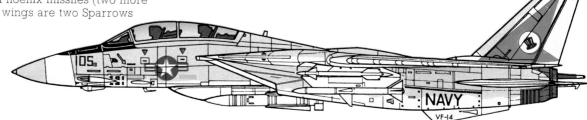

This is an F-14A from the US Navy fighter squadron VF-32 'Swordsmen', with home base at NAS Oceana, Virginia. It is depicted with a full load of six Phoenix missiles, two of them being hung on the underwing pylons. The IR seeker is absent from this aircraft.

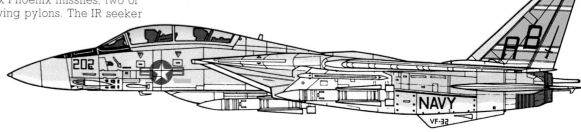

Favouring one of the more flamboyant colour schemes, VF-84 is known as 'The Jolly Rogers' and certainly does not subscribe to the low-visibility air-combat camouflage! Home base is NAS Oceana, but VF-84 is part of Air Wing CVW-8 embarked aboard USS *Nimitz*.

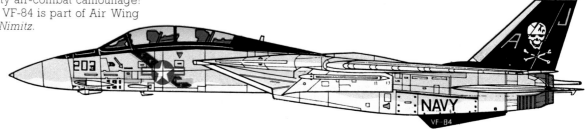

The badge of Navy fighter squadron VF-111 is a setting sun, the unit's popular name being 'The Sundowners'. Based at NAS Miramar, California, it is part of the Pacific Fleet's CVW-19 Air Wing, embarked aboard *Coral Sea* and due to go aboard *Carl Vinson* as this book went to press.

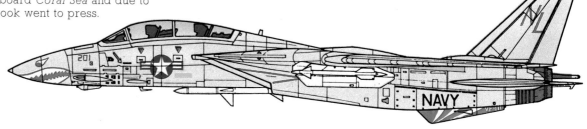

Many F-14s have an infra-red seeker under the nose in place of the ALQ-100 antenna; others will in future carry the Northrop TCS (TV Camera System). This aircraft of Navy squadron VF-124 'The Moonshiners' has the IR sensor, and, unusually, drop tanks. It serves in the training role at NAS Miramar.

Distinctive for its checkerboard rudders, VF-211 squadron is known as 'The Checkmates' and is part of the Pacific Fleet's CVW-9, normally embarked aboard USS *Constellation* but with home base at NAS Lemoore.

After a period when hardly any F-14s were serviceable the Islamic Iranian Air Force has since 1980 striven to keep its force (originally 80) of Tomcats operational, and several participated in the war against Iraq. Main bases are Khatami (Isfahan) and Shiraz.

Lack of money is the main reason for the failure of the Navy to go ahead with the more powerful and avionically updated F-14B and F-14C planned at the start of the VFX programme. All that funding allowed was flight-testing the F-14B, with the 12700kg (28,000lb) F401 engine, in September 1973.

Subsequently General Electric produced a newer and generally more advanced powerplant in the F101-DFE (Derivative Fighter Engine), in the 13600kg (30,000lb) class. This outstanding augmented turbofan was flown in the Super Tomcat in 1981, and may power the planned F-14D which the Navy hopes to buy.

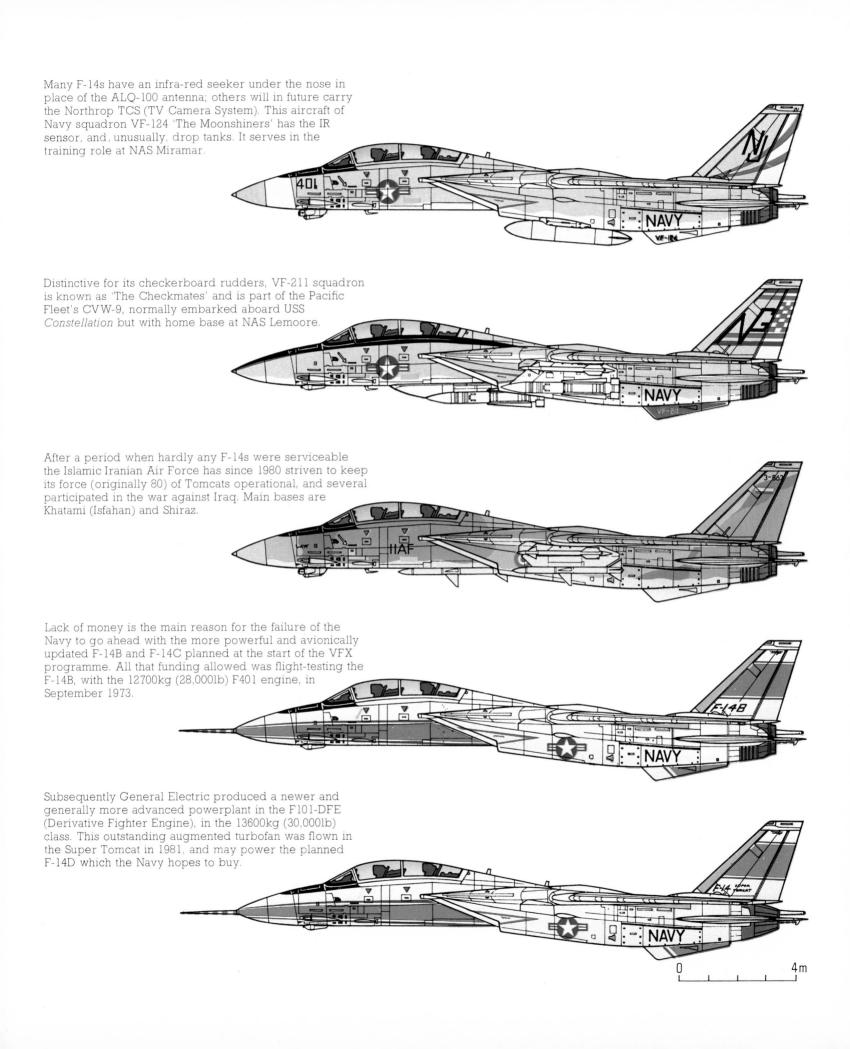

0   4m

Grumman F-14 Tomcat

When Congress halted development of the unsuccessful F-111B in mid-1968, Grumman (a major F-111B contractor) already had an outline design for a superior carrier-based fighter for the US Navy. This project won the ensuing VFX competition in January 1969, and the first F-14A prototype flew on 21 December 1970. It was envisaged that the F-14A would quickly be superseded by the F-14B with later engines and the F-14C with new engines, avionics and weapons. In the event, although the F-14 proved outstandingly successful, rising costs nearly wrecked the programme, caused litigation and delay and, despite prolonged trouble with the TF30 engine, has so far prevented later versions from being produced.

Like the contemporary F-15, the F-14 has twin vertical tails carried on widely spaced twin engines, with the crew in a nose fuselage emerging from between the inlets. Unlike the Air Force fighter it has variable-sweep wings, with a Mach sweep programmer automatically setting the optimum sweep angle and high-lift features for the flight condition or manoeuvre demand, an added feature being automatic extension of glove vanes (small foreplanes) to control the shift of centre of pressure at supersonic Mach numbers. Although it can fight at weights lighter than the F-111B, and has a much better all-round performance, in fact the maximum weight with six Phoenix missiles is even greater, and part of the reason for the high price is that the F-14 is a large aircraft and costly in all respects including fuel. It offers in return a long-range interception capability unrivalled by any aircraft.

Hughes Aircraft played a significant role in developing the AWG-9 radar and Phoenix missile (initially for the YF-12 and F-111B in 1959–62), with the ability to track up to 24 targets simultaneously at ranges (depending on target-aircraft size and aspect) up to 314km (195 miles). The system can simultaneously attack any six of these targets, though it is not usual to carry six of these large missiles. No other aircraft has the versatility of selecting long-range missiles (Phoenix), medium-range missiles (Sparrow), short-range missiles (Sidewinder) or an internal gun.

The F-14 was designed not only for the basic Navy fighter missions of DLI (deck-launched intercept) and CAP (combat air patrol) but also for attack on ground targets with heavy bombloads. Though normally deployed in conjunction with E-2C control aircraft the F-14A has sufficiently comprehensive navigation and weapon-delivery systems to operate independently. The crew of pilot and naval flight officer sit in Martin-Baker GRU-7A seats under a long canopy hinged upwards from the rear. Catapult take-offs use the nose-tow bar on the twin-wheel nose gear, while the main gears have single wheels with carbon brakes and retract forwards with the wheels turning 90° to lie flat in the fixed wing glove. The outer wings carry full-span slats and single-slotted flaps. Roll control is by the differential tailplanes (able to be driven in opposite directions), augmented at sweep angles less than 55° by wing spoilers which also provide direct lift control on the landing approach. A retractable refuelling probe is on the right side of the nose.

Apart from the loss of the first prototype, flight testing was outstandingly successful and by September 1974 squadrons VF-1 and -2 were embarked aboard USS *Enterprise* with the Pacific Fleet. By 1983 almost 450 F-14As had been delivered, of a planned total of 491, replacing the F-4J in most embarked fighter wings. In the absence of any other aircraft 49 F-14s were fitted with Tarps (tac air recon pod system) with optical cameras and infra-red, retaining full weapons capability. Another recent fit is Northrop TCS (TV camera set) for long-range target identification.

In 1975–8 Grumman delivered 80 F-14As to Iran, but after the revolution they fell into disuse. In September 1973 a prototype F-14B was flown with F401 engines, and the same aircraft was used in 1981 to fly the F101-DFE engines, much more powerful than the troublesome TF30s. The only firm plan in 1983 is to switch to an F-14C with TF30-414A engines with strengthened parts.

COUNTRY OF ORIGIN USA.

CREW 2.

TOTAL PRODUCED By 1983 about 450 of 491.

DIMENSIONS Wingspan, 20°: 19·54m (64ft 1½in), 68°: 11·65m (38ft 2½in), overswept to 75° for carrier stowage: 10·15m (33ft 3½in); length 19·1m (62ft 8in); wing area 52·49m² (565·0ft²).

WEIGHTS Empty 18036kg (39,762lb); maximum loaded 33724kg (74,348lb).

ENGINES Two 9480kg (20,900lb) Pratt & Whitney TF30-412A or -414A augmented turbofans.

MAXIMUM SPEED 2517km/h (1,564mph, Mach 2·34).

SERVICE CEILING Over 15.24km (50,000ft).

RANGE Not published but ferry range with external fuel is about 4500km (2,800 miles).

MILITARY LOAD One M61A-1 20mm gun with 675 rounds; four Phoenix AAMs carried under fuselage on special pallets, or four Sparrow AAMs recessed under fuselage; pylons under fixed wing gloves carry total of four Sidewinder AAMs or two Phoenix or Sparrow plus two Sidewinder; in surface-attack role, various bombs or other weapons to total of 6577kg (14,500lb).

USERS Iran, USA (Navy).

Lockheed C-130 Hercules

Perhaps conscious of the fact that it has been flying for almost 30 years, the Lockheed-Georgia Company advertises the C-130 as 'the tactical airlifter that keeps acting newer and newer'. Its record speaks for itself; in what must be its twilight production years it keeps finding new customers, appearing in fresh versions and rolling off the production line while proposed replacements either are out of production or have never entered it.

The original customer for what is today universally called The Herky Bird was the USAF Tactical Air Command, which in 1951 issued a requirement for a new transport to carry 92 troops, 64 paratroops or 11340kg (25,000lb) of cargo and use rough front-line airstrips. The Lockheed Model 82 was selected on 2 July 1951, and the first flight by a YC-130 took place at Burbank in August 1954. Lockheed had taken over the vast wartime B-29 plant at Marietta to build B-47s, and there was spare capacity there to make the C-130 as well. The first C-130A built by the Lockheed-Georgia Company flew on 7 April 1955.

Little about the C-130 was radical, but never before had all desirable features been incorporated in one military transport. The structure was stressed skin and flush-riveted, with a long-span wing for cruise efficiency and high-lift flaps. Allison at last got the T56 turboprop working, to produce a compact package of great power for sparkling performance. The cargo hold was completely unobstructed, 3m (10ft) wide and 2·74m (9ft) high, with a level floor at convenient height accessed by side doors and by a giant powered ramp at the rear across which trucks or other large loads could pass. In flight the rear ramp could be lowered for paradropping twin sticks of troops or heavy cargo and then closed to restore the streamline shape (then a very rare feature). The entire interior could be pressurized for comfortable high-altitude cruise, and noise and vibration (though noticeable) were much lower than in piston aircraft. Large tandem wheels on each side were matched to unpaved airstrips and, despite retracting into

fuselage side boxes, gave adequate track for stability on rough ground.

Seldom has any aircraft received such universal acclaim as the C-130A when it entered service with the 463rd Troop Carrier Wing at Ardmore AFB in December 1956. Lockheed built 219 of the C-130A model, with projecting APS-59 nose radar, provision for eight assisted-take-off rockets and underwing drop tanks, and stronger rear fuselage and tail. Conversions or new models included the RC-130 photomapping family, GC-130 drone directors (later DC-130 family), JC-130 ICBM and spacecraft tracker and retriever, C-130D Arctic radar support series, and AC-130A night attack gunships.

Next, in 1957, came the C-130B with Dash-7A engines swinging four-blade propellers to lift a greater internal load of fuel. This was the first model widely exported, and sub-variants include the WC-130B for weather reconnaissance, LC-130F with skis for the Navy, KC-130F tankers for the Marines and JC-130B spacecraft retrievers.

In 1960 the predecessor of today's USAF Military Airlift Command urgently called for a long-range model, and the result was the C-130E with 5145 litre (1,132 gal, 1,359 US gal) drop tanks and a further rise in gross weight. Again there were many sub-variants, but in 1963 the HC-130H for the USAF Aerospace Rescue and Recovery Service introduced a more powerful T56 used in current sub-types. Many are stretched, examples including the RAF Hercules C.3 and the civil L-100-20 and L-100-30 (see data), which need greater volume for low-density commercial cargoes.

Today Lockheed has sold well over 1,700 of all versions, for 50 nations. New variants include a cargo aircraft minelayer, a battlefield command and control model (EC-130E), the high-capacity commercial L-100-50, the proposed L-400 Twin Hercules with two T56 engines, the EC-130ARE (airborne radar extension) low-cost surveillance platform by Lockheed Aircraft Service Company with radar 'saucer' on its tail, and a maritime patrol and rescue model for Japan.

COUNTRY OF ORIGIN USA.

CREW Normal flight crew: 4.

TOTAL PRODUCED About 1,700.

DIMENSIONS Wingspan 40·41m (132ft 7in); length, standard: 29·79m (97ft 9in), **L-100-20**: 32·33m (106ft 1in), **Hercules C.3, L-100-30, C-130H-30:** 34·37m (112ft 9in), **L-100-50:** 40·97m (134ft 5in); wing area 162·12m² (1,745ft²).

WEIGHTS Empty, **C-130H:** 33063kg (72,892lb); maximum payload 19685kg (43,399lb); maximum loaded, **C-130A:** 52616kg (116,000lb), **C-130E:** 79380kg (175,000lb).

ENGINES Four Allison T56 turboprops, **C-130A:** 3,750ehp T56-1A, **C-130B:** 4,050ehp T56-7A, **C-130H:** 4,910ehp (flat-rated at 4,508ehp) T56-15.

MAXIMUM SPEED Also maximum cruising speed: typically 602km/h (374mph).

SERVICE CEILING **C-130E** at 58970kg (130,000lb): 10·06km (33,000ft).

RANGE **C-130E** with maximum payload and full allowances: 4002km (2,487 miles).

MILITARY LOAD Normally 92 troops, 64 paratroops, 74 litters (stretchers) and attendants or wide range of cargo within weight limit; stretched 34·37m versions: 128 troops, 92 paratroops or 97 litter patients.

USERS Abu Dhabi, Angola, Argentina, Australia, Belgium, Bolivia, Brazil, Cameroun, Canada, Chile, Colombia, Denmark, Dubai, Ecuador, Egypt, Gabon, Great Britain (RAF), Greece, Indonesia, Iran, Israel, Italy, Japan, Jordan, Kuwait, Libya, Malaysia, Morocco, New Zealand, Nigeria, Norway, Oman, Pakistan, Peru, Philippines, Portugal, Saudi Arabia, Singapore, South Africa, South Korea, Spain, Sudan, Sweden, Thailand, Tunisia, Turkey, Uganda, USA (AF, ANG, Marines, Navy), Venezuela, Zaïre.

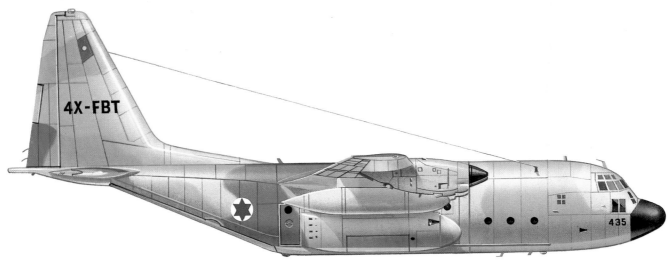

Israel's Heyl Ha'Avir received a total of eight Lockheed C-130Hs, 12 C-130Es, and two KC-130H tanker/transports. Four of the long-range H models were used on the daring raid to Entebbe, Uganda, on 4 July 1976, to rescue the 103 airline passengers from a hijacked Airbus. It is almost impossible to tell an E from an H, and the Heyl Ha'Avir would not confirm whether the particular aircraft depicted went to Entebbe. Most views feature the 5146-litre (1,132 gal, 1,359 US gal) pylon tanks; the left side elevation shows the loading ramp lowered but tanks not carried. Heyl Ha'Avir transports carry civil registration as well as national insignia.

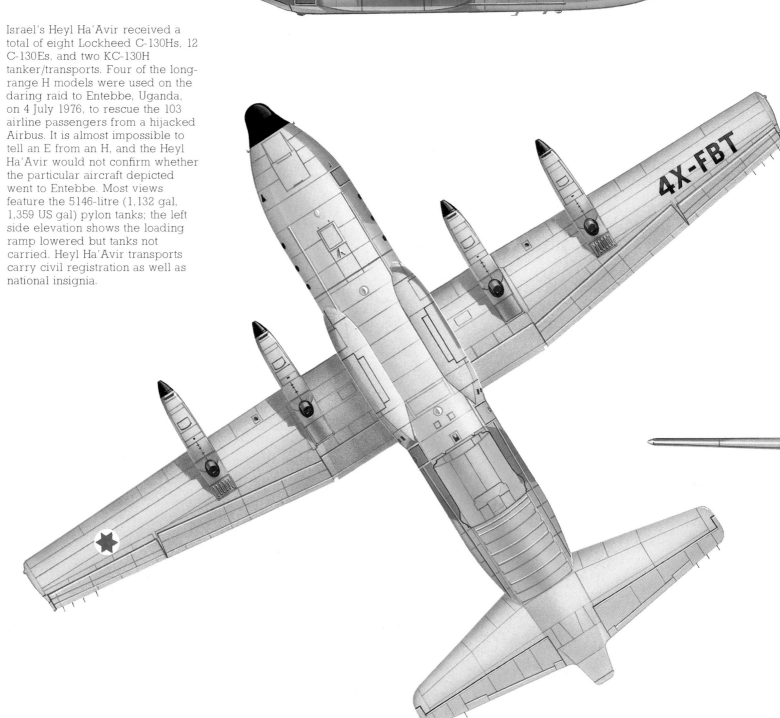

Lockheed C-130 Hercules

0   4m

Lockheed C-130 Hercules

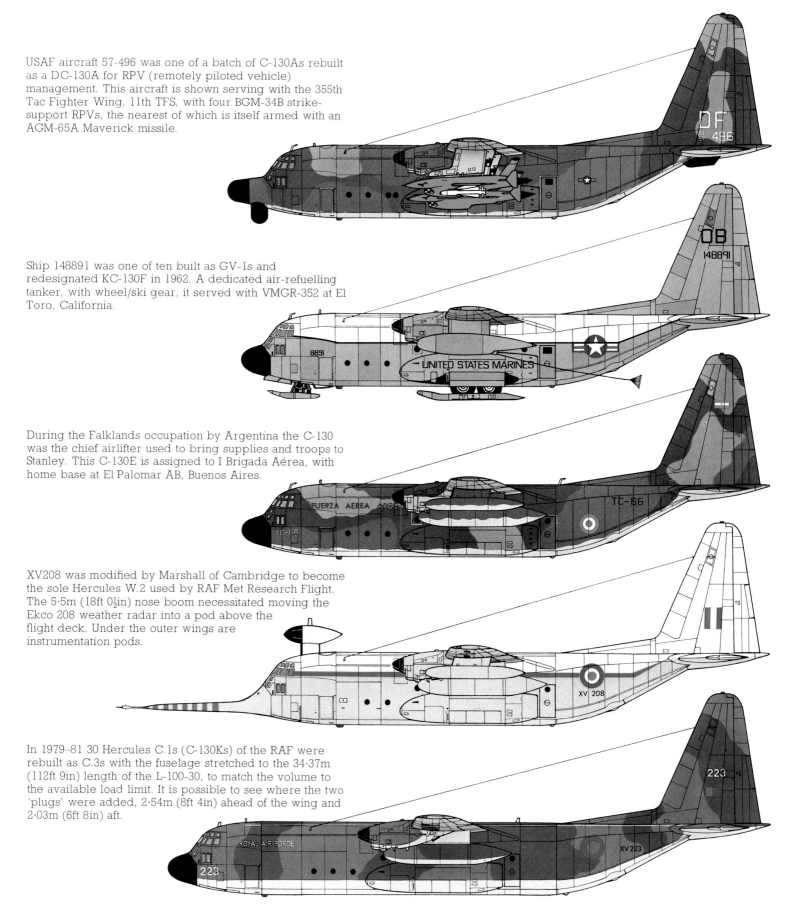

USAF aircraft 57-496 was one of a batch of C-130As rebuilt as a DC-130A for RPV (remotely piloted vehicle) management. This aircraft is shown serving with the 355th Tac Fighter Wing, 11th TFS, with four BGM-34B strike-support RPVs, the nearest of which is itself armed with an AGM-65A Maverick missile.

Ship 148891 was one of ten built as GV-1s and redesignated KC-130F in 1962. A dedicated air-refuelling tanker, with wheel/ski gear, it served with VMGR-352 at El Toro, California.

During the Falklands occupation by Argentina the C-130 was the chief airlifter used to bring supplies and troops to Stanley. This C-130E is assigned to I Brigada Aérea, with home base at El Palomar AB, Buenos Aires.

XV208 was modified by Marshall of Cambridge to become the sole Hercules W.2 used by RAF Met Research Flight. The 5·5m (18ft 0½in) nose boom necessitated moving the Ekco 208 weather radar into a pod above the flight deck. Under the outer wings are instrumentation pods.

In 1979–81 30 Hercules C.1s (C-130Ks) of the RAF were rebuilt as C.3s with the fuselage stretched to the 34·37m (112ft 9in) length of the L-100-30, to match the volume to the available load limit. It is possible to see where the two 'plugs' were added, 2·54m (8ft 4in) ahead of the wing and 2·03m (6ft 8in) aft.

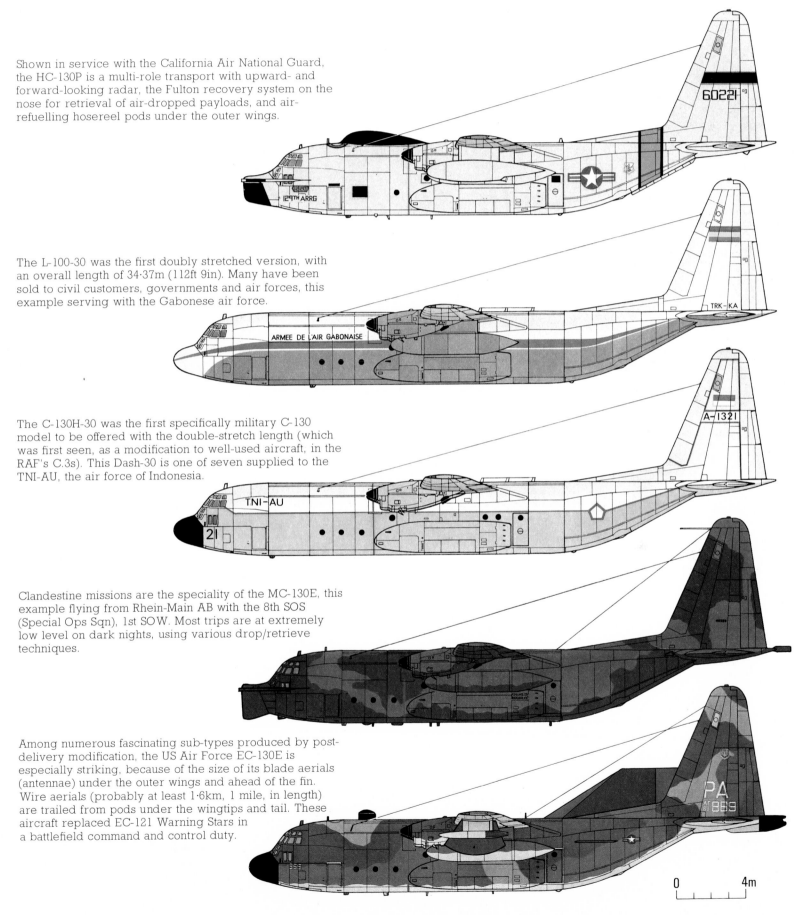

Shown in service with the California Air National Guard, the HC-130P is a multi-role transport with upward- and forward-looking radar, the Fulton recovery system on the nose for retrieval of air-dropped payloads, and air-refuelling hosereel pods under the outer wings.

The L-100-30 was the first doubly stretched version, with an overall length of 34·37m (112ft 9in). Many have been sold to civil customers, governments and air forces, this example serving with the Gabonese air force.

The C-130H-30 was the first specifically military C-130 model to be offered with the double-stretch length (which was first seen, as a modification to well-used aircraft, in the RAF's C.3s). This Dash-30 is one of seven supplied to the TNI-AU, the air force of Indonesia.

Clandestine missions are the speciality of the MC-130E, this example flying from Rhein-Main AB with the 8th SOS (Special Ops Sqn), 1st SOW. Most trips are at extremely low level on dark nights, using various drop/retrieve techniques.

Among numerous fascinating sub-types produced by post-delivery modification, the US Air Force EC-130E is especially striking, because of the size of its blade aerials (antennae) under the outer wings and ahead of the fin. Wire aerials (probably at least 1·6km, 1 mile, in length) are trailed from pods under the wingtips and tail. These aircraft replaced EC-121 Warning Stars in a battlefield command and control duty.

Aeritalia/Lockheed F-104S Starfighter

The Aeritalia/Lockheed F-104S was the ultimate production Starfighter, both technically and in timing. It marked a surprising return to the original defensive purpose of the F-104, although it is used principally as a missile-armed interceptor rather than a close-combat dogfighter. It does have an internal gun, but the small wing area has always been a problem in the close-combat mode, and the F-104S is heavier than any other variant at up to 14060kg (31,000lb). The aircraft shown is assigned to the Aeronautica Militare Italiano 53° Stormo's 21° Gruppo CI (*caccia intercettore*, interceptor fighter) at Cameri, west of Milan. It carries AIM-9J Sidewinders and the Italian-developed Aspide AAM, claimed to have a range of up to 100km (62 miles), well over twice that of the US Sparrow from which it was derived, even though it uses the identical rocket motor. The inflight-refuelling probe is detachable. The Dash-19 engine nozzle and canted ventral fins are other features peculiar to this version.

0   4m

Lockheed F-104 Starfighter

Pakistan was one of very few countries to use the F-104 in combat. The US government supplied 10 ex-USAF F-104As, completely refurbished, plus 2 two-seat trainers. Based at Sargodha, they saw action in the 1965 war with India, but were withdrawn soon afterwards.

The CF-104s of the Canadian Armed Forces operate almost entirely in the ground attack and reconnaissance role, the principal unit being the 1st Air Group at Baden-Söllingen in West Germany. This machine served with 417 Sqn at Cold Lake, Alberta, the training unit (note practice bomb pod).

The koala bear insignia (see opposite page below) of 203 Sqn appears on the fin of this F-104J of the Japanese Air Self-Defence Force. In 1982–8 the 169 aircraft of this type are to be replaced by Mitsubishi-assembled F-15 Eagles.

By the time this book appears many of the F-104G Starfighters of the West German Marineflieger MFG 2 will already have been replaced by Tornados. This aircraft has the MFG 2 shield high on the fin; the missile is an old French-supplied AS.20 anti-ship weapon.

Canadair-built CF-104D trainers still serve with Denmark's ESK 726 at Ålborg alongside a motley collection of other Lockheed, European and Canadian-built F-104s, some of them dedicated EW (electronic warfare) platforms.

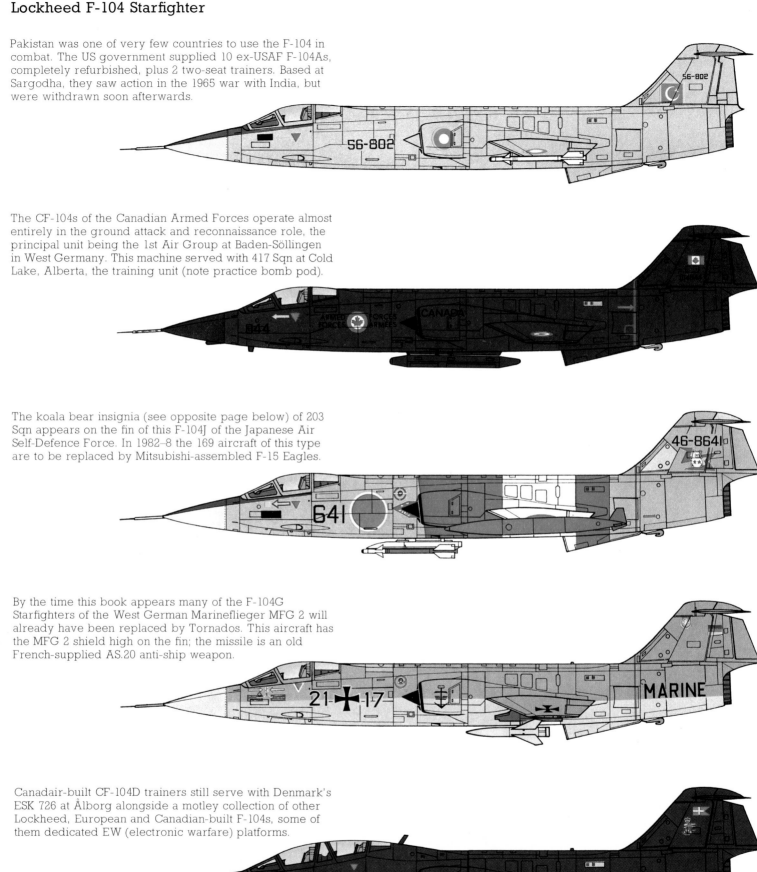

The Hellenic Air Force has a wing, 116ª based at Araxos, equipped with F-104Gs and (as illustrated) TF-104G trainers. The wing has diminished in size until it is effectively a single squadron, No 335.

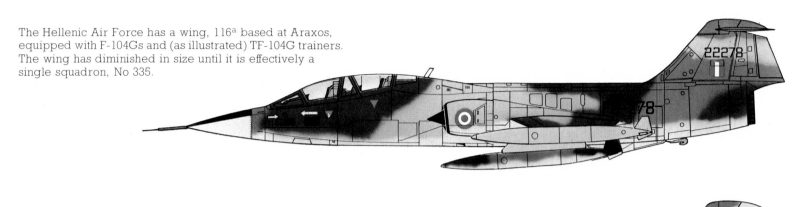

Taiwan's reconnaissance strength is vested mainly in a squadron of eight RF-104G Starfighters which, with about 60 F-104Gs (of 63 supplied), forms the 5th Fighter Wing. The camera installation projects under the fuselage.

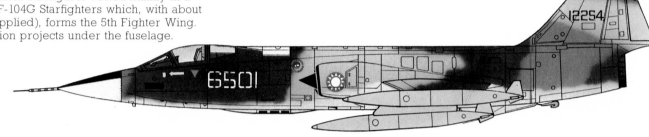

This curious Starfighter is the F-104G-CCV, the initials signifying control-configured vehicle. CCV technology is aimed at making aircraft more manoeuvrable by designing them to be inherently unstable, and then fitting a powerful, reliable and instant-reacting control system. This F-104 was rebuilt by MBB; one of its features is an extra tailplane and fin-top.

Turkey bought 40 Italian-built F-104S interceptors, which supplemented the earlier F-104G and F-4E with the emphasis on all-weather defence. This example flies with 143 Sqn at Murted AB.

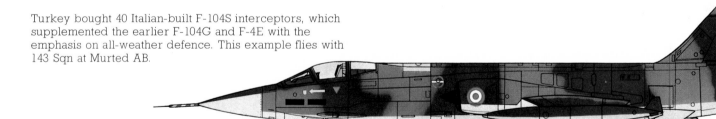

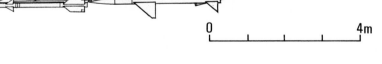

0   4m

Marineflieger
(Germany/Federal Republic)

ESK 726
(Denmark)

MFG 2
(Germany/Federal Republic)

203 Squadron
(Japan)

Lockheed F-104 Starfighter

Clarence L. 'Kelly' Johnson, one of the most famous American aircraft designers, spent much time in the early 1950s trying to build the best possible air-combat fighter to succeed his F-80 Shooting Star. The worried F-86 pilots in Korea clamoured for more and more speed and height, at the expense of almost everything else. There was a strongly held belief that fighters were getting too big, too complicated, too heavy and too expensive. This powerful reaction resulted in the F-104, and although it made fine copy for the publicity media, it did not produce the best fighter. Indeed the F-104 was hardly used at all by the US Air Force, and would have been a very limited programme had not Lockheed succeeded in selling a heavier and more complicated version as a nuclear attack bomber, at first to West Germany.

Development began in 1951 and, after prolonged study, settled on a tiny unswept wing of unprecedented thinness and with sharp edges for minimum supersonic drag. The leading edge was hinged to droop at low speeds, and the plain flaps were in most production aircraft fitted with high-velocity air jets fed by the engine compressor; this flap-blowing technique had been discovered just in time. The first XF-104 was built with plain side inlets to a J65 engine (a British Sapphire made by Wright in the USA), and a novel downward ejection seat to avoid problems with the canopy and the high T-tail. It first flew on 7 February 1954.

On 17 February 1956 the first flight took place of the F-104A with the much more powerful J79 engine in a fully developed duct leading from variable inlets with central shock-bodies to a variable-profile nozzle system. This gave thrust that greatly exceeded drag to well beyond Mach 2, then almost twice as fast as any other Western fighter. An M61 gun was fitted on the left side, a removable flight-refuelling probe on the nose and Sidewinder AAMs on the wingtips. Of 153 built, about half entered USAF service, initially with the 83rd Fighter Interceptor Sqn in January 1958. They were soon passed to the Air National Guard and to Pakistan and Jordan, although 27 later returned to the USAF with the J79–19 engine.

The F-104B was a tandem dual trainer with a broader vertical tail, while the 77 F-104Cs were fighter/bombers for USAF Tactical Air Command, with the F-104D as the corresponding two-seater. But what revitalized the dying programme was Lockheed's success in selling the F-104G to the Luftwaffe in 1960. This looked little different, apart from having the broad tail, but in fact it had a stronger airframe, Nasarr radar, inertial navigation, manoeuvre flaps and many other new features. A vast multi-national manufacturing programme was set up to build 970 in European groups, 110 by Canadair (plus 200 CF-140s for Canada) and 207 Japanese F-104Js resembling F-104Cs.

The first F-104G flew on 5 October 1960. The Luftwaffe and Marineflieger received 750, using them as low-level strike and reconnaissance machines; at that time no other type could fly all-weather electronically guided missions of the kind needed. Sadly, there were high casualties among inexperienced pilots, and among other modifications the seat was changed to the fast-reacting Martin-Baker Q-7 series. Lockheed supplied large numbers of F-104F and TF-104G trainers, the RF-104G recon model and RTF-104G1 all-weather two-seat recon aircraft.

In 1966 Lockheed flew the first of a new interceptor version developed jointly with Aeritalia for the Italian air force. This type, the F-104S, marked a return to the fighter role, with updated systems, R21G/F15G radar and Sparrow AAMs, though it retained attack capability and also had the option of the Orpheus multi-sensor recon pod. Aeritalia delivered 205, and completed the programme in 1976 with a further 40 for Turkey.

Since 1974 the German MBB company, an industrial giant embracing companies which once made the F-104G, has been engaged in a CCV (control-configured vehicle) research project using a modified F-104G with various arrangements of canard foreplane, ballast and fuel transfer systems.

COUNTRY OF ORIGIN USA.

CREW 1, trainers: 2.

TOTAL PRODUCED 2,446.

DIMENSIONS Wingspan (without tip tanks or missiles) 6·68m (21ft 11in); length 16·69m (54ft 9in); wing area 18·21m² (196ft²).

WEIGHTS Empty, **F-104A:** 5698kg (12,562lb), **F-104G:** 6387kg (14,082lb), **F-104S:** 6758kg (14,900lb); maximum loaded, **F-104A:** 8891kg (19,600lb), **F-104G:** 13054kg (28,779lb), **F-104S:** 14061kg (31,000lb).

ENGINE One General Electric J79 augmented turbojet, **F-104A:** 6713kg (14,800lb) J79-3, **F-104G:** 7167kg (15,800lb) J79-11A, **F-104S:** 8119kg (17,900lb) J79-19.

MAXIMUM SPEED Clean, high-altitude: 2334km/h (1,450mph, Mach 2·2), sea level: 1464km/h (910mph, Mach 1·2).

SERVICE CEILING Clean: 17·68km (58,000ft).

RANGE **F-104A, C:** 1770km (1,100 miles), **F-104G:** 3510km (2,180 miles), **F-104s:** 2920km (1,815 miles).

MILITARY LOAD One 20mm M61A-1 gun in some versions (can be fitted in G with reduced fuel, standard in S); provision for two Sidewinder AAMs on wingtips; **F-104C** can carry two 454kg (1,000lb) bombs; **F-104G** can carry one 907kg (2,000lb) weapon under fuselage plus two 454kg (1,000lb) stores under wings; and **F-104S** can carry two Sparrow or Aspide AAMs plus two or four Sidewinders.

USERS Belgium, Canada, Denmark (stored after replacement by F-16), Germany (Federal Republic), Greece, Italy, Japan, Jordan, Netherlands, Norway (replaced by F-16), Pakistan, Spain, Taiwan, Turkey.

Lockheed P-3 Orion

During World War 2 the long-range ocean patrol and ASW mission was flown by flying boats and converted heavy bombers. The first aircraft designed for the task was the Lockheed P2V (later P-2) Neptune, built in large numbers for many air forces. Although it proved capable of exceptional development, by the mid-1950s it was clear a successor should be ordered, with greater interior volume for more sensor operators, and with much greater ability to lift sensors and ASW weapons. Instead of a purpose-designed aircraft the Navy called for off-the-shelf submissions based on existing types.

In April 1958 the choice fell on Lockheed's proposal for a modified Electra passenger transport. This aircraft had been designed for domestic routes and had excellent performance and handling, even with three of its four turboprop engines shut down. The engine was similar to the T56 used in the C-130, but with the gearbox mounted low and the inlet duct high instead of the other way round. Features of the aircraft included a short-span integral-tank wing, circular-section pressurized fuselage longer than the wingspan, twin-wheel landing gears and hydraulically boosted flight controls.

After testing a modified Electra in August 1958 Lockheed flew a fully equipped YP-3A in November 1959 and the first production P-3A on 15 April 1961. Although an unpressurized weapon bay was added forward of the wing, no fewer than ten underwing pylons were added for a wide variety of stores. Sonobuoys are launched from the rear fuselage; a MAD (magnetic-anomaly detector) is extended from the tail and the nose houses the Texas Instruments radar developed from the APS-88A used in the Grumman S-2E. More than 35 advanced electronic items were installed for ASW search and attack, navigation, communications and other purposes. A searchlight was fitted under the right wing, comprehensive photo installations provided for day or night use and accommodation for a crew of 12, five of them in the central tactical compartment. With sonobuoy racks removed, seats can be installed for 50 equipped combat troops.

Lockheed delivered 157 of the P-3A version, three going to Spain. This model was retired in 1978, but some are still in the USN Reserve, and rebuilds include the RP-3A (special recon) and WP-3A (weather). In 1965 production switched to the Lockheed P-3B with more powerful engines, which eliminated water/alcohol boosting, as well as improved navigation and sensing. Later, Bullpup missiles were added on wing pylons. This version was sold to Australia, New Zealand and Norway, and while some were rebuilt as EP-3B electronic recon aircraft (Navy squadrons VQ-1 and -2), others were progressively modified by Lear Siegler and Boeing to improve ASW capability.

By far the most important model, the P-3C entered production in 1968, and by 1983 Lockheed had delivered 240 of a planned total of 316 to the US Navy, the last due in 1990. The P-3C has been built in basic, Update, Update II and Update III versions, each incorporating significant increased ASW capability with better sensors, data-processing and weapons, as well as revisions throughout the aircraft. P-3C sales to foreign countries have taken production of all models close to 600 by 1983. Japan's 45 include 38 licence-built by Kawasaki. Iran's six have the designation P-3F.

While the P-3C continues as the basic ASW model, Canada bought the CP-140 Aurora which is essentially the same aircraft but completely redesigned from the ASW viewpoint with the sensor, avionics and data-processing of the S-3A. The interior is revised and the whole aircraft equipped for search/rescue, fisheries protection, ice recon and many other missions, which after the fitting of an extra weapon-bay sensor installation will include resource survey, pollution control and aerial survey. Other models include the US Navy EP-3E (rebuilds of EP-3A and -3B with large canoe radars), the WP-3D airborne research centres and a single RP-3D used in a worldwide study of the Earth's magnetic field. In 1971 a P-3C set various world turboprop records.

COUNTRY OF ORIGIN USA.

CREW 12.

TOTAL PRODUCED About 600 of more than 670 ordered or programmed by 1990.

DIMENSIONS Wingspan 30·38m (99ft 8in); length overall 35·61m (116ft 10in); wing area 120·77m² (1,300ft²).

WEIGHTS Empty, **P-3A:** 26444kg (58,300lb), **P-3C:** 27890kg (61,491lb); maximum loaded, **P-3A:** 60781kg (134,000lb), **P-3C:** 64410kg (142,000lb).

ENGINES Four Allison T56 turboprops, **P-3A:** 4,500hp T56-10W, **P-3B** and **-3C:** 4,910hp T56-14.

MAXIMUM SPEED At medium height, reduced weight: 761km/h (473mph); set record speed of 806·1km/h (500·89mph).

SERVICE CEILING 8·63km (28,300ft).

RANGE Mission radius (no time on station): 3835km (2,383 miles), **CP-140** ferry range: 8024km (4,986 miles).

MILITARY LOAD Maximum can include six 907kg (2,000lb) mines externally, plus 3289kg (7,252lb) internal load comprising two Mk 101 depth bombs, four Mk 44 or similar AS torpedoes, 87 sonobuoys, 42 Mk 7 marine markers and various other buoys, signals and flares. **CP-140** weapon bay is restricted to 2177kg (4,800lb) but ten underwing pylons retain original limits from 277kg (611lb) to 1111kg (2,450lb) each.

USERS Australia, Canada, Iran, Japan, Netherlands, New Zealand, Norway, Spain, USA (Navy).

Lockheed P-3C Orion

It is extraordinary that the P-3C Orion should have ten external stores pylons, while its RAF counterpart, the Nimrod, should have only two pylons, which were soon removed because they were seldom used! Part of the answer lies in the Orion's shallow internal weapon bay, occupying a short compartment under the forward fuselage floor. The rest of the underside of the fuselage is occupied by a camera compartment (in the Update II replaced by an FLIR) ahead of the nose gear, a mass of electronics aerials, an APU and hydraulic service centre, and a battery of sonobuoy launch tubes aft of the wing: 48 A-size unpressurized tubes loaded from outside, three A-size pressurized tubes that can be reloaded with sonobuoys carried on board, and one large B-size tube. This P-3C of US Navy Patrol Squadron VP-50 is normally based at Moffett Field, south of San Francisco, California. It is shown with AXR-13 (LLLTV, low light level TV) under the root of the right wing and ALQ-78 (ECM) under the left. Mk 25 mines are carried on the outer pylons.

0   4m

Lockheed P-3 Orion

The original production model, the P-3A, is no longer used in US Navy front-line squadrons, but continues to serve in second-line duties. This aircraft was completely rebuilt by the Navy as a VIP transport on the strength of VP-30 normally based at NAS Jacksonville, Florida.

Externally almost indistinguishable from the P-3A, the P-3B is still operated by its export customers in its original ASW and maritime patrol role. This P-3B is on the strength of RNZAF No 5 Sqn, based at Whenuapai, near the capital, Auckland.

Many of the operational aircraft of the Norwegian air force are painted medium sea grey overall, including the force of five (intended to be increased) P-3B Orions operated by 333 Squadron from Andøya. Upper surfaces of the wing flaps are painted bright red, visible after landing.

Several Orions have been rebuilt for use as special EW (electronic warfare) platforms, or for weather reconnaissance or geomagnetic mapping programmes. This EP-3E of Navy Squadron VQ-2 is one of the least grotesquely changed examples, used by this squadron to gather information on signals emitted by Soviet warships the world over. Most VQ-2 aircraft have large ventral blisters.

The Islamic Iranian Air Force continues to operate at least three of its six P-3Fs, which are basically P-3Cs with the under-nose compartment with forward and lateral windows for a gimbal-mounted KA-74A surveillance camera. Originally they had probes for taking fuel from 707 and 747 tankers.

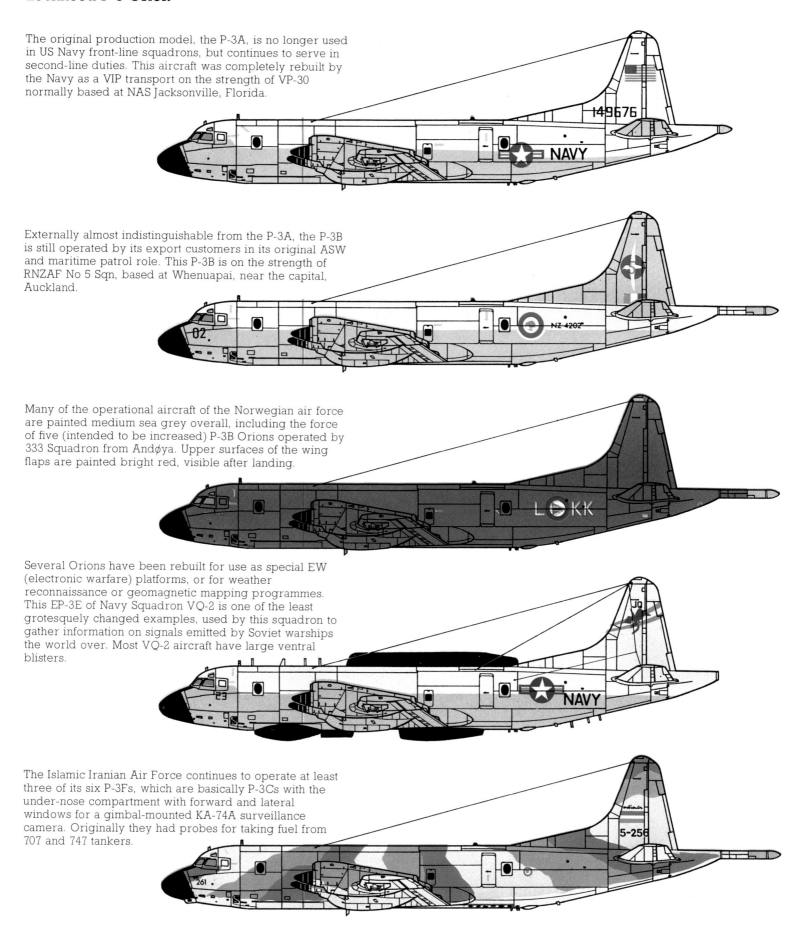

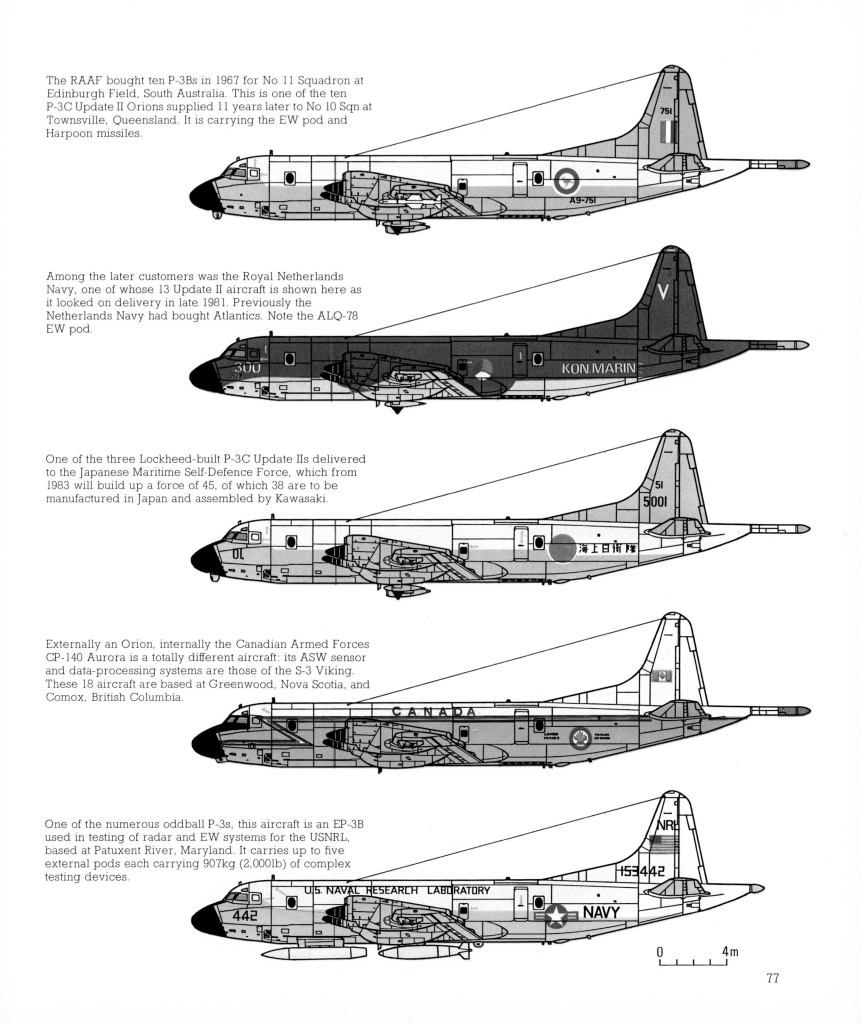

The RAAF bought ten P-3Bs in 1967 for No 11 Squadron at Edinburgh Field, South Australia. This is one of the ten P-3C Update II Orions supplied 11 years later to No 10 Sqn at Townsville, Queensland. It is carrying the EW pod and Harpoon missiles.

Among the later customers was the Royal Netherlands Navy, one of whose 13 Update II aircraft is shown here as it looked on delivery in late 1981. Previously the Netherlands Navy had bought Atlantics. Note the ALQ-78 EW pod.

One of the three Lockheed-built P-3C Update IIs delivered to the Japanese Maritime Self-Defence Force, which from 1983 will build up a force of 45, of which 38 are to be manufactured in Japan and assembled by Kawasaki.

Externally an Orion, internally the Canadian Armed Forces CP-140 Aurora is a totally different aircraft: its ASW sensor and data-processing systems are those of the S-3 Viking. These 18 aircraft are based at Greenwood, Nova Scotia, and Comox, British Columbia.

One of the numerous oddball P-3s, this aircraft is an EP-3B used in testing of radar and EW systems for the USNRL, based at Patuxent River, Maryland. It carries up to five external pods each carrying 907kg (2,000lb) of complex testing devices.

0   4m

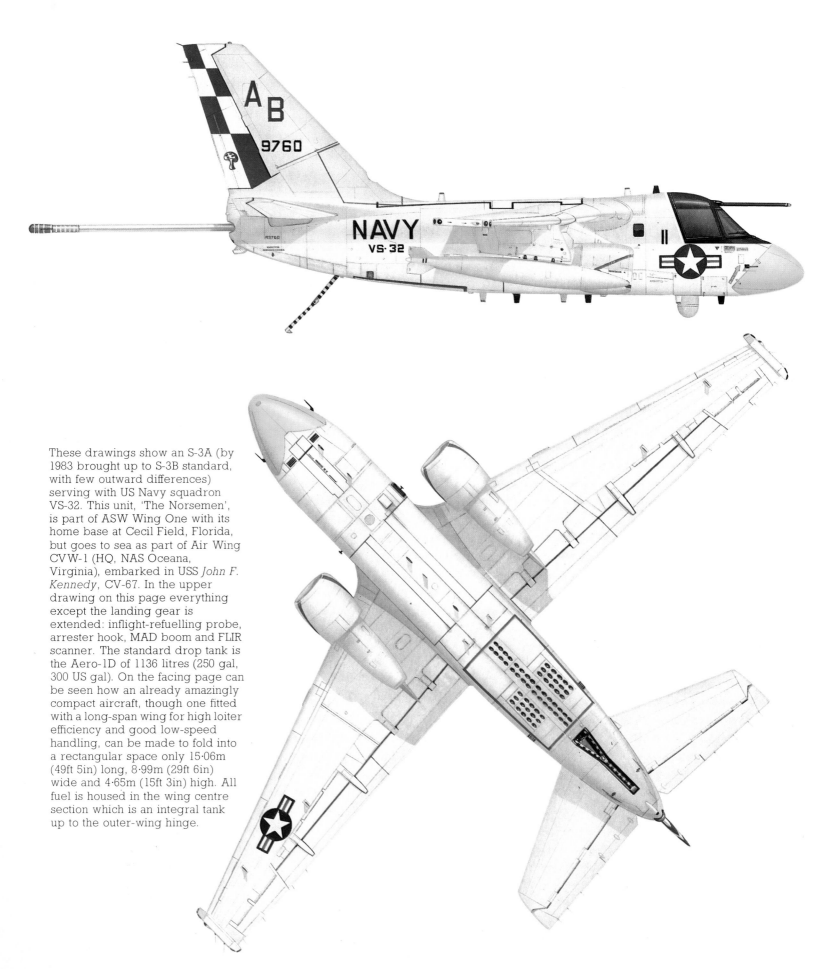

These drawings show an S-3A (by 1983 brought up to S-3B standard, with few outward differences) serving with US Navy squadron VS-32. This unit, 'The Norsemen', is part of ASW Wing One with its home base at Cecil Field, Florida, but goes to sea as part of Air Wing CVW-1 (HQ, NAS Oceana, Virginia), embarked in USS *John F. Kennedy*, CV-67. In the upper drawing on this page everything except the landing gear is extended: inflight-refuelling probe, arrester hook, MAD boom and FLIR scanner. The standard drop tank is the Aero-1D of 1136 litres (250 gal, 300 US gal). On the facing page can be seen how an already amazingly compact aircraft, though one fitted with a long-span wing for high loiter efficiency and good low-speed handling, can be made to fold into a rectangular space only 15·06m (49ft 5in) long, 8·99m (29ft 6in) wide and 4·65m (15ft 3in) high. All fuel is housed in the wing centre section which is an integral tank up to the outer-wing hinge.

Lockheed S-3 Viking

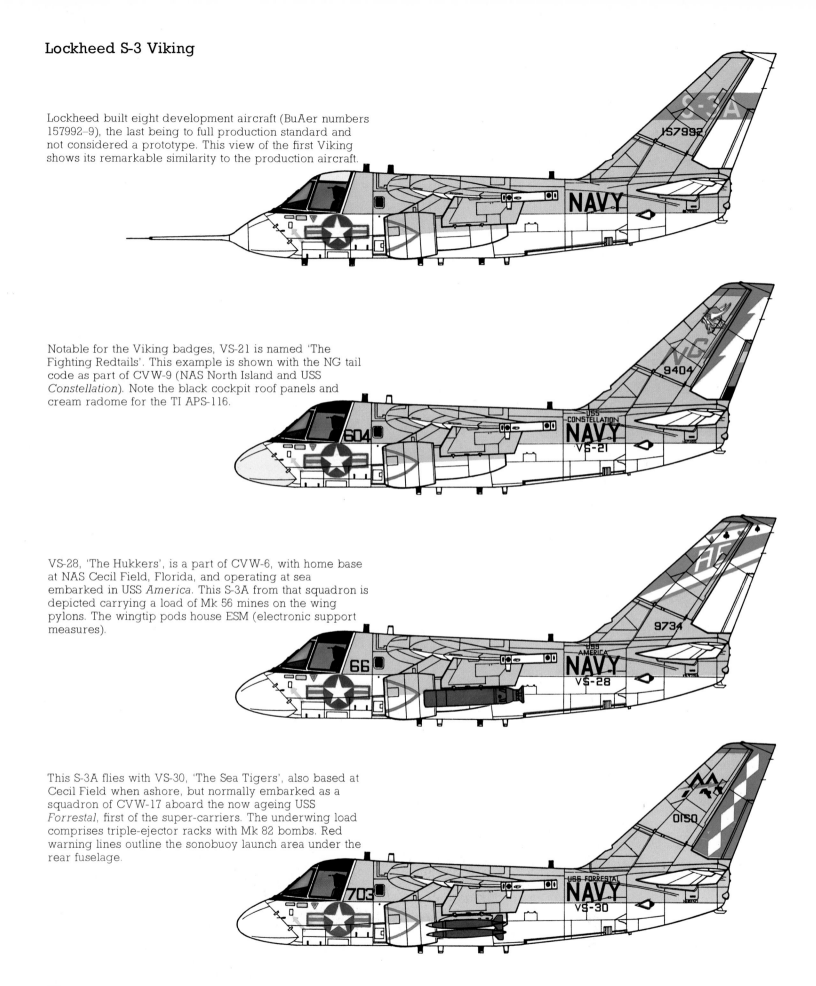

Lockheed built eight development aircraft (BuAer numbers 157992–9), the last being to full production standard and not considered a prototype. This view of the first Viking shows its remarkable similarity to the production aircraft.

Notable for the Viking badges, VS-21 is named 'The Fighting Redtails'. This example is shown with the NG tail code as part of CVW-9 (NAS North Island and USS *Constellation*). Note the black cockpit roof panels and cream radome for the TI APS-116.

VS-28, 'The Hukkers', is a part of CVW-6, with home base at NAS Cecil Field, Florida, and operating at sea embarked in USS *America*. This S-3A from that squadron is depicted carrying a load of Mk 56 mines on the wing pylons. The wingtip pods house ESM (electronic support measures).

This S-3A flies with VS-30, 'The Sea Tigers', also based at Cecil Field when ashore, but normally embarked as a squadron of CVW-17 aboard the now ageing USS *Forrestal*, first of the super-carriers. The underwing load comprises triple-ejector racks with Mk 82 bombs. Red warning lines outline the sonobuoy launch area under the rear fuselage.

One of several US military aircraft painted (usually temporarily) in colourful Bicentennial livery in 1976 was this S-3A of VS-41 'The Shamrocks', from NAS North Island and used in the crew-training role. Instead of the usual tail code RA on a shamrock, this aircraft displayed the famous Navy Jack of 1775 on its tail.

Carefully painted spectrum colours between black outlines adorn the tail of this US-3A COD (Carrier On-board Delivery) transport Viking, with underwing cargo containers. The unit is VS-38 'Claw Clan', of Pacific Fleet CVW-14, whose ship is the nuclear USS *Enterprise*. The national flag is displayed by a red griffin.

Like the US-3A above, the KS-3A tanker has the pre-amp VHF blade aerial removed from above the leading edge, but the hosereel installation calls for major changes at the rear including removal of the sonobuoy tubes. No individual markings are visible on this tanker trials aircraft, which is shown with 1137-litre (250 gal, 300 US gal) underwing tanks.

A black-and-white AGM-84A Harpoon cruise missile is seen on this S-3B development aircraft, whose test flying has involved prolonged debugging of the greatly augmented avionics systems. The Harpoon gives an anti-ship capability from ranges up to 92km (57 miles), beyond the limit of most ship-to-air weapon systems.

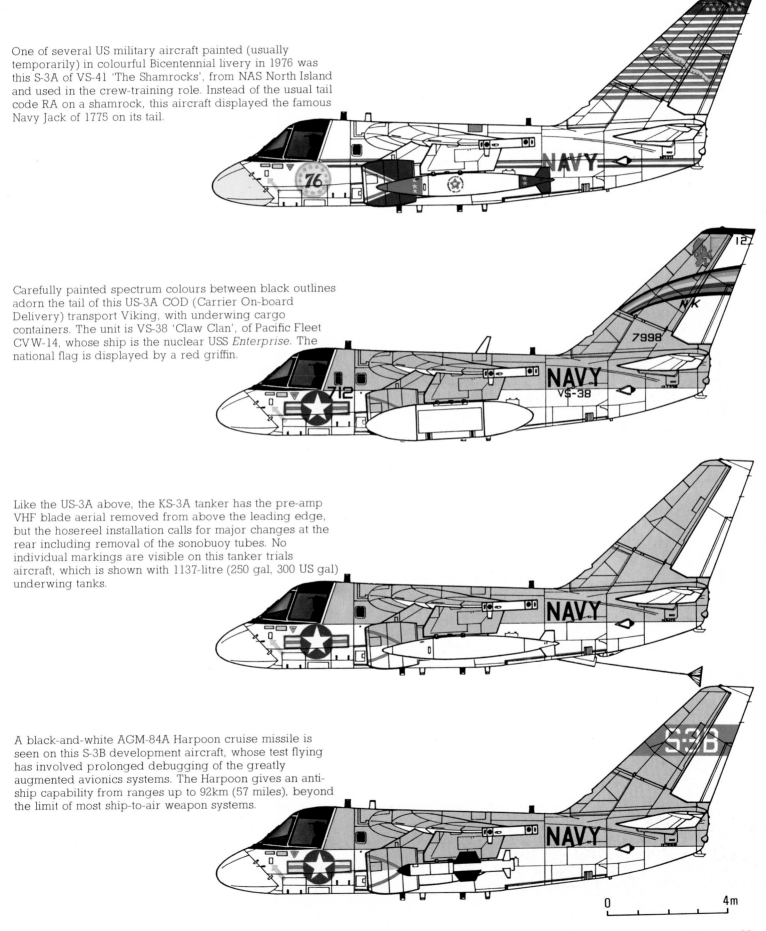

0   4m

81

Lockheed S-3 Viking

The Viking is not only perhaps the most remarkable exercise in packaging yet seen in aircraft design, but it is also rare among modern military aircraft in that there was only one production model and the whole programme was completed in six years. At the same time, new versions might yet be ordered, and the original S-3As are being updated.

While the P-3 Orion is the standard US Navy shore-based ASW aircraft, the S-3A is the corresponding platform embarked aboard carriers. At the end of World War 2 carrier-based ASW machines could not carry both sensors and weapons, and thus had to operate in pairs, one being the hunter and the other the killer. Then with the twin-engined S-2 Tracker, built by Grumman, a hunter/killer aircraft was at last made to suit a carrier, but this aircraft was slow and increasingly deficient in sensor power. It is remarkable that it was not until 1967 that a replacement was sought, and in August 1969 Lockheed's submission was chosen, with associate LTV (Vought) responsible for the wings, pylons, pods, aft fuselage, tail, landing gear and assurance of carrier suitability. The first of eight test aircraft flew on 21 January 1972, and the Viking entered fleet service on 20 February 1974. A total of 187 was delivered, the last in mid-1978.

The simplest part of the S-3 design was the basic aircraft, although even this had to be extremely carefully planned to house the mass of systems and still be carrier-compatible. Shorter than a fighter's, the fuselage has a Texas Instruments APS-116 radar in the nose, with the crew compartment ahead of the wings seating pilot and co-pilot in front and Tacco (tactical co-ord) and Senso (sensor operator) to the rear. There is a split internal weapons bay, augmented by underwing pylons, and ASW sensors include a MAD boom which can be extended from the tail (normally housed in the upper fuselage), sonobuoys ejected from the rear fuselage and an infra-red sensor extended below the cockpit. All nav/attack systems are linked through a Univac computer, with separate acoustic data processor. ECM

receivers are carried on the tips of the very efficient high-lift wings, which fold on skewed hinges so that the tips can overlap. The large vertical tail also folds. General Electric specially developed the high bypass ratio turbofan engines which give fine performance with good range and endurance, fuel consumption being less than half that of earlier jet engines of similar power.

From 1974 the S-3A rapidly replaced the S-2E aboard carriers, at the same time that the old ASW carriers were decommissioned. Under today's concept the ASW force forms part of the CVW carrier air wing of each of the giant attack carriers, with a basic force of six VS squadrons in the Atlantic Fleet and six in the Pacific, likely to be increased to seven in each fleet. At the start of the S-3A programme it was thought probable that the same basic type would be used for a number of other roles, and for several years the Navy has been evaluating a KS-3 tanker, with a single hosereel and drogue in the rear fuselage, and a US-3A COD (carrier on-board delivery) transport version. After studying various US-3 models with enlarged fuselages and rear ramp doors the decision was taken to use almost the existing fuselage in the US-3A and carry 907kg (2,000lb) of cargo in large pods hung on the wing pylons. This was the arrangement in the US-3A prototype, but in late 1982 it was expected that, if a COD version is ordered, it will have a wider fuselage with rear door.

Meanwhile, as the jigs and tooling lie in storage awaiting a US-3 go-ahead, up to 160 of the 179 production Vikings are likely to be updated under an extensive long-term WSIP (weapon-system improvement programme) from which they will emerge with the designation S-3B. Though little changed externally, the S-3B will have greater acoustic processing capacity, expanded ESM (electronic support measures) coverage, greater and faster radar processing, a new sonobuoy receiver system and provision for firing the Harpoon missile from the wing pylons against shipping.

COUNTRY OF ORIGIN USA.

CREW 4.

TOTAL PRODUCED 187.

DIMENSIONS Wingspan 20·93m (68ft 8in); length 16·26m (53ft 4in); wing area 55·55m² (598ft²); when folded, wingspan and length are respectively 8·99m (29ft 6in) and 15·06m (49ft 5in).

WEIGHTS Empty 12088kg (26,650lb); maximum loaded 23831kg (52,539lb).

ENGINES Two 4207kg (9,275lb) General Electric TF34-400A turbofans.

MAXIMUM SPEED 834km/h (518mph).

SERVICE CEILING 11km (36,000ft).

RANGE Combat range: more than 3700km (2,300 miles), ferry range: more than 5560km (3,450 miles).

MILITARY LOAD Internal weapon bay for four Mk 36 destructors, or four Mk 46 torpedoes, or four Mk 82 bombs, or four Mk 54 depth bombs or four Mk 53 mines. Underwing pylons can be equipped with triple ejector racks enabling each side to carry three rocket pods, three Mk 20 cluster bombs, flare launchers, Mk 36 destructors, Mk 82 bombs or a single AGM-84A Harpoon long-range missile.

USER USA (Navy).

Lockheed U-2 and SR-71

First, and possibly only, totally clandestine aircraft ever to serve with a major power, the **Lockheed U-2** was revealed in 1957 as a high-altitude research aircraft built for NASA (US National Aeronautics and Space Administration). In fact its design had begun in 1954 as a covert spy aircraft for the CIA (Central Intelligence Agency).

It was one of the biggest of many challenges met by the Lockheed Advanced Development Projects team at Burbank, led by C.L. 'Kelly' Johnson. In a secure building called The Skunk Works a hand-picked team created the strange bird to meet a secret specification for a strategic reconnaissance aircraft able to fly so high that it could not be shot down. Thus, long overflights could be made across the Soviet Union and other territories whose governments often never even knew!

The basic U-2 could hardly have been simpler, the structure being extremely light and resembling a jet sailplane with long-span wings for efficient high-altitude flight. To save weight no ejection seat was fitted, and the only landing gear comprised a tandem pair of twin wheels on the centreline with stabilizing wheels under the wings. On take-off these wing wheels fall away, and the landing is completed with one wingtip sliding on the ground. The U-2 proved to be unbelievably difficult to fly and especially to land, with a highly flexible but weak airframe, and with the approach speed almost the same as the stalling speed.

Tony LeVier made the first flight in mid-1955, and the 1956 budget paid (secretly) for 48 U-2As and five two-seat U-2Ds, but increasing demands for range and mission equipment led to a switch in 1958 to the U-2B with a larger engine; at least 14 U-2As were completed to this standard. Most had integral wing fuel tanks. The two-seat version of the U-2B was the U-2C, and the U-2CT conversion trainer with raised rear cockpit is still in use. Most U-2Ds were modified for missile monitoring and fall-out study, while JU-2D and WU-2D versions also flew important research programmes. But the main U-2As

and Bs carried out clandestine missions with impunity until on 1 May 1960 one was shot down by a SAM battery near Sverdlovsk, USSR, the civilian CIA pilot being sentenced for espionage.

This put a damper on proceedings, although USAF pilots took over for Cuban missions during the 1962 missile crisis. Some 24 had been lost over hostile territory or in accidents when in 1968 a fresh batch of 12 greatly enlarged WU-2Cs was ordered, these being redesignated U-2R. With almost twice the wing area, these carry far more fuel and equipment, and altogether 25 were produced including rebuilds. Two same-size rebuilds were delivered to NASA as ER-2 Earth-resource aircraft. The latest version is the TR-1 tactical reconnaissance aircraft of the USAF, of which the total order comprises 33 TR-1As plus two 2-seat TR-1Bs. These costly machines are packed with advanced avionics, including synthetic-aperture side-looking radars. The first TR-1A was completed in July 1981.

Another highly secret Lockheed aircraft is the **SR-71A**, the incredible Mach 3-plus monster, marking the second-generation strategic reconnaissance aircraft to emerge from The Skunk Works. Originally developed as the A-11 (another cover, like 'U-2') in 1960, it flew in 1962 as the YF-12A interceptor, the larger long-range SR-71 following in December 1964. A total of 31 SR-71As was built, two being converted to SR-71B trainers. The SR-71C was a trainer converted from the A-11. First used by the 4200th Strategic Recon Wing in 1966, and passed to the 9th SRW a year later, these black giants —popularly called Blackbirds—fly missions in many parts of the world and are based at Beale AFB, California, and RAF Mildenhall, England. Flying twice as high as almost all other aircraft, their crew of pilot and a recon systems operator wear astronaut suits and carry personal environmental systems. The airframe is almost wholly of titanium alloy, and at Mach 3 most of the lift comes from the broad sharp-sided body and the thrust from the suction around the large variable spike in the engine inlets.

COUNTRY OF ORIGIN USA.

CREW 1 or 2.

TOTAL PRODUCED **U-2:** 65; **ER:** 2; **TR:** 6 of 35 planned; **A-11/YF-12:** 18; **SR-71:** 31.

DIMENSIONS Wingspan, **U-2A and derivatives:** 24·38m (80ft 0in) **U-2R/ER/TR:** 31·39m (103ft 0in), **SR:** 16·94m (55ft 7in); length, **U-2A and derivatives:** 15·11m (49ft 7in), **U-2R/ER/TR:** 19·2m (63ft 0½in), **SR:** 32·74m (107ft 5in); wing area, **U-2A and derivatives:** 52·49m² (565ft²), **U-2R/ER/TR:** 92·9m² (1,000ft²), **SR:** 167·2m² (1,800ft²).

WEIGHTS Empty, **U-2A:** 4241kg (9,350lb), **U-2R:** 7212kg (15,900lb), **TR-1A:** about 8165 kg (18,000lb), **SR:** about 31400kg (69,000lb); maximum loaded, **U-2A:** 7190kg (15,850lb), **U-2B** with slipper tanks: 7834kg (17,270lb), **U-2R:** 13154kg (29,000lb), **TR:** 18143kg (40,000lb), **SR:** 77110kg (170,000lb).

ENGINE(S) **U-2A:** one 5080kg (11,200lb) Pratt & Whitney J57-37A turbojet, **U-2B** and all later variants: one 7711kg (17,000lb) P&W J75-13B turbojet, **SR:** two 14742kg (32,500lb) P&W J58/JT11B-20D augmented bypass turbojets.

MAXIMUM SPEED **U-2s:** typically 837km/h (520mph) at high altitude, **SR:** set world record at 3529·56km/h (2,193·17mph, Mach 3·32).

SERVICE CEILING **U-2A:** about 22·8km (75,000ft), **all later versions, including TR:** 27·43km (90,000ft), **SR:** over 24·4km (80,000ft).

RANGE **U-2A:** 4828km (3,000 miles), **U-2B:** 6437km (4,000 miles), **U-2R/ER/TR:** about 5633km (3,500 miles), **SR:** 4168km (2,590 miles).

MILITARY LOAD No weapons, but comprehensive systems for various kinds of optical, electronic, infra-red and other reconnaissance, depending on mission.

USER USA (AF, NASA, Navy).

Lockheed SR-71A

The SR-71B trainer has a second cockpit, the extra drag of which has a significant effect on maximum speed.

Fastest military aircraft in the world, and current holder of the world absolute speed record, the Lockheed SR-71A continues to fly on a limited scale with the USAF 9th Strategic Reconnaissance Wing, whose home base is Beale AFB, California. In the past ten years great efforts have been made to apply 'stealth' technology to a replacement aircraft, and small modifications may be introduced to the regular SR-71s in the inventory to reduce radar signature. Little can be done about the IR emission, which to a heat-sensitive seeker makes the whole 'Blackbird' family glow like lighthouses. In cruising flight most of the thrust comes from the favourable pressure distribution round the inlet spikes, while much of the lift is generated by the sharp-chined body. The inwards-canted vertical tails pivot as single units, there being no fixed fin.

0   4m

Lockheed U-2/TR-1

The original procurement, on a hidden vote, comprised 48 U-2As which initially flew without markings, although several were painted in NACA (later NASA) insignia to support the cover story. Later they received USAF numbers 56-6675/6722, and some USAF insignia and various paint schemes. More than half were completed as U-2Bs.

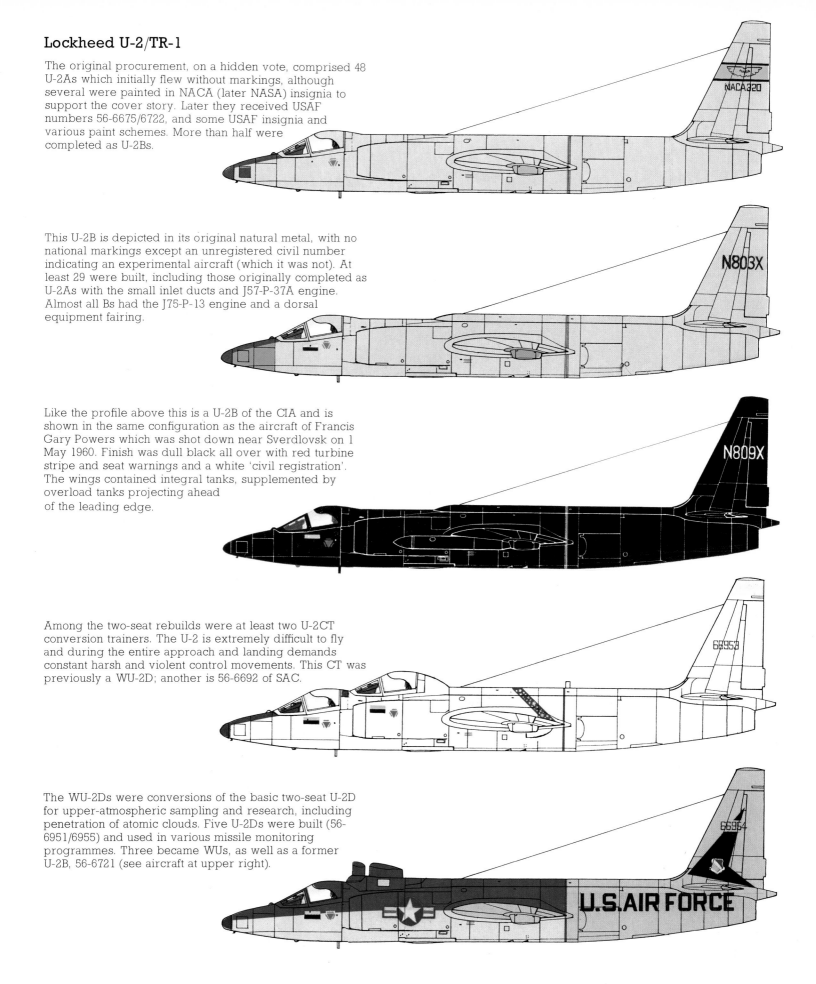

This U-2B is depicted in its original natural metal, with no national markings except an unregistered civil number indicating an experimental aircraft (which it was not). At least 29 were built, including those originally completed as U-2As with the small inlet ducts and J57-P-37A engine. Almost all Bs had the J75-P-13 engine and a dorsal equipment fairing.

Like the profile above this is a U-2B of the CIA and is shown in the same configuration as the aircraft of Francis Gary Powers which was shot down near Sverdlovsk on 1 May 1960. Finish was dull black all over with red turbine stripe and seat warnings and a white 'civil registration'. The wings contained integral tanks, supplemented by overload tanks projecting ahead of the leading edge.

Among the two-seat rebuilds were at least two U-2CT conversion trainers. The U-2 is extremely difficult to fly and during the entire approach and landing demands constant harsh and violent control movements. This CT was previously a WU-2D; another is 56-6692 of SAC.

The WU-2Ds were conversions of the basic two-seat U-2D for upper-atmospheric sampling and research, including penetration of atomic clouds. Five U-2Ds were built (56-6951/6955) and used in various missile monitoring programmes. Three became WUs, as well as a former U-2B, 56-6721 (see aircraft at upper right).

Perhaps the most-rebuilt U-2 of all began life as a CIA U-2B and in about 1961 reappeared as a two-seat U-2D. Next it was fitted with a giant vertical fairing drum as a JU-2D for special upper-atmospheric sampling, still painted black, before finally going to the Air Force Flight Test Center at Edwards AFB as a WU-2D with special features and attractive white/red livery.

By 1966 half the U-2s had been lost, mainly because they were too difficult to fly, and Lockheed delivered a further batch of 25 which incorporated parts of surviving aircraft but were largely new and were assigned numbers 68-10329/10353. Designated U-2R, the dimensions increased considerably, and take-off weight jumped from 7834 to 13154kg (17,270 to 29,000lb), allowing for an electronic-reconnaissance payload of 5443kg (12,000lb) in large wing pods. Ship 10336 is a long-nose model.

Based on the U-2R but cleared to a further increased weight of 18144kg (40,000lb), the TR-1 draws on extensive U-2 experience in having a synthetic-aperture radar, which behaves as if it had a scanner hundreds of metres across, to obtain sharp magnified pictures of what goes on up to 55km (35 miles) across a foreign frontier. Flown on 1 August 1981, this was the first of 33 TR-1As assigned to SAC, 18 of them based in Europe (initially at RAF Alconbury).

Included in the 1980 budget were two TR-1As, plus this special NASA aircraft designated ER-2 for Earth-resources research. Based at Ames Research Center it carries radars, cameras, IR scanner, Lidar (laser radar), samplers, a gas chromatograph and many other sensors. Thus after 27 years the U-2 really has become a 'NASA research aircraft'.

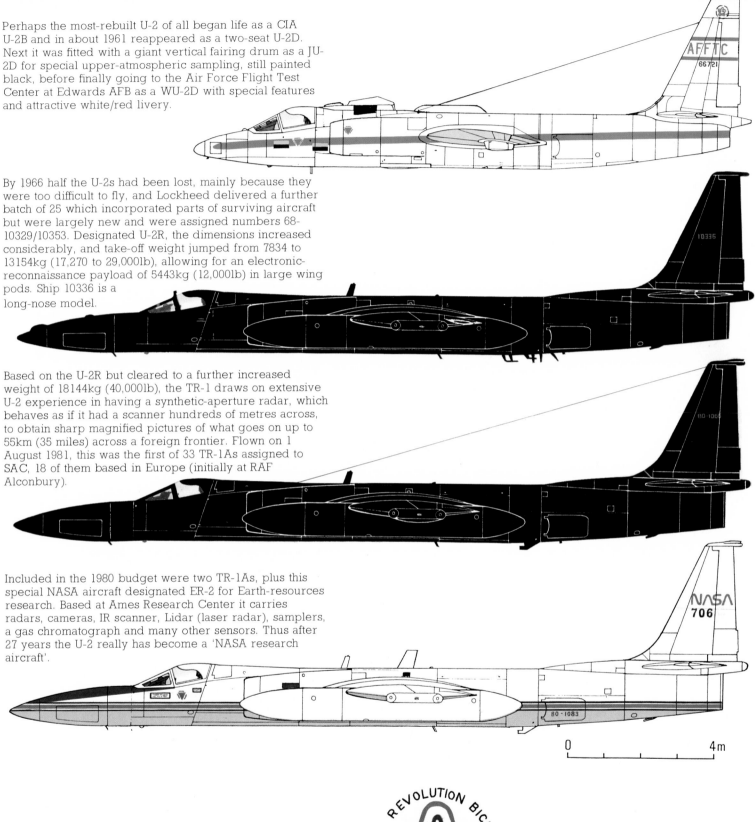

0   4m

Lockheed emblem (USA)

Bicentennial badge (USA)

NASA

NASA emblem (USA)

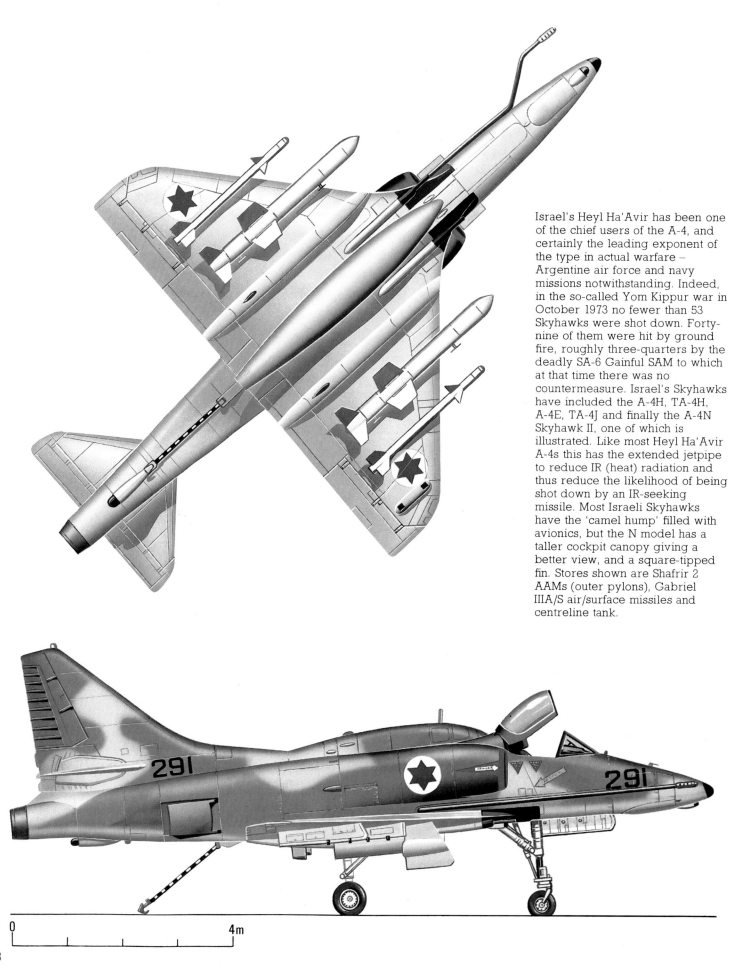

Israel's Heyl Ha'Avir has been one of the chief users of the A-4, and certainly the leading exponent of the type in actual warfare – Argentine air force and navy missions notwithstanding. Indeed, in the so-called Yom Kippur war in October 1973 no fewer than 53 Skyhawks were shot down. Forty-nine of them were hit by ground fire, roughly three-quarters by the deadly SA-6 Gainful SAM to which at that time there was no countermeasure. Israel's Skyhawks have included the A-4H, TA-4H, A-4E, TA-4J and finally the A-4N Skyhawk II, one of which is illustrated. Like most Heyl Ha'Avir A-4s this has the extended jetpipe to reduce IR (heat) radiation and thus reduce the likelihood of being shot down by an IR-seeking missile. Most Israeli Skyhawks have the 'camel hump' filled with avionics, but the N model has a taller cockpit canopy giving a better view, and a square-tipped fin. Stores shown are Shafrir 2 AAMs (outer pylons), Gabriel IIIA/S air/surface missiles and centreline tank.

0   4m

McDonnell Douglas A-4N Skyhawk II

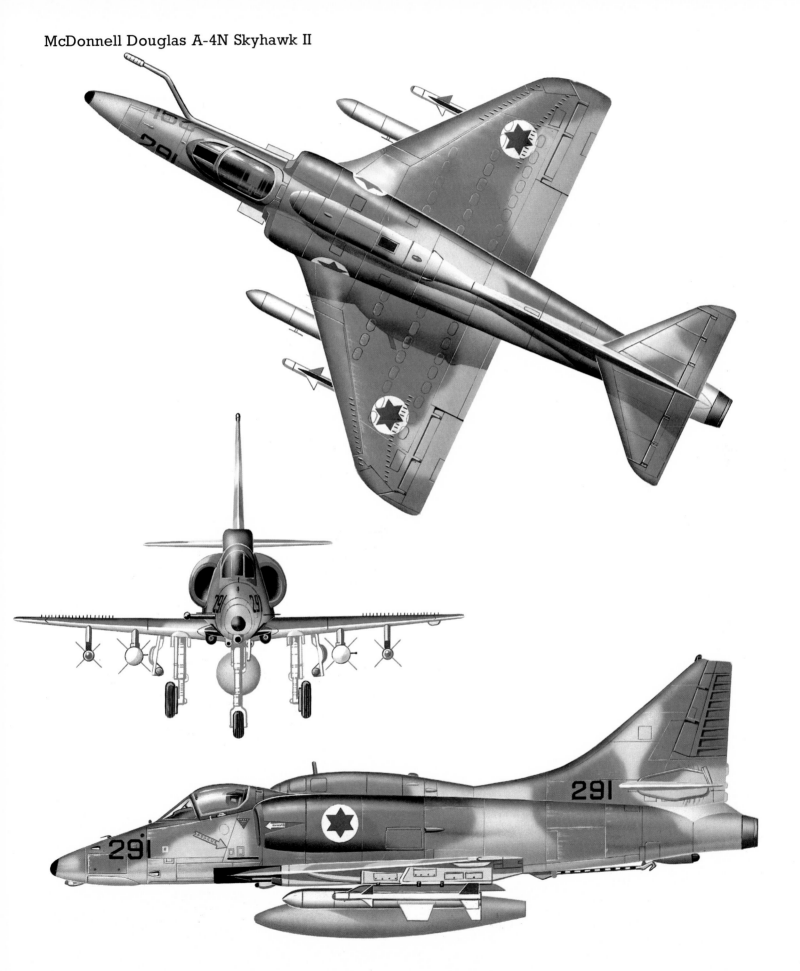

McDonnell Douglas A-4 Skyhawk

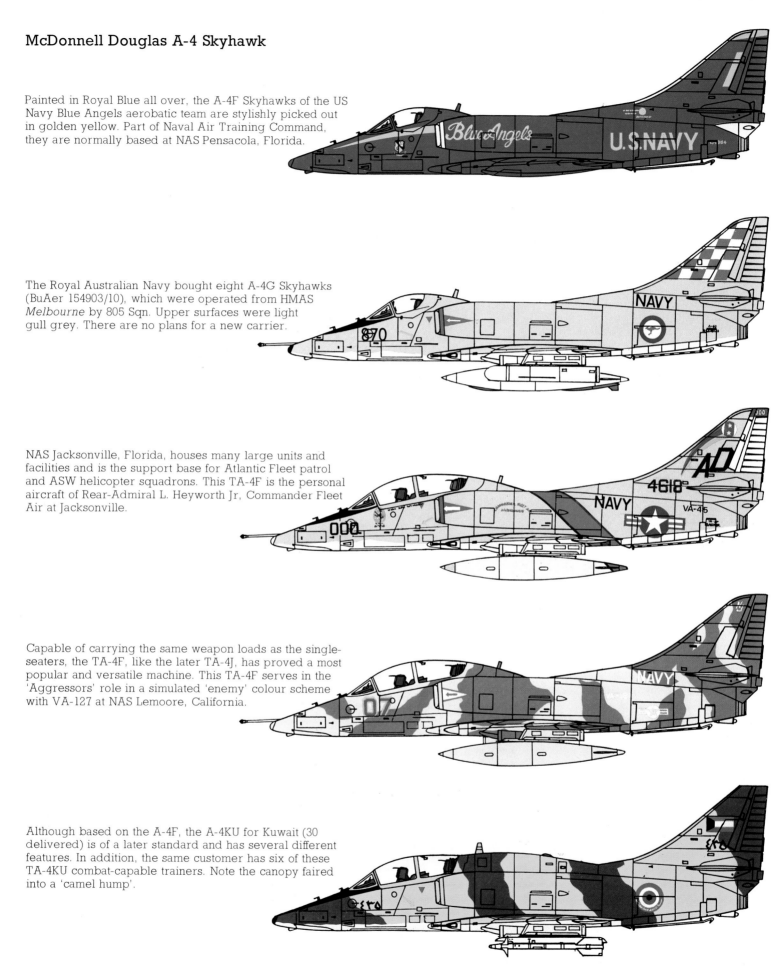

Painted in Royal Blue all over, the A-4F Skyhawks of the US Navy Blue Angels aerobatic team are stylishly picked out in golden yellow. Part of Naval Air Training Command, they are normally based at NAS Pensacola, Florida.

The Royal Australian Navy bought eight A-4G Skyhawks (BuAer 154903/10), which were operated from HMAS *Melbourne* by 805 Sqn. Upper surfaces were light gull grey. There are no plans for a new carrier.

NAS Jacksonville, Florida, houses many large units and facilities and is the support base for Atlantic Fleet patrol and ASW helicopter squadrons. This TA-4F is the personal aircraft of Rear-Admiral L. Heyworth Jr, Commander Fleet Air at Jacksonville.

Capable of carrying the same weapon loads as the single-seaters, the TA-4F, like the later TA-4J, has proved a most popular and versatile machine. This TA-4F serves in the 'Aggressors' role in a simulated 'enemy' colour scheme with VA-127 at NAS Lemoore, California.

Although based on the A-4F, the A-4KU for Kuwait (30 delivered) is of a later standard and has several different features. In addition, the same customer has six of these TA-4KU combat-capable trainers. Note the canopy faired into a 'camel hump'.

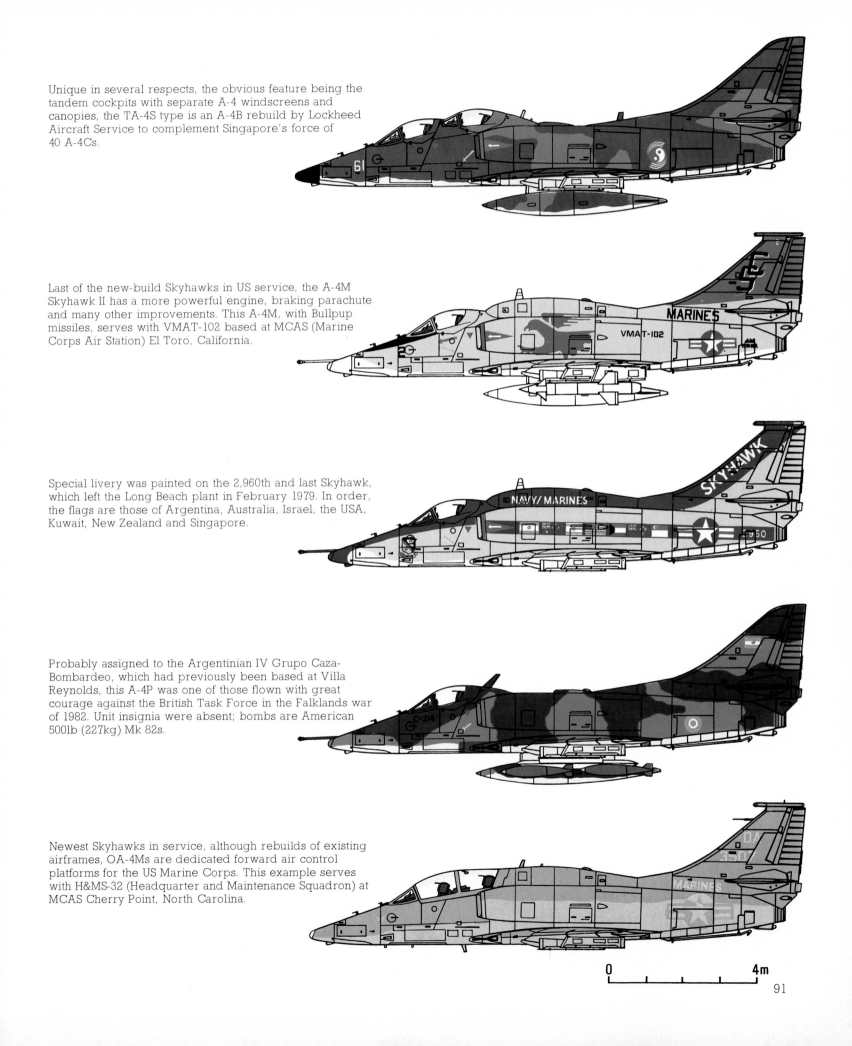

Unique in several respects, the obvious feature being the tandem cockpits with separate A-4 windscreens and canopies, the TA-4S type is an A-4B rebuild by Lockheed Aircraft Service to complement Singapore's force of 40 A-4Cs.

Last of the new-build Skyhawks in US service, the A-4M Skyhawk II has a more powerful engine, braking parachute and many other improvements. This A-4M, with Bullpup missiles, serves with VMAT-102 based at MCAS (Marine Corps Air Station) El Toro, California.

Special livery was painted on the 2,960th and last Skyhawk, which left the Long Beach plant in February 1979. In order, the flags are those of Argentina, Australia, Israel, the USA, Kuwait, New Zealand and Singapore.

Probably assigned to the Argentinian IV Grupo Caza-Bombardeo, which had previously been based at Villa Reynolds, this A-4P was one of those flown with great courage against the British Task Force in the Falklands war of 1982. Unit insignia were absent; bombs are American 500lb (227kg) Mk 82s.

Newest Skyhawks in service, although rebuilds of existing airframes, OA-4Ms are dedicated forward air control platforms for the US Marine Corps. This example serves with H&MS-32 (Headquarter and Maintenance Squadron) at MCAS Cherry Point, North Carolina.

0   4m

McDonnell Douglas
A-4 Skyhawk

With great boldness and imagination, Ed Heinemann, in 1952 chief engineer of Douglas's Navy plant at El Segundo, designed the XA4D prototype to a gross weight of 15,000lb (6804kg), exactly half what the specification allowed. So effective was this design that, with a long series of updates to engine, systems and avionics, it remained in production 22 years longer than planned, and was bought by many land-based air forces. In fact an Israeli pilot said in 1981 'How can we ever replace it?'.

During the Korean war (1950–3) Heinemann's A-1 Skyraider could fly a 10-hour mission with a heavy bombload but was slow; jets were fast but carried few bombs and had cripplingly short endurance. What was needed was a jet attack aircraft with good endurance with a heavy bombload. The Navy asked Heinemann to scheme a design to fly a particular set of missions and reach a speed of 495mph (797km/h) within a stipulated weight limit of 30,000lb (13608kg). He came up with a design even smaller than jet fighters. It had a wing forming an integral fuel tank from tip to tip, with slats along the leading edge, so small it did not need to fold. He never even considered a turboprop, and selected a British turbojet made in the USA, mounted above the wing with side inlets. He used a one-piece skin to cover the entire wing, both above and below, with no cut-out for the landing gears, which retracted forwards so that the leg lay under the skin while the wheel fitted ahead of the spar inside the leading edge. Leaving out a weapons bay saved 2268kg (5,000lb), and the radical ideas even extended to the design of the ejection seat and the electronic packages.

The gross weight came out at 12,000lb (5443kg). Nobody, not even Heinemann's own team, could believe it. The Navy asked for twice the bombload and another 100 nautical miles (185km) of range; the weight became 14,300lb (6486kg). Still incredulous, the Navy authorized the XF4D-1 prototype. This flew on 22 June 1954, and soon set a world 500km (311-mile) circuit record at more than 695mph (1118km/h),

just 200mph faster than specification!

By this time the doubters had become enthusiastic converts, and the A4D-1 entered fleet service in October 1956, powered by the Wright J65 Sapphire engine rated at 3493kg (7,700lb) thrust and carrying a weapon load of 2268kg (5,000lb) on three pylons. In 1962 this model was redesignated A-4A. It was followed by 542 A4D-2s (A-4Bs) with provision for guiding the Bullpup missile and with a demountable flight-refuelling probe. The most numerous version was the A4D-2N (A-4C) of 1959, which introduced terrain-clearance radar, Labs (see Glossary), a better autopilot, Escapac seat and angle-of-attack indicator; 638 were built.

Pratt & Whitney produced an improved engine, the J52, but the A4D-3 and -4 with this powerplant were not built. Finally the A-4E of 1961 launched the second generation of Skyhawks, with the J52 not only stretching the range but also lifting greater weapon loads from five external stations. In 1962 the load was increased further, to 4153kg (9,155lb), about the same as the empty weight. The A-4F introduced a dorsal avionics pack as the first of the 'Camel' Skyhawks; other updates included a steerable nosewheel, zero/zero seat, wing spoilers and greater thrust. The TA-4F was the first dual trainer, but it was outnumbered by the simplified TA-4J.

The A-4M Skyhawk II introduced a more powerful J52, redesigned vertical tail and braking parachute (previously used on the Israeli A-4H which has 30mm guns). The Israeli A-4N has a longer jetpipe to protect against heat-seeking missiles. Last of the new-build versions was the A-4Y with British Marconi HUD and other improved avionics, finally closing the production line at Long Beach at 2,405 attack models and 555 trainers after 26 years.

New and reconditioned Skyhawks sold well. The Singapore TA-4S is unique in having separate tandem canopies. The final US version is the OA-4M forward-air control model of the Marines with Camel hump and tandem cockpits.

COUNTRY OF ORIGIN USA.

CREW Attack: 1, training and FAC: 2.

TOTAL PRODUCED 2,960.

DIMENSIONS Wingspan 8·38m (27ft 6in); length, **A-4B** excluding probe 12·04m (39ft 6in), **most single-seat:** 12·29m (40ft 4in), **two-seat:** 12·99m (42ft 7¼in); wing area 24·16m² (260ft²).

WEIGHTS Empty, **A-4A:** 3493kg (7,700lb), **A-4F:** 4581kg (10,100lb), **A-4M:** 4747kg (10,465lb); maximum loaded, **A-4A:** 7711kg (17,000lb), **A-4B:** 9979kg (22,000lb), **all others**, shipboard: 11113kg (24,500lb), land-based: 12437kg (27,420lb).

ENGINE **A-4B, C, L, P, Q** and **S:** one 3493kg (7,700lb) Wright J65-16A, **A-4E, J:** one 3856kg (8,500lb) Pratt & Whitney J52-6, **A-4F, G, H, K:** one 4218kg (9,300lb) J52-8A, **A-4M, N:** one 5080kg (11,200lb) J52-408A.

MAXIMUM SPEED All versions, clean: 1078–1102km/h (670–685mph).

SERVICE CEILING All versions, clean: about 15km (49,000ft).

RANGE Late versions, clean, or with max fuel plus 1814kg (4,000lb) bombload: 1480km (920 miles), **A-4M** ferry range with max internal and external fuel: 3307km (2,055 miles).

MILITARY LOAD Normally two 20mm Mk 12 guns in wing roots with 200 (late models, 400) rounds each; **A-4A, B, C:** three pylons for 2268kg (5,000lb) weapon load, **A-4E, F, G, H, K, L, P, Q, S:** five pylons for 3720kg (8,200lb), **A-4M, N, Y:** five pylons for 4153kg (9,155lb).

USERS Argentina, Australia, Indonesia, Israel, Kuwait, Malaysia, New Zealand, Singapore, USA (Marine Corps, Navy, Reserve).

McDonnell Douglas F-4 Phantom II

In May 1953 the young McDonnell Aircraft Company at St Louis lost the US Navy's first award of a supersonic fighter to a rival (Vought). Undaunted, MAC carried on with studies and eventually produced a fighter that was far superior to anything else in sight. Though nobody called it beautiful, it was such a fabulous performer that it was soon bought not only for the Navy and Marines but also for the US Air Force, and by foreign customers. Throughout the 1960s it was the standard against which other fighters were judged (and found wanting), and when the last Phantom came off the line it completed a programme worth $27 billion.

In the mid-1950s the project was for an attack fighter, but the Navy then asked for 10 of its 11 weapon pylons to be removed, leaving just a centreline rack for a large drop tank. On 27 May 1958 the first prototype flew as a pure fleet defence fighter, with recesses under its broad fuselage for four Sparrow AAMs guided by the large nose radar and managed by a second crew member in the back seat. Later development prototypes introduced flap blowing to reduce the landing speed, a larger radar scanner in a bulged radome, an infra-red detector in a separate pod under the nose, underwing pylons each able to carry either an extra Sparrow or a pair of close-range Sidewinder AAMs, and a flight-refuelling probe. Early Phantom IIs collected more world speed, height and climb records than any other aircraft in history.

Service with the US Navy and Marine Corps began in December 1960, the first production model being the F-4B of which 637 were built. Apart from the larger radome this was distinguished from the F-4A by a raised cockpit canopy. Although these were not originally requested, the F-4B was fitted with extra pylons and tested with heavy bombloads of up to 7257kg (16,000lb). In the Vietnam war the F-4B flew attack missions at low level as well as air combat and even FAC sorties, with conspicuous success.

For the first time here was a naval fighter that outperformed anything in the US Air Force. After careful study the McDonnell fighter was adopted for Tactical Air Command as the F-110 (changed to F-4 in the 1962 rationalization of designations). TAC received F-4Bs on loan pending delivery of its own F-4C which introduced a few minor changes the Air Force judged essential, among them larger brakes with anti-skid, larger main tyres, a boom receptacle instead of a probe, dual flight controls, pneumatic/cartridge engine starters and a few new avionic items. MAC delivered 583 of this model, all but the first batch being camouflaged.

The F-4C led straight to an unarmed reconnaissance model, the RF-4C, with extremely comprehensive sensors. In turn the equipment fitted to this was put into the original naval model to produce the RF-4B for the Marines. No fewer than 505 of the RF-4C type were built, and alongside them MAC built 825 of the F-4D type which closely resembled the F-4C externally, but incorporated completely revised navigation and weapon-aiming systems tailored to land warfare. The D was meant to be the ideal USAF version, but experience in Vietnam showed the urgent need for an internal gun and other changes, resulting in the F-4E which also introduced extra power, more internal fuel and a new radar in a slim nose. The USAF took 831, all but the first batches having a slatted wing for better manoeuvring with heavy bombloads. A further 538 were sold to numerous export customers (see list), as well as to Japan where 130 F-4EJs were assembled under licence.

Britain bought a largely redesigned model with Spey engines of greater power, but this did not give the expected boost in performance. The Royal Navy had 52 F-4Ks (Phantom FG.1s) and the RAF 118 F-4Ms (Phantom FGR.2s). Latest US model is the F-4G Wild Weasel II ECM version, of which 116 were produced by rebuilding F-4Es with APR-38 electronic systems. Many users are updating these useful aircraft; the Luftwaffe, for example, is fitting new digital nav/attack systems, and the RAF has added fin-cap ECM aerials and Sky Flash missiles.

COUNTRY OF ORIGIN USA.

CREW 2.

NUMBER PRODUCED 5,195 not including 16 RF-4Es for Iran (not assembled).

DIMENSIONS Wingspan 11·68m (38ft 4in); length, **B, C, D, J, N, S:** 17·75m (58ft 3in), **E, EJ, F, G** and **RF:** 19·2m (63ft 0in); wing area 49·24m² (530ft²).

WEIGHTS Empty, **B, C, D, J, N:** about 12700kg (28,000lb); **E, EJ, F, G, RF:** 13154kg (29,000lb), **K, M:** 14061kg (31,000lb); maximum loaded, **B:** 24766kg (54,600lb), **C, D, G, J, K, M, N, RF:** 26308kg (58,000lb), **E, EJ, F:** 27379kg (60,360lb).

ENGINES Two General Electric J79 augmented turbojets, **B, RF-4B:** 7711kg (17,000lb) J79-8, **C, D:** 7711kg (17,000lb) J79-15, **E, EJ, F, G:** 8120kg (17,900lb) J79-17, **J, N, S:** 8120kg (17,900lb) J79-10, **K, M:** 9305kg (20,515lb) Rolls-Royce Spey 202/203 augmented turbofans.

MAXIMUM SPEED Clean except for Sparrow AAMs, J79 versions: 1464km/h (910mph, Mach 1·20) at low altitude, 2414km/h (1,500mph, Mach 2·27) at high altitude; Spey versions: 1481km/h (920mph Mach 1·21) low, 2231km/h (1,386mph, Mach 2·10) high.

SERVICE CEILING **E:** 18·97km (62,250ft), **M:** 17·98km (59,000ft).

RANGE **Most versions:** 3700km (2,300 miles), **E, EJ, G:** 4184km (2,600 miles).

MILITARY LOAD No internal gun except **E, EJ, F:** one 20mm M61A-1 with 639 rounds; four Sparrow or Sky Flash AAMs recessed under fuselage, centreline pylon for any tac store up to 1370kg (3,020lb) M118 bomb, or missile, tank, gun pod or tow target installation; four wing pylons for all tac bombs or missiles including Maverick, Hobos, Paveway, Walleye or AAMs: F-4G carries Standard ARM, HARM and Shrike missiles.

USERS Egypt, Germany (Federal Republic), Great Britain (RAF), Greece, Iran, Israel, Japan, South Korea, Spain, Turkey, USA.

McDonnell Douglas
F-4J Phantom II

Although the Phantom no longer flies as a first-line combat aircraft with the US Navy, hundreds serve in secondary duties in three main variants: the F-4J, F-4N (remanufactured and updated F-4B) and F-4S (remanufactured F-4J with outer-wing manoeuvring slats). The aircraft depicted is a special F-4J used by VX-4 'The Evaluators', the Navy Air Test and Evaluation squadron based at NAS Point Mugu, California. Painted in Thunderbird-style 1976 Bicentennial colours, it is the 18th production aircraft (BuAer 153088) and is shown clean except for centreline tank. Another early F-4J (153783) serving with VX-4 is the subject of the side elevation at the foot of the opposite page, with bunny tail badge and Sparrow missiles.

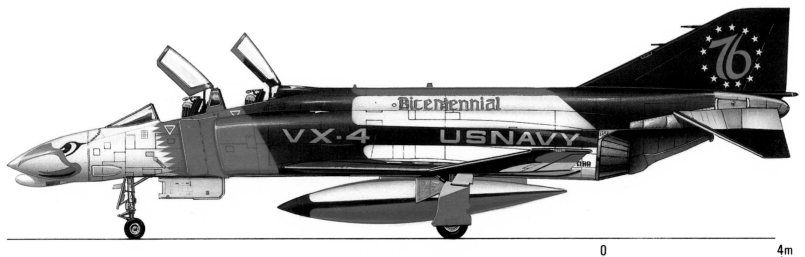

0   4m

McDonnell Douglas F-4 Phantom II

Spain's Ejército del Aire uses various Mirages and also the Phantom F-4C(S) to equip its NACOM (air combat command). This F-4C(S) bears the badge of Escuadrón 121 on its fin. Esc 121 and 122 both operate their Phantoms from Torrejón, near Madrid. They expect to re-equip with the F/A-18A in about 1987.

The RF-4B is a unique unarmed multisensor reconnaissance derivative of the F-4B used only by the US Marine Corps. It equips the Marine recon squadron VMFP-3, home base El Toro, California, and part of Marine Aircraft Group 11. The nose closely resembles that of the RF-4C as originally built (not as modified below).

The camera and sensor systems of many RF-4C reconnaissance aircraft have been modified as shown in this aircraft of the Alabama Air National Guard. There is a larger forward-looking radar and a large bulged underside to the main camera bay, to the rear of which is hung one of the ubiquitous ALQ-119 series of ECM pods. Electroluminescent formation lights adorn the forward and mid-fuselage, fin and wingtips. The badge is that of the 106th Tac Recon Sqn.

First developed at the US Naval Air Development Center, Warminster, Pennsylvania, the remotely piloted QF-4B is a versatile drone used chiefly by the Pacific Missile Test Center (previously Naval Missile Center, hence fin letters) at Point Mugu, California. Black walkways are used on the high-visibility colour scheme. QF-4Bs remain in production at NADC and the Rework Facility at Cherry Point, North Carolina.

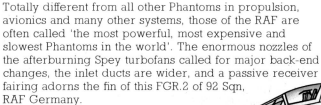

Totally different from all other Phantoms in propulsion, avionics and many other systems, those of the RAF are often called 'the most powerful, most expensive and slowest Phantoms in the world'. The enormous nozzles of the afterburning Spey turbofans called for major back-end changes, the inlet ducts are wider, and a passive receiver fairing adorns the fin of this FGR.2 of 92 Sqn, RAF Germany.

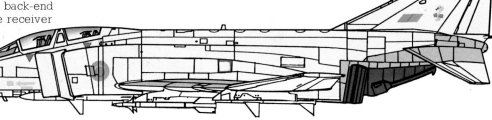

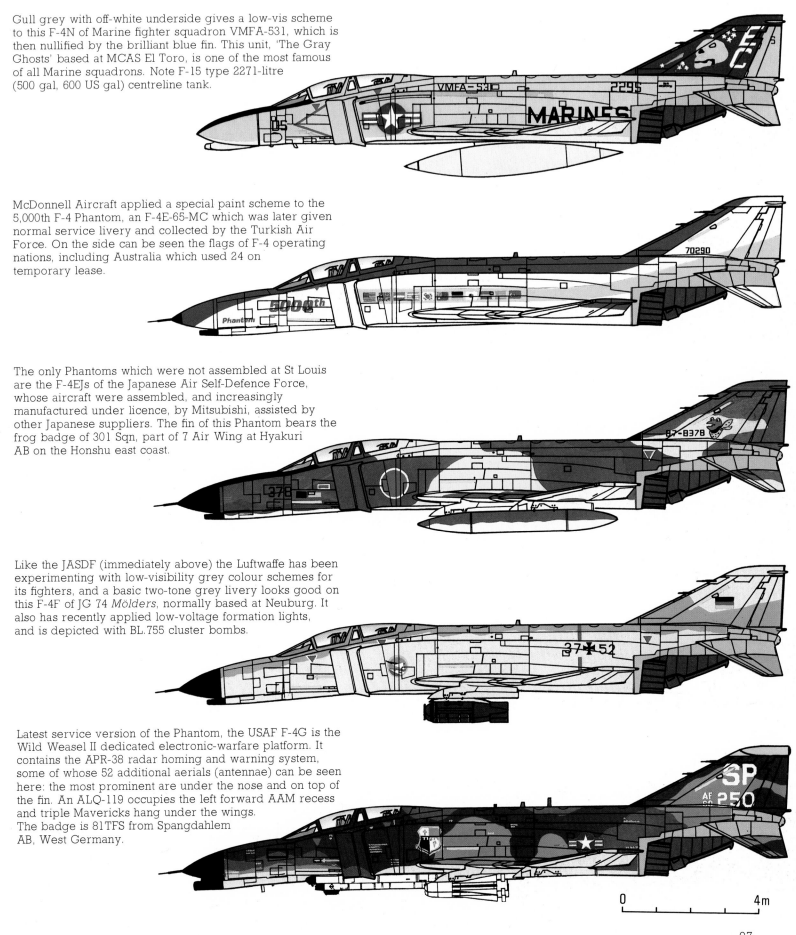

Gull grey with off-white underside gives a low-vis scheme to this F-4N of Marine fighter squadron VMFA-531, which is then nullified by the brilliant blue fin. This unit, 'The Gray Ghosts' based at MCAS El Toro, is one of the most famous of all Marine squadrons. Note F-15 type 2271-litre (500 gal, 600 US gal) centreline tank.

McDonnell Aircraft applied a special paint scheme to the 5,000th F-4 Phantom, an F-4E-65-MC which was later given normal service livery and collected by the Turkish Air Force. On the side can be seen the flags of F-4 operating nations, including Australia which used 24 on temporary lease.

The only Phantoms which were not assembled at St Louis are the F-4EJs of the Japanese Air Self-Defence Force, whose aircraft were assembled, and increasingly manufactured under licence, by Mitsubishi, assisted by other Japanese suppliers. The fin of this Phantom bears the frog badge of 301 Sqn, part of 7 Air Wing at Hyakuri AB on the Honshu east coast.

Like the JASDF (immediately above) the Luftwaffe has been experimenting with low-visibility grey colour schemes for its fighters, and a basic two-tone grey livery looks good on this F-4F of JG 74 *Mölders*, normally based at Neuburg. It also has recently applied low-voltage formation lights, and is depicted with BL.755 cluster bombs.

Latest service version of the Phantom, the USAF F-4G is the Wild Weasel II dedicated electronic-warfare platform. It contains the APR-38 radar homing and warning system, some of whose 52 additional aerials (antennae) can be seen here: the most prominent are under the nose and on top of the fin. An ALQ-119 occupies the left forward AAM recess and triple Mavericks hang under the wings. The badge is 81TFS from Spangdahlem AB, West Germany.

Despite its formidable cost the McDonnell Douglas F-15 was adopted by the Japanese Air Self-Defence Force as the successor to the F-4EJ. Like the latter, the bulk of the 100 aircraft is being made under licence, by a group led by Mitsubishi Heavy Industries. The first two F-15Js were delivered from St Louis and the next eight were assembled by Mitsubishi. The Japanese group is now engaged in producing the final 78 aircraft of the total of 88 of this single-seat version, and a batch of 12 two-seat F-15DJs is being supplied from MAC. It is expected that all the Js, and possibly the DJs, will be equipped to carry the conformal FAST (Fuel And Sensor, Tactical) fuel pallets shown on the starboard (right side) of the plan view on this page and in the side elevation below. FAST packs increase internal fuel capacity from 6103kg (13,455lb) to a remarkable 10,523kg (23,200lb).

This aircraft is the first Mitsubishi-assembled F-15J, 12-8803, delivered to the JASDF at Gifu in 1982. Colours are the standard two shades of grey. On the facing page it is shown with full air-defence armament of Sparrows and Sidewinders, plus a 2273-litre (500 gal, 600 US gal) external tank. In the side elevation below, the canopy and speed brake are open, the arrester hook deployed, and the pivoted engine inlets are depressed to the low-speed high-AOA (angle of attack) position.

12-8803

0   4m

McDonnell Douglas F-15J Eagle

12-8803

McDonnell Douglas F-15 Eagle

Standard colours for USAF F-15 Eagles are the two Compass Ghost grey shades, and this is shown here on an F-15A of the crack 32TFS in USAFE, based at Camp Amsterdam, Netherlands. It is usual not to suppress the yellow, red, white and blue in the insignia and other stencilling.

This F-15A serves with the first combat-ready operator of the type, the 49th TFW at Holloman AFB, New Mexico. It is shown with Sparrows, Sidewinders and centreline tank (which is also carried by the F-4G).

The only other USAF F-15 wings outside the United States (considering Alaska as being inside) are the 36TFW at Bitburg AB, West Germany, and the 18th at Kadena AB, Okinawa. This F-15A-15 serves with the German-based unit, whose badge appears in the preferred place on the side of the inlet.

The second two-seat F-15B, at the time designated TF-15A, was aircraft 71-291, which in 1976 appeared in this Bicentennial livery. It is a tribute to modern finishes that the aircraft looked immaculate after 1,000 hours of arduous display flying.

The Israelis are notoriously sensitive about identification of units, but it has been reported that the badge on the tail of Heyl Ha'Avir aircraft 669 is that of 133 Squadron. Like some USAF Eagles, this aircraft has a red outline to the cockpit.

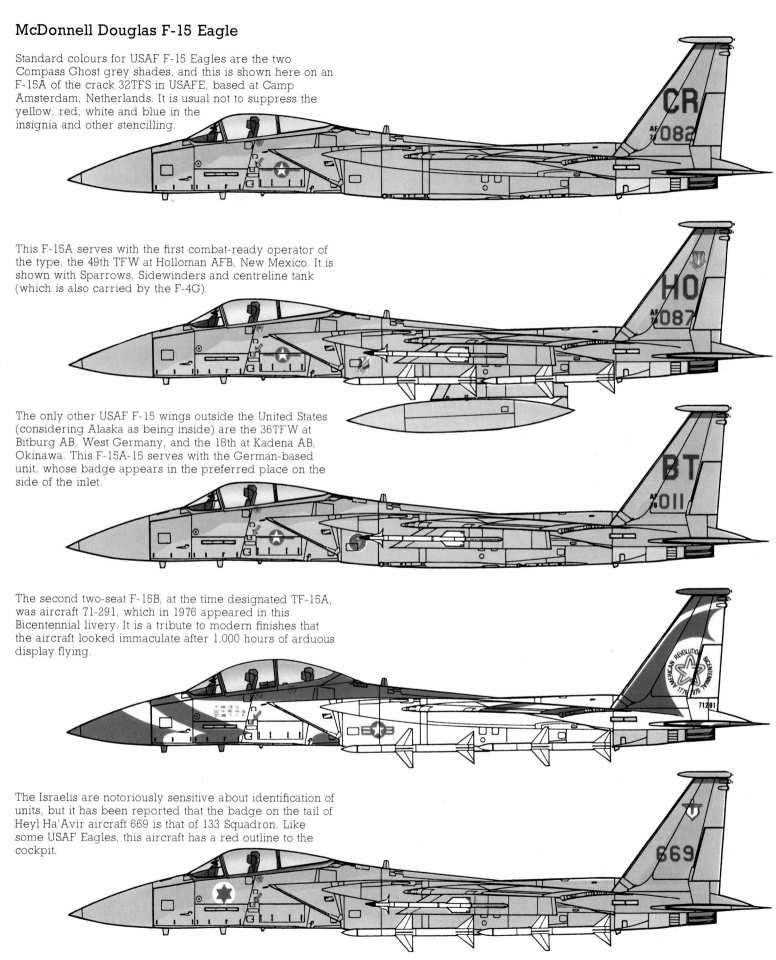

Delivery of an initial 62 Eagles to Saudi Arabia began in August 1981, representing a force more than double the original Israeli purchase. This is one of the two-seaters, which are approximately to F-15D standard. All should have been delivered in 1984, replacing Lightnings.

Fast packs adding 4422kg (9,770lb) of fuel without extra drag are seen on this F-15C, with programmable radar processor, serving with 18TFW (67TFS) at Kadena AB, Okinawa. The PacAf shield appears on the fin.

McDonnell Douglas has proposed this Wild Weasel version, which by 1984 is almost certain to be in production. Demonstration F-15D No 78-527 is shown with centreline tank, Sparrows, Sidewinders, and AGM-88 Harm and Snakeye bomb attack weapons.

The two-seater 71-291 has been transformed into the demonstrator for the proposed F-15E Strike Eagle, seen here in Charcoal Lizard colours and carrying Sidewinders, Fast packs, Pave Tack sensor pod and eight Mk 82 bombs. It is competing for selection against the F-16E (F-16XL).

0   4m

'Eagle Driver'
pilot's patch (USA)

49th Tactical
Fighter Wing (USA)

36th Tactical
Fighter Wing (USA)

USAF Tactical
Air Command

101

McDonnell Douglas F-15 Eagle

Generally considered the world's leading air-superiority fighter, the F-15 was planned as the FX in 1965 partly because of the obvious inability of the F-111 to perform in this role and partly because of the appearance of the Soviet MiG-25, which was able to fly much faster and higher than any US aircraft. By 1965 the USAF had no good air-combat fighter, though the gun and slatted wing of the F-4E had helped that aircraft to remain in the picture. What was urgently needed was an aircraft which at low levels had an engine thrust greater than the clean loaded weight, as well as a lower wing loading for exceptional power of manoeuvre. The FX contest was won by McDonnell Aircraft in December 1969, with the prospect of a 729-aircraft programme, one in seven being a two-seater.

The first of 20 development F-15 aircraft flew on 27 July 1972, and on 14 November 1974 the 21st aircraft, a two-seat F-15B, became the first to be delivered. Initially regarded as a relatively light aircraft, in comparison with the F-4 and F-111, it gradually became recognized as large and astronomically costly, although sheer power has kept it in the forefront of flight performance, and sustained high-rate production has fought inflation to keep the price well below that of smaller machines such as the F-18 and Mirage 2000. Increasing fuel costs spurred the search for a cheaper partner that was met by the F-16, and predictably the F-15 was later adapted as an outstandingly capable attack, reconnaissance and ECM aircraft.

The wing is enormous, but has a fixed cambered leading edge with 45° taper and plain flaps and outboard ailerons. It is set high on the broad fuselage with wide boxed engine ducts and a nose projecting ahead from the inlets; the latter have horizontal ramps and are pivoted across the bottom to incline forward and down for flight at high angles of attack. Unlike the F-14, the engines are close together, but there is room for some fuel between the inlet ducts. Left and right vertical and horizontal tails are carried on booms projecting aft of the engine nozzles. Despite the weight, there are only three landing wheels. There is no probe, but a flight-refuelling boom receptacle is incorporated into the top of a bulged fairing at the root of the left wing. The gun is in the corresponding fairing on the right (it had been planned to use a new 25mm gun firing caseless ammunition, but this was never fitted). A giant door-type airbrake hinges upwards above the fuselage.

As with the propulsion system of the earlier F-111, the engine gave Pratt & Whitney severe and prolonged problems in several regimes of flight, but it gradually matured to take its place as an outstanding powerplant subsequently adopted in almost identical form for the F-16. Much of the rear of the F-15 is titanium, and graphite and boron composites are used for numerous skin panels. The Hughes APG-63 radar gives all-aspect look-down, shoot-down capability, and the outstanding cockpit offers near-perfect visibility and 'Hotas' (hands on throttle and stick) control with virtually no need to move the hands.

By 1983 about 700 Eagles had been delivered to several TAC fighter wings, to the 36th TFW at Bitburg in Germany, the 32nd TFS at Camp Amsterdam (Netherlands) and the 48th Fighter Interceptor Sqn, which was the first US defence unit to re-equip from the old F-106. Other F-15s have been delivered to Israel, Japan and Saudi Arabia; 86 of the 100 for Japan are being assembled by Mitsubishi, like the F-4EJ.

From mid-1980 deliveries switched to the F-15C and two-seat F-15D with even more internal fuel, Fast packs (fuel and sensor, tactical) housing further fuel and optional sensors, and programmable radar signal processors giving better combat capability. In 1980 McDonnell rebuilt an F-15B as the Strike Eagle to demonstrate improved attack capability, and 400 F-15E attack aircraft are now to be bought for the USAF with advanced all-weather avionics which may include synthetic-aperture radar for sharp definition of surface targets. An RF-15 recon and Wild Weasel ECM model have yet to be ordered.

COUNTRY OF ORIGIN USA.

CREW Fighters: 1, trainers: 2.

TOTAL PRODUCED About 700 of planned 1,584-plus.

DIMENSIONS Wingspan 13·05m (42ft 9¾in); length, all versions: 19·44m (63ft 9½in); wing area 56·49m² (608ft²).

WEIGHTS Empty, **F-15A:** about 12247kg (27,000lb), **F-15B:** about 12610kg (27,800lb); maximum loaded, **A**, **B:** 25401kg (56,000lb), **C**, **D:** 30844kg (68,000lb).

ENGINES Two Pratt & Whitney F100-100 augmented turbofans each rated at 10810kg (23,830lb) with maximum afterburner.

MAXIMUM SPEED For brief periods cleared to 1506km/h (936mph, Mach 1·23) at sea level or 2655km/h (1,650mph, Mach 2·5) at high altitude, in each case in clean condition.

SERVICE CEILING 19·2km (63,000ft).

RANGE **F-15A:** 4631km (2,878 miles), **F-15C:** 5552km (3,450 miles).

MILITARY LOAD One 20mm M61A-1 gun with 940 rounds; four AIM-7E2 or AIM-7F Sparrow AAMs nestled along flanks of fuselage and two pairs of AIM-9L (or other) Sidewinder (Israel, Rafael Shafrir) AAM on side extensions of inboard wing pylons; five pylons for total external load of 7257kg (16,000lb); **F-15E:** provision for three external gun pods or total external load of 10886kg (24,000lb); **Wild Weasel:** HARM anti-radiation missiles and Snakeye bombs, plus usual complement of AAMs.

USERS Israel, Japan, Saudi Arabia, USA (AF).

McDonnell Douglas F/A-18 Hornet

Planned as a VFAX lightweight naval fighter, much cheaper than the costly F-14, the F-18 has matured as an excellent and versatile aircraft but costing even more than its larger partner. From 1979 to 1982 the programme was often close to termination, but it survived and, assisted by foreign sales, and great efforts at reducing costs, it is planned to continue and to replace the last F-4s in the carrier-based or Marine Corps fighter role and the A-4 and A-7 in the attack mission.

The gestation of the Hornet was unique. The USN intended to buy a new-design VFAX, but in August 1974 Congress instructed the Navy instead to purchase a carrier-based derivative of one of the rival lightweight fighters already on test. McDonnell Douglas, which had no design to offer, managed to conclude a remarkable deal in which it became prime contractor for a navalized version of the Northrop YF-17, Northrop becoming a mere associate responsible for the mid and rear fuselage and the twin vertical tails. This submission was ordered into full-scale development in January 1976. At that time it was planned to produce three basic versions: the F-18A Hornet fighter, the A-18A for attack missions and the TF-18A trainer with full combat capability but slightly less fuselage fuel. In the event the two single-seat models proved so similar that all have the same designation of F/A-18A.

Compared with the original Northrop fighter the F/A-18A has a larger wing (area increased from 32·5m²/350ft² to 37·16m²/400ft²) of greater span, a wider fuselage housing 2000kg (4,400lb) more fuel, a larger radar (Hughes APG-65 with doppler beam sharpening to give an even clearer picture) and structure strengthened for catapult launch and arrested landing. The twin engines were modified from bypass jets to turbofans; the seat was changed to the Martin-Baker US10S; quad digital fly-by-wire flight controls drive both tailplanes and ailerons for roll control (which was one of the major problems in development); the proportion of graphite epoxy composite structure was greatly in-creased; the large wing-root extensions were given axial slots to control airflow over the inner wing (flight at angles of attack as high as 60° is possible); and the cockpit was completely redesigned so that three electronic displays replaced almost all conventional instruments, and virtually every pilot input control for air/air or air/surface combat is mounted either on the throttles or on the stick.

The steerable twin-wheel nose gear retracts forwards and is stressed for nose-tow catapult launch, while the main legs fold to the rear with the single wheels turning 90° to lie under the engine air ducts. The speed brake is on the upper surface of the rear fuselage, while the full span of the wing is provided with powered leading-edge flaps and single-slotted flaps and 45° drooping ailerons. The wing folds at the inner ends of the ailerons. Very great effort has been applied to reducing the time and cost of maintenance and fault diagnosis and rectification, and although cost has soared alarmingly, the F/A-18A has won foreign orders.

The first of 11 YF-18s flew at St Louis on 18 November 1978. Despite serious difficulties, initial carrier trials were completed within a year, all 11 development Hornets had flown by March 1980, and in November 1980 VFA-125 had formed as the Hornet development squadron at NAS Lemoore, California. The first combat squadrons for both the Atlantic and Pacific fleets, and the first Marines unit, were all in being by early 1983, by which time about 100 Hornets had flown of a planned 1,377 for the Navy and Marines, including more than 150 TF/A-18A trainers. Between 1982 and '88 Canadian Armed Forces will receive 137 with designation CF-18, to replace the obsolescent CF-101 and CF-104. In 1984 deliveries are to begin of 75 Hornets for the Royal Australian Air Force, replacing the Mirage IIIO. These aircraft will have some Australian content, despite a further increase in price on this account, and will be assembled by GAF, Melbourne.

Northrop is trying to sell a land-based F-18L, somewhat lighter and simpler and with better performance.

COUNTRY OF ORIGIN USA.

CREW **F/A:** 1, **TF/A:** 2.

TOTAL PRODUCED By 1983 over 100 of at least 1,589 planned.

DIMENSIONS Wingspan, excluding AAMs: 11·43m (37ft 6in), including AAMs: 12·31m (40ft 4¾in); length 17·07m (56ft 0in); wing area 37·16m² (400ft²).

WEIGHTS Empty: not published but about 10000kg (22,050lb); loaded, fighter mission: 15234kg (33,585lb); loaded, attack mission: 21319kg (47,000lb).

ENGINES Two General Electric F404-400 augmented turbofans each with maximum afterburner rating 'in 16,000lb (7258kg) class'.

MAXIMUM SPEED Clean, high altitude: about 1912km/h (1,188mph, Mach 1·8).

SERVICE CEILING About 15·24km (50,000ft).

RANGE Combat radius, fighter mission: 740km (460 miles); ferry range: 3706km (2,303 miles).

MILITARY LOAD One 20mm M61A-1 gun in top of nose with 570 rounds; centreline station for tank or weapon(s), attachments on flanks of engine ducts for two Sparrow AAMs (or laser spot tracker and camera pods or forward-looking infra-red pods), inboard wing stations for tanks or air/ground weapons, outboard wing stations for various weapons, including Sparrow AAMs, and wingtip shoes for AIM-9L Sidewinder AAMs; maximum total load for unspecified high-g acceleration limit: 7711kg (17,000lb).

USERS Australia, Canada, USA (Marines, Navy).

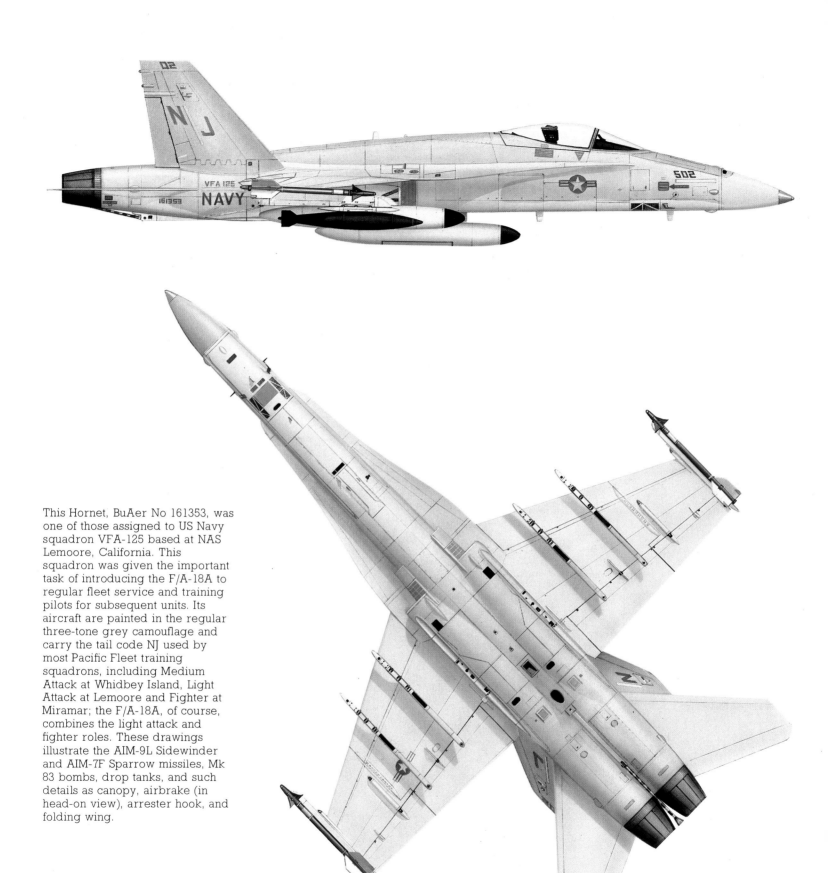

This Hornet, BuAer No 161353, was one of those assigned to US Navy squadron VFA-125 based at NAS Lemoore, California. This squadron was given the important task of introducing the F/A-18A to regular fleet service and training pilots for subsequent units. Its aircraft are painted in the regular three-tone grey camouflage and carry the tail code NJ used by most Pacific Fleet training squadrons, including Medium Attack at Whidbey Island, Light Attack at Lemoore and Fighter at Miramar; the F/A-18A, of course, combines the light attack and fighter roles. These drawings illustrate the AIM-9L Sidewinder and AIM-7F Sparrow missiles, Mk 83 bombs, drop tanks, and such details as canopy, airbrake (in head-on view), arrester hook, and folding wing.

McDonnell Douglas F/A-18A Hornet

0   4m

McDonnell Douglas F/A-18 Hornet

Superficially similar to the Hornet, the Northrop YF-17 prototypes were first flown on 9 June and 21 August 1974, and spent the first year in a fly-off against the two General Dynamics YF-16 prototypes. This is the No 1 aircraft. In recent years these company-operated machines have been used to support marketing of the proposed F-18L.

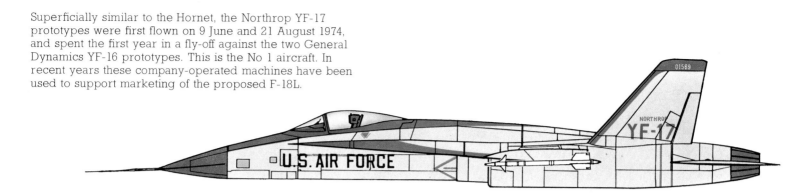

The first prototype Hornet Navy Air Combat Fighter, not at that time designated F/A-18A, flew at St Louis on 18 November 1978. With BuAer No 160775 it was painted in this attractive blue/white/yellow livery with hornet badge. Almost every part of the airframe differed from the YF-17.

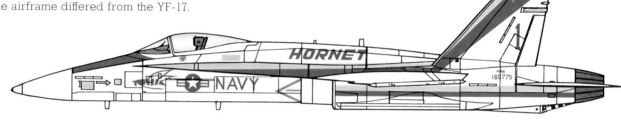

The fifth prototype, BuAer 160780, is shown as it was first flown in 1979 with designation F-18A and a wing with a large leading-edge dogtooth. Radar is fitted and weapons comprise two AIM-7 and two AIM-9 AAMs.

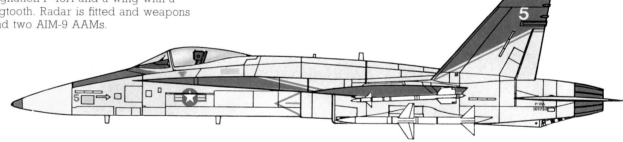

Two tandem dual-pilot trainers were included in the first 11 development Hornets and this version has formed a small proportion of every contract placed subsequently. Fully combat-capable, it differs mainly in its added rear cockpit, with new one-piece canopy (which like the windshield can be opened upwards) and reduced fuselage fuel. This TF/A-18A was assigned to VFA-125 at NAS Lemoore, California.

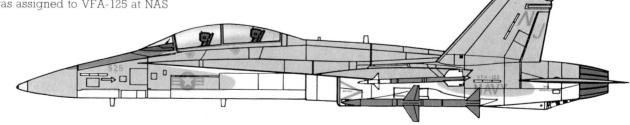

In the interdiction (long-range attack) role the F/A-18A can carry a wide range of weapons including the AGM-84A Harpoon cruise missiles shown on this aircraft of VX-5, the Navy Test & Evaluation Squadron. Also visible are a centreline tank and wingtip AIM-9L missiles, but a FLIR (forward-looking infra-red) and laser spot tracker are hidden by the Harpoons.

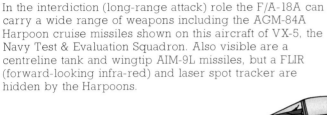
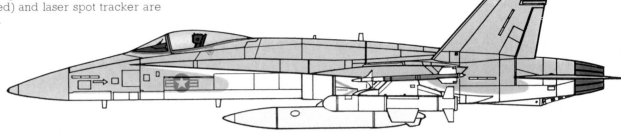

The first Canadian Armed Forces CF-18, a two-seater, flew in this low-visibility scheme on 29 July 1982, and since October 1982 two have been delivered each month. Note the spotlight on the left side for identifying other aircraft at night, and false canopy painted on the underside. CF-18s are replacing the CF-101; later they will replace the CF-104 and CF-5.

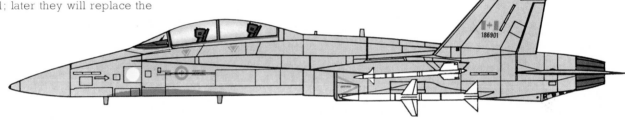

No F/A-18A had been built for the RAAF as this book went to press, and deliveries are not scheduled to begin until late 1984, with assembly of numbers 3 to 75 to be handled by Government Aircraft Factories in Melbourne. This aircraft is shown with GBU-15 stand-off attack missiles.

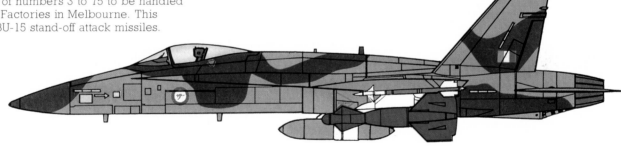

In Spain the F/A-18A Hornet will replace the Mirage III, just as it will in Australia. Again no details of the EdA (Spanish air force) Hornet are yet available, but 84 are to be delivered from 1986. The weapons shown include eight Mk 83 bombs.

0   4m

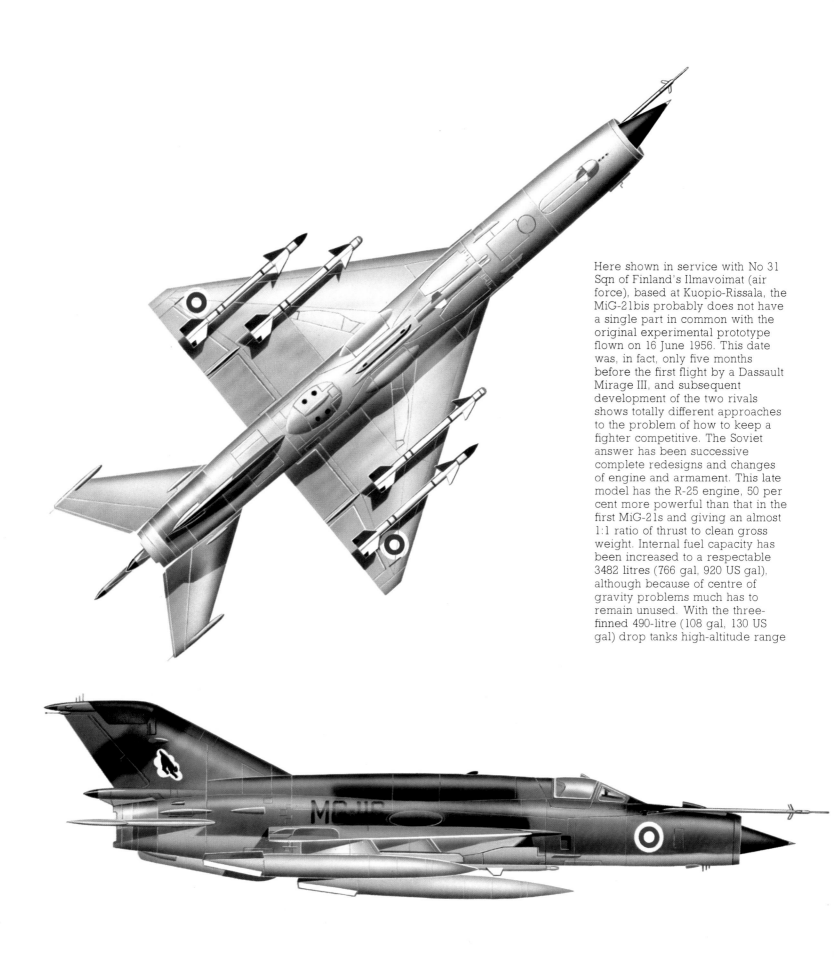

Here shown in service with No 31 Sqn of Finland's Ilmavoimat (air force), based at Kuopio-Rissala, the MiG-21bis probably does not have a single part in common with the original experimental prototype flown on 16 June 1956. This date was, in fact, only five months before the first flight by a Dassault Mirage III, and subsequent development of the two rivals shows totally different approaches to the problem of how to keep a fighter competitive. The Soviet answer has been successive complete redesigns and changes of engine and armament. This late model has the R-25 engine, 50 per cent more powerful than that in the first MiG-21s and giving an almost 1:1 ratio of thrust to clean gross weight. Internal fuel capacity has been increased to a respectable 3482 litres (766 gal, 920 US gal), although because of centre of gravity problems much has to remain unused. With the three-finned 490-litre (108 gal, 130 US gal) drop tanks high-altitude range

Mikoyan/Guryevich MiG-21bis

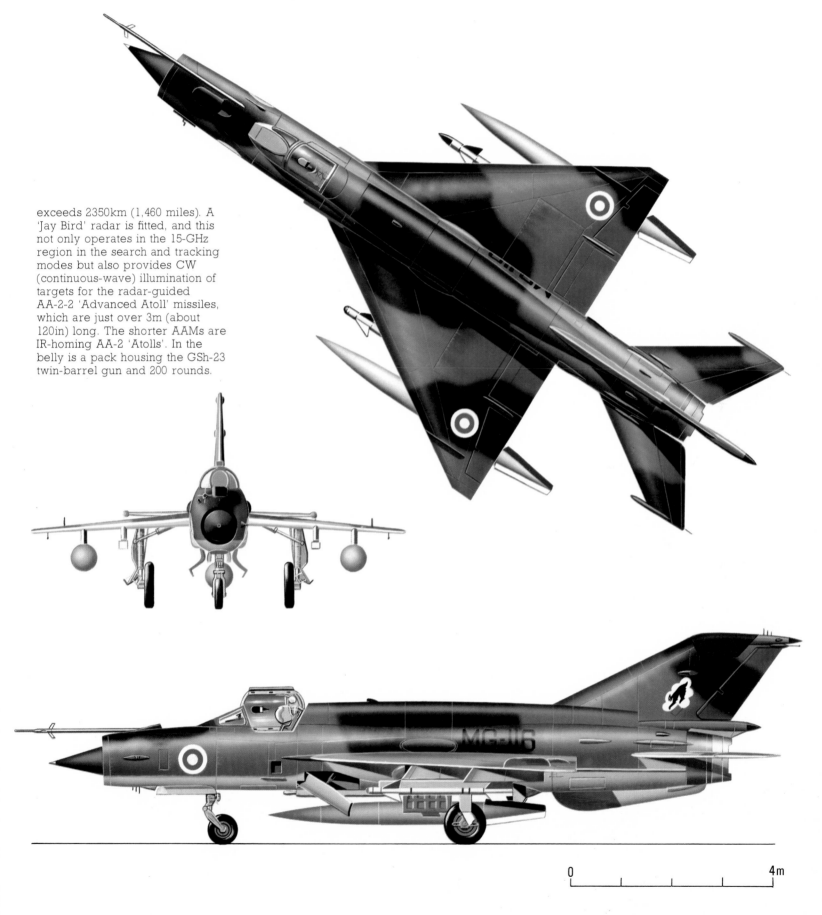

exceeds 2350km (1,460 miles). A 'Jay Bird' radar is fitted, and this not only operates in the 15-GHz region in the search and tracking modes but also provides CW (continuous-wave) illumination of targets for the radar-guided AA-2-2 'Advanced Atoll' missiles, which are just over 3m (about 120in) long. The shorter AAMs are IR-homing AA-2 'Atolls'. In the belly is a pack housing the GSh-23 twin-barrel gun and 200 rounds.

0   4m

Mikoyan/Guryevich MiG-21

There is little point in attempting to give precise Soviet designations even to the small selection of MiG-21s illustrated here. This example, one of the clandestine 'squadron' flown by the USAF, is a MiG-21F of about 1960 vintage. Czech-built F-models lacked the rear-view transparencies.

This Yugoslav aircraft typifies the first sub-types of MiG-21PF, or Fishbed-D, with an R1L ('Spin Scan-A') radar in an enlarged inlet. The engine was usually an R-11F. Note the broader vertical tail.

There have been dual-pilot trainer versions of every major series of MiG-21, all with the NATO name Mongol. This Czech example is one of the later versions, with R-11F or R-13 engine, R1L radar and a separate windscreen.

Like the trainer above, this MiG-21FL has a braking-parachute container beneath the rudder and the R-11-300 engine. This aircraft is one made under licence by HAL in India as a Type 77; it served with IAF No 8 Sqn.

This aircraft, probably a MiG-21M Fishbed-J, has the plain ejection seat and separate windscreen and side-hinged canopy used on all later versions. Some have a zero/zero seat, usable under all conditions. The operator is the Somali Aeronautical Corps, Hargeisa.

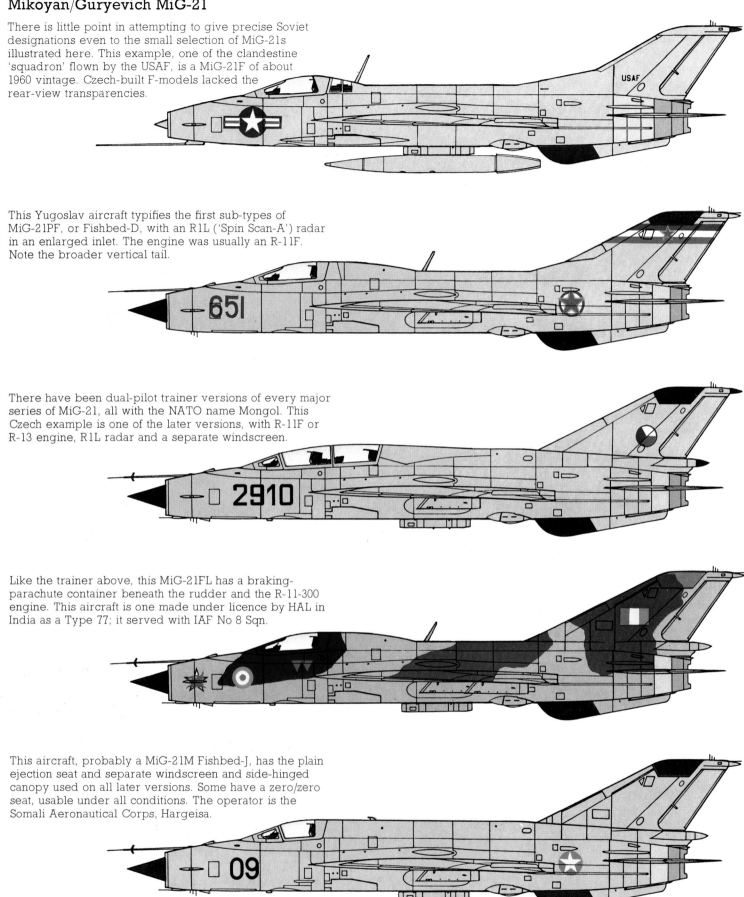

The Nigerian Air Force received at least 25 of the MiG-21MF type with the R-13-300 engine (with debris deflection strakes below the auxiliary inlet doors ahead of the wing root), GSh-23 twin-barrel gun and a much-needed rear-view mirror in the canopy. This example was seen at Kano.

Even before the start of the war with Iran, the Iraqi Air Force had put over 100 of these MiG-21PFM (Fishbed-F) fighters into service, and most have seen combat duty. The usual radar is the R2L ('Spin Scan-B') also fitted to the M and MF, and the GP-9 centreline gun pack is installed.

Among the nine variants of the MiG-21 supplied to Egypt, to a total of more than 400 aircraft, one of the less common is the MiG-21RF reconnaissance version, seen here with No 26 Sqn based at Inchas. Instead of the GSh-23 it has a three-camera pack under the cockpit, and centreline sensor pod, but this aircraft lacks the wingtip ECM pods sometimes carried.

Shown with two AA-2-2 'Advanced Atoll' and two AA-8 'Aphid' new-generation AAMs, this Soviet aircraft is of the third-generation MiG-21bis family with a very large dorsal fairing and the excellent R-25 engine. The nose badge is awarded to all FA regiments that reach a specified standard of proficiency and readiness.

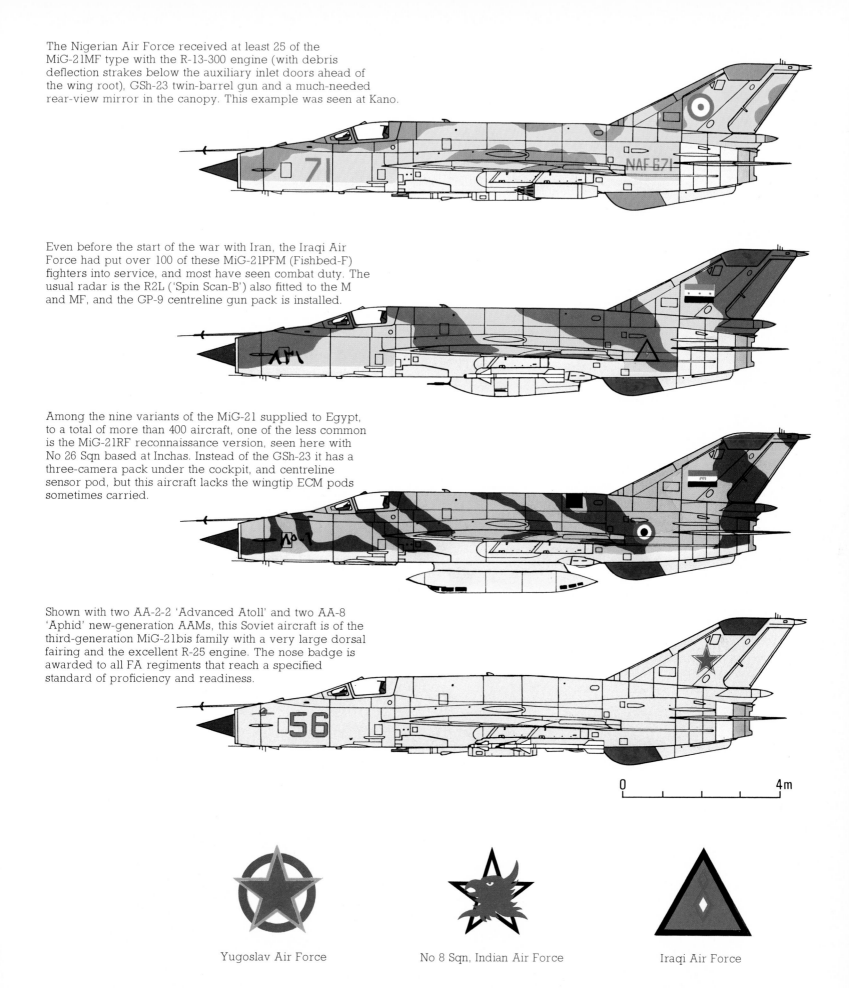

0   4m

Yugoslav Air Force   No 8 Sqn, Indian Air Force   Iraqi Air Force

111

Mikoyan/Guryevich MiG-21

The most numerous military aircraft of the past quarter-century, the MiG-21 has always been a warplane in the same class as the F-104 and Mirage, limited in sensors and weapons but quite pleasant to fly on a fine day and useful for a country trying to acquire numbers of Mach 2 aircraft at a modest price. But the prolonged development of the MiG-21 transformed it over the years into a modern aircraft far greater in capability than the early models. Whereas the latter were strictly based on Korean experience, today's MiG-21s are based on the technology of the 1970s.

After the Korean war, TsAGI, the Soviet central aero and hydrodynamic research agency, concluded that the best shape for air-combat aircraft was either a slender conventional wing swept at the acute angle of 57°–60° or a 50°–55° delta, in either case with a swept horizontal tail (unlike the Dassault formula). The newly formed Sukhoi OKB was assigned the task of creating large aircraft to both configurations, while the MiG (Mikoyan and Guryevich) OKB was given the vital job of building the next-generation air-combat fighter.

Some of the early MiG prototypes were closely related to the MiG-19, the Ye-50 of 1955 achieving the remarkable speed of 2460km/h (1,529mph) on an afterburning RD-9B turbojet and a rocket. The main series with essentially a new airframe began with the Ye-2A (swept wing) and Ye-5 (delta), both of which were displayed at the Aviation Day show in 1956. In the West it was a great surprise to discover years later that the production choice had been the delta. Via the Ye-6 with much less-prominent fences, and the new R-11 engine, was developed the Ye-66 which as well as being the first MiG-21 also set speed and height records.

Pre-production MiG-21 fighters reached VVS (air force) units in 1958. Extremely compact and neat, they were agile and popular, despite having hardly anything inside except 2340 litres (515 gal, 618 US gal) of fuel and two 30mm guns in the wing roots. The fully powered flight controls included slab tailplanes and area-increasing flaps,

and the canopy formed a single moulding complete with the windscreen and forming a windbreak to screen the pilot during ejection. By 1959 the Atoll AAM was carried on wing pylons, but despite the use of an uprated engine the left gun was usually removed to save weight. The MiG-21F also introduced a broader fin, and was made in Czechoslovakia, China and India.

Various further changes were combined in the PF in 1961, including the R-11F engine fed by an enlarged inlet with radar in the movable centrebody, another increase in fin chord, extra fuel, larger spine, larger main tyres (causing bulges for the retracted wheels above and below the wing), the drag chute relocated above the jetpipe and the pitot boom relocated above the nose. By 1963 the GP-9 gunpack was fitted, the PFS introduced blown flaps, the FL the R-11-300 engine and R2L improved radar, and the PFM a further increase in fin chord and a new sideways-hinged hood with separate windscreen. The PFMA had an extra pair of wing pylons and a larger spine containing additional fuel. Most batches also had an internal gunpack and zero/zero seat. Several recon versions are generally known as the MiG-21R, while all main variants had MiG-21U trainer versions.

By 1970 the -21M introduced the F2S-300 engine, but this was replaced in the MF by the R-13-300. The SMT further enlarged the dorsal spine and added optional wingtip ECM pods. Last of the main sub-families, the MiG-21bis brought in the R-25 engine and also features a revised airframe with a still larger dorsal fairing and improved equipment such as harpoon-like yaw vanes on the pitot boom. Called 'Fishbed-N' by NATO, the bis family includes interceptors with more powerful radar and various ECM and reconnaissance variants.

Altogether about 10,000 MiG-21s must have been built. Experimental versions include the Ye-166 record-breaker, a STOL conversion with lift jets in the fuselage, and the tailless MiG-21 Analog which tested a scaled-down wing for the Tu-144 SST.

COUNTRY OF ORIGIN Soviet Union.

CREW Fighters: 1, trainers: 2.

TOTAL PRODUCED At least 10,000 not including production in Czechoslovakia, India and China.

DIMENSIONS Wingspan 7·15m (23ft 5½in); length, typical of all models, including probe: 15·76m (51ft 8½in); wing area 23·0m² (248ft²).

WEIGHTS Empty, **21F:** about 5670kg (12,500lb), **21M:** 5950kg (13,117lb), **21bis:** about 6300kg (13,890lb); maximum loaded, **21F:** 7500kg (16,535lb), **21M:** 9400kg (20,725lb), **21bis:** about 9800kg (21,600lb).

ENGINE One Tumanskii augmented turbojet, **21:** 5100kg (11,240lb) R-11, **21F:** 5750kg (12,676lb) R-11F, **21FL:** 6200kg (13,668lb) R-11-300, **21MF:** 6600kg (14,550lb) R-13-300, **21bis:** 7500kg (16,535lb) R-25.

MAXIMUM SPEED Clean, high altitude, all models: about 2230km/h (1,385mph, Mach 2·1).

SERVICE CEILING 18km (59,055ft).

RANGE High-altitude maximum, with drop tank(s), **21F:** 885km (550 miles), **21M:** 1800km (1,118 miles).

MILITARY LOAD **21:** one or two 30mm NR-30 guns, two K-13A Atoll AAMs; **21M:** one GSh-23 twin-barrel 23mm gun, four Atoll or (radar guided) Advanced Atoll AAMs or various other loads such as four UV-16-57 rocket pods (16 57mm rockets) or two 500kg (1,102lb) and two 250kg (551lb) bombs; **21bis:** two AA-7 and two AA-8 AAMs.

USERS Afghanistan, Albania, Algeria, Angola, Bangladesh, Bulgaria, China, Cuba, Czechoslovakia, Germany (Democratic Republic), Egypt, Ethiopia, Finland, Hungary, India, Iraq, Jugoslavia, Laos, Mozambique, Nigeria, North Korea, Poland, Romania, Somalia, South Yemen, Soviet Union (FA, PVO, AV-MF), Sudan, Syria, Tanzania, Uganda, Vietnam, possibly Zambia. Evaluation examples with Israel and USAF.

Mikoyan/Guryevich MiG-23/-27

By the early 1960s the MiG OKB, by this time led only by Col.-Gen. Artem I. Mikoyan, was searching for a superior tactical aircraft to replace the MiG-21. The task was paralleled by Dassault, the main difference being that the MiG delta had a tail. Like the French company the Soviet team reached the conclusion that the future lay with the variable-geometry swing-wing configuration. The first simple and effective VG layout had been discovered in Britain, using widely spaced pivots on the ends of a triangular fixed portion of wing called a glove, and finally perfected by NASA in the USA. This formula was the basis for the F-111, and also for the Dassault and the Soviet aircraft.

In fact, two configurations were explored in the Soviet Union. One was a modification of existing swept-wing aircraft, and it was used by Sukhoi to improve the Su-7, by Tupolev to improve the Tu-22. The other was an uncompromised 'clean sheet of paper' design. Initially refined during model testing at TsAGI, the national aerodynamic centre, it was adopted by Sukhoi for the Su-24 and by Mikoyan for the family of warplanes described here. Like the smaller and simpler MiG-21, the replacement was planned both as an air-combat fighter with the PVO (air defence forces) and as a formidable attack aircraft for the FA (frontal aviation, or tactical air forces). But there was no risk of running into 'commonality' problems of the kind the F-111 encountered because all versions were to stem from the same basic aircraft.

The prototype in the OKB's Ye-23 family was the Ye-231, probably first flown in late 1966. It was powered by a large afterburning turbojet—almost certainly a Lyul'ka AL-21—and featured a high-mounted wing, large vertical tail plus a folding ventral fin, efficient variable inlets with Phantom-style splitter plates and ramps, large single mainwheels folding into the fuselage, and a single-seat cockpit with a canopy level with the top of the fuselage.

The prototype gave a smooth display at the last Aviation Day show, in July 1967, where it was dubbed Flogger by NATO. Early in production the aircraft was redesigned to take a much better engine, the R-27, as a result of which the rear fuselage was shortened and the wings moved forward some 60cm (24in). The outer wings were improved by adding extended leading edges (which at minimum sweep leave narrow slots between the dogtooth discontinuity at the inner end and the fixed glove) incorporating large leading-edge flaps, which are drooped in the low-speed regime with the central fin retracted. Once the definitive model was refined, in 1973, production was launched at a rate far greater than that of any Western aircraft, with some 300 delivered each year from 1975.

The basic air-combat model was the MiG-23MF, with a High Lark radar, gun and growing complement of AAMs. It can also carry air/surface weapons, and has an excellent array of sensors and ECM installations. Export models have generally had a smaller Jay Bird radar and lacked the doppler radar, laser ranger and ECM gear of the Soviet machines. The same smaller radar is usually fitted to MiG-23U trainer versions. Except for the latter, Soviet MiG-23s switched in 1977 to a more powerful engine, the R-29.

The similar R-29B engine was used from the start in the FA's attack version, the MiG-27; this has fixed inlets and a new front end (called 'ducknose' by its pilots) which gives a good forward view and contains all necessary attack sensors and weapon-delivery systems, but no radar. The MiG-27 has extra pylons under the rear fuselage, drop-tank pylons on the outer wings usable only at minimum sweep, extra cockpit armour, a multi-barrel gun and low-pressure tyres for use from rough airstrips.

Yet another sub-family, widely exported, is the MiG-23BN series. These aircraft have the attack nose of the -27 but the variable inlets and gun of the fighter. Since 1981 four new sub-types have been identified of this attack family alone. There is little doubt that new species of 'Flogger' will continue to appear in the future.

COUNTRY OF ORIGIN Soviet Union.

CREW Fighters: 1, trainers: 2.

TOTAL PRODUCED About 2,200 to date.

DIMENSIONS Wingspan, at 16° sweep: 14·25m (46ft 9in), at 72°: 8·17m (26ft 9½in); length, closely similar for all except early AL-21 version: 16·8m (55ft 1½in); wing area, 16°: 37·2m² (400ft²).

WEIGHTS (estimated) Empty, **23MF:** 11300kg (25,000lb), **27:** 10890kg (24,000lb); maximum loaded, **23MF:** 16000kg (35,275lb), **27:** 20500kg (45,195lb).

ENGINE Prototype and pre-production: one 11200kg (24,700lb) Lyul'ka AL-21F-3 augmented turbojet, **MiG-23MF (early), -23U** and export: one 10200kg (22,485lb) Tumanskii R-27 augmented turbofan, **MiG-23MF, BN** and **-27**: one 11500kg (25,350lb) Tumanskii R-29 augmented turbofan.

MAXIMUM SPEED High altitude, **23MF** with AAMs: 2447km/h (1,520mph, Mach 2·3), **27** (clean): 1700km/h (1,057mph, Mach 1·6).

SERVICE CEILING **MiG-23MF:** 18·6km (61,000ft), **27:** 15·5km (51,000ft).

RANGE Combat radius, **23MF** on high intercept mission: 1200km (745 miles), **27** on all-low bombing mission: 390km (240 miles).

MILITARY LOAD **MiG-23MF:** one 23mm GSh-23 gun, two AA-7 Apex AAMs on inlet-duct pylons, up to eight AA-8 Aphid close-range AAMs on glove pylons, other stores for attack mission; **MiG-27:** one six-barrel gun (unknown type), up to 4500kg (9,920lb) of weapons including AS-7 Kerry precision missile.

USERS Algeria, Bulgaria, Cuba, Czechoslovakia, Egypt, Ethiopia, Germany (Democratic Republic), Hungary, India, Iraq, Libya, Poland, Soviet Union, Syria and Vietnam.

The MiG-23 was the first application of the Soviet Union's standard shape for an optimized variable-geometry 'swing-wing' aircraft (as distinct from a modification of an existing design, such as the Su-7 or Tu-22). Such aerodynamic configurations are perfected at TsAGI, the national centre for such work, and used with minimal change by the OKBs which produce the actual designs for new aircraft. The MiG-23 is an almost ideal single-engined multi-role tactical aircraft (which has been complemented by the Sukhoi OKB's use of the same shape scaled up to use two similar engines). Within the family are dedicated ground-attack aircraft, some of which have simplified sea-level propulsion and are designated MiG-27, and air-combat interceptors such as the two PVO aircraft depicted here. Features of the MiG-23MF include a large pulse-doppler radar operating in the J-band of wavelengths, a cockpit canopy designed for minimum drag at the expense of poor all-round view, main landing gear reminiscent of the F-111 with legs almost horizontal, and a folding ventral fin to enhance yaw stability, especially with a full load of AAMs. The aircraft below is carrying two AA-7 'Apex' and two close-range AA-8 'Aphid' missiles.

Mikoyan/Guryevich MiG-23MF

In the view from above on this page the wings are shown at the maximum sweep angle of 72°, clearly revealing the enormous dogtooth discontinuities on the leading edges which in tight turns generate strong spiral vortices and keep the upper-surface flow attached. Unlike the American F-111 there is a large gap between the wings and horizontal tails at maximum sweep, and of course the US type is larger and much heavier. The MiG-23 is more a counterpart to the F-16, but using earlier technology and designed for stand-off interception and surface attack rather than dogfighting. It has long been supposed that a carrier-based version will shortly appear. Below, aircraft of Frontal Aviation with four AA-8s.

0   4m

Mikoyan/Guryevich MiG-23/-27

The original Ye-231 swing-wing prototype was displayed publicly in July 1967, and subsequently between 20 and 50 similar aircraft were produced as the MiG-23. Engine was the AL-21F. Basic problems including pitch instability demanded complete redesign.

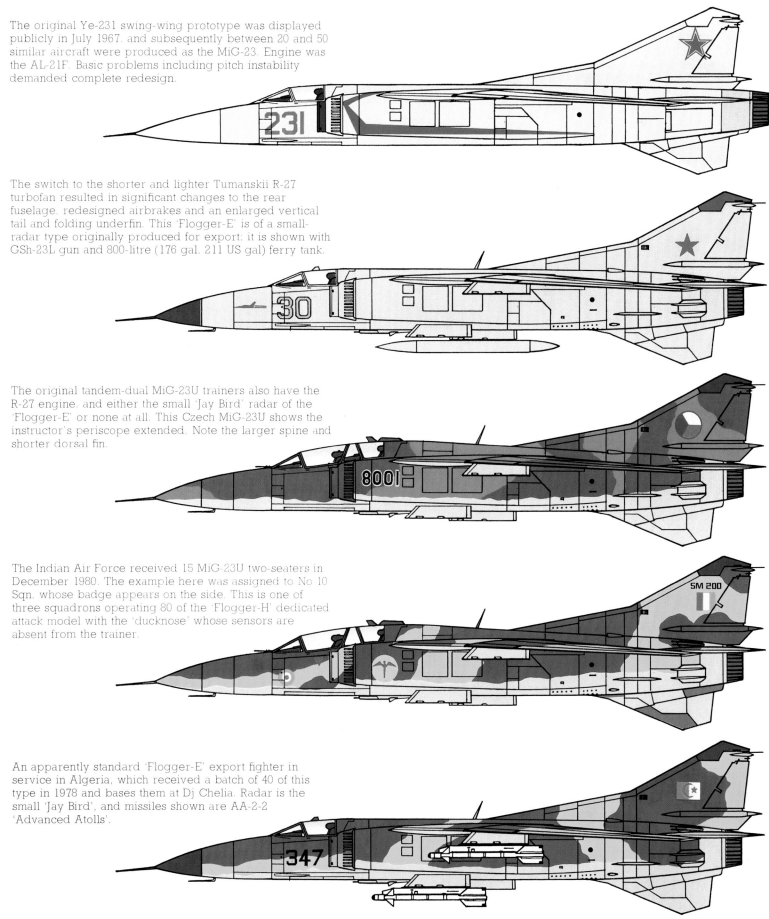

The switch to the shorter and lighter Tumanskii R-27 turbofan resulted in significant changes to the rear fuselage, redesigned airbrakes and an enlarged vertical tail and folding underfin. This 'Flogger-E' is of a small-radar type originally produced for export; it is shown with GSh-23L gun and 800-litre (176 gal, 211 US gal) ferry tank.

The original tandem-dual MiG-23U trainers also have the R-27 engine, and either the small 'Jay Bird' radar of the 'Flogger-E' or none at all. This Czech MiG-23U shows the instructor's periscope extended. Note the larger spine and shorter dorsal fin.

The Indian Air Force received 15 MiG-23U two-seaters in December 1980. The example here was assigned to No 10 Sqn, whose badge appears on the side. This is one of three squadrons operating 80 of the 'Flogger-H' dedicated attack model with the 'ducknose' whose sensors are absent from the trainer.

An apparently standard 'Flogger-E' export fighter in service in Algeria, which received a batch of 40 of this type in 1978 and bases them at Dj Chelia. Radar is the small 'Jay Bird', and missiles shown are AA-2-2 'Advanced Atolls'.

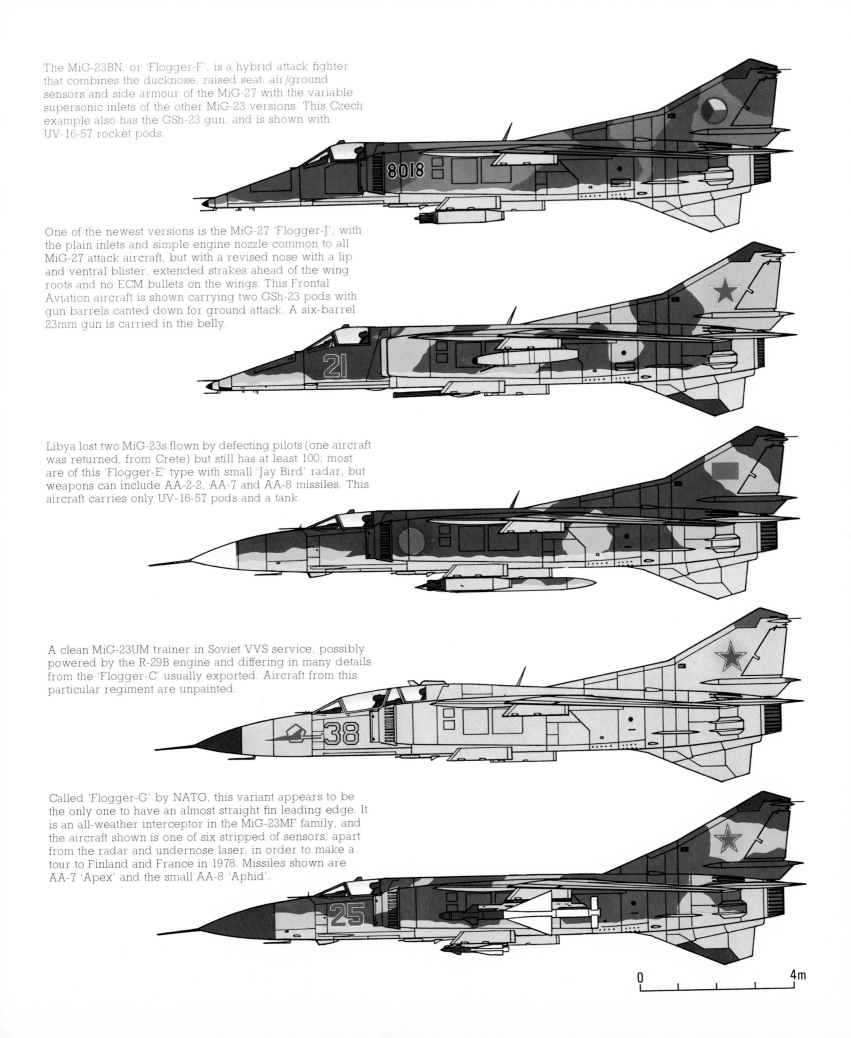

The MiG-23BN, or 'Flogger-F', is a hybrid attack fighter that combines the ducknose, raised seat, air/ground sensors and side armour of the MiG-27 with the variable supersonic inlets of the other MiG-23 versions. This Czech example also has the GSh-23 gun, and is shown with UV-16-57 rocket pods.

One of the newest versions is the MiG-27 'Flogger-J', with the plain inlets and simple engine nozzle common to all MiG-27 attack aircraft, but with a revised nose with a lip and ventral blister, extended strakes ahead of the wing roots and no ECM bullets on the wings. This Frontal Aviation aircraft is shown carrying two GSh-23 pods with gun barrels canted down for ground attack. A six-barrel 23mm gun is carried in the belly.

Libya lost two MiG-23s flown by defecting pilots (one aircraft was returned, from Crete) but still has at least 100; most are of this 'Flogger-E' type with small 'Jay Bird' radar, but weapons can include AA-2-2, AA-7 and AA-8 missiles. This aircraft carries only UV-16-57 pods and a tank.

A clean MiG-23UM trainer in Soviet VVS service, possibly powered by the R-29B engine and differing in many details from the 'Flogger-C' usually exported. Aircraft from this particular regiment are unpainted.

Called 'Flogger-G' by NATO, this variant appears to be the only one to have an almost straight fin leading edge. It is an all-weather interceptor in the MiG-23MF family, and the aircraft shown is one of six stripped of sensors, apart from the radar and undernose laser, in order to make a tour to Finland and France in 1978. Missiles shown are AA-7 'Apex' and the small AA-8 'Aphid'.

0   4m

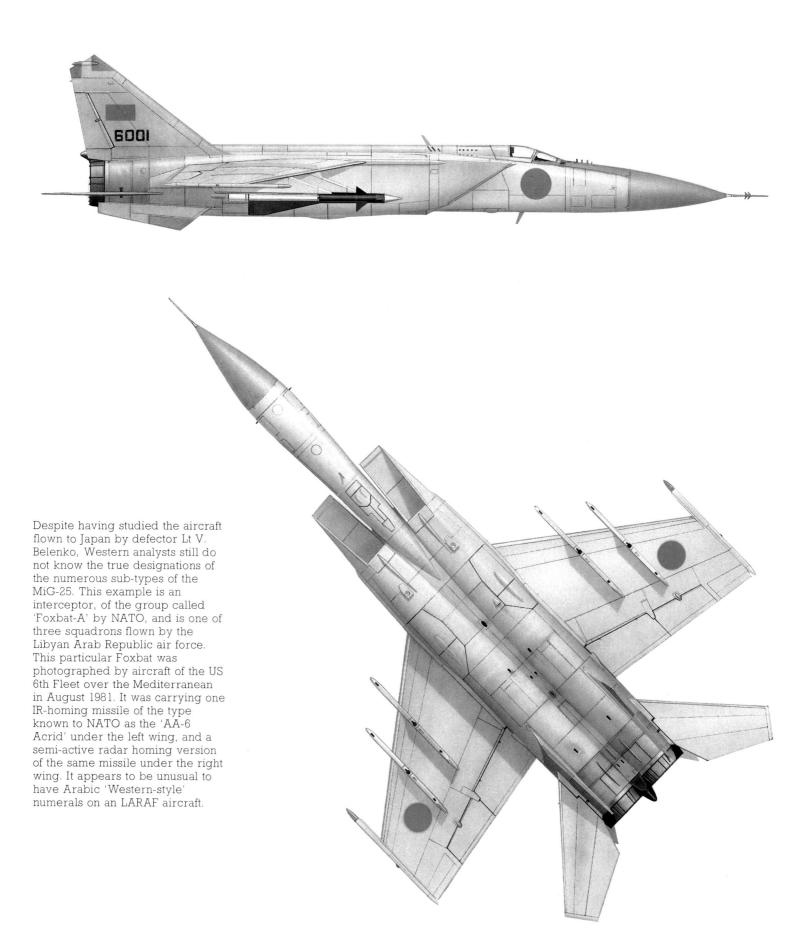

Despite having studied the aircraft flown to Japan by defector Lt V. Belenko, Western analysts still do not know the true designations of the numerous sub-types of the MiG-25. This example is an interceptor, of the group called 'Foxbat-A' by NATO, and is one of three squadrons flown by the Libyan Arab Republic air force. This particular Foxbat was photographed by aircraft of the US 6th Fleet over the Mediterranean in August 1981. It was carrying one IR-homing missile of the type known to NATO as the 'AA-6 Acrid' under the left wing, and a semi-active radar homing version of the same missile under the right wing. It appears to be unusual to have Arabic 'Western-style' numerals on an LARAF aircraft.

Mikoyan/Guryevich MiG-25 (Foxbat-A)

Mikoyan/Guryevich MiG-25

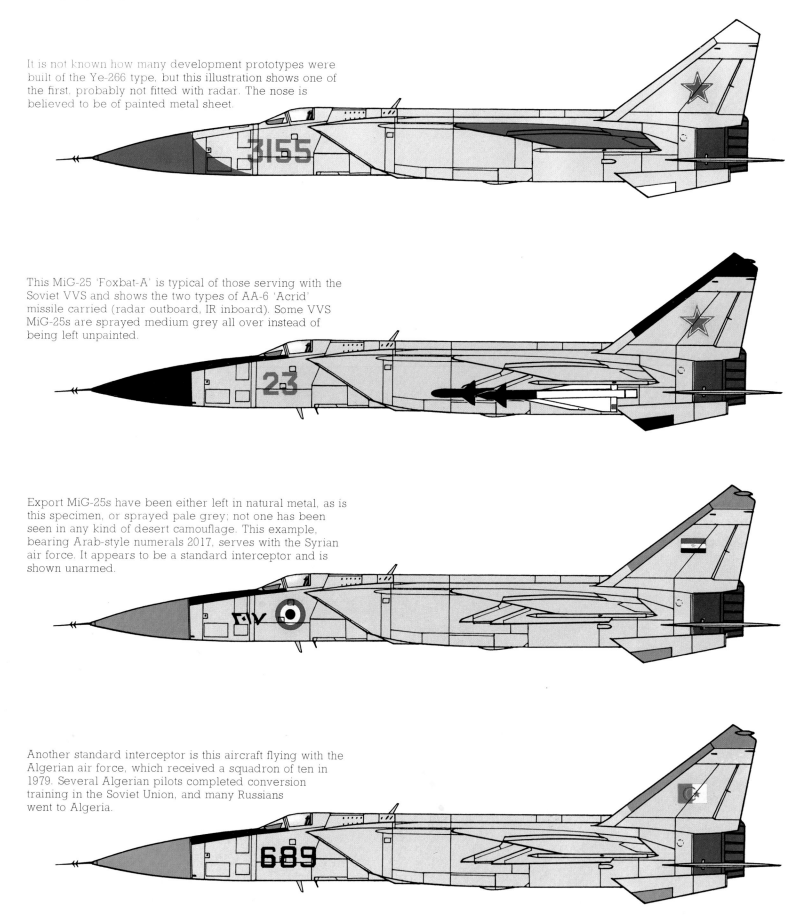

It is not known how many development prototypes were built of the Ye-266 type, but this illustration shows one of the first, probably not fitted with radar. The nose is believed to be of painted metal sheet.

This MiG-25 'Foxbat-A' is typical of those serving with the Soviet VVS and shows the two types of AA-6 'Acrid' missile carried (radar outboard, IR inboard). Some VVS MiG-25s are sprayed medium grey all over instead of being left unpainted.

Export MiG-25s have been either left in natural metal, as is this specimen, or sprayed pale grey; not one has been seen in any kind of desert camouflage. This example, bearing Arab-style numerals 2017, serves with the Syrian air force. It appears to be a standard interceptor and is shown unarmed.

Another standard interceptor is this aircraft flying with the Algerian air force, which received a squadron of ten in 1979. Several Algerian pilots completed conversion training in the Soviet Union, and many Russians went to Algeria.

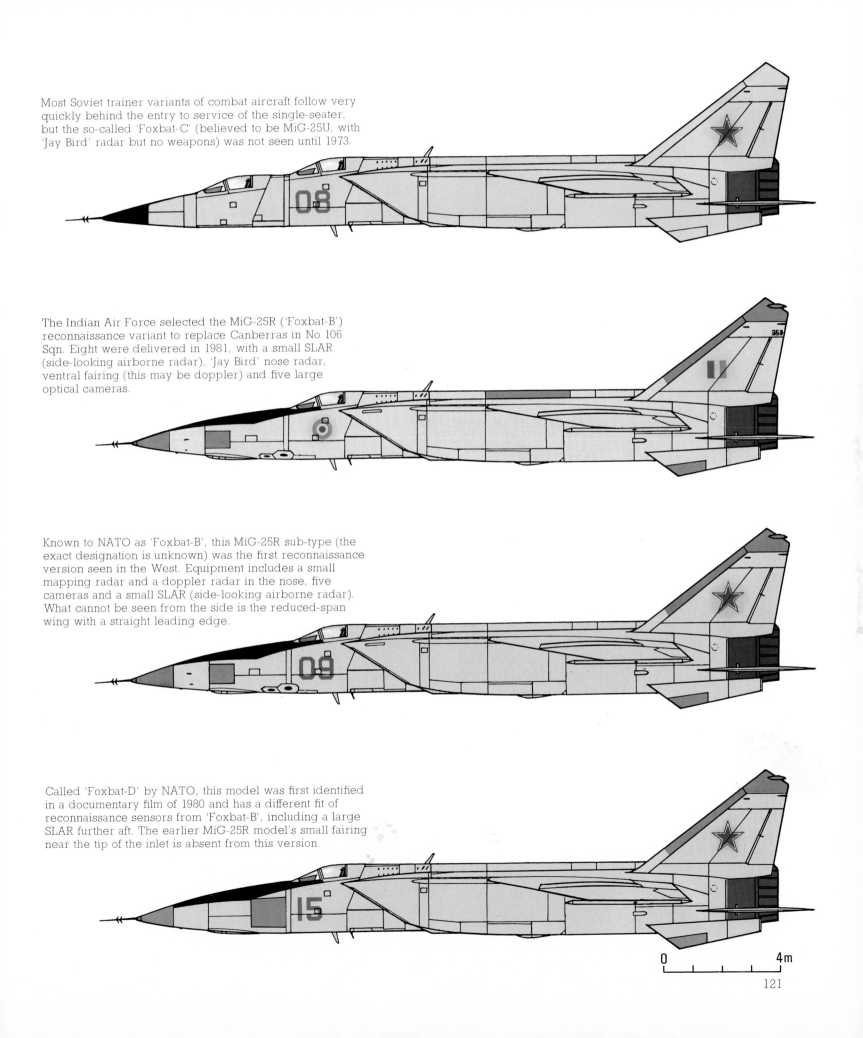

Most Soviet trainer variants of combat aircraft follow very quickly behind the entry to service of the single-seater, but the so-called 'Foxbat-C' (believed to be MiG-25U, with 'Jay Bird' radar but no weapons) was not seen until 1973.

The Indian Air Force selected the MiG-25R ('Foxbat-B') reconnaissance variant to replace Canberras in No 106 Sqn. Eight were delivered in 1981, with a small SLAR (side-looking airborne radar), 'Jay Bird' nose radar, ventral fairing (this may be doppler) and five large optical cameras.

Known to NATO as 'Foxbat-B', this MiG-25R sub-type (the exact designation is unknown) was the first reconnaissance version seen in the West. Equipment includes a small mapping radar and a doppler radar in the nose, five cameras and a small SLAR (side-looking airborne radar). What cannot be seen from the side is the reduced-span wing with a straight leading edge.

Called 'Foxbat-D' by NATO, this model was first identified in a documentary film of 1980 and has a different fit of reconnaissance sensors from 'Foxbat-B', including a large SLAR further aft. The earlier MiG-25R model's small fairing near the tip of the inlet is absent from this version.

0   4m

Mikoyan/Guryevich MiG-25

In the mid-1950s the USAF initiated the development of a next-generation strategic bomber, to cruise at Mach 3 or about 3200km/h (2,000mph). Although prototypes of the resulting B-70 (RS-70) were built and flown, the bomber was eventually cancelled. The chief result of the programme was the Soviet Union's MiG-25, the fastest combat aircraft ever put into service. Designed to intercept the B-70, it was not cancelled but continued both for long-range interception and as an advanced reconnaissance aircraft.

To intercept a Mach 3 bomber, a fighter needs a very high flight performance itself, as well as powerful radar and AAMs able to steer accurately towards a distant target at a much higher or lower level. Inevitably the resulting aircraft has to be optimized for high-speed flight, paying the penalty of extremely long take-off and landing, very high fuel consumption and, in particular, poor manoeuvrability and virtually no dogfight capability. At high supersonic speeds the MiG-25 flies essentially in a straight line, normally under precise ground control, until its radar locks on to its quarry. In the reconnaissance role it flies at extreme altitude at full throttle where it is vulnerable only to larger SAM defences. At low altitudes it is slower than modern attack aircraft, the limitation being its structural strength.

Initial development of the large engine was probably carried out with the single-engined Ye-166, which set speed and altitude records in 1961–2. The Ye-266, prototype of the interceptor, flew three years later, and from April 1965 set many records for speed, height and for rate of climb. Four flew past at the 1967 Aviation Day display. They caused a profound shock in Washington. Given the name Foxbat, they were at first thought to be MiG-23s; it took some years for the correct VVS designation to be identified in the West.

Utterly unlike previous Soviet aircraft, the MiG-25 has two very large propulsion systems with electronically controlled variable inlets; fuel in structural inner metal tanks between and above the inlet ducts and in integral tanks in the high-mounted wings; and a fuselage projecting ahead from between the inlets. The thin wings make no concessions to low-speed efficiency and have no movable surfaces other than plain flaps and inboard ailerons. For the first time, twin canted vertical tails were used on a modern fighter. Most structure was steel, leading edges being titanium, and to cool the inlet airflow at Mach 3 water/methanol was sprayed into each inlet duct via an external pipe ahead of the wing. The large high-pressure tyres of the main gear retract forwards to lie vertically outboard of the inlet ducts.

The original radar, called Fox Fire by NATO, is a large and primitive set using vacuum tubes, and relying on sheer power to burn through ECM and lock on to distant targets. No gun was fitted, reliance being placed on the largest long-range AAMs in the world carried on four underwing pylons. Continuous-wave target-illuminating radars look ahead from the wingtip anti-flutter bodies, which also house passive warning receivers and ECM.

The MiG-25U trainer has a second (pupil) cockpit lower and further forward, with a similar side-hinged canopy, and no sensors or AAMs. Instead of radar and AAMs, the various MiG-25R recon versions have a pointed nose with five cameras and various SLAR and infra-red installations, as well as more sophisticated internal navigation systems. Another sub-type has a very large SLAR on the right side. Oddly, these -25R models have a slightly different wing with reduced span and a straight (not kinked) leading edge.

In 1971 MiG-25Rs were detached to Egypt for overflights of Israel. By 1976 the VVS force was complete and exports began to Algeria, Libya and Syria. By this time production was switching to a developed (-25MF?) version with up-rated engines, a stronger structure for manoeuvres and low-level flight at full power, and new AAMs. This is a two-seater. In 1982 the US Defense Department allocated the name Foxhound to this aircraft.

COUNTRY OF ORIGIN Soviet Union.

CREW **25, 25R:** 1, **25U** and **Foxhound:** 2.

TOTAL PRODUCED About 550.

DIMENSIONS Wingspan, **25, 25U:** 13·95m (45ft 9in), **25R:** 13·4m (44ft 0in); length 23·82m (78ft 1¾in); wing area, **25, 25U:** 56·83m² (611·7ft²), **25R:** 55m² (592ft²).

WEIGHTS Empty, **25:** over 20000kg (44,090lb), **25R:** 19600kg (43,200lb); maximum loaded, **25:** 36200kg (79,800lb), **25R:** 33400kg (73,635lb).

ENGINES Two 11000kg (24,250lb) Tumanskii R-31 augmented turbojets; **Ye-266M, Foxhound:** two 14000kg (30,865lb) R-31F.

MAXIMUM SPEED Clean, 3400km/h (2,115mph, Mach 3·2); with AAMs: 3000km/h (1,864mph, Mach 2·8).

SERVICE CEILING **25:** 24·4km (80,000ft), **25R:** 27km (88,600ft).

RANGE Maximum combat radius, **25** or **25R:** 1300km (805 miles).

MILITARY LOAD **25:** four AAMs on underwing pylons, initially two IR and two radar Anab or Ash, from 1979 two IR and two radar Acrid, possibly with option of Apex as alternative. **Foxhound** rumoured to have a gun. **MiG-25U, 25R:** no weapons but 25R carries wide range of reconnaissance sensors including optical cameras, IR linescan, SLAR and Elint systems.

USERS Algeria, India, Libya, Soviet Union, Syria.

Northrop F-5

Always an attractive small fighter costing less to buy and operate than any Western competitor, the F-5 family will soon notch up its 3,000th sale. This is remarkable, in view of the fact that it was never bought by any of the US forces except in small evaluation batches or as a specialized mount to act the part of MiG-21s in training combat pilots.

The basic design had its origins in the N-102 Fang light interceptor designed on the basis of Korean experience in 1953. By several steps this led to the N-156F fighter and N-156T trainer of 1956. The trainer was built to the tune of 1,189 examples as the T-38 Talon—but nobody wanted the fighter, although the Department of Defense funded three prototypes, the first of which flew on 30 July 1959. But in May 1962 the design was chosen for supply to allies of the United States, and the first F-5A flew on 31 July 1963, a two-seat F-5B following on 24 February 1964.

Compared with the N-156F, the F-5 had more powerful engines, seven external pylons for a heavier weapon load and a landing gear with larger tyres on stronger legs for operations from rough airstrips. From 1964 Northrop delivered over 1,100 As and Bs, some having a camera-filled nose (retaining the guns) as the RF-5A, and numerous improvements were phased in, including anti-icing, a bird-proof windscreen, arrester hook, extending nose leg, flight-refuelling probe, more powerful J85 engines, take-off rockets, manoeuvre flaps under the wings, larger drop tanks, auxiliary engine inlets, doppler radar and improved weapon aiming.

On 28 March 1969 a two-seater with more powerful engines, the YF-5B-21, led to the F-5E Tiger II and F-5F two-seater, a second generation which won the Department of Defense contest to find a successor to the F-5A and B. Hard to tell at a distance from the earlier model, the Tiger II has a wider fuselage housing more fuel, improved inlets with wing LEXs (leading-edge extensions) alongside, and many other updates including an Emerson APQ-153 radar, as well as the improvements previously added to the A/B models. The Tiger II proved an enormous success, and since 1973 sales have exceeded 1,300.

Unlike the A/B models the E has been put to limited use by the US forces, in all cases simulating hostile fighters such as the MiG-21. Important units that fly it include the USAF 57th Tactical Training Wing at Nellis AFB (Air Force Base) near Las Vegas; the 527th squadron at RAF Alconbury, England, home of the famed Aggressors who serve as sparring partners for all the élite fighter units in NATO; the Navy Fighter Weapons School at NAS (Naval Air Station) Miramar, California; and squadron VF-43 at NAS Oceana, Virginia. Foreign users have introduced successive modifications: particularly well-equipped Tiger IIs are used by Saudi Arabia with inertial navigation, internal radar warning and chaff/flare dispensers, and Maverick precision-guided missiles.

In 1980 the Carter administration authorized a third generation, but this time Northrop had to find the money. In developing today's F-5G Tigershark the main change is a switch to the F404 engine, one of which provides 63 per cent more thrust than the two engines used previously. This has had a dramatic effect on performance, and to go with it Northrop revamped the airframe with a broad 'shark nose', bigger canopy, larger tailplanes, new-technology cockpit, improved flight controls, new weapon options and, in later Tigersharks, a General Electric G-200 pulse/doppler radar and HUD.

Northrop built a mock-up with the tail number 71983 to emphasize the promise of deliveries in July 1983. The F-5G is likely to sell extremely well, offering almost the combat capability of an F-16 for less cost, and with a price Northrop expects to be one-sixth that of a Mirage 2000. For the second half of the 1980s a new wing is being designed, of composite structure and much greater area and, for the first time in any F-5, containing fuel. From the start the F-5 family has sold because air forces all over the world knew they could handle it. Now the F-5G is interesting even major powers.

COUNTRY OF ORIGIN USA; licence-built in Canada, Netherlands, Spain, Taiwan.

CREW Fighters: 1, trainers: 2.

TOTAL PRODUCED About 2,500 to date.

DIMENSIONS Wingspan, excluding missiles, **5A/B:** 7·7m (25ft 3in), **E/F/G:** 8·13m (26ft 8in); length, including probe on A/B/E/F, **A:** 14·38m (47ft 2in), **B:** 14·12m (46ft 4in), **E:** 14·68m (48ft 2in), **F:** 15·72m (51ft 7in), **G:** 14·19m (46ft 6⅔in); wing area, **A/B:** 15·79m² (170ft²), **E/F/G:** 17·3m² (186ft²).

WEIGHTS Empty, **A:** 3667kg (8,085lb), **B:** 3792kg (8,361lb), **E:** 4392kg (9,683lb), **F:** 4793kg (10,567lb), **G:** 5089kg (11,220lb); maximum loaded, **A:** 9379kg (20,677lb), **B:** 9299kg (20,500lb), **E:** 11193kg (24,676lb) **F:** 11442kg (25,225lb), **G:** 11857kg (26,140lb).

ENGINES **A/B:** two 1850kg (4,080lb) General Electric J85-GE-13 augmented turbojets; **E/F:** two 2268kg (5,000lb) J85-GE-21A; **G:** one 7434kg (16,390lb) F404-GE-400 augmented turbofan.

MAXIMUM SPEED Clean, 10·67km (35,000ft), **F-5A:** 1487km/h (924mph, Mach 1·4), **B:** 1423km/h (884mph, Mach 1·34), **E:** 1734km/h (1,077mph), Mach 1·63), **F:** 1646km/h (1,024mph, Mach 1·55); **G:** 2234km/h (1,388mph, Mach 2·1).

SERVICE CEILING **A/B:** 15·5km (50,900ft), **E:** 15·79km (51,800ft), **F:** 15·48km (50,800ft), **G:** 16·76km (55,000ft).

RANGE Combat radius, max payload, **A:** 346km (215 miles), **B:** 362km (225 miles), **E:** lo-lo-lo mission, 222km (138 miles), **E**, max fuel, two Sidewinders: 1056km (656 miles), **G**, full weapon load: 667km (415 miles).

MILITARY LOAD Two Pontiac M-39A2 20mm cannon. **A/B:** five pylons for 2812kg (6,200lb) including Sidewinder AAMs on wingtips, **E/F:** total raised to 3175kg (7,000lb); **G:** three GPU-5/A Gepod 30mm gun pods, four Sparrows or Amraams, six AIM-9L Sidewiders or four Mavericks.

USERS See pages 124/125.

Northrop F-5 (continued from page 123)
USERS Brazil, Canada, Chile, Egypt,
Ethiopia, Greece, Indonesia, Iran,
Jordan, Kenya, Libya, Malaysia,
Mexico, Morocco, Netherlands,
Norway, Pakistan, Peru, Philippines,
Saudi Arabia, South Korea, Singapore,
Spain, Sudan, Switzerland, Taiwan,
Thailand, Tunisia, Turkey, USA (AF,
Navy), Vietnam, Yemen Arab
Republic.

USAF
01530

U.S. AIR FORCE

30

Northrop F-5E Tiger II

The subject of these illustrations is the F-5E Tiger II with US Air Force number 70-1530, serving in the 'Aggressor' role with the 64th FITS (Fighter Interceptor Training Squadron) of the famed 57th FWW (Fighter Weapons Wing) at Nellis, AFB, outside Las Vegas, Nevada. Aircraft flying in the 'Aggressor' role, like the corresponding Navy 'Top Gun' fighters, are usually painted in colour schemes loosely resembling Warsaw Pact aircraft, with prominent numbers on the nose. This F-5E is in a 'Lizard' light tan and dark tan scheme, with the unit badge on the side of the inlet duct and the TAC badge on the fin. Most aircraft of the 64th have the unit's black-and-yellow checker stripe across the top of the fin, except for those in Heatley/Ferris and similar low-visibility schemes, when the national insignia is also painted in non-contrasting shades of grey. The only weapon carried here is a wingtip AIM-9L Sidewinder, and an instrumentation data-link pod.

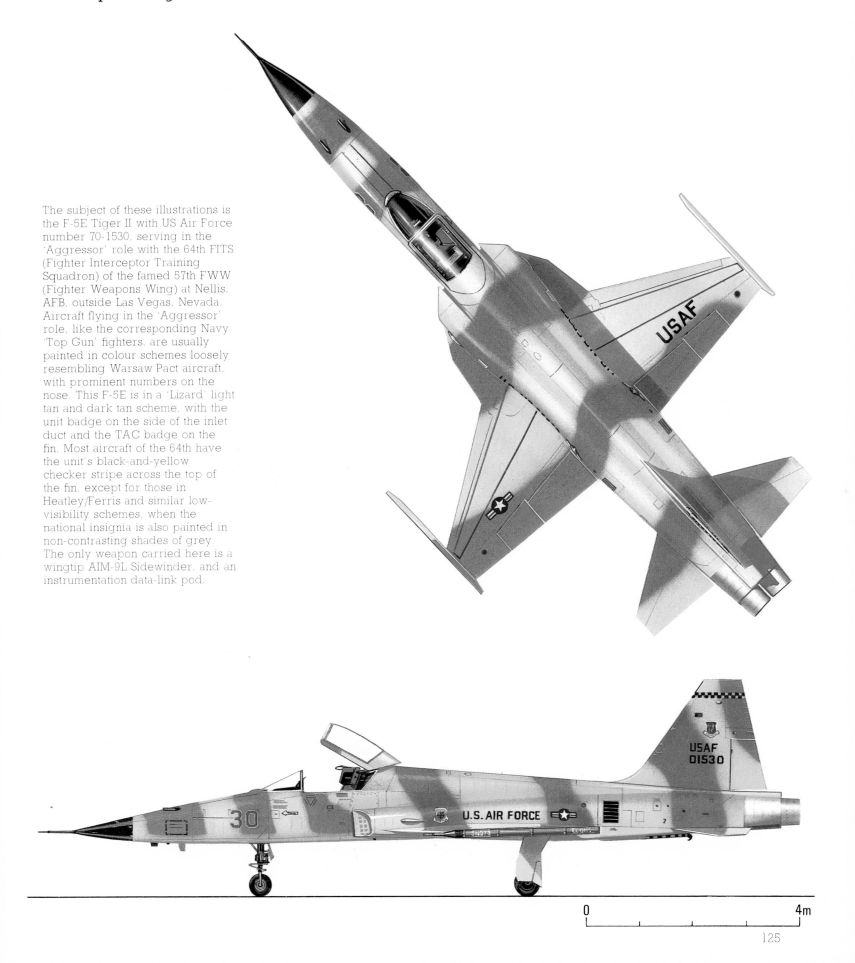

Northrop F-5

The Força Aérea Portuguesa does most of its advanced
pilot training on T-37s and venerable T-33As, but at Monte
Real it also has six ex-USAF T-38A Talons. These
supersonic tandem-seaters may be followed by a
purchase of F-5 fighters.

The only example of the first-generation F-5A (Freedom
Fighter) family illustrated here is this CR-9 (Spanish
designation) serving with the Ejército del Aire's Escuadrón
211, based at Morón. The CR-9 is better known as the
SRF-5A, Spanish photo-recon version of the F-5A.

Brazil, the world's fifth-largest country, has made giant
strides towards self-sufficiency in military aircraft, but has
to import supersonic fighters: the newest are 42 F-5E Tiger
IIs bought in 1974. No 4820 is assigned to 1° Esquadrão of
the I Grupo de Aviação de Caça, based at Santa Cruz (Rio).

Among the best-known fighters in the world are the
various 'Aggressor' units whose role is to test and
improve the air-combat capability of US and allied pilots.
This F-5E was seen in a typical non-standard colour
scheme at the 57th Fighter Weapons Wing, USAF,
at Nellis AFB, near Las Vegas.

The US Navy's counterpart is the 'Top Gun' school at the
Fighter Weapons School at NAS (Naval Air Station)
Miramar, California. As in the USAF, some Navy F-5s have
been flown in the jagged camouflage planned according to
the Heatley/Ferris schemes, but this example has
rounded outlines.

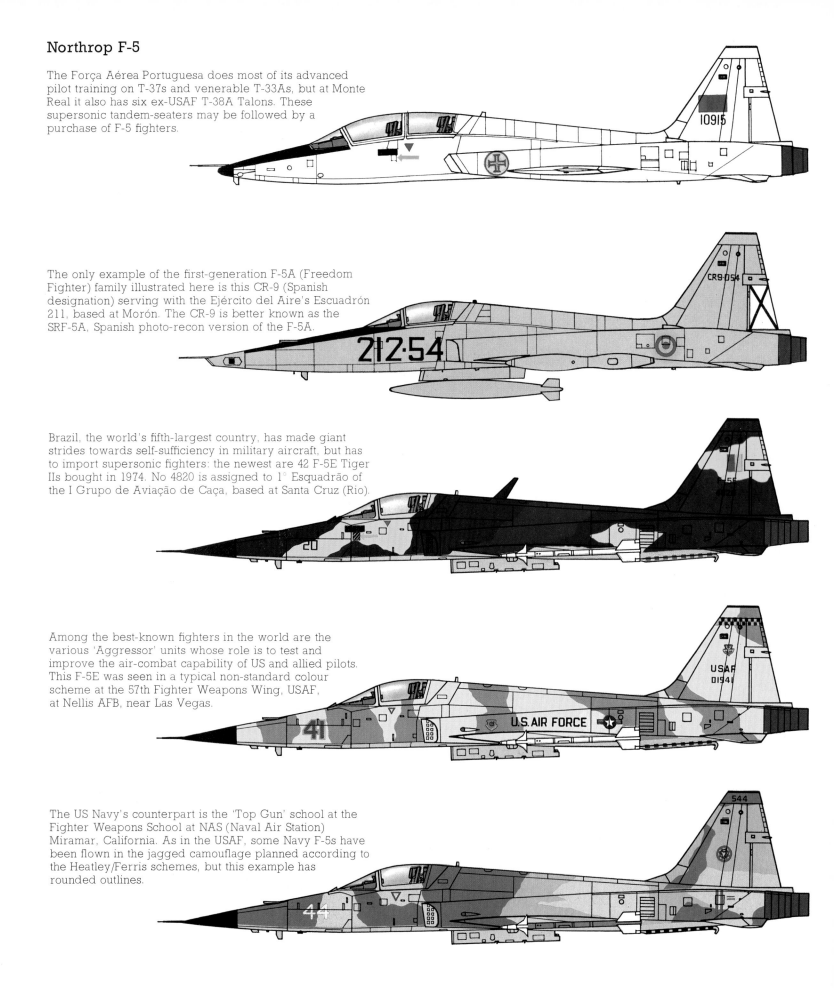

Few fighters are in such a politically sensitive position as the F-5E Tiger IIs of the Royal Saudi Air Force, whose borders are ringed by conflicts. The F-5s operate mainly in the surface-attack role; this example was assigned to 10 Sqn at Khamis Mushayt. They are the best-equipped F-5Es in the world.

Another Middle East F-5 operator is Jordan, whose AQAA (Arabic initials for Royal Jordanian Air Force) has used both the F-5A and the more modern F-5E shown here. The F-5Es have extremely small roundels, less than half the normal diameter.

Since 1979 a total of 66 F-5E Tiger IIs and six two-seat F-5Fs have replaced some Hunters in the Swiss air force, for both interception (as here, with 20mm guns and Sidewinders) and ground-attack missions. The Federal Aircraft factory at Emmen completed their assembly in 1981 and is now working on a second batch of 32 Es and six Fs.

Longest of all the Northrop T-38/F-5 family, the F-5F is the tandem dual version of the Tiger II, with unchanged fuel capacity but only one gun. The USAF uses 118 of these cost-effective combat-capable trainers, first delivered in summer 1976.

One of the most effective of all re-engining programmes led to the F-20A Tigershark, whose F404 augmented turbofan generates almost double the thrust of the combined pair of J85-21s in the Tiger II. Much of the airframe is also new; examples are the flattened 'shark' nose, larger canopy and important wing-root strakes alongside the extended inlet ducts.

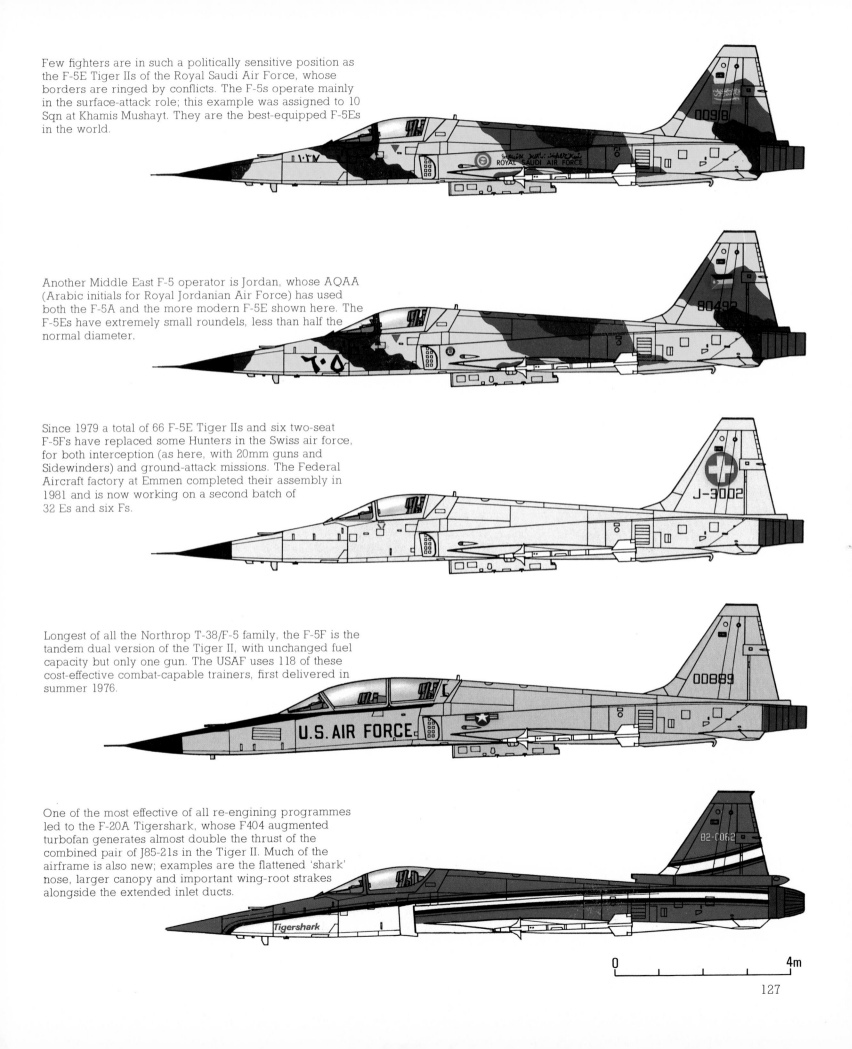

ZA327

ZA327

B-51

Panavia Tornado GR.1

After five years of test-flying with the nine prototypes and six pre-series aircraft, production IDS Tornados followed in the second half of 1979. By April 1981 the first batch of 40 had been completed, the number rising to 100 in April 1982 and 170 in April 1983. This example is a Tornado IDS of the RAF, with British designation Tornado GR.1 (GR from Ground attack and Reconnaissance), with serial number ZA327. It serves at the TTTE (Tornado Trinational Training Establishment) at RAF Cottesmore, where 50 handle type conversion of crews from all three customer countries. The fin code B-51 means that this Tornado is the 51st British aircraft. In the left-side elevation (below) it is seen with gear down, wings forward, canopy open, flaps down and reversers deployed. The underside view opposite shows the wings at minimum sweep (the pylons swivel to remain fore/aft) and the flight refuelling probe extended. In the front, top and right-side views the wings are fully swept. The external load shown comprises eight BL.755 cluster dispensers, two 1500-litre (330 gal, 396 US gal) tanks and two ARI.23246/1 ECM pods (also known as Ajax and Sky Shadow). Note the laser under the nose in the right-side view.

0   4m

129

Panavia Tornado

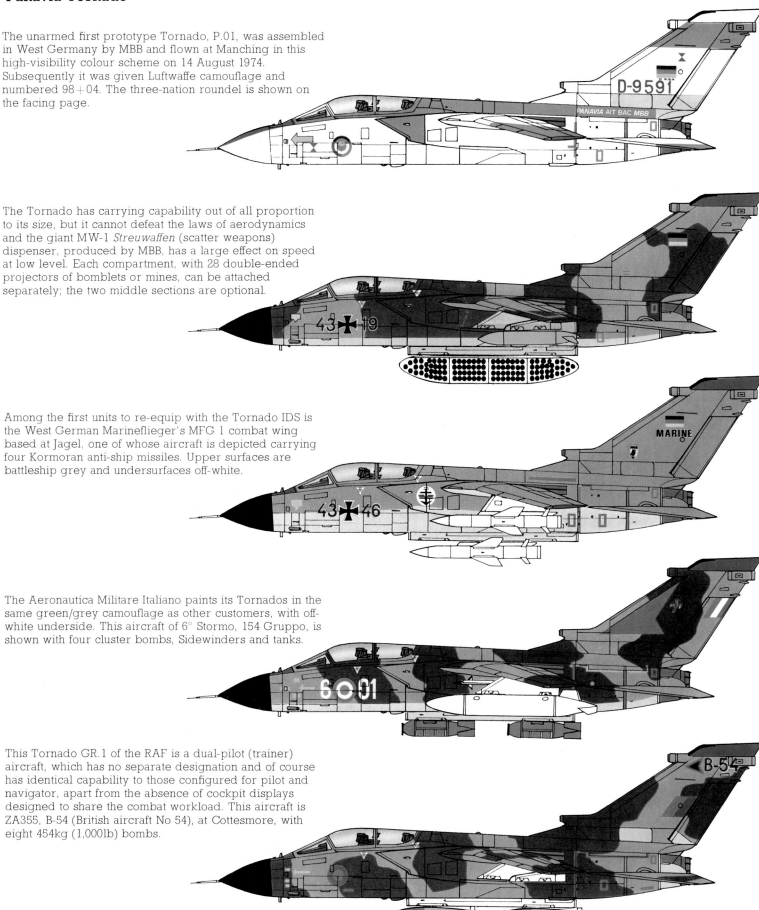

The unarmed first prototype Tornado, P.01, was assembled in West Germany by MBB and flown at Manching in this high-visibility colour scheme on 14 August 1974. Subsequently it was given Luftwaffe camouflage and numbered 98+04. The three-nation roundel is shown on the facing page.

The Tornado has carrying capability out of all proportion to its size, but it cannot defeat the laws of aerodynamics and the giant MW-1 *Streuwaffen* (scatter weapons) dispenser, produced by MBB, has a large effect on speed at low level. Each compartment, with 28 double-ended projectors of bomblets or mines, can be attached separately; the two middle sections are optional.

Among the first units to re-equip with the Tornado IDS is the West German Marineflieger's MFG 1 combat wing based at Jagel, one of whose aircraft is depicted carrying four Kormoran anti-ship missiles. Upper surfaces are battleship grey and undersurfaces off-white.

The Aeronautica Militare Italiano paints its Tornados in the same green/grey camouflage as other customers, with off-white underside. This aircraft of 6° Stormo, 154 Gruppo, is shown with four cluster bombs, Sidewinders and tanks.

This Tornado GR.1 of the RAF is a dual-pilot (trainer) aircraft, which has no separate designation and of course has identical capability to those configured for pilot and navigator, apart from the absence of cockpit displays designed to share the combat workload. This aircraft is ZA355, B-54 (British aircraft No 54), at Cottesmore, with eight 454kg (1,000lb) bombs.

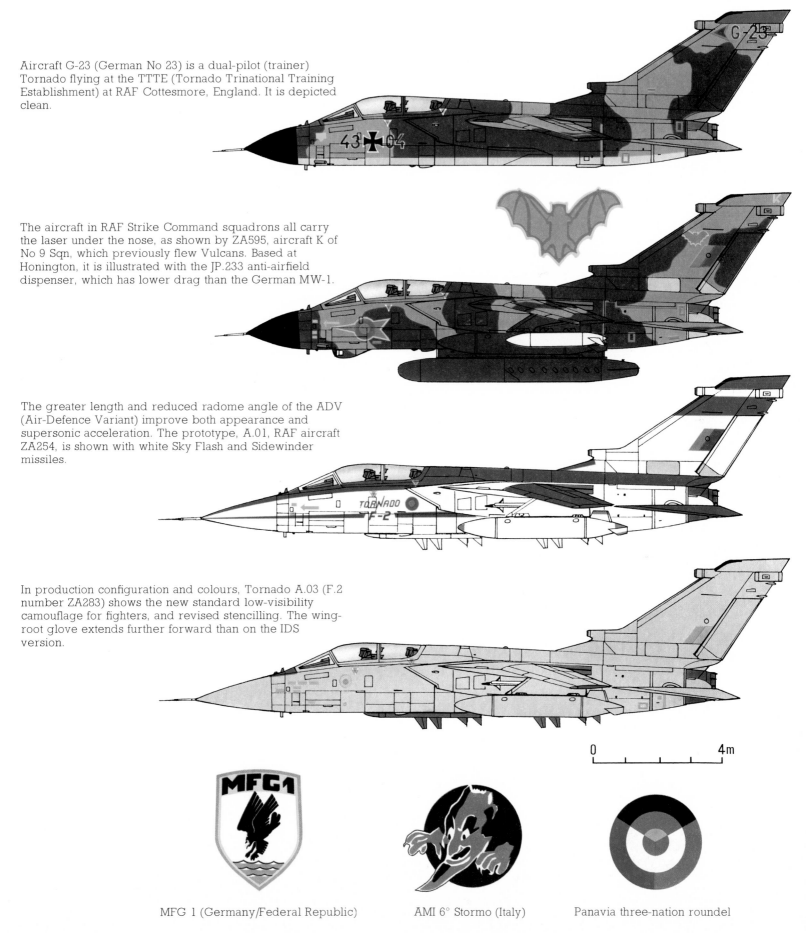

Aircraft G-23 (German No 23) is a dual-pilot (trainer) Tornado flying at the TTTE (Tornado Trinational Training Establishment) at RAF Cottesmore, England. It is depicted clean.

The aircraft in RAF Strike Command squadrons all carry the laser under the nose, as shown by ZA595, aircraft K of No 9 Sqn, which previously flew Vulcans. Based at Honington, it is illustrated with the JP.233 anti-airfield dispenser, which has lower drag than the German MW-1.

The greater length and reduced radome angle of the ADV (Air-Defence Variant) improve both appearance and supersonic acceleration. The prototype, A.01, RAF aircraft ZA254, is shown with white Sky Flash and Sidewinder missiles.

In production configuration and colours, Tornado A.03 (F.2 number ZA283) shows the new standard low-visibility camouflage for fighters, and revised stencilling. The wing-root glove extends further forward than on the IDS version.

0   4m

MFG 1 (Germany/Federal Republic)   AMI 6° Stormo (Italy)   Panavia three-nation roundel

Panavia Tornado

Critics of multinational programmes may point to the Tornado—originally known as the MRCA, for Multi-Role Combat Aircraft—as evidence that such enterprises take longer than firmly directed national ones; but they will find it hard to fault the end-product. No other aircraft in history has ever had to meet the numerical requirements of four of the world's toughest customers in three countries, and although both the aircraft and its engines were totally new 'clean sheet of paper' designs the final hardware has set new standards of reliability and trouble-free operation.

After almost four years of discussion at the political and engineering levels, the baseline MRCA brochure was printed in March 1969, outlining a variable-sweep aircraft with two very modern engines intended to meet the demands of the RAF (which wanted two seats in a primarily attack role), Luftwaffe (which wanted a multi-role single-seater), Marineflieger (which was concerned with anti-ship missions), Aeronautica Militare Italiano (which wanted a single-seater) and the Dutch Koninklijke Luchtmacht (which required a single-seat fighter). The Dutch pulled out, and eventually Panavia was established as a three-nation group with British Aerospace and West Germany's MBB each holding 42·5% and Italy's Aeritalia 15%. Also, Turbo-Union was set up to produce the extremely advanced new engine in the ratio Rolls-Royce and MTU 40% each and Fiat 20%.

The first Tornado flew at Manching, Germany, on 14 August 1974, and after extremely trouble-free development the production aircraft was first delivered for service tests in February 1978, followed by the setting up of a Tri-national Training Establishment at RAF Cottesmore, England, in early 1982 with 48 aircraft. As this book went to press the RAF expected to receive 200 Tornado GR.1s (instead of 220, twenty being switched to the interceptor version), the West German Luftwaffe 212, the Marineflieger 112 and the Aeronautica Militare 100. All these are basically similar attack aircraft with advanced navigation, electronic-warfare and weapon-aiming systems. Features include outer wings pivoting from 25° (with very advanced high-lift systems) to 68° for automatic terrain following at over 1480km/h (920mph, Mach 1·2); plus differential tailplanes for roll control, with quad fly-by-wire flight control under authority of a digital computer; a powerful Texas Instruments multi-mode radar tied in with the Decca doppler for the highest possible navigation precision; outstandingly short take-off and landing with anti-skid brakes, lift dumpers and engine reversers; and an unrivalled set of electronic displays for the pilot and backseat navigator. Tornado can fly lower and faster than any other aircraft.

In early 1982 the 100th of this version was delivered, with the rest of the 624 following at the rate of 110 (44 UK, 42 Germany and 24 Italy) per year. In parallel the RAF has ordered a long-range all-weather interceptor to replace the Lightning and Phantom, the Tornado F.2, which differs mainly in having a new track-while-scan pulse-doppler radar, a longer fuselage housing more fuel and providing length for four Sky Flash (or Amraam) missiles recessed nose-to-tail, extended wing-root gloves, a longer and more pointed nose radome giving better supersonic acceleration, a retractable flight-refuelling probe (the RAF IDS model has provision for a removable probe), and one gun instead of two.

The first fighter Tornado flew on 27 October 1979 and development has since progressed swiftly. The RAF purchase of F.2s has been increased to 185, and orders from other Panavia partner countries, and from export customers, are being discussed. It may be that in the long term this will be the variant built in the greatest numbers. Meanwhile the Luftwaffe's Jabo 31, 32, 33 and 34, the Marineflieger MFG 1 and 2, and RAF No 9 Sqn at Honington (site of the tri-national Weapon Conversion Unit) and 617 at Marham will all have begun to equip by the time this book appears. The AMI's 20°, 102°, 154° and 186° *gruppi* are following close behind, in an 809-aircraft programme.

COUNTRIES OF ORIGIN Germany (Federal Republic), Great Britain and Italy.

CREW 2.

TOTAL PRODUCED About 195 by early 1983.

DIMENSIONS Wingspan, 25°: 13·9m (45ft 7in), 68°: 8·6m (28ft 2½in); length, **IDS:** 16·7m (54ft 9½in), **F.2:** 18·06m (59ft 3in); wing area (estimated): 30m² (323ft²).

WEIGHTS Empty, **IDS:** about 14000kg (30,865lb), **F.2:** about 14515kg (32,000lb); maximum loaded, **IDS:** 26490kg (58,400lb), **F.2:** 23587kg (52,000lb).

ENGINES Two 7200kg (15,900lb) class Turbo-Union RB.199 Mk 101 augmented turbofans.

MAXIMUM SPEED Clean, high altitude: 2337km/h (1,452mph, Mach 2·2).

SERVICE CEILING 18·5km (60,700ft).

RANGE **IDS:** about 3890km (2,420 miles), **F.2:** about 4350km (2,700 miles).

MILITARY LOAD **IDS:** Two 27mm Mauser guns, plus over 400 combinations of external stores (including every NATO bomb, air/ground missile, ECM/gun/rocket pod or tank) to total of about 8200kg (18,000lb) with 10000kg (22,000lb) in emergency circumstances; **F.2:** one 27mm Mauser gun, four Sky Flash recessed under fuselage and two (or more) AIM-9L Sidewinder AAMs externally.

USERS Germany (Federal Republic—Luftwaffe, Marineflieger), Great Britain (RAF), Italy.

Rockwell International B-1B

In 1968 a wit said that the initials AMSA stood for 'America's Most Studied Aircraft' rather than for Advanced Manned Strategic Aircraft. Even at that time there had been six years of study on how to build the next bomber for USAF Strategic Air Command. But nothing had been built by 1968. Time dragged on and eventually in 1970 Rockwell was awarded a contract for the B-1; General Electric was to produce the engines. The first B-1 flew on 23 December 1974, and the USAF announced a force of 244. Three further prototypes flew with great success, but in June 1977 President Jimmy Carter cancelled the entire production programme. Arguments—and inflation—continued, but in October 1981 President Reagan announced a force of 100 B-1B bombers, to enter service from 1988. At a cost of some $28 billion, they will tide SAC over until a still later 'stealth' bomber arrives in the early 1990s.

At the political level many powerful people with little technical knowledge cannot comprehend the arguments why a bomber is necessary, nor how its design can protect it against enemy defences. Even well into the B-1 flight programme there was a belief that in some way speed was an advantage. Today it is finally understood that the first design priority is to reduce the bomber's radar signature (its appearance on enemy radar displays), and the B-1B has special shapes, special RAM (radar-absorbent material) structure and very comprehensive and powerful defensive avionics able to mask, confuse and in various other ways interfere with hostile electronics of every kind used in air defence systems.

The high-speed design features of the B-1 have been eliminated in the B-1B. The crew of four have ejection seats instead of a jettisonable capsule. The four engines under the rear of the fixed glove portion of the wing are fed by simple fixed inlets instead of complex variable inlets. Even the swing wing was almost replaced by a wing fixed at 50°; the pivoted arrangement was retained only because at maximum sweep the aircraft is better able to make low-level

attacks at about 960km/h (600mph). Even so, the B-1B can just exceed the speed of sound at high altitude but this is not regarded as important, and it greatly increases fuel consumption.

One of the vital requirements is the ability to 'scramble' from the home base in the few minutes that would elapse between the first warning of an ICBM attack and the destruction of the base. The main point of a bomber is that it can be sent off as soon as an enemy attack appears likely; unlike a retaliatory ICBM, the bomber can be recalled if the attack should not develop. Bombers also have very great capability in conventional warfare, and the B-1B is so large because it has to be able to fly to anywhere in the world. Even without using its flight-refuelling capability the B-1B can fly 12000km (7,460 miles)— although not with the maximum load of 22 ALCMs (cruise missiles) or 128 free-fall bombs because, with all these on board, many are hung on eight pylons under the fuselage and this creates considerable additional drag.

Like the original B-1, the B-1B has three 4·57m (15ft) long weapon bays. Each can carry an eight-round drum of SRAM missiles, but the ALCM grew in length and only a single eight-round launcher can be accommodated internally, although 14 can be hung on the external pylons.

Rockwell received new development contracts in early 1982. Measured from the date of such a decision the first representative aircraft (the rebuilt second B-1) could fly in 21 months, the first production B-1B in 38 months, and the last of the planned first batch of 15 in 57 months. This last date coincides with the B-1B becoming ready for use, although the first 15 are mainly for training. The first B-1B may fly in February 1985 and the operationally ready date would be March 1988. It would take a further 22 months, to early 1990, to deliver the remaining 85 B-1Bs of the combat squadrons. But by this time, even allowing for improvements that may be developed in the meanwhile, the B-1B will find it hard to penetrate hostile airspace.

COUNTRY OF ORIGIN USA.

CREW 4.

TOTAL PRODUCED None.

DIMENSIONS Wingspan, 15° sweep: 41·67m (136ft 8½in), 67·5° sweep: 23·84m (78ft 2½in); length 45·78m (150ft 2½in); wing area about 181·2m² (1,950ft²).

WEIGHTS Empty about 80000kg (176,000lb); maximum loaded 216800kg (477,954lb).

ENGINES Four 13600kg (30,000lb) class General Electric F101-GE-102 augmented turbofans.

MAXIMUM SPEED Clean, high altitude: 1275km/h (792mph, Mach 1·2).

SERVICE CEILING About 14·6km (48,000ft).

RANGE 12000km (7,460 miles).

MILITARY LOAD Free-fall conventional bombs: 128 Mk 82 (84 internal) or 38 Mk 84 (24 internal); free-fall nuclear bombs: 20 B28 (12 internal), 26 B43 (12 internal) or 38 B61 or B83 (24 internal); missiles: 38 AGM-69A SRAM (24 internal) or 22 AGM-86B ALCM (eight internal).

USER USA (AF).

The subject of all these illustrations is the fourth prototype B-1, which in late 1981 was restored to flight status to underpin the B-1B programme. In 1982 work began on reconstructing the No 2 prototype to incorporate most of the airframe and systems features of the production B-1B, and it flew again in early 1983. The No 4 aircraft has meanwhile been even more completely updated with the B-1B offensive and defensive avionics systems, together with a number of airframe and systems changes; on resuming flight development in 1984 it was to be virtually a B-1B. The first completely new production B-1B aircraft was expected to be ready ahead of time in December 1984. These illustrations depict the No 4 prototype as it was in 1982, when it still had variable engine inlets for Mach 2 performance at high altitude. The B-1B will have fixed backward-sloping inlets to give a much reduced radar cross section; speed can still be maintained at over 966km/h (600mph) at a height of 91m (200ft). Other changes are elimination of the long dorsal spine and relocation of the nose probe on the right side of the nose. Another visible difference will be in the simpler overwing fairings, although the range of wing sweep from 15° to 67·5° will not be altered. One way in which the No 4 prototype has resembled the B-1B from the start is its blunt electronics-packed tail end; another is its use of four separate ejection seats instead of a jettisonable crew capsule as on the first three prototypes shown overleaf.

0   4m

Rockwell International B-1

The first B-1 prototype is depicted as it looked at the roll-out ceremony from Rockwell's works at Palmdale on 26 October 1974. Painted glossy white all over, it had a jettisonable crew capsule, fully variable engine inlets and a pointed tail, and was used in a very successful programme to explore flight qualities.

The second prototype was the structural test aircraft, and was rolled out on 11 May 1976 and flown on 14 June (both dates are later than for the third aircraft). It was finally stored after a shorter flying life than any other B-1, only 282·5 hours in 60 flights.

B-1 prototype No 3 was the vital testbed for the avionics, especially the offensive (electronic-warfare) systems, which were of unparalleled complexity and power. It is shown after being camouflaged for the low-level mission. It had flown 829·4 hours when the original flight testing ended in April 1981.

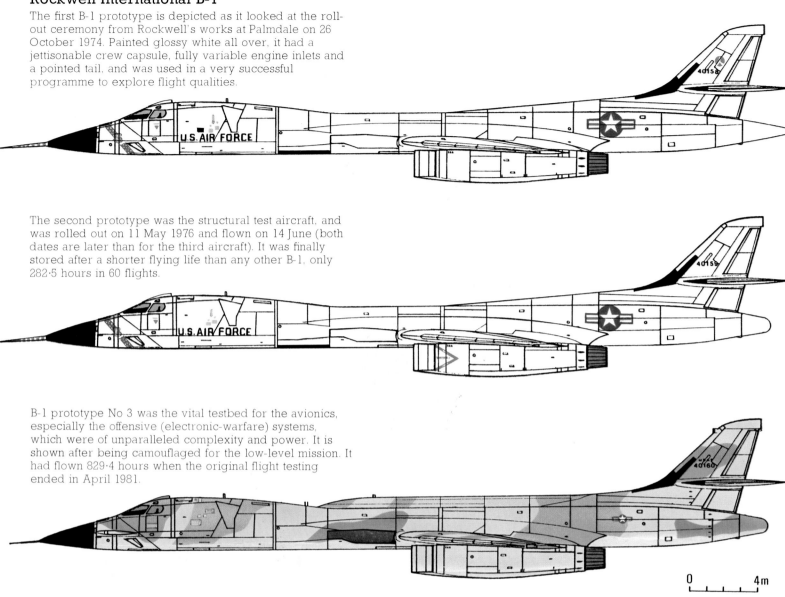

Originally the ALCM (Air-Launched Cruise Missile) was the same size as the SRAM (Short-Range Attack Missile), but the production ALCM is much longer. Thus only eight can be carried inside a B-1B, compared with 24 SRAMs. External pylons can carry another 14 of either weapon.

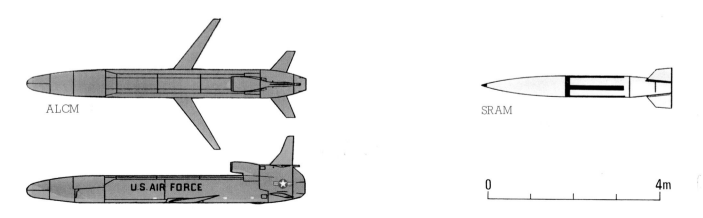

ALCM

SRAM

Rockwell International B-1B

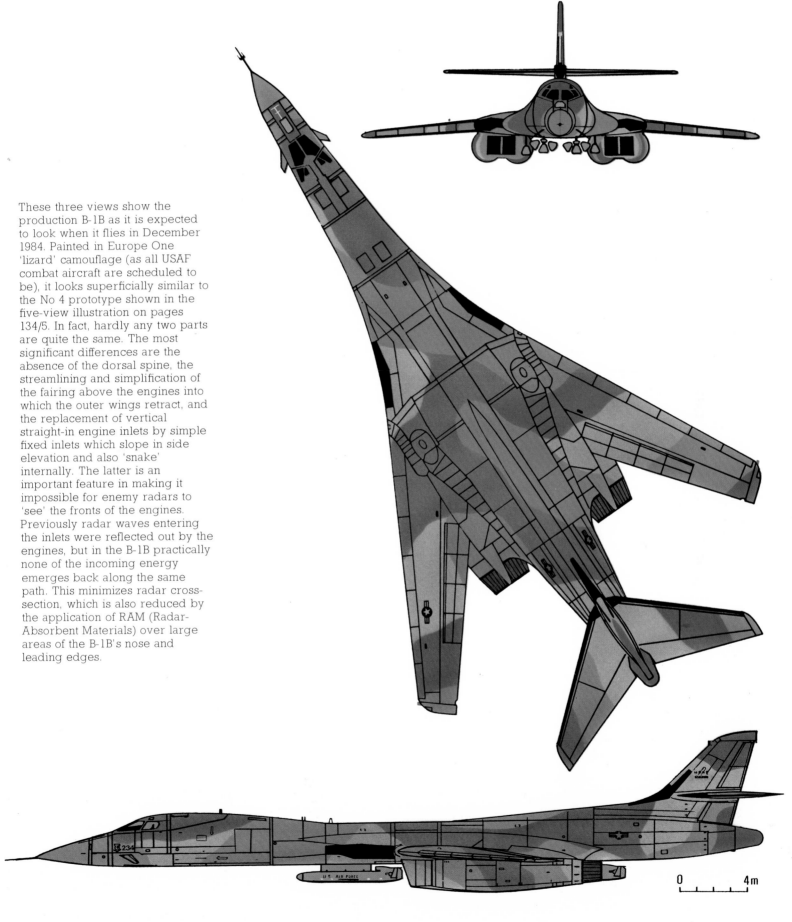

These three views show the production B-1B as it is expected to look when it flies in December 1984. Painted in Europe One 'lizard' camouflage (as all USAF combat aircraft are scheduled to be), it looks superficially similar to the No 4 prototype shown in the five-view illustration on pages 134/5. In fact, hardly any two parts are quite the same. The most significant differences are the absence of the dorsal spine, the streamlining and simplification of the fairing above the engines into which the outer wings retract, and the replacement of vertical straight-in engine inlets by simple fixed inlets which slope in side elevation and also 'snake' internally. The latter is an important feature in making it impossible for enemy radars to 'see' the fronts of the engines. Previously radar waves entering the inlets were reflected out by the engines, but in the B-1B practically none of the incoming energy emerges back along the same path. This minimizes radar cross-section, which is also reduced by the application of RAM (Radar-Absorbent Materials) over large areas of the B-1B's nose and leading edges.

0   4m

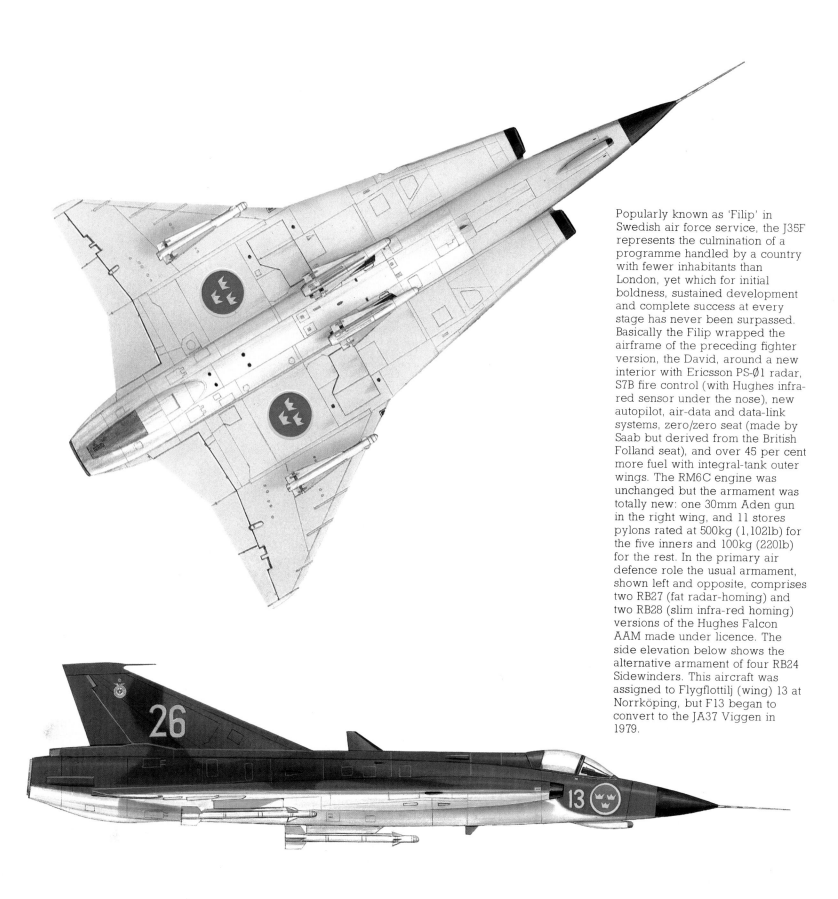

Popularly known as 'Filip' in Swedish air force service, the J35F represents the culmination of a programme handled by a country with fewer inhabitants than London, yet which for initial boldness, sustained development and complete success at every stage has never been surpassed. Basically the Filip wrapped the airframe of the preceding fighter version, the David, around a new interior with Ericsson PS-Ø1 radar, S7B fire control (with Hughes infra-red sensor under the nose), new autopilot, air-data and data-link systems, zero/zero seat (made by Saab but derived from the British Folland seat), and over 45 per cent more fuel with integral-tank outer wings. The RM6C engine was unchanged but the armament was totally new: one 30mm Aden gun in the right wing, and 11 stores pylons rated at 500kg (1,102lb) for the five inners and 100kg (220lb) for the rest. In the primary air defence role the usual armament, shown left and opposite, comprises two RB27 (fat radar-homing) and two RB28 (slim infra-red homing) versions of the Hughes Falcon AAM made under licence. The side elevation below shows the alternative armament of four RB24 Sidewinders. This aircraft was assigned to Flygflottilj (wing) 13 at Norrköping, but F13 began to convert to the JA37 Viggen in 1979.

Saab J35F Draken

Saab-35 Draken

The Saab-35 design was developed with the low-powered Saab 210 research aircraft followed by three Saab-35 prototypes, of which this was the first, flown on 25 October 1955. The engine was an RM5A (licensed Avon RA.7R with twin-eyelid nozzle, as used on the British Swift).

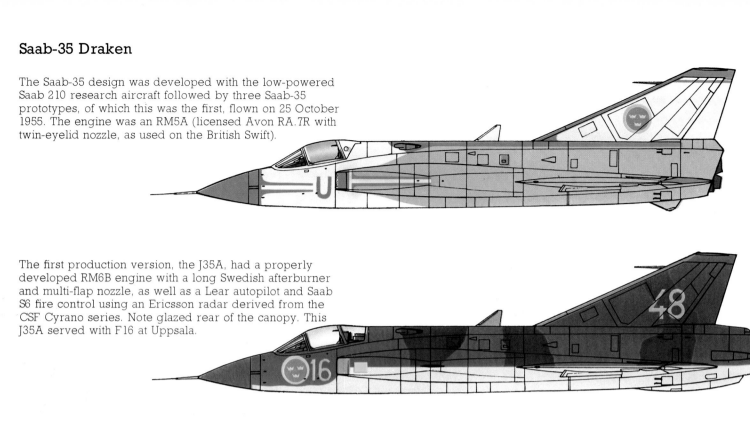

The first production version, the J35A, had a properly developed RM6B engine with a long Swedish afterburner and multi-flap nozzle, as well as a Lear autopilot and Saab S6 fire control using an Ericsson radar derived from the CSF Cyrano series. Note glazed rear of the canopy. This J35A served with F16 at Uppsala.

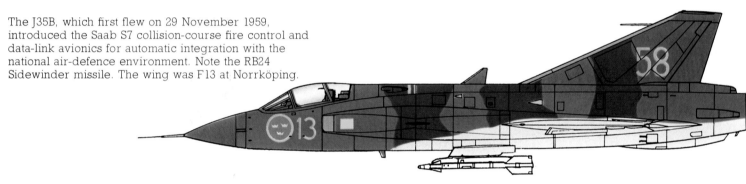

The J35B, which first flew on 29 November 1959, introduced the Saab S7 collision-course fire control and data-link avionics for automatic integration with the national air-defence environment. Note the RB24 Sidewinder missile. The wing was F13 at Norrköping.

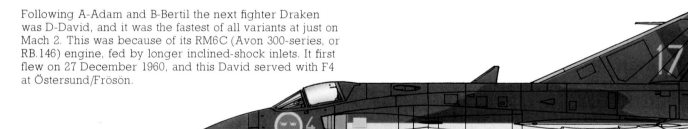

Following A-Adam and B-Bertil the next fighter Draken was D-David, and it was the fastest of all variants at just on Mach 2. This was because of its RM6C (Avon 300-series, or RB.146) engine, fed by longer inclined-shock inlets. It first flew on 27 December 1960, and this David served with F4 at Östersund/Frösön.

The S35E (Erik) used the airframe and propulsion of David but with equipment for reconnaissance only. The pressurized nose housed four cameras, and there were also three long-focal-length cameras, one in the nose and one in each gun bay in the wing. The unit was F11 at Nyköping/Skavsta (Södermanland).

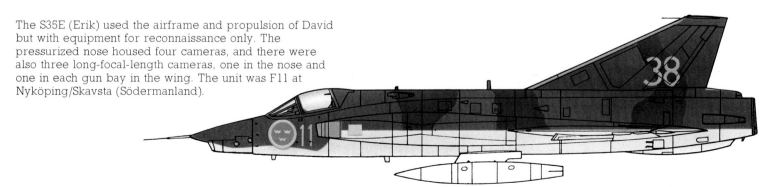

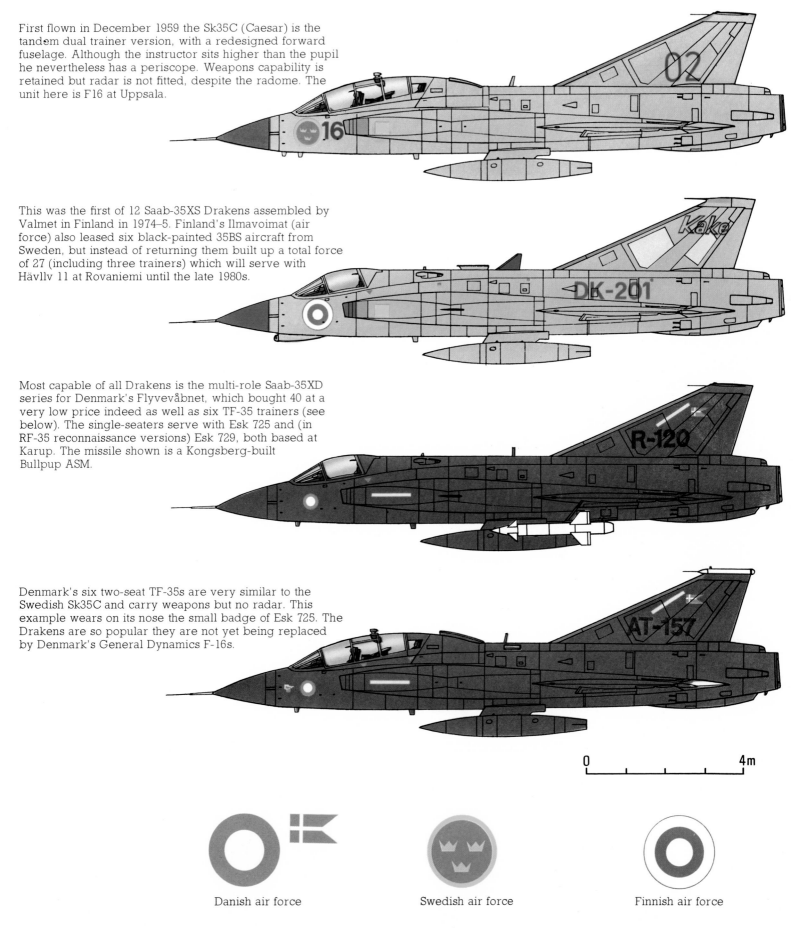

First flown in December 1959 the Sk35C (Caesar) is the
tandem dual trainer version, with a redesigned forward
fuselage. Although the instructor sits higher than the pupil
he nevertheless has a periscope. Weapons capability is
retained but radar is not fitted, despite the radome. The
unit here is F16 at Uppsala.

This was the first of 12 Saab-35XS Drakens assembled by
Valmet in Finland in 1974–5. Finland's Ilmavoimat (air
force) also leased six black-painted 35BS aircraft from
Sweden, but instead of returning them built up a total force
of 27 (including three trainers) which will serve with
Hävllv 11 at Rovaniemi until the late 1980s.

Most capable of all Drakens is the multi-role Saab-35XD
series for Denmark's Flyvevåbnet, which bought 40 at a
very low price indeed as well as six TF-35 trainers (see
below). The single-seaters serve with Esk 725 and (in
RF-35 reconnaissance versions) Esk 729, both based at
Karup. The missile shown is a Kongsberg-built
Bullpup ASM.

Denmark's six two-seat TF-35s are very similar to the
Swedish Sk35C and carry weapons but no radar. This
example wears on its nose the small badge of Esk 725. The
Drakens are so popular they are not yet being replaced
by Denmark's General Dynamics F-16s.

0   4m

Danish air force   Swedish air force   Finnish air force

141

Saab-35 Draken

In the early 1960s a British air expert caused a furore by praising Sweden's military procurement programmes. His native critics perhaps deliberately failed to understand the point he was making. Whereas since 1945 Britain has put into service 7 per cent of the types of combat aircraft on which public money has been spent, the Swedes have achieved a 100 per cent rate of success. They have explained this by saying that they cannot afford ever to create the wrong aircraft; but they have never shirked when the answer seemed to be a radically unconventional design. The Draken, the so-called double-delta, still looks modern today, and it is hard to believe that it was designed over 30 years ago when even the swept wing was a new idea.

It was in 1949 that the Royal Swedish Air Board issued Project 1250 calling for a fighter able to reach at least Mach 1·4, yet operate from existing airbases. Saab's small engineering team under Erik Bratt knew that the thickness of the wing had to be no more than about one-twentieth as great as the chord (distance from leading edge to trailing edge, measured parallel to the fore/aft axis). They were attracted to the idea of making the aircraft virtually an all-wing delta; this made the chord three or more times the usual value, so the thickness could be several times greater than with a normal wing. It was also found possible to package the fuel, avionics and armament inside such a shape quite conveniently, the only unusual feature being that everything was arranged in a front-to-rear sequence, with a small gap amidships for the main wheels. The leading-edge sweep was an amazing 70°, just twice the usual 1949 value.

The engine for the fighter was obtained from England, as were the two 30mm Aden guns fitted in the leading edge of what had become a double-delta wing with sweep of 80° inboard and 57° on the thin outer sections. The first of three Saab-35 prototypes flew on 25 October 1955, and the production J35A went into service with the Flygvapnet in March 1960. The J35A was a day interceptor, although its early

French-designed radar, autopilot and Saab lead-pursuit fire control did give some all-weather capability. The important factors were that J35A, called Adam by its pilots, had a flashing Mach 1·8 performance despite its simple fixed-geometry inlets, was easy to fly even from Sweden's dispersed bases on country roads, and was well within the Flygvapnet's capability to look after it in harsh environments.

In 1961 Adam was fitted with Swedish-made Sidewinder missiles and an infra-red sight, and a year later it began to be supplemented and then replaced by the J35B (Bertil), with an automatic link to the Swedish national air-defence net, and a more powerful engine. Next came the Sk35C (Caesar), a dual-control trainer version. In late 1963 deliveries began of the J35D (David), with a much more powerful Swedish-made Rolls engine, more internal fuel and a new PS-Ø3 radar. The S35E (Erik) was an unarmed reconnaissance version.

Having got a first-rate basic aircraft with David, Saab then packed it with advanced avionics to produce the most important of all models, the J35F (Filip). This entered service in 1966 as a true all-weather multi-role aircraft with an S7B collision-course intercept system, only one gun but four Swedish-made Falcon missiles, two being radar-guided and two infra-red homing. About 300 Filips had been delivered by 1972, at the unbelievably low price of about £420,000 each. Thus the 300 cost about as much as five Mirage 2000s.

Saab rounded off the Draken programme at 606 by selling further developed attack/reconnaissance versions to Denmark and Finland, in each case offering not only a bargain aircraft but impressive industrial benefits as well: the Finns also assembled their dozen J35XS aircraft themselves. Sweden has always resisted arms sales, and her strictly neutral stance has been in sharp contrast to the aggressive selling of, for example, France. Few air forces have taken the trouble to study the exceptionally good service record of the Drakens from Adam to Filip, which despite their appearance have no vices.

COUNTRY OF ORIGIN Sweden.

CREW Fighters: 1, trainers: 2.

TOTAL PRODUCED 606.

DIMENSIONS Wingspan 9·4m (30ft 10in); length, **E:** 15·85m (52ft 0in), **F:** 15·4m (50ft 4in); wing area 49·2m² (529·6ft²).

WEIGHTS Empty, **F:** 8250kg (18,188lb); maximum loaded, **F:** 12270kg (27,050lb), **35XD:** 16000kg (35,274lb).

ENGINE One Rolls-Royce Avon augmented turbojet made under licence by Svenska Flygmotor, **A/B/C:** 6804kg (15,000lb) RM6B, **D/E/F/XD:** 7761kg (17,110lb) RM6C.

MAXIMUM SPEED Clean, **E/F/XD:** 2128km/h (1,322mph, Mach 2).

SERVICE CEILING Clean, **E/F/XD:** 19·5km (64,000ft).

RANGE **F/XD**, internal fuel only plus bombs: 1300km (808 miles), max fuel: 3250km (2019 miles).

MILITARY LOAD **F:** one 30mm Aden M/55 gun with 90 rounds, two RB27 and two RB28 Falcon AAMs plus two or four RB324 Sidewinder AAMs; **XD:** no gun, or with reduced fuel two Aden M/55, plus nine weapon pylons each rated at 454kg (1,000lb), all usable simultaneously, plus four RB24 or 324 Sidewinders.

USERS Denmark, Finland, Sweden.

Saab-37 Viggen

Although Saab-Scania (in 1968 the Saab company merged with the Scania group) eventually managed to hang nine 454kg (1,000lb) bombs under the Draken, much greater capability was needed for the final quarter of the 20th century. In 1958 the outline for System 37 was agreed, the basic design and equipment was settled by 1963, and the first of seven prototypes flew on 8 February 1967. From the start System 37 had been planned as a platform only slightly larger than a Draken but one versatile enough to be equipped for a wide range of missions. In the event, no attempt was made to alter the basic role of each aircraft once it had been built, although it would not be impossible to convert any Viggen into one of a different sub-type (with the exception of the last model, the JA37 fighter, which is virtually a new aircraft type).

From the start two overriding requirements strongly influenced the design. The Flygvapnet was anxious not to give up its vital capability of basing its front-line aircraft in country areas where there are no airbases, making take-offs and landings on ordinary farm roads. Recognizing better than other air forces that in any European war fixed airbases would be wiped out in the first few minutes, Sweden thus demanded STOL capability, and precise landing at low speeds under full control. This led to the unique configuration with powered flaps on both the main wing and the canard foreplane, and to such features as tandem main wheels with anti-skid brakes, and a reverser on the augmented turbofan engine. The second basic demand was that System 37 should be not only a family of aircraft but also an integrated defence network including all the ground equipment, training devices, simulators and interfaces with the STRIL-60 electronic net that covers Sweden.

An exceptional proportion of the airframe is made of bonded metal honeycomb, which gives a smooth exterior finish for very low weight. The propulsion was always envisaged as a single large augmented engine, but the choice of the British Medway was thwarted by its cancellation, leaving the only choice an American airline turbofan for which Svenska Flygmotor developed an afterburner and variable nozzle with integral reverser. Every nook and cranny in all versions is occupied by electronics or fuel. Many advanced-technology items use British design assistance, including the HUD and autothrottle/speed control for landings, but the rocket-assisted seat is Saab's design.

The first variant to enter service, in June 1971, was the AJ37 attack Viggen (the name means 'thunderbolt'). This single-seater was the baseline for all other variants, and has a powerful Ericsson radar and digital computer for precision air/ground delivery in all weathers. There is no internal armament, everything being hung on seven pylons, three under the broad fuselage and two under each wing.

The SF37 is an all-weather armed reconnaissance model which replaced the S35E between 1977 and 1980. The SH37 is another reconnaissance version, this time with radar and special equipment for missions over water and with attack capability; it replaced the S32C Lansen. The SK37 is a dual tandem trainer, with an instructor cockpit replacing some fuel and electronics and fitted with a bulged hood and twin periscopes.

Another feature of the SK37 is a taller kinked-top fin, and this was also used in the final version, the JA37 interceptor. This is a largely new aircraft packaged into an almost unchanged airframe, with a modified engine, very modern pulse-doppler radar, permanently installed gun with exceptional kinetic energy from each shot, a completely new digital fire-control designed for the air-to-air mission and a powerful missile armament. After a colossal development effort lasting ten years, the first production JA37 flew in 1977, and 149 are being delivered in 1979–85 to replace 8 squadrons of Drakens.

Production of the AJ, SF, SH and SK versions totalled 180, and by mid-1982 about 60 JAs had been delivered. Total deliveries for Sweden will be 329.

COUNTRY OF ORIGIN Sweden.

CREW **AJ**, **SH**, **SF** and **JA:** 1, **SK:** 2.

TOTAL PRODUCED About 240 by mid-1982.

DIMENSIONS Wingspan 10·6m (34ft 9½in); length, including probe, **AJ**, **SF**, **SH**, **SK:** 16·3m (53ft 5¾in), **JA:** 16·4m (53ft 9¾in); wing area 46m² (495·1ft²).

WEIGHTS Empty, not published; maximum loaded, **AJ:** 20500kg (45,195lb), **JA:** 17000kg (37,478lb).

ENGINE One P&W JT8D augmented turbofan built under licence by SFA with SFA afterburner (except JA): 11790kg (25,970lb) RM8A, **JA:** 12750kg (28,108lb) RM8B.

MAXIMUM SPEED All versions, clean: over 2127km/h (1,322mph, Mach 2) at high altitude, 1468km/h (912mph, Mach 1·2) at sea level.

SERVICE CEILING About 19km (62,300ft).

RANGE Tactical radius with unspecified external armament, hi-lo-hi flight profile, over 1000km (620 miles).

MILITARY LOAD **AJ:** total load of 6000kg (13,228lb) of stores on seven pylons including RB04E and RB05A heavy surface-attack missiles, RB75 (TV Maverick) precision missiles, 16 bombs, gun pods, rocket pods, ECM pods, tanks and self-protection RB24 Sidewinder or RB28 Falcon AAMs. **JA:** one 30mm Oerlikon KCA gun, up to six RB71 (British Aerospace Sky Flash) or other mixes including RB24 Sidewinders; bombs or rockets in attack missions, e.g. four pods each of six 135mm rockets.

USER Sweden.

Saab JA37 Viggen

Having delivered 180 Viggens of earlier versions, Saab-Scania AB of Sweden is now producing the JA37 interceptor, intended primarily for the air-to-air role. The subject of these drawings is a JA37 serving with the second squadron to be equipped with this type, an element of wing F17 based at Ronneby. Most views show it with the standard air-to-air armament of one 30mm Oerlikon KCA gun with 150 rounds, two RB 71 (BAe Sky Flash) and four RB 24 (Sidewinder) missiles. The left-side view below shows the aircraft with missiles removed and with the fin folded and canopy open. The gun (which is offset on the left side in a box which forms the fairing for the centreline drop tank) is one of the most powerful in service outside the Soviet Union. It has a firing rate of 1,350 rounds per minute, an extremely high muzzle velocity of 1050m (3,445ft)/min and a projectile weight of 360g (0.79 1lb), resulting in impact energy considerably greater than that of the British Aden or French DEFA of the same calibre. Unlike most modern combat aircraft (except the Tornado), the Viggen has an engine thrust reverser. Its exit apertures can be seen on the sides and underside ahead of the jet nozzle.

0   4m

Saab-37 Viggen

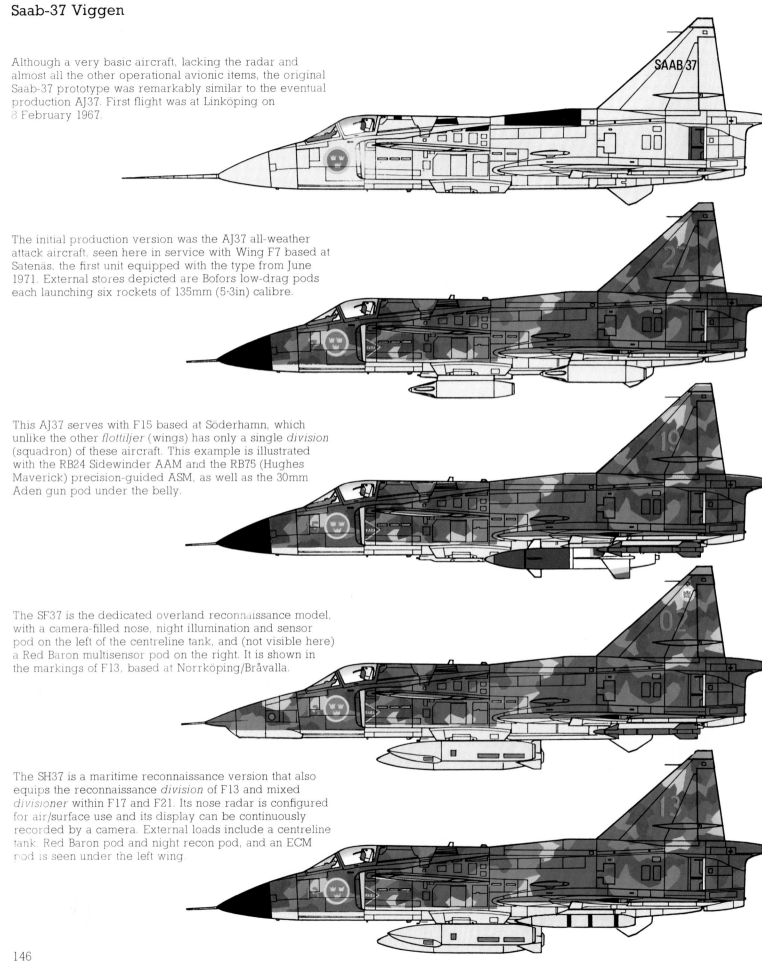

Although a very basic aircraft, lacking the radar and almost all the other operational avionic items, the original Saab-37 prototype was remarkably similar to the eventual production AJ37. First flight was at Linköping on 8 February 1967.

The initial production version was the AJ37 all-weather attack aircraft, seen here in service with Wing F7 based at Satenäs, the first unit equipped with the type from June 1971. External stores depicted are Bofors low-drag pods each launching six rockets of 135mm (5·3in) calibre.

This AJ37 serves with F15 based at Söderhamn, which unlike the other *flottiljer* (wings) has only a single *division* (squadron) of these aircraft. This example is illustrated with the RB24 Sidewinder AAM and the RB75 (Hughes Maverick) precision-guided ASM, as well as the 30mm Aden gun pod under the belly.

The SF37 is the dedicated overland reconnaissance model, with a camera-filled nose, night illumination and sensor pod on the left of the centreline tank, and (not visible here) a Red Baron multisensor pod on the right. It is shown in the markings of F13, based at Norrköping/Bråvalla.

The SH37 is a maritime reconnaissance version that also equips the reconnaissance *division* of F13 and mixed *divisioner* within F17 and F21. Its nose radar is configured for air/surface use and its display can be continuously recorded by a camera. External loads include a centreline tank, Red Baron pod and night recon pod, and an ECM pod is seen under the left wing.

Because of its extra cockpit, the SK37 trainer was the first variant to be fitted with an extended fin, the added upper section being swept back and housing a VHF aerial. All Viggen vertical tails can be folded down to the left. This model serves with the Viggen OCU (operational conversion unit), administered by wing F15, based at Söderhamn.

The first JA37 Viggen interceptor was a rebuilt AJ37, and had only some of the new version's features. This illustration shows the fifth development aircraft, first flown on 15 December 1975, which was the first to be built as a JA37 from the start. Apart from the new tail, a small blade aerial can be seen above the tail fairing and the KCA gun pod under the belly.

Aircraft 38 of wing F13 is a typical production JA37, seen in a new low-visibility air-combat scheme which may become standard after various alternatives have been evaluated. The external stores are four RB71 Sky Flashes and two RB24 Sidewinders.

This Viggen, basically a JA37, is being used as the main development aircraft for the JAS 39 next-generation aircraft. It has a complete fly-by-wire digital flight-control system which was first flown on 14 September 1982. ESS is the Swedish equivalent of FBW (fly-by-wire).

Not due to fly until 1986, for Flygvapen service from 1990, the Saab-39 JAS, named Gripen, will be considerably smaller and much more fuel-efficient than the Viggen, but is expected to be even more capable. Missiles shown are RB05A, RB71 and RB24. Gripen means 'Griffin'.

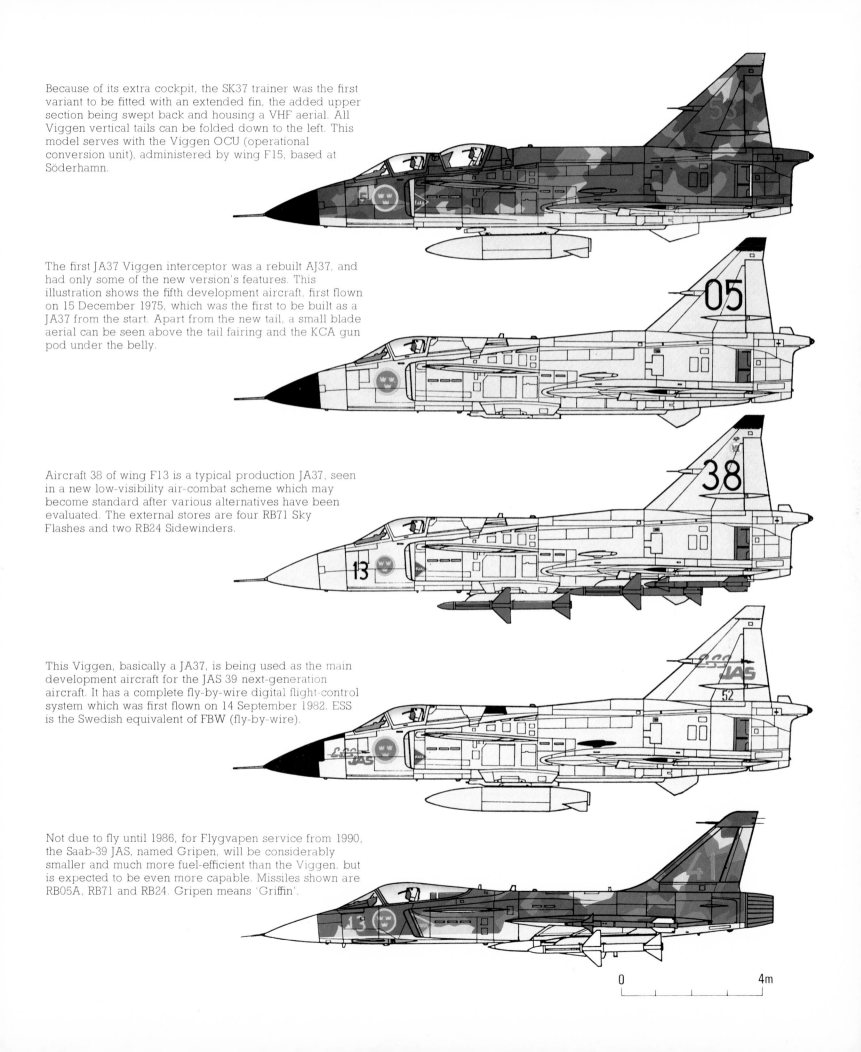

0   4m

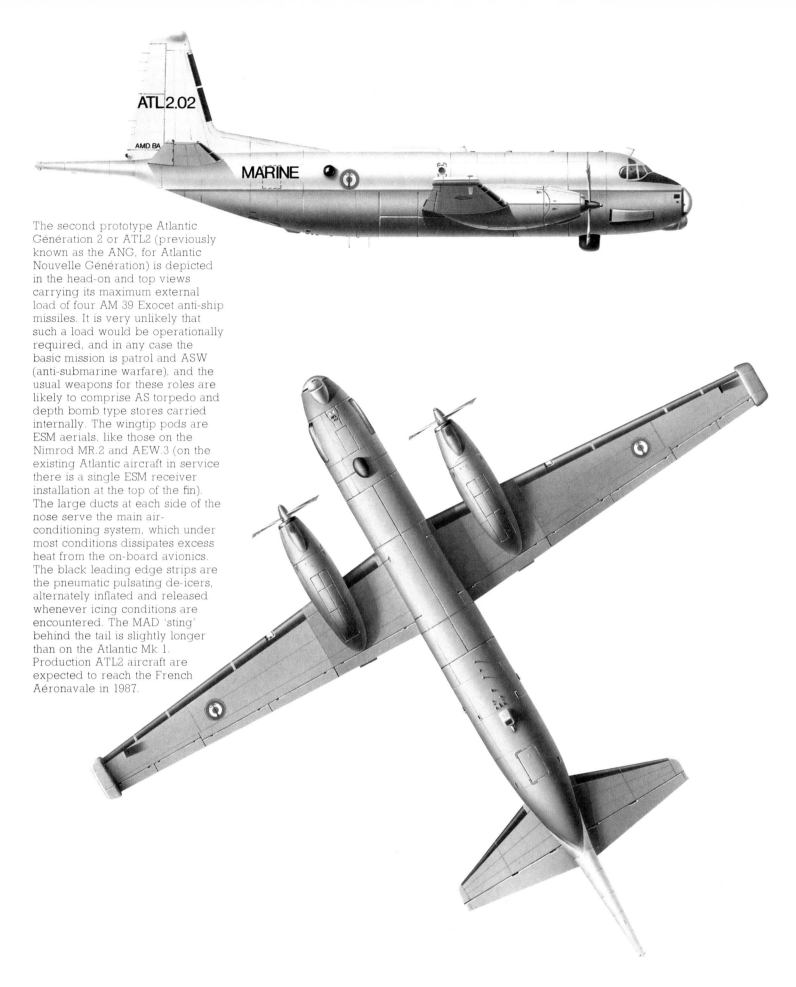

The second prototype Atlantic Génération 2 or ATL2 (previously known as the ANG, for Atlantic Nouvelle Génération) is depicted in the head-on and top views carrying its maximum external load of four AM 39 Exocet anti-ship missiles. It is very unlikely that such a load would be operationally required, and in any case the basic mission is patrol and ASW (anti-submarine warfare), and the usual weapons for these roles are likely to comprise AS torpedo and depth bomb type stores carried internally. The wingtip pods are ESM aerials, like those on the Nimrod MR.2 and AEW.3 (on the existing Atlantic aircraft in service there is a single ESM receiver installation at the top of the fin). The large ducts at each side of the nose serve the main air-conditioning system, which under most conditions dissipates excess heat from the on-board avionics. The black leading edge strips are the pneumatic pulsating de-icers, alternately inflated and released whenever icing conditions are encountered. The MAD 'sting' behind the tail is slightly longer than on the Atlantic Mk 1. Production ATL2 aircraft are expected to reach the French Aéronavale in 1987.

SECBAT (Dassault-Breguet)
Atlantic ATL2

ATL2.02

AMD.BA

MARINE

0   4m

SECBAT (Dassault-Breguet) Atlantic

The first prototype Br.1150 flew in the regular grey/white colour scheme on 21 October 1961. Several years later while on instrumented research it appeared in this Day-Glo orange. It has a forward fuselage 1m (39·4in) shorter than the production aircraft; other differences include tip pods (searchlight on right tip) and absence of an MAD boom.

In service with the French Aéronavale, the Atlantic formed the basic standard adopted by most other customers, with CSF DRAA-2B radar (shown in the operating position), CSF magnetometer in the tailboom (replaced by an advanced Crouzet product in the later ATL2 variant), a large dorsal spine incorporating communications and ADF aerials, and ARAR/ARAX ESM aerial array at the top of the fin.

The West German Marineflieger adopted almost exactly the same equipment fit as the Aéronavale, other items including Julie/Jezebel active sonobuoy systems and the Autolycus diesel sniffer, all today regarded as obsolete. Equipment is now being completely updated. This aircraft serves with MFG 3 at Nordholz.

The Netherlands shared in production from the start but were a bit late in organizing their order, so they finally received nine from the first block and five from the reopened line in 1970–2. They fly with VSQ-321 at Valkenburg with the Marine Luchtvaartdienst designation SP-13A.

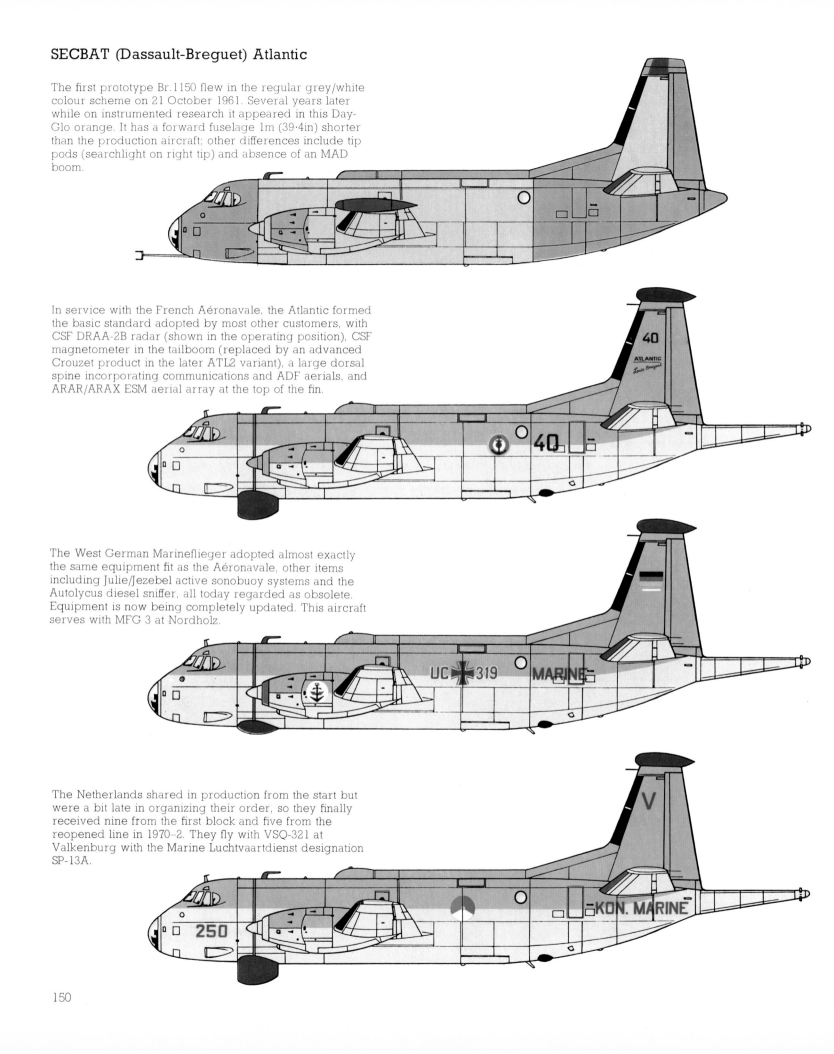

Italy bought 18 of the second block from the reopened production line, although build-standard is essentially the same as for the first batch. This example serves with the Marinavia 30° Stormo based in Sardinia at Cagliari-Elmas.

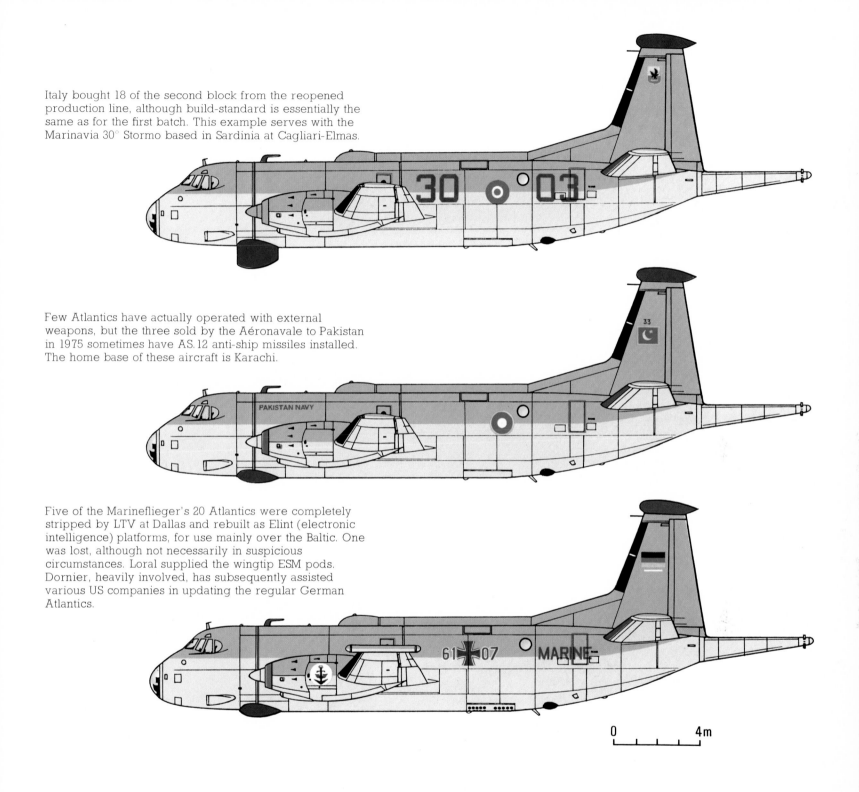

Few Atlantics have actually operated with external weapons, but the three sold by the Aéronavale to Pakistan in 1975 sometimes have AS.12 anti-ship missiles installed. The home base of these aircraft is Karachi.

Five of the Marineflieger's 20 Atlantics were completely stripped by LTV at Dallas and rebuilt as Elint (electronic intelligence) platforms, for use mainly over the Baltic. One was lost, although not necessarily in suspicious circumstances. Loral supplied the wingtip ESM pods. Dornier, heavily involved, has subsequently assisted various US companies in updating the regular German Atlantics.

Marineflieger (Germany/Federal Republic)

Marinavia 30° Stormo (Italy)

Aéronavale (France)

SECBAT (Dassault-Breguet) Atlantic

Although the total numbers involved have been so restricted that manufacture has been costly and unprofitable, the Atlantic has always been a notably efficient maritime patrol and ASW (anti-submarine warfare) aircraft which has been updated into a second generation for service well into the next century. At the same time its history underscores the apparent inability of NATO nations to adopt common defence hardware, and the fact that one Atlantic user, the Netherlands, has now bought P-3C Orions does not augur well for the sales prospects of the new version.

The programme was the result of an attempt in 1958 to find a common NATO aircraft to replace the P-2 Neptune. The Breguet Br.1150 won over 24 other submissions, and the first of two prototypes ordered in 1959 made its maiden flight on 22 October 1961. The Br.1150 was a completely conventional twin-turboprop with a wing of considerable span for long-range efficiency, and a double-bubble section fuselage: the upper bubble is fully pressurized and, together with the doors to the large weapon bay in the lower lobe, skinned with smooth, internally stiffened sandwich panels. Because of the modest speed it was possible to use pneumatic inflatable rubber boots to de-ice all leading edges.

Over a length of 15m (50ft) the upper fuselage lobe has a constant cross-section as large as a short-haul jet. Accommodation is provided for a total crew of 12, plus (on long patrol missions) a relief crew of 12. The main tactical compartment extends from the flight deck back across the wing and has seats for an ECM/ESM/MAD operator, radar operator, tactical coordinator and two sonobuoy operators, all facing display and control panels along the right side. Further aft is the rest area and then beam positions for two observers and, at the rear, the large compartment for sonobuoys, flares and the main entrance ladder.

Avionics and armament were typical of the 1959 era, the main radar being a CSF DRAA-2B in a retractable bin extended from under the forward fuselage. CSF also supplied the MAD (magnetic anomaly detector) at the tip of the tailboom for detecting the distortion of the Earth's magnetic field caused by a submerged submarine. ECM receiver aerials were grouped in a fairing on the fin, and weapons in the large main bay could be supplemented by four small AS.12 or other missiles on wing pylons.

Breguet (later Dassault-Breguet) formed a consortium called SECBAT including Sud-Aviation (now Aérospatiale), Fokker, ABAP (a Belgian sub-group) and Seeflug (a West German group), and the British engines and propellers were likewise assigned to a multinational combine. By 1968 France's Aéronavale had received 40 Atlantics and the Federal German Marineflieger 20; after a costly break, production was resumed with 9 for the Netherlands and 18 for Italy, while France sold three of its Atlantics to Pakistan.

By 1972 improved versions were being studied, and eventually the first ANG (Atlantic Nouvelle Génération), a rebuilt Mk 1, flew on 8 May 1981. The ANG has a refined structure giving longer life and increased serviceability, and almost totally updated systems. The latter include Thomson-CSF Iguane main radar, an FLIR (forward-looking infra-red) pod under the nose, two inertial systems and enormously enhanced data-processing speed and memory. External changes include a new fin tip with ESM (electronic support measures) frequency analysis aerials instead of the former fairing, added ESM direction-finding receivers at the wing-tips, a lengthened MAD boom and a large cabin air-conditioning fairing on the left of the nose.

The SECBAT consortium has, as far as possible, been re-formed to make a substantial run of ANGs from 1986 onwards. France has a requirement for 42, and the type is being keenly marketed not only for its original roles but for Elint (electronic intelligence, a role for which five West German Mk 1s were converted), air-refuelling tanker, passenger and cargo transport, mine-laying and civil offshore patrol and rescue.

COUNTRY OF ORIGIN France (built by international group).

CREW 12.

TOTAL PRODUCED 87 of Mk 1 version.

DIMENSIONS Wingspan, **1:** 36·3m (119ft 1in), **ANG:** 37·36m (122ft 7in); length, **1:** 31·75m (104ft 2in), **ANG:** 32·62m (107ft 0½in); wing area (both, excluding ANG tip pods): 120·34m² (1,295ft²).

WEIGHTS Empty, **1:** 24000kg (52,910lb), **ANG:** 25000kg (55,115lb); maximum loaded, **1:** 43500kg (95,899lb), **ANG:** 46200kg (101,852lb).

ENGINES Two 5,665shp Rolls-Royce Tyne 21 turboprops made under licence by group led by SNECMA of France.

MAXIMUM SPEED 658km/h (409mph).

SERVICE CEILING **1:** 10km (32,800ft), **ANG:** 9·1km (29,850ft).

RANGE 9000km (5,590 miles).

MILITARY LOAD Internal bay can accommodate all standard NATO bombs, mines, depth charges or torpedoes, typical loads being up to 12 depth charges, nine mines or eight Mk 46 torpedoes; two AM 39 missiles can be launched, supplemented by four more launched from wing pylons which add a further 3500kg (7,715lb) to weapon weight; rear fuselage houses up to 78 sonobuoys.

USERS France, Germany (Federal Republic), Italy, Netherlands, Pakistan.

SEPECAT Jaguar

One of the most cost-effective attack aircraft of modern times, the Jaguar was developed to meet a joint need of the French Armée de l'Air and British RAF for a supersonic trainer and light attack aircraft in 1965. In May 1966 the joint SEPECAT company was formed by the industrial partners BAC (since replaced by British Aerospace) and Breguet (since replaced by Dassault-Breguet), the augmented turbofan engines being assigned to a joint company formed by Rolls-Royce and Turboméca. The basis for the aircraft was the Br 121, but—mainly at the instigation of Britain—this was developed into an aircraft which, although no larger, was able to carry more than four times the military load plus all-weather avionics. As a result the Jaguar became far more important as an attack aircraft than as a trainer, a role for which augmented engines and supersonic performance are not justifiable.

The first to fly was a French Jaguar E (trainer) on 8 September 1968, followed by the Jaguar A (French single-seat attack), Jaguar S (RAF attack), Jaguar B (RAF trainer) and, for export customers, the first Jaguar International in August 1976. The basic aircraft has a small high-mounted wing with high-lift leading-edge slats and full-span double-slotted flaps, lateral control being by means of spoilers. The two small engines are fed by plain lateral inlets, and the landing gear has twin wheels throughout and is designed for operations from rough front-line airstrips. An RAF Jaguar has been landed on an incomplete section of motorway, and it took off again with full bombload.

The French Jaguars were handicapped by being deliberately austerely equipped, with a twin-gyro platform and doppler in place of the full inertial system of the RAF Jaguar S, and lacking the latter's chisel nose with a laser. Later a CSF laser ranger was added, together with a computer for Martel missiles, and, in the last 30 of the 160 Jaguar As, an Atlis II pod on the centreline pylon with a laser and a TV camera aligned with it, for use with the AS.30L missile and various precision-guided bombs. About one-third of the As have a panoramic camera in the nose for 180° horizon-to-horizon coverage.

The RAF Jaguar S, designated Jaguar GR.1, has full digital/inertial navigation and weapon aiming, and can also carry a flush-fitting reconnaissance pallet on the underside of the fuselage with cameras and infra-red linescan. Other equipment includes a HUD (head-up display), projected map display, and a retractable flight-refuelling probe. The RAF received 165 of this version, as well as 38 two-seat T.2s with only one gun; the 40 French two-seaters retain both guns.

Manufacture was shared: Britain built the wings, tail, inlets and rear fuselage and France the front and mid-fuselage sections. RAF Jaguars were assembled at Warton and French aircraft at Toulouse. All 402 aircraft for the original customers were delivered by late 1981. Many have since been updated; the RAF GR.1s have all received more powerful engines and upgraded avionics.

Sadly for the programme the French partner, taken over by Dassault in 1971, has since promoted the Mirage instead of Jaguar, but despite this the type has been sold to Ecuador (12), Oman (24) and India (18 leased from the RAF, 40 supplied from Britain and 45 assembled in India from British components). All export aircraft are Jaguar Internationals with uprated engines and a wide range of customer options for avionics and weapons. A maritime strike version is available, and all models can have Magic or other close-range missiles carried on overwing pylons.

Lack of money has curtailed possible major improvements to the RAF Jaguars. Current planning is to withdraw the type in 1987, although a life-extension programme now appears likely in view of absence of a replacement. BAe is making a carbon-fibre wing of greater area, and in partnership with Marconi Avionics and Dowty has also flown one of the world's most advanced 'fly-by-wire' flight control systems with quadruplicated signalling and no mechanical back-up. This Jaguar is now flying in a deliberately de-stabilized condition to assist the design of future fighters.

COUNTRIES OF ORIGIN Great Britain/France jointly.

CREW Attack: 1, trainers: 2.

TOTAL PRODUCED About 485, of 550 plus, by late 1982.

DIMENSIONS Wingspan 8·69m (28ft 6in); length, including probe, **A/S/International:** 16·83m (55ft 2½in), **B/E:** 17·53m (57ft 6¼in); wing area 24·18m² (260·27ft²).

WEIGHTS Empty, typical: 7000kg (15,432lb); maximum loaded 15700kg (34,612lb).

ENGINES Two Rolls-Royce Turboméca Adour augmented turbofans, **A/E:** 3314kg (7,305lb) Adour 102, **B/S/early exports:** 3647kg (8,040lb) Adour 804, **International:** 3810kg (8,400lb) Adour 811.

MAXIMUM SPEED At sea level: 1350km/h (840mph, Mach 1·1); at 11km (36,000ft): 1699km/h (1,056mph, Mach 1·6).

SERVICE CEILING Over 13·7km (45,000ft).

RANGE Typical attack radius, external tanks: 1408km (875 miles), ferry range: 3524km (2,190 miles).

MILITARY LOAD Two (RAF **T.2** trainer: 1) 30mm guns (Aden in RAF, DEFA in French and most export); total of 4763kg (10,500lb) of external stores carried on five pylons (fuselage centreline plus two under each wing) including almost complete range of British or French bombs, tanks, pods and ECM and AS.30L or Martel AS.37 missiles (cleared also to use other missiles including Harpoon); **International** has overwing pylons for Magic or other close-range AAMs.

USERS Ecuador, France, Great Britain (RAF), India, Oman.

XZ 368

XZ 368

EL

EL

XZ 101

S

0   4m

SEPECAT Jaguar GR.1

Except for the drawing at lower left (opposite page) the subject on these pages is a Jaguar GR.1 of No 6 Sqn, based at RAF Coltishall, Norfolk, in 38 Group. No 6 gained the nickname 'The Can Openers' from their exploits in the Western Desert in 1942 with Hurricane IIDs armed with 40mm guns that could pierce Rommel's armour. The can-opener badge is displayed on the engine inlet, and a zigzag marking is painted on the ARI.18223 passive radar-warning receiver installation near the top of the fin. External load shown in some views comprises two 1200-litre (264 gal, 317 US gal) drop tanks and two 454kg (1,000lb) GP bombs. The side elevation below shows the tandem centreline pylon installed but not loaded. Two views show the neat flight-refuelling probe extended.

Opposite page, below, is a Jaguar GR.1 from No 2 (written II) Squadron, which operates from RAF Laarbruch, Germany, in the tactical reconnaissance role. Optical cameras and an infra-red sensor are carried in the large ventral pod, but this can quickly be removed for operations in the strike role. Note the open canopy and airbrakes, and the tough long-stroke landing gear suitable for rough unsurfaced runways.

SEPECAT Jaguar

A.03 was the first single-seater to fly (on 29 March 1969) and differed from production A-series Jaguars in such respects as the straight top to the fuselage and the splitter plates inboard of the inlets. A carrier-based version was also flown but cancelled by France.

The final 30 Jaguar As (single-seat attack model for the Armée de l'Air) have been fitted with the Atlis II laser target designation pod (which also has a TV acquisition capability) and can carry the AS.30L laser-homing missile. It is possible all 160 Jaguar A aircraft may be thus equipped.

This Jaguar T.2 from RAF No 31 Sqn at Brüggen, Germany, is one of 38 two-seaters supplied to the RAF as squadron conversion and weapons trainers, with considerable combat capability. Only one gun is carried, and neither the nose laser nor fin-mounted passive warning receivers are fitted.

The Armée de l'Air's EC 1/7, based at St Dizier, was the first unit to equip with the Jaguar E (École), the initial two-seat training version. A total of 40 was delivered, with twin 30mm DEFA guns but austere avionics. The only external load depicted is two 1200-litre (264 gal, 317 US gal) tanks.

Ecuador purchased 12 Jaguars, ten of them single-seat versions based on the RAF Jaguar GR.1 and fitted with almost identical avionics. They were delivered in early 1977 and replaced aged F-80s. External loads shown here include tandem BL.755 cluster bombs, two tanks and two Matra 155 rocket launchers each with 18 SNEB rockets.

156

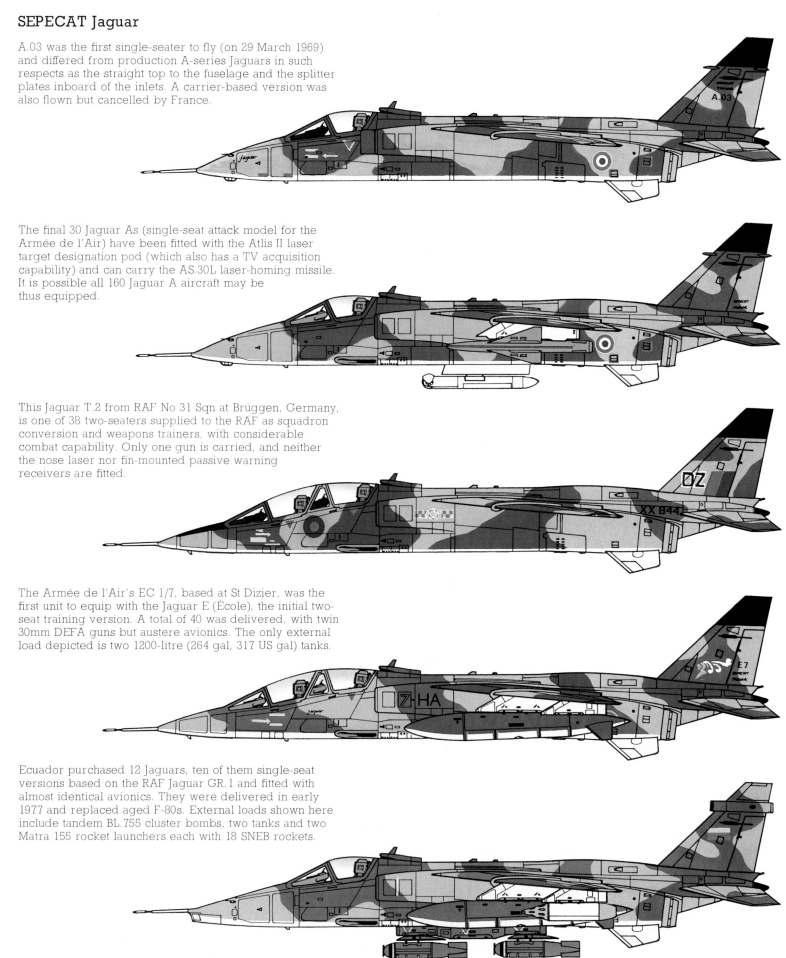

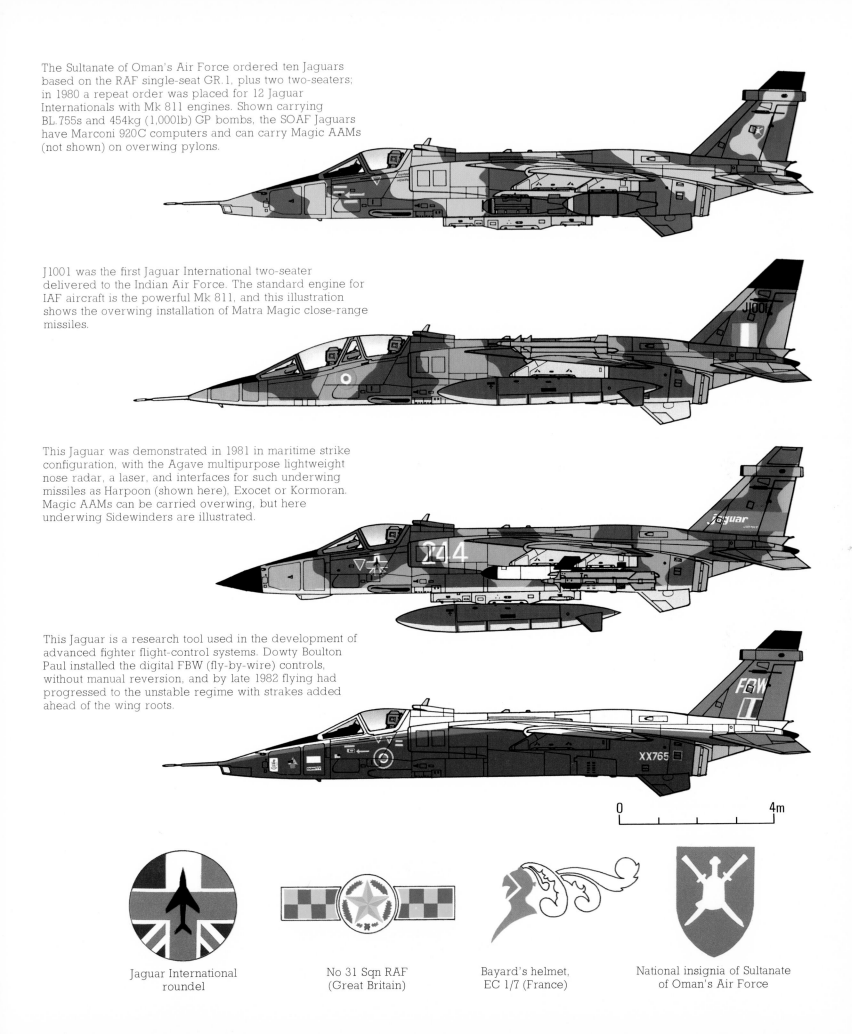

The Sultanate of Oman's Air Force ordered ten Jaguars based on the RAF single-seat GR.1, plus two two-seaters; in 1980 a repeat order was placed for 12 Jaguar Internationals with Mk 811 engines. Shown carrying BL.755s and 454kg (1,000lb) GP bombs, the SOAF Jaguars have Marconi 920C computers and can carry Magic AAMs (not shown) on overwing pylons.

J1001 was the first Jaguar International two-seater delivered to the Indian Air Force. The standard engine for IAF aircraft is the powerful Mk 811, and this illustration shows the overwing installation of Matra Magic close-range missiles.

This Jaguar was demonstrated in 1981 in maritime strike configuration, with the Agave multipurpose lightweight nose radar, a laser, and interfaces for such underwing missiles as Harpoon (shown here), Exocet or Kormoran. Magic AAMs can be carried overwing, but here underwing Sidewinders are illustrated.

This Jaguar is a research tool used in the development of advanced fighter flight-control systems. Dowty Boulton Paul installed the digital FBW (fly-by-wire) controls, without manual reversion, and by late 1982 flying had progressed to the unstable regime with strakes added ahead of the wing roots.

0   4m

Jaguar International roundel

No 31 Sqn RAF (Great Britain)

Bayard's helmet, EC 1/7 (France)

National insignia of Sultanate of Oman's Air Force

Until 1981 it was thought that this Chinese fighter-bomber was built at Shenyang, and it was often called A-5 in the West (earlier it was mistakenly dubbed 'Type 6B'). It is now known to be in production at the Nanzhang (Nancheng) factory, and its designation is Q-5, from Qianjiji (attack aircraft). Derived from the J-6 (Chinese-built MiG-19PF, see overleaf). it has an internal bomb bay, longer fuselage, which provides increased internal capacity for fuel behind the redesigned cockpit and avionics in the nose, and a slightly extended wing able to carry a considerably greater external weapon load. These illustrations also show the larger vertical tail, twin canted ventrals and completely new doors for the nose landing gear, which remain open after the gear is extended. The side elevation below shows a camouflage scheme first seen during the war with Vietnam in 1979. The other views show the more common natural metal finish with 250kg (551lb) bombs on the external body pylons and (facing page) S-5 type pods for seven 57mm rockets. All views show 800-litre (176 gal, 211 US gal) drop tanks.

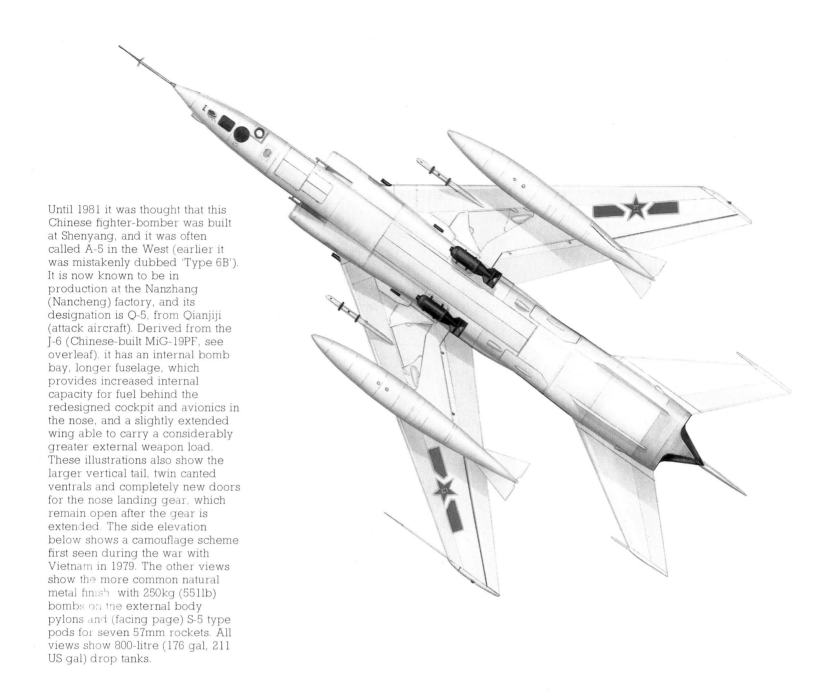

20690

0   4m

Nanzhang Q-5

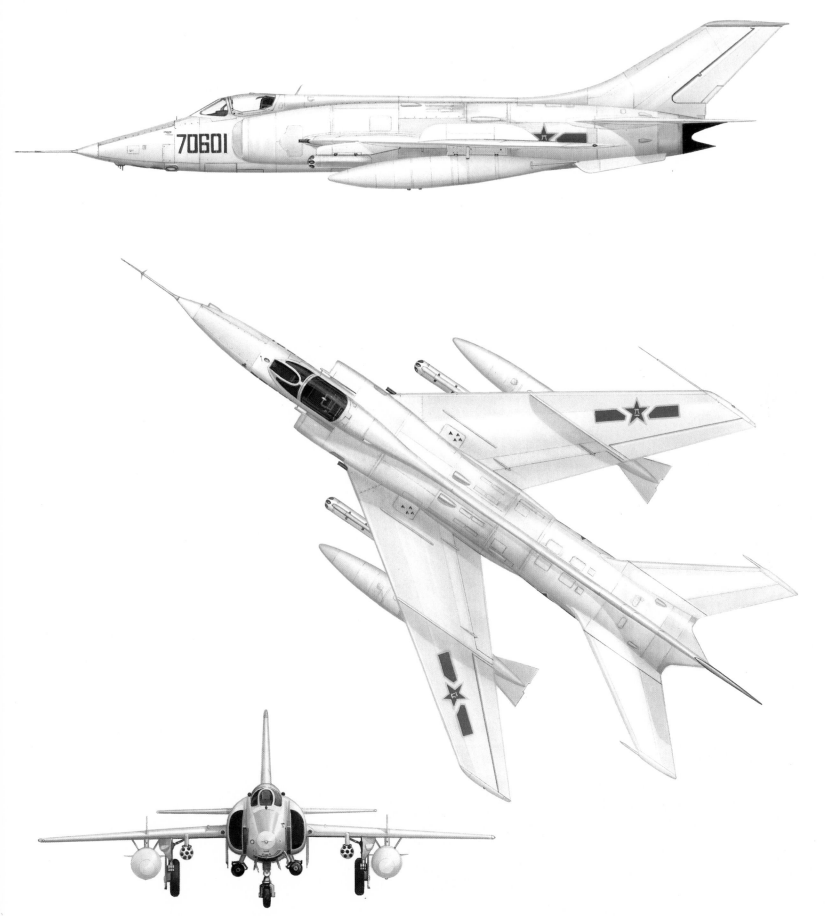

Shenyang J-6 and Nanzhang Q-5

The Chinese Air Force of the People's Liberation Army still uses a considerable number of the basic J-6 (Jianjiji-6, fighter type 6), which is a day fighter equivalent to the MiG-19SF. A minority which appears to be distributed throughout the 33-odd regiments have their beautifully finished skin painted with a camouflage scheme as shown. About 10 per cent are JZ-6 reconnaissance models.

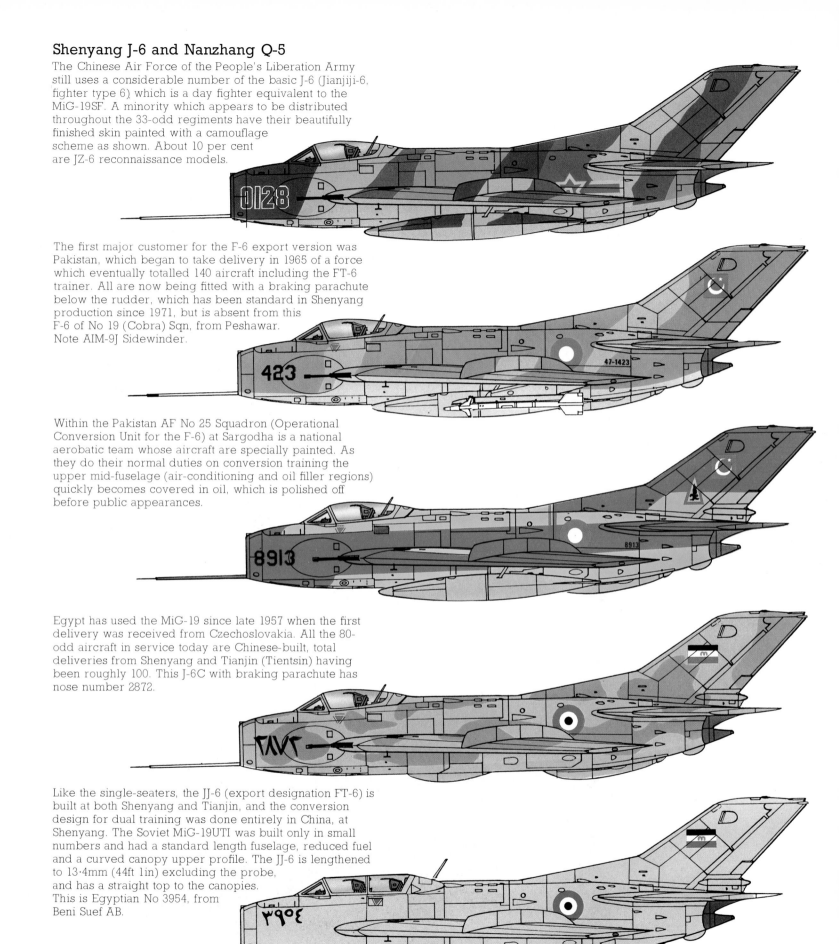

The first major customer for the F-6 export version was Pakistan, which began to take delivery in 1965 of a force which eventually totalled 140 aircraft including the FT-6 trainer. All are now being fitted with a braking parachute below the rudder, which has been standard in Shenyang production since 1971, but is absent from this F-6 of No 19 (Cobra) Sqn, from Peshawar. Note AIM-9J Sidewinder.

Within the Pakistan AF No 25 Squadron (Operational Conversion Unit for the F-6) at Sargodha is a national aerobatic team whose aircraft are specially painted. As they do their normal duties on conversion training the upper mid-fuselage (air-conditioning and oil filler regions) quickly becomes covered in oil, which is polished off before public appearances.

Egypt has used the MiG-19 since late 1957 when the first delivery was received from Czechoslovakia. All the 80-odd aircraft in service today are Chinese-built, total deliveries from Shenyang and Tianjin (Tientsin) having been roughly 100. This J-6C with braking parachute has nose number 2872.

Like the single-seaters, the JJ-6 (export designation FT-6) is built at both Shenyang and Tianjin, and the conversion design for dual training was done entirely in China, at Shenyang. The Soviet MiG-19UTI was built only in small numbers and had a standard length fuselage, reduced fuel and a curved canopy upper profile. The JJ-6 is lengthened to 13·4mm (44ft 1in) excluding the probe, and has a straight top to the canopies. This is Egyptian No 3954, from Beni Suef AB.

160

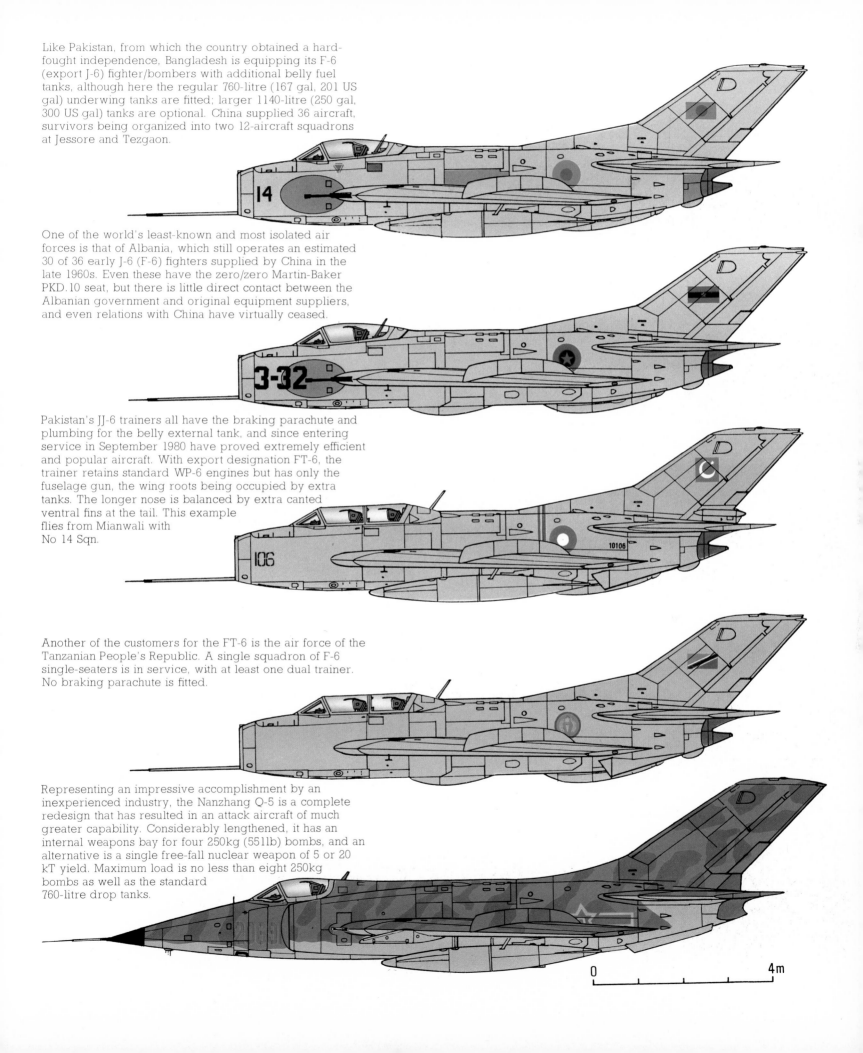

Like Pakistan, from which the country obtained a hard-fought independence, Bangladesh is equipping its F-6 (export J-6) fighter/bombers with additional belly fuel tanks, although here the regular 760-litre (167 gal, 201 US gal) underwing tanks are fitted; larger 1140-litre (250 gal, 300 US gal) tanks are optional. China supplied 36 aircraft, survivors being organized into two 12-aircraft squadrons at Jessore and Tezgaon.

One of the world's least-known and most isolated air forces is that of Albania, which still operates an estimated 30 of 36 early J-6 (F-6) fighters supplied by China in the late 1960s. Even these have the zero/zero Martin-Baker PKD.10 seat, but there is little direct contact between the Albanian government and original equipment suppliers, and even relations with China have virtually ceased.

Pakistan's JJ-6 trainers all have the braking parachute and plumbing for the belly external tank, and since entering service in September 1980 have proved extremely efficient and popular aircraft. With export designation FT-6, the trainer retains standard WP-6 engines but has only the fuselage gun, the wing roots being occupied by extra tanks. The longer nose is balanced by extra canted ventral fins at the tail. This example flies from Mianwali with No 14 Sqn.

Another of the customers for the FT-6 is the air force of the Tanzanian People's Republic. A single squadron of F-6 single-seaters is in service, with at least one dual trainer. No braking parachute is fitted.

Representing an impressive accomplishment by an inexperienced industry, the Nanzhang Q-5 is a complete redesign that has resulted in an attack aircraft of much greater capability. Considerably lengthened, it has an internal weapons bay for four 250kg (551lb) bombs, and an alternative is a single free-fall nuclear weapon of 5 or 20 kT yield. Maximum load is no less than eight 250kg bombs as well as the standard 760-litre drop tanks.

0   4m

Shenyang J-6 and Nanzhang Q-5

When the team of engineers at the Mikoyan/Guryevich OKB (experimental design collective, or bureau) in the Soviet Union began work on their I-350 fighter in 1951 they little thought that derivatives of this aircraft would be in production in China more than 30 years later. In fact, although the MiG-19, as the production I-350 was called, soon faded from the scene in the land of its birth, its great qualities were better recognized by the Chinese and used to support an outstandingly successful programme that has seen Chinese-built aircraft exported for the first time.

There are several reasons for the longevity of this classic basic design, which in parallel with the North American F-100 was the first supersonic military aircraft in the world. Its wing was a technical *tour de force*, with leading edge swept back at almost 60° yet with a slender form leading to an almost pointed tip. Combining this shape with powered ailerons in the usual outboard location was bold in the extreme; the F-100 designers put their ailerons inboard (prohibiting the use of flaps) because they were afraid of the wing twisting. Another good feature was the engine, a particularly neat axial turbojet designed by S.K. Tumanskii at the Mikulin OKB. After his boss Mikulin's political disgrace in 1956 Tumanskii took over and developed this engine (its designation was then changed from AM-5 to R-9) into a series used in all subsequent MiGs and many other types, made in thousands. The engine was so slim that two could be used with less frontal area than the single British-derived engine used in the earlier MiG-15 and -17. A third plus was the hard-hitting 30mm gun.

Taken together these and other factors added up to an air-combat fighter of no mean capability. But in the Soviet Union the fact that the small delta-wing MiG-21 was faster caused the MiG-19 to be phased out of production in about 1958, and most countries then regarded it as becoming obsolete. Mach-2 fighters were all the rage, and few people noticed that in 1958 China signed a licence to make the MiG-19 in

versions corresponding to three Soviet originals: the basic 19SF day fighter/bomber, the 19PF interceptor with only two guns and with all-weather radar, and the 19PM with four missiles instead of guns.

The Chinese called the type the J-6, from Jianjiji (fighter). The workmanship on the J-6 variants was superb, and new versions designed in China (different from Soviet counterparts) include the FT-6 trainer with two side-hinged canopies and a reconnaissance version with cameras filling the underside of the nose. In 1965 Pakistan began building up a force of J-6s: it was here that Western observers encountered the type and quickly reappraised it. Its great performance and manoeuvrability, and the devastating firepower of its guns, made a deep impression. Later Pakistan J-6s were fitted with underbelly tanks and Sidewinder missiles, and in some air forces, including the Egyptian, British equipment has been introduced.

During the 1960s China studied ways of increasing the potential of this great basic design and by 1970 had produced the Q-5 (Qianjiji, attack aircraft). This has an extended fuselage with an internal bomb bay—today rare but, in the view of the Chinese, essential for a modern attack machine—and a redesigned nose which in some Q-5s is fitted with a multi-mode radar. Most have only small ranging radar but are progressively being fitted with improved navigation and weapon-aiming systems, including a twin-gyro platform, doppler, laser ranger and reconnaissance camera.

The new nose necessitated the use of lateral air inlets. The cockpit lies between these, moved well forward of the wing making room for the bomb bay below and extra fuel above. The canopy is of the hinged clamshell type (on the MiG-19/J-6 it slides), and other new features include extended wings with kinked trailing edges, a modified tail and six pylons for external stores. At press time the precise engines of the Q-5 remained unknown, but the author's opinion is that the increase in weight makes a more powerful unit, such as the Chinese-built R-11, essential.

COUNTRY OF ORIGIN J-6: Soviet Union, made in China; Q-5: China.

CREW Fighters: 1, trainers: 2.

TOTAL PRODUCED Estimated, MiG-19: 4,000, J-6: 5,000, Q-5: 500 by 1982.

DIMENSIONS Wingspan, J-6: 9·2m (30ft 2¼in), Q-5: 10·2m (33ft 5in); length, J-6 (excluding probe): 12·6m (41ft 4in), Q-5: 15·25m (50ft 0in); wing area, J-6: 25m² (269ft²), Q-5: unknown but about 28m² (300ft²).

WEIGHTS Empty, J-6: 5760kg (12,700lb), Q-5: estimated 6200kg (13,670lb); maximum loaded, J-6: 8700kg (19,180lb), Q-5: estimated 10700kg (23,590lb).

ENGINES Two augmented turbojets, J-6: 3250kg (7,165lb) WP-6 (based on R-9BF), Q-5: unknown but higher thrust.

MAXIMUM SPEED Clean, high-altitude, J-6: 1452km/h (902mph, Mach 1·365), Q-5: estimated 1435km/h (890mph, Mach 1·346).

SERVICE CEILING J-6: 17·9km (58,725ft), Q-5: about 16km (52,500ft).

RANGE J-6 combat radius, hi-lo-hi with two 800-litre (176 gal, 211 US gal) tanks, 686km (426 miles), Q-5: same mission plus four 250kg (551lb) bombs internal, 650km (404 miles).

MILITARY LOAD J-6: three NR-30 guns (only two on interceptor and none on FT-6), six pylons for load of 1400kg (3,086lb) including two tanks of up to 1520-litre (334 gal, 402 US gal) size, plus two 250kg bombs plus two Sidewinder AAMs; Q-5: two NR-30 guns, four 250kg bombs in internal bay, two 250kg on belly pylons, two 250kg or two S-5 pods each for seven 57mm rockets on inboard wing pylons, plus two 800- or 1520-litre tanks or two 1000kg (2,205lb) bombs outboard; maximum bombload 4000kg (8,818lb).

USERS J-6: Albania, Bangladesh, China, Egypt, Kampuchea, Pakistan, Tanzania, Vietnam, Zambia; Q-5: China, Pakistan.

Sukhoi Su-7/-17/-22

It is commonly said of the Russians that they never throw anything away. It is certainly true that, having developed something that works, they will go on building and improving it rather than take the risk of designing something new as a replacement. Thus, when in the mid-1950s the Sukhoi OKB (design bureau) produced a new attack aircraft, it was reasonably certain to last for several years with the FA (frontal aviation, the vast tactical attack arm of the Soviet air forces). What was unexpected was that it would keep on being improved even into the 1980s, so that new models are still pouring off the assembly line!

Pavel O. Sukhoi had had a run of bad luck in the late 1940s and his OKB was shut by Stalin's command. On Stalin's death in 1953 Sukhoi was allowed to reopen, and this coincided with the development by TsAGI, the national aerodynamic laboratory, of two shapes which appeared to be the best for future supersonic aircraft. One had an acutely swept wing (62° on the leading edge) and the other a pure delta. In both cases the configuration had a conventional swept horizontal tail. Like Mikoyan, Sukhoi was instructed to design supersonic aircraft to both shapes, but Sukhoi's were considerably larger, matched to the powerful AL-7 augmented turbojet by Arkhip Lyul'ka. The T-series deltas are discussed in the next entry in this book. The S-series swept-wing aircraft eventually led to the Su-7 (service designation) of 1957, which went into production as the standard attack aircraft of the FA.

Superficially the Su-7 resembled its delta sisters, except for the wing, but internal equipment was very different. The aircraft was of considerable size, almost in the class of the mighty American F-105, and from the start was not only beautifully made but also a joy to fly. Handling at all speeds was smooth, precise and viceless, and despite the fixed leading edge and short-span area-increasing flaps the landing speed was modest. Like all FA aircraft the Su-7 was intended to be capable of operation from rough airstrips, and it was typically Russian in its tough simplicity. The only real fault was that there was room inside for a mere 3970 litres (873 gal, 1049 US gal) of fuel, and with a very large augmented engine this meant that the twin drop tanks almost always had to be carried on the fuselage pylons—making the air/ground ordnance load trivial.

Despite this, very large numbers of Su-7s were made, followed by the 7U trainer, 7BKL with soft-field skids added, 7BM with increased power and 7BMK with take-off rockets and braking parachutes for off-airfield operation.

In the early 1960s the current vogue for variable-sweep aircraft led Sukhoi to produce the Su-7IG (IG is the Russian abbreviation for variable-geometry), with OKB designation S-22I. It used another TsAGI scheme, intended for application to existing swept-wing types, in which only the outer part of the wing was pivoted. This seemed to the West hardly worth doing, and nobody was surprised when the 7IG shown at the 1967 Aviation Day appeared to sink without trace. But in 1972 pictures appeared of developed 7IGs in squadron strength!

Sukhoi had combined the swing-wing with still more power and improved nav/attack avionics to produce a new family with designations Su-17, -20 and -22. Even the earliest -17 can carry twice the bombload of any Su-7, fly out of an airstrip little more than half as long and attack a target 30 per cent further away! But even the realization in the West of the magnitude of the improvement gave no inkling of the prolonged further increase in capability that the Sukhoi bureau (led by Ye.A. Ivanov since Sukhoi's death in 1975) has achieved. With first the AL-21F-3 and now the Tumanskii R-29B engine, the latest versions (whose designations are unknown) include single- and two-seaters with a wealth of new avionics for precision all-weather attack, much extra fuel in large dorsal fairings, redesigned vertical tails, better pilot view ahead, a wider range of ordnance items and extremely comprehensive electronic-warfare systems. (See also the next-generation Su-24, page 182.)

(See also the next-generation Su-24, page 182.)

COUNTRY OF ORIGIN Soviet Union.

CREW Most: 1, trainers: 2.

TOTAL PRODUCED Probably more than 3,500.

DIMENSIONS Wingspan, **7**: 8·93m (29ft 3½in), **17**, **'Fitter-J'** (swept 28°): 14·0m (45ft 11¼in), (swept 62°): 10·6m (34ft 9½in); length, including probe, **7BMK**: 17·37m (57ft 0in), **17**: 18·75m (61ft 6¼in); wing area, **7**: about 30m² (323ft²), **17**, **'Fitter-J'** (swept 28°): 40·1m² (431·6ft²). 'Fitter-J' is NATO name for Su-22.

WEIGHTS Empty, **7**: about 8620kg (19,000lb), **17**: about 10000kg (22,050lb), **'Fitter-J'**: about 10800kg (23,800lb); maximum loaded, **7**: 13500kg (29,750lb), **17**: about 17700kg (39,020lb), **'Fitter-J'**: about 20000kg (44,090lb).

ENGINE **7**: one 9000kg (19,841lb) Lyul'ka AL-7 augmented turbojet, **7BM/BMK/UMK**: 10000kg (22,046lb) AL-7F-1, **17**: one 11200kg (24,690lb) Lyul'ka AL-21F-3 augmented turbojet, **'Fitter-J'** and several other late models: one 11500kg (25,350lb) Tumanskii R-29B augmented turbofan.

MAXIMUM SPEED **7**, clean at high altitude: 1700km/h (1,055mph, Mach 1·6), **17**, **'Fitter-J'**: 2310km/h (1,434mph, Mach 2·17).

SERVICE CEILING **7**: 15·15km (49,700ft), **17**, **'Fitter-J'**: 18km (59,050ft).

RANGE **7**: 1450km (900 miles), **17**: 2250km (1,400 miles), **'Fitter-J'**: about 2500km (1,550 miles).

MILITARY LOAD **7**: two 30mm NR-30 guns, four external pylons for two 750kg (1,650lb) and two 500kg (1,102lb) bombs, or equivalent loads of rocket pods or other stores, but more often two drop tanks plus two bombs of 500kg (1,102lb); **17** and later versions including **'Fitter-J'**: two NR-30s each with 70 rounds, plus eight external pylons for total of 4000kg (8,820lb) of bombs, rockets or missiles such as AS-7 Kerry.

USERS See pages 164/165.

USERS See pages 164/165.

Sukhoi Su-7/-17/-20/-22
(continued from page 163)
USERS **7:** Afghanistan, Algeria,
Czechoslovakia, Egypt, Hungary,
India, Iraq, North Korea, Poland,
Romania, Soviet Union, Syria,
Vietnam, Yemen (South); **17/20/22:**
Algeria, Czechoslovakia, Egypt,
Germany (Democratic Republic),
India, Iraq, Libya, Peru, Poland,
Soviet Union, Syria, Vietnam, Yemen
(North and South).

0   4m

Sukhoi Su-22 Fitter-J

Known to NATO forces as Fitter-J, this Sukhoi swing-wing attack aircraft of the Libyan Arab Republic air force is believed to be a version of the Su-22, but there is no clear understanding in the West of the true designations of aircraft in the Su-17, -20 and -22 family. This model is one of the advanced single-seat versions with a large dorsal spine (believed to contain fuel), taller fin and added ventral fin, an augmented avionics suite (although nothing like as comprehensive as that of aircraft of the Soviet Frontal Aviation) and a Tumanskii R-29B turbofan engine of 11500kg (25,350lb) thrust. As usual these illustrations show the aircraft with the wings at both extremes of sweep (leading-edge angles of 28° opposite and 62° at right), two of the views showing AA-2 'Atoll' AAMs and 800-litre (176 gal, 211 US gal) drop tanks. Bomb or air/surface missile loads of up to 4000kg (8,820lb) can be carried on the eight pylons, and two 30mm guns are retained.

Sukhoi Su-7/-17/-20/-22

Big, enjoyable to fly, and extremely strong and reliable, the Su-7 at all times has been popular with its pilots. The Su-7BM introduced duct fairings along the fuselage, twin brake parachutes below the rudder, an uprated engine, tail warning radar, a zero/zero seat and many other additions. This BM is Algerian, one of four squadrons supporting Polisario guerrillas.

Egypt received over 150 Su-7 single-seaters, but many were lost in accidents or in action, and the 60 remaining are only gradually being restored to active status and fitted with new (mainly Western) avionics. This BM at Katamia airbase is shown with twin tanks and UV-16-57 rocket pods.

The Su-7UM conversion trainer is used in Egypt to prepare pupils for both the Su-7BM and the small force of 19 swing-wing Su-20s. The instructor and pupil both have clamshell canopies; the former has his own sloping windscreens and bulged side panels giving a better view than the pupil in front!

Another big recipient of the massive Sukhoi was India, whose air force took at least 140. Today only two squadrons remain, although the type is popular. This BM serves with No 222 'The Killers' squadron, which like rival No 32 sports numerous colour schemes, including fins painted orange, or in red/white stripes, or left unpainted.

Indian Su-7UM trainers are unpainted, except for a handful still showing the last vestiges of former camouflage. They have two NR-30 guns, but lack air-conditioning for the hot climate and have even less fuel than the single-seaters. Mission endurance, always an Su-7 problem, is thus extremely poor.

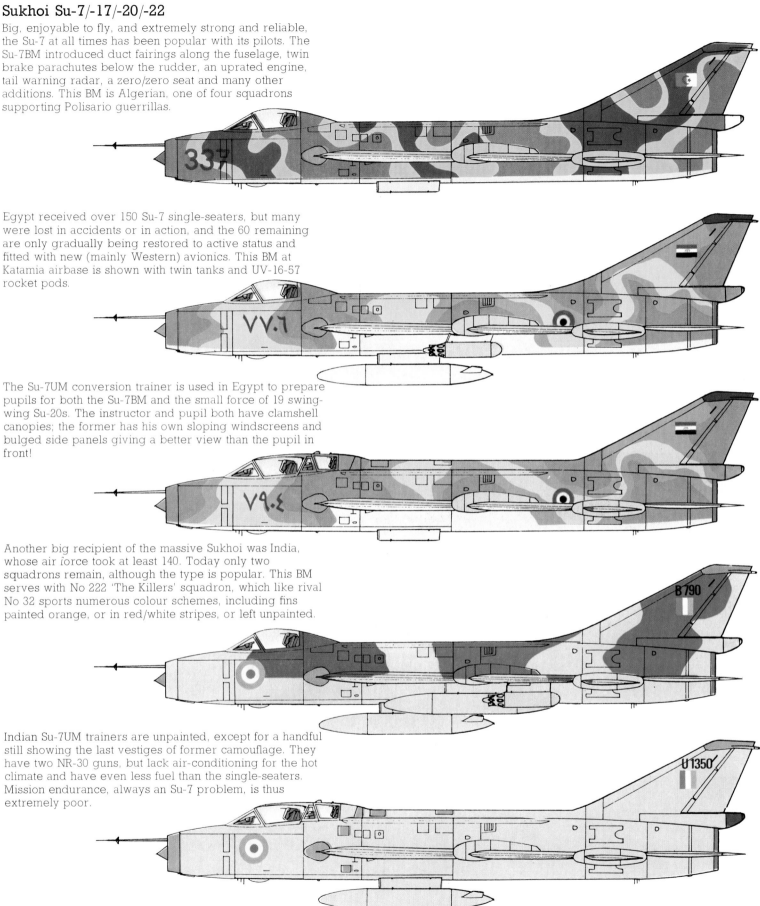

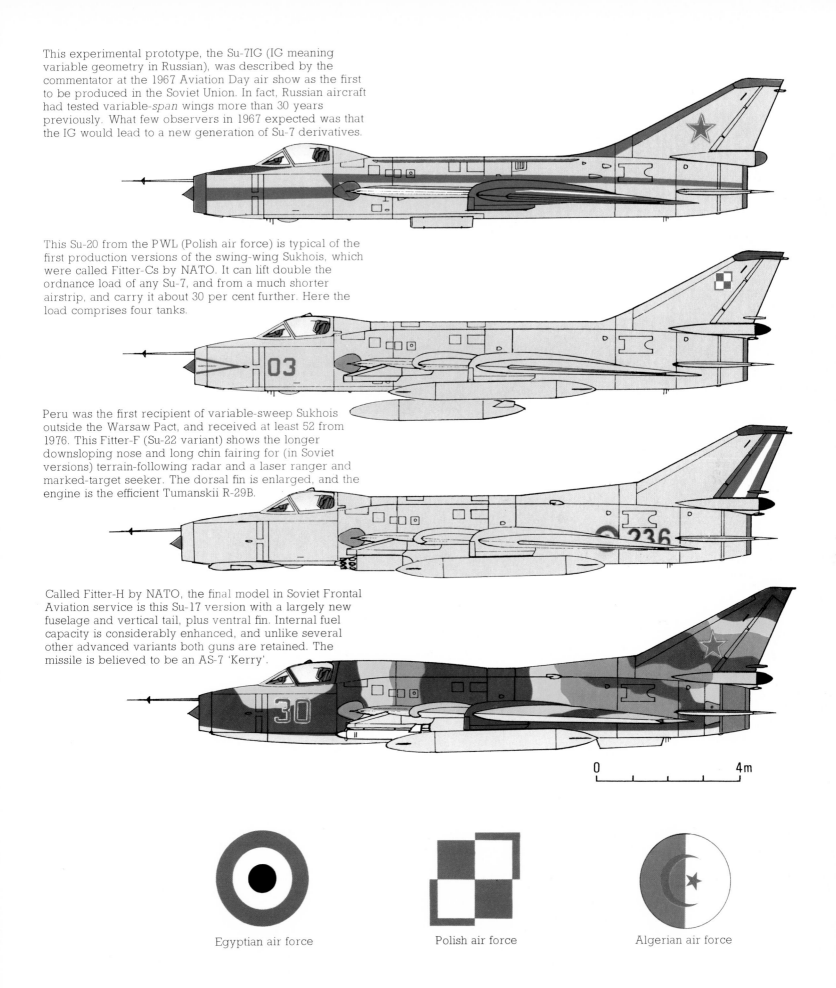

This experimental prototype, the Su-7IG (IG meaning variable geometry in Russian), was described by the commentator at the 1967 Aviation Day air show as the first to be produced in the Soviet Union. In fact, Russian aircraft had tested variable-*span* wings more than 30 years previously. What few observers in 1967 expected was that the IG would lead to a new generation of Su-7 derivatives.

This Su-20 from the PWL (Polish air force) is typical of the first production versions of the swing-wing Sukhois, which were called Fitter-Cs by NATO. It can lift double the ordnance load of any Su-7, and from a much shorter airstrip, and carry it about 30 per cent further. Here the load comprises four tanks.

Peru was the first recipient of variable-sweep Sukhois outside the Warsaw Pact, and received at least 52 from 1976. This Fitter-F (Su-22 variant) shows the longer downsloping nose and long chin fairing for (in Soviet versions) terrain-following radar and a laser ranger and marked-target seeker. The dorsal fin is enlarged, and the engine is the efficient Tumanskii R-29B.

Called Fitter-H by NATO, the final model in Soviet Frontal Aviation service is this Su-17 version with a largely new fuselage and vertical tail, plus ventral fin. Internal fuel capacity is considerably enhanced, and unlike several other advanced variants both guns are retained. The missile is believed to be an AS-7 'Kerry'.

0   4m

Egyptian air force

Polish air force

Algerian air force

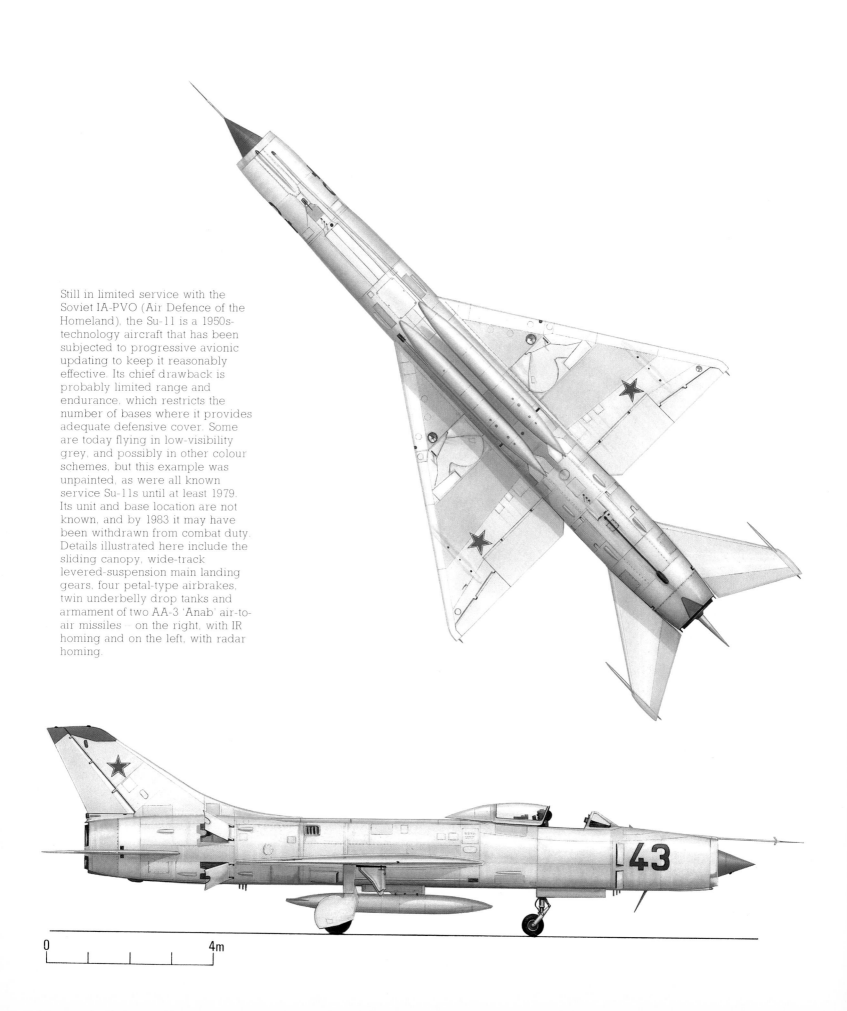

Still in limited service with the Soviet IA-PVO (Air Defence of the Homeland), the Su-11 is a 1950s-technology aircraft that has been subjected to progressive avionic updating to keep it reasonably effective. Its chief drawback is probably limited range and endurance, which restricts the number of bases where it provides adequate defensive cover. Some are today flying in low-visibility grey, and possibly in other colour schemes, but this example was unpainted, as were all known service Su-11s until at least 1979. Its unit and base location are not known, and by 1983 it may have been withdrawn from combat duty. Details illustrated here include the sliding canopy, wide-track levered-suspension main landing gears, four petal-type airbrakes, twin underbelly drop tanks and armament of two AA-3 'Anab' air-to-air missiles — on the right, with IR homing and on the left, with radar homing.

0   4m

Sukhoi Su-11

Sukhoi Su-9/-11

The first prototype built by the reconstituted Sukhoi OKB in 1954–5 was the T-1 (T for Tre-oogolnyi, three-angled, i.e. delta). This was refined in 1956 into the T-3 illustrated, with a wide oval inlet and broad wedge above.

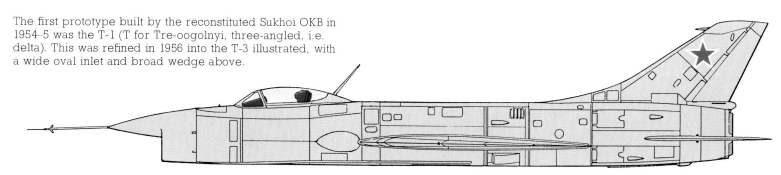

Sukhoi's team had great difficulty trying to design a nose inlet with variable geometry and space for radar. In the T-7 research prototype the inlet was two-dimensional, with pivoted upper and lower lips.

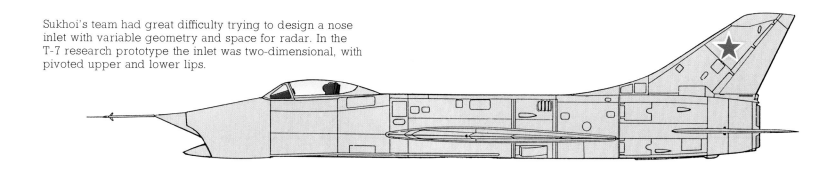

In the PT-8 (P for Perekhvatchik, interceptor) a conical centrebody was added for R1L radar, but the initial flying was done without variable geometry, in early 1958.

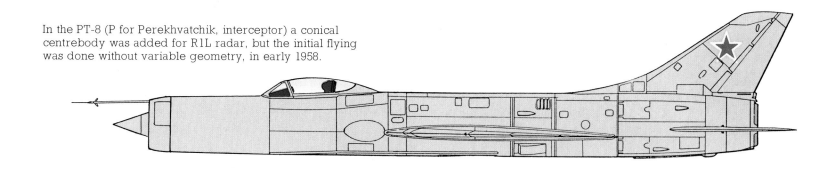

Fastest of all the early Sukhoi T-series prototypes was the T-37, which had a variable multi-shock inlet and larger afterburner with convergent/divergent nozzle. The related T-431 set various world records.

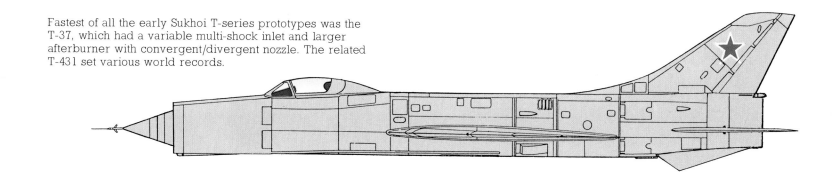

By 1960 Sukhoi could confidently design what became the Su-9 all-weather interceptor, produced in quantity for the PVO. The AL-7F engine was fed by an inlet very similar to that of the Su-7, with the small Izumrud radar, and four obsolescent AA-1 missiles.

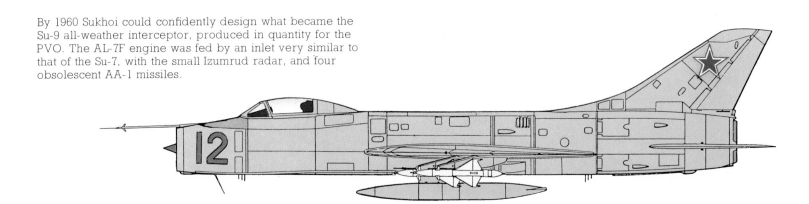

Pilot conversion to the Su-9 was assisted by the tandem dual Su-9U trainer, which retained radar and (seldom fitted) provision for missiles, but had even less fuel. NATO name is Maiden; the interceptor is dubbed Fishpot.

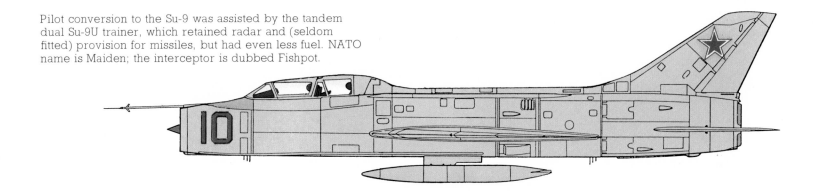

By 1967 the Su-9 had been replaced in production by the Su-11, with the more powerful AL-7F-1 engine and new radar (Uragan 5B) and weapons (AA-3 and AA-8). To accommodate the radar the inlet was enlarged and lengthened.

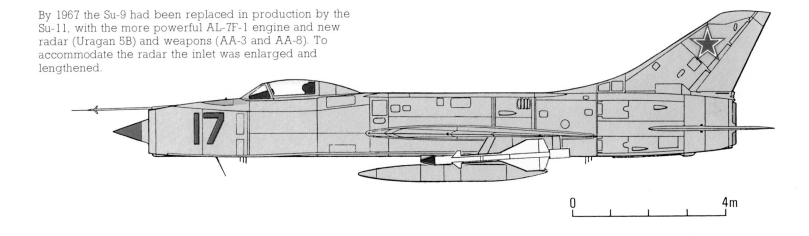

0   4m

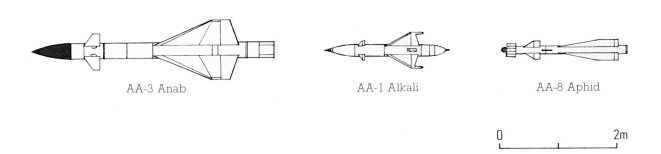

AA-3 Anab   AA-1 Alkali   AA-8 Aphid

0   2m

Sukhoi Su-9/-11

In the past at least, Soviet aircraft designers have faced public disgrace and even prison, should one of their creations prove in any serious way to be faulty. This naturally led them to choose solutions involving the least technical risk. When it came to the thorny task of selecting a basic configuration, especially a new one for a new realm of flight performance, they were extremely happy to adopt a layout suggested by TsAGI, the national aerodynamic centre. Thus at any given point in time as many as four OKBs (design bureaux) would be found working on aircraft of identical shape, though possibly of different size and power.

One of the shapes to emerge from the Korean war in 1953 was the tailed delta, and in 1956 flight trials with prototypes by the MiG and Sukhoi OKBs resulted in this configuration being adopted for the next generation of fighters (the swept wing was thought preferable for attack aircraft). The main difference was that, while both OKBs built large aircraft powered by the AL-7 engine, the MiG OKB went into production only with a smaller machine powered by the R-11 engine (the MiG-21). Size is therefore the main difference between the two families of fighters, with the result that the MiG-21 was initially a day air-combat fighter and the Sukhoi design was a radar-equipped night and all-weather interceptor.

Sukhoi's prototypes were given T numbers. There was no problem in the low-mid position of the wing and mid-mounted slab tailplane, nor in the four door-type airbrakes around the rear fuselage, but prolonged research was needed to discover the best arrangement of variable air inlet(s) and radar. The T-3 of January 1956 had a nose like the American F-86D with the radar in the upper lip of a fixed circular pitot inlet. The PT-7 had a curious inlet with rectangular section and a hinged lower wedge lip. The PT-8 had an advanced circular nose inlet with a large movable conical centrebody housing the radar. The P-1 of 1957 had variable side inlets and a very large nose containing a big radar and crew of two in tandem, the

only two-seater in the family apart from trainers. Another unusual feature of the P-1 was that its armament comprised batteries of unguided rockets fired from internal boxes.

For the production interceptor the least risky answer appeared to be the T-43 with a simple nose inlet, small centrebody for R1L radar (called Spin Scan by NATO) and armament of four rather primitive guided AAMs (air-to-air missiles) called Alkali by NATO, fired from underwing rails. Exactly the same radar and AAMs were carried by a version of the MiG-19, the 19PF. No guns were fitted. This machine went into production in 1958 as the Su-9 (a designation previously used as an internal OKB number for a fighter of 1948). Service with the PVO (air-defence forces) began in 1959. Like the Su-7, two drop tanks under the fuselage were needed to supplement the modest 2145-litre (472 gal, 567 US gal) internal fuel. Large numbers were built, about one in six being a two-seat Su-9U trainer. The T-431 research prototype set a height record at 28852m (94,659ft) in 1959 and a speed record around a 500km (311-mile) circuit at 2337km/h (1,452mph) in 1962.

Production was being switched by 1965 to the Su-11, with a more powerful AL-7 engine and completely new radar and weapons. To accommodate the powerful Uragan 5B (NATO, Skip Spin) radar the nose centrebody was greatly enlarged, the surrounding duct being lengthened and enlarged in consequence. The new long-range missiles (NATO, Anab) were carried in pairs, a radar-guided one under one wing and an IR (heat-homing) missile under the other. Two slim duct fairings were added along the fuselage past the central tankage, as on the Su-7B.

Probably about 1,000 of each type were built, all the production Su-11s appearing to be single-seaters. By late 1982 almost all Su-9s had been withdrawn, the majority being converted as RPV (remotely piloted vehicle) targets for use in air-defence research and training. About 390 Su-11s still remained in PVO service.

COUNTRY OF ORIGIN Soviet Union.

CREW Interceptors: 1, trainers: 2.

TOTAL PRODUCED Possibly 2,000.

DIMENSIONS Wingspan 8·43m (27ft 8in); length, excluding probe, **9:** 16·3m (53ft 5¾in), **11:** 17·2m (56ft 5in); wing area 24·4m² (263ft²).

WEIGHTS (estimated) Empty, **9:** 8650kg (19,070lb), **11:** 8900kg (19,630lb); maximum loaded, **9:** 11800kg (26,000lb), **11:** 13600kg (30,000lb).

ENGINE One Lyul'ka augmented turbojet, **9:** 9000kg (19,841lb) AL-7F, **11:** 10000kg (22,046lb) AL-7F-1.

MAXIMUM SPEED Both, clean, high-altitude: 1915km/h (1,190mph, Mach 1·8).

SERVICE CEILING Both 17km (55,700ft).

RANGE Both, high-altitude, with tanks: 1450km (900 miles).

MILITARY LOAD **9:** four K-13A (Atoll) air-to-air missiles; **11:** two Anab air-to-air missiles (one IR, one radar).

USER Soviet Union.

Sukhoi Su-15

The most remarkable feature of Soviet fighters is that their wing loading (aircraft weight divided by wing area) was much less than other fighters of 1950–70. Relatively large wings and light weights were inherited from a line of extremely agile dogfighters, and with very few exceptions the Soviet fighters could out-turn all the opposition. In Vietnam even the Chinese F-4 (MiG-17) could fly rings round the US fighter of the same designation. It was able to do so in practice because political restraints robbed the US fighter of its main advantage over the old Soviet design: its ability to kill at long range.

In the late 1950s the Soviet planners conceded that the radar-equipped interceptor did not need to be quite so agile. The extreme expression of this belief was the MiG-25, but the Sukhoi OKB was also informed and the result was the impressive interceptor called Su-15 by the VVS (air force). We do not know any of the OKB designations for the prototypes. The basic thinking was that, if you could count on a long concrete runway—which is a luxury enjoyed by the PVO (air-defence forces), in sharp contrast to the FA (frontal aviation)—then it is possible to pack much more into a fighter to make it go faster and/or further, and to carry a heavier load. So a heavily loaded twin-engined version of the Su-11 was the natural outcome.

Sukhoi had already explored high-speed flight with highly loaded wings in the P-1 and in the T-37, a single-engined research prototype of 1960 designed for 3000km/h (1,864mph). The Su-15 may have been a fairly straightforward exercise, almost the only part needing much thought being the lateral inlets. In the P-1 these had been oval, standing away from the fuselage wall and housing sliding centrebodies to adjust the geometry to the speed of the aircraft. In the Su-15 the more modern vertical box was chosen, with a large sharp-edged perforated ramp on the inner side, as in the F-4 Phantom. Compared with the Su-11 the fuselage was considerably lengthened, and internal fuel more than doubled by the tankage between the ducts. Ahead of the cockpit was installed the large Uragan 5B radar device in a surprising purely conical radome with a sharp kink at the junction with the fuselage. Electronics and weapons were basically the same as for the Su-11. For all-round access to the engines, the rear fuselage and tail is removable.

With so much now proven, and an engine already built by the thousand, the only real risk concerned the new inlets—and perhaps the ability of pilots to fly such a 'hot' aircraft in bad weather. The first Su-15 was probably the all-black prototype flown by Sukhoi test pilot Vladimir Ilyushin, son of the famed rival designer Sergei Ilyushin. It probably flew in 1965, and ten were in a display in 1967. There is no reason to doubt that the Su-15 maintained the Sukhoi tradition of good handling at all airspeeds, and clearance for production was exceptionally swift: the first Su-15s reached PVO regiments before 1970. This version was called Flagon-A by NATO.

At a relatively early stage the wing was improved by extending the outer portions, outboard of a small unswept portion giving a kink at the leading edge. The longer span greatly improved lift at low speeds, reducing field length from the 2km (6,500ft) needed by Flagon-A. The new wing went into production on Flagon-D in 1970, but it was first seen in 1967 on a variant with three lift jets in the fuselage (Flagon-B) not built in numbers. Flagon-C is the two-seat trainer, and the main production versions are the latest, called Flagon-E and -F. Both have the long-span wing and each introduced an engine offering an increase in power. Flagon-F also at last has an aesthetically pleasing ogival (curved) radome.

One of the world's fastest combat aircraft, the Su-15 is believed still to be in limited production. The number in service peaked at nearly 1,000 in the late 1970s, and has now declined to around 700, all of late versions. It has not been seen with later radar or missiles even though the Uragan 5B and Advanced Anab are now obsolescent, nor have any Su-15s been exported. Several units have re-equipped with the MiG-23MF.

COUNTRY OF ORIGIN Soviet Union.

CREW Interceptors: 1, trainers: 2.

TOTAL PRODUCED About 2,000.

DIMENSIONS Wingspan, **Flagon-A:** 9·14m (30ft 0in), **Flagon-B** and later: 10·53m (34ft 6in); length, excluding probe, 20·0m (65ft 7½in); wing area, **E/F:** 35·8m² (385ft²).

WEIGHTS (estimated) Empty, **D/E/F:** 11800kg (26,000lb); loaded, **D/E/F:** 21000kg (46,300lb).

ENGINES Two Tumanskii augmented turbojets, **A/B/C/D:** 6200kg (13,668lb) R-11F2-300 (**B:** the same plus three lift jets), **E:** 6600kg (14,550lb) R-13F-300, **F:** 7200kg (15,875lb) R-13F2-300.

MAXIMUM SPEED 2655km/h (1,650mph, Mach 2·5), reduced to about 2450km/h (1,520mph, Mach 2·3) with missiles.

SERVICE CEILING 20km (65,600ft).

RANGE With internal fuel only: 2250km (1,400 miles).

MILITARY LOAD Two AA-3-2 Advanced Anab missiles, one IR and one radar homing.

USER Soviet Union.

Called Flagon-F by NATO, this is thought to be the newest and final production variant of the Sukhoi Su-15 interceptor, of which an estimated 750 are still serving with the PVO-Strany (air defence forces) around the sensitive borders of the Soviet Union. PVO combat aircraft are exclusively long-range stand-off interceptors. They are uncompromised by any need for attack on surface targets, reconnaissance or any other missions of the kind that aircraft of the Frontal Aviation have to fly. Another fundamental difference is that, whereas FA aircraft must be able to operate for lengthy periods away from proper airfields, PVO interceptors can count on long paved runways. The Su-15, like the MiG-25, is a very high performance aircraft with a take-off and landing speed in the 350km/h (217mph) region, which may explain why this version appears to have twin nosewheels. Wing loading is high, but this is no problem as the Su-15 does not engage in close combat. It normally carries either one or two AA-3 'Anab' missiles with radar guidance, plus one or two similar

0   4m

missiles with IR (heat) homing, or a pair of close-range AA-8 'Aphids'. The radar missiles have pointed conical noses; the IR version has an ogival (curved) nose. The simultaneous use of two forms of guidance considerably increases the destructive power of an interception in almost all environmental conditions, although the Su-15/Anab is an old combination with uncertain results against ground-hugging cruise missiles.

Sukhoi Su-15

The Sukhoi OKB's first attempt to build a faster, longer-ranged interceptor based on the 1954 tailed-delta shape was the P-1 of 1957. A tandem two-seater, it had a large pointed radome matched to the design speed of 2050km/h (1,275mph, Mach 1·93). The lateral inlets had fixed geometry, the wings drooped outer leading edges, and armament comprised a battery of rockets.

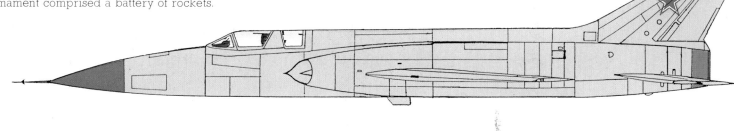

Little is known of the timing, designation or other details of the Sukhoi prototypes that led to the Su-15. The earliest example known was this all-black aircraft flown at the 1967 Aviation Day display by chief OKB pilot Vladimir Ilyushin (son of the famed founder of a rival OKB, Sergei V. Ilyushin). It is believed that the first flight was in 1964.

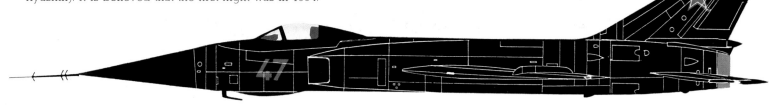

The first production version, called Flagon-A by NATO, was an extremely fast single-seat interceptor with a wing little changed from that of the Su-9 and Su-11, but powered by two R-11 engines fed by sharp-lipped rectangular inlets. This aircraft, of the *Zolotistyi Jastreb* (Golden Hawks) display team, had a large rear warning radar above the fin, as did most of this series.

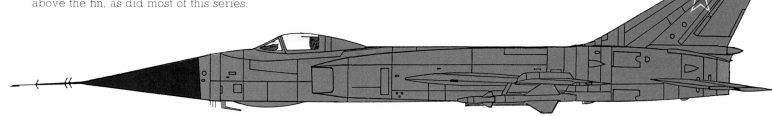

Flagon-B, or Su-15VD (vertical engines), another prototype flown at the 1967 Aviation Day display, was one of at least four jet-lift STOL conversions of existing fighters which were evaluated against swing-wings as a way of reducing field length. Three lift jets were installed in the fuselage, in place of fuel, and the wings were increased in span by reducing sweep on the outer sections. The metal nose was black, as were triangles ahead of the main-engine inlets.

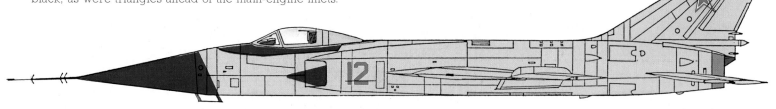

About 100 examples were built of the Su-15U tandem dual trainer, which NATO calls the Flagon-C. Like all subsequent versions, which are the only ones now in service, it has a wing with short extra unswept sections alongside fences at the junction of the 53° inner wing with the 37° outer sections. There are two upward-hinged canopies and a large periscope for the instructor.

Designations of most Su-15 variants are unknown in the West, but the first major production version was called Flagon-D by NATO. It introduced the new wing, with a kinked leading edge and span increased from 9·15 to 10·53m (30 to 34½ft), and doubled the armament from two AAMs (usually AA-3 'Anab') to four.

Possibly half the 700-odd Su-15s in service are of this Flagon-E type (although it is thought the radomes are being changed for the ogival pattern). This is basically a Flagon-D with enlarged inlets and more powerful R-13F2-300 engines, which were probably required to reduce the time taken to reach hostile intruders from the moment a warning is given.

Final Su-15 model identified in IA-PVO (air defence forces) service is so-called Flagon-F, known to have augmented avionic systems, and externally distinguished by its ogival radome which should offer lower drag and give improved supersonic acceleration and speed. All Su-15s seen in regular service have been unpainted. The white A-3 'Anab' AAM is of the IR species.

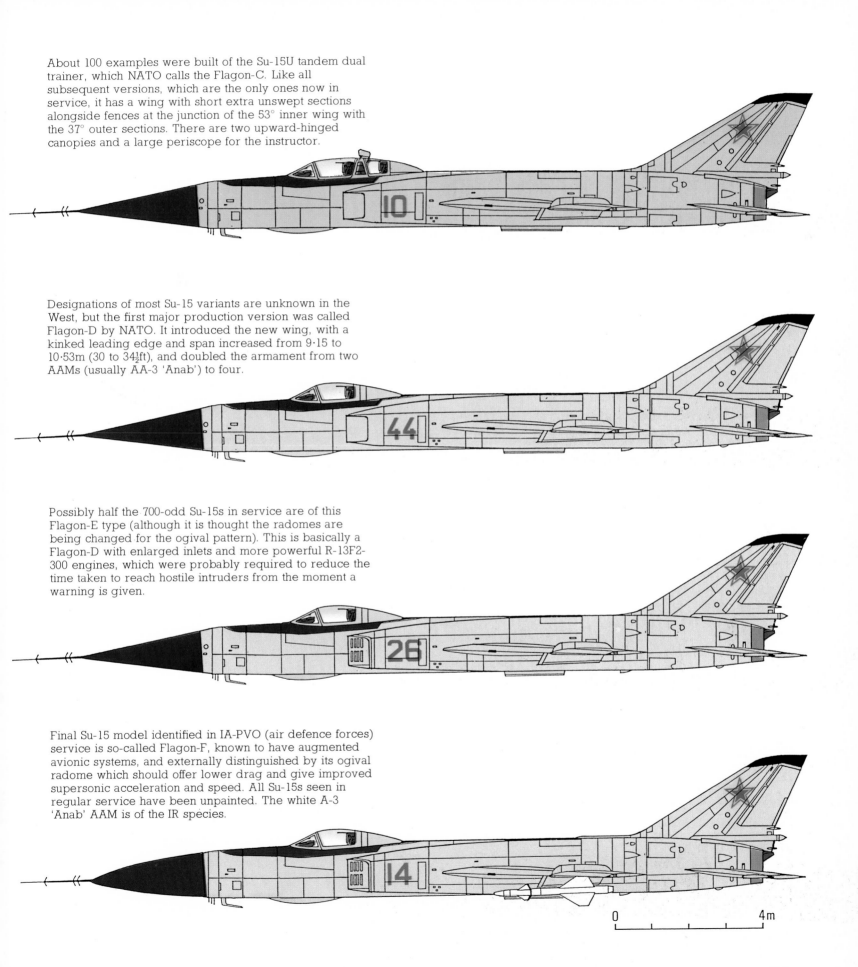

0   4m

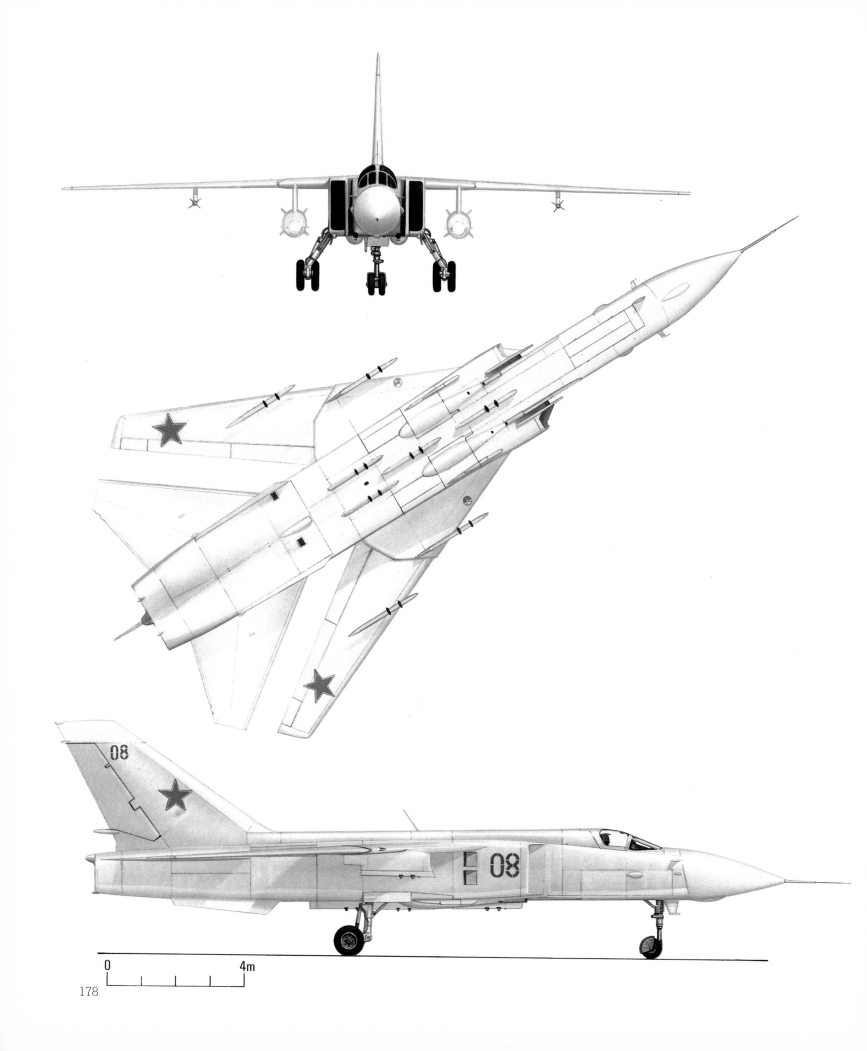

0   4m

The artist experienced considerable difficulty in establishing some details of this now widely used Soviet attack aircraft, which has capabilities almost identical to the West's Tornado (although the Russian aircraft is much larger and more powerful, and burns about 70 per cent more fuel). One of the problems concerned the arrangement of fairings at the tail; that shown in aircraft 17 (side elevation above) is different from the aircraft depicted in the other four views. It is believed that each of the eight external stores pylons is rated at 1000kg (2,205lb). Loads shown are four cluster bombs on the fuselage, AA-2-2 'Advanced Atoll' self-defence missiles on the outer wing pylons (both this and AA-8 'Aphid' are believed to be carried singly or in pairs) and the very large drop tanks, which have small canard fins to pull down the tank noses on release. The artist is confident that the ventral blisters, often thought to be of different sizes, are in fact identical and cover two guns of unknown type. A large part of each blister is formed by the two airbrakes whose hinge fairings were at one time thought to be small stores pylons. Limits of wing sweep, both illustrated, are 16° and 68°.

0   4m

Yakovlev Yak-36MP

Called 'Forger' by NATO, this
unique ship-based VTOL combat
aircraft from the Soviet Union
carries all its weapons externally
on four pylons. Because the
inboard pair appear extremely
close to the legs of the main
landing gear, this apparently
restricts what can be carried there
to single AA-2-2 'Advanced Atoll'
or AA-8 'Aphid' close-range
AAMs. On the outer pylons it is
possible to carry tanks, rocket
pods, bombs and various other
stores including the gun pods
illustrated, each of which houses a
GSh-23 twin-barrel 23mm cannon
and its ammunition. The left-side
view opposite shows one of the
Yak-36MP aircraft carried aboard
Minsk on its 1976 'shakedown'
cruise. It is depicted with cockpit
canopy, lift-jet doors and efflux
doors all open, main-engine
nozzles vectored to 90° and the
wings folded. The other views
show one of the aircraft carried
aboard the same ship in 1981, with
upper-fuselage fences added to
improve airflow around the top of
the lift-jet bay and gun pods on the
outer pylons. The suffix letters
almost certainly signify 'maritime
interceptor' in Russian.

Sukhoi Su-24 and Yakovlev Yak-36MP

The Su-24 and Yak-36MP are two of the latest Soviet combat aircraft to enter service. As yet, no variants of the Su-24 are known, and only a single (two-seat) version of the Yak-36MP, so it is possible to deal with both here in the space normally alotted a single basic type.

Both are representatives of a class rare in the Soviet Union, the completely new design. Even that is not quite correct, because the Yakovlev is (on paper at least) derived from the experimental Yak-36, and the Sukhoi is based on exactly the same TsAGI-developed aerodynamic shape as was used by the Tupolev bureau to turn the Tu-22 into the swing-wing 22M.

This particular swing-wing shape has an ideal uncompromised wing, unlike that used in the Su-17, -20 and -22 described earlier, where only the outer and relatively small portion of wing is pivoted. In the **Su-24** the whole wing panel is pivoted, except for a small fixed triangular portion at the root known as a glove. The same configuration is seen in the MiG-23 and -27, and in any case TsAGI got the original configuration from the NASA and the F-111, so they knew it worked.

As the same shape had been adopted for the MiG-23 family, why was Sukhoi OKB assigned the task of building what the VVS (air force) calls the Su-24? The answer is that in the 1960s the main thrust of development for FA (frontal aviation) aircraft changed from close-support and defensive roles to long-range offensive missions, and for the first time the FA was to be provided with strike aircraft able to cover the whole of Western Europe as far as Portugal and the Outer Hebrides of Scotland. This reflected a profound change of thinking in the Politburo and military staffs. The Su-24 is, more than any other warplane except the F-111, the modern 'fighter' type aircraft which is actually today's counterpart to yesterday's four-engined heavy bombers, flying missions at least as long (in distance, not time) while carrying if anything even heavier bombloads.

We in the West know little of the detail engineering of the Su-24, although as far back as 1974 it was the subject of awed appraisals in Washington. Just as the big Bison and Bear bombers had caused consternation among the NATO nations in the 1950s, so has Fencer (its Western reporting name) become the big scare of the 1980s. And not without reason, because it has every modern navigation and weapon-aiming sensor for all-weather precision. It is an exact counterpart to the West's Tornado IDS, but bigger and more powerful, and available in larger numbers, sooner.

As for the **Yak-36MP**, called Forger by NATO, this is the only jet-lift aircraft in military use apart from the Harrier. It appears to bear scant family likeness to the Yak-36 VTOL (vertical take-off and landing) research aircraft of the mid-1960s, apart from having the same propulsion system of a vectored main engine and two separate lift jets. At take-off the aircraft rises on the thrust of the two rear nozzles of the main engine and the two jets from the lift engines, which are operated only during take-off and landing. The lift jets are inclined slightly aft, so the main-engine nozzles are rotated past the 90° position to cancel fore/aft thrust.

The Yak-36MP was designed to fly from the big multi-role warships of the *Kiev* class, in such missions as local air defence, surface attack and reconnaissance. It is less versatile than the Sea Harrier in that it cannot make a rolling take-off with a heavy attack load but has to rise vertically. Features include folding wings, a small ranging radar, lateral inlet ducts and armament hung on four underwing pylons. It is evident from the rock-steady precision of its landing approaches that some form of electronic ship guidance is linked to the autopilot in the aircraft. There is a two-seat conversion trainer, known as Forger-B to NATO, which has a fuselage extended both ahead of and behind the wing.

Although attractive and neat, and capable of supersonic speed in the clean condition, the Yak-36MP is regarded as an interim type. The West expects a much more formidable successor to appear.

COUNTRY OF ORIGIN Soviet Union.

CREW **Yak-36MP Forger-A:** 1, rest: 2.

TOTAL PRODUCED **Su-24:** about 700 by 1983, **Yak-36MP:** about 150 (estimate).

DIMENSIONS (estimated) Wingspan, **Su-24**, 16°: 17·15m (56ft 3in), 68°: 9·53m (31ft 3in), **Forger-A/B:** 7·32m (24ft 0in); length, **Su-24:** 21·29m (69ft 10in), **Forger-A:** 15·25m (50ft 0in), **Forger-B:** 17·68m (58ft 0in); wing areas, not accurately determined.

WEIGHTS (estimated) Empty, **Su-24:** 19000kg (42,000lb), **Forger-A:** 7375kg (16,260lb), **Forger-B:** 8200kg (18,100lb); maximum loaded, **Su-24:** 39500kg (87,080lb), **Forger-A/B:** 11565kg (25,500lb).

ENGINES **Su-24:** two augmented turbofans, probably 12500kg (27,560lb) Tumanskii R-29B, **Forger-A/B:** one vectored-thrust main engine plus two lift turbojets each rated at about 3630kg (8,000lb).

MAXIMUM SPEED Clean, high-altitude, **Su-24:** 2340km/h (1,454mph, Mach 2·2), **Forger-A/B:** 1170km/h (725mph, Mach 1·1).

SERVICE CEILING (estimated) **Su-24:** 17·5km (57,400ft), **Forger-A/B:** 12km (39,400ft).

RANGE Combat radius, **Su-24**, hi-lo-hi mission with 2000kg (4,409lb) bombload: 1800km (1,115 miles), **Forger**, maximum weapons, hi-lo-hi mission: 370km (230 miles).

MILITARY LOAD **Su-24:** four pylons under body and four under wings, for load of at least 8000kg (17,635lb), including range of guided air/surface missiles, plus at least one fuselage-mounted gun (probably two of differing calibres); **Forger-A:** four wing pylons for total estimated at 1360kg (3,000lb) of bombs, rocket or gun pods, ECM/EW sensors or jammers, reconnaissance pods, air-to-air missiles (AA-2-2 Advanced Atoll or AA-8 Aphid) or drop tanks.

USER Soviet Union.

Tupolev Tu-16

Called Badger by NATO, the Soviet Tu-16 has been in service for 30 years. This is remarkable by any standard, and it is striking testimony to the soundness of the original structural design, which has resisted fatigue over a lifespan several times greater than envisaged when the prototype flew in late 1952.

At that time Tupolev's OKB (design bureau) had taken the pirated American B-29 strategic bomber design a very long way via the Tu-80 and Tu-85, and ultimately moved on to the great Tu-20 described in the next entry. The Tu-88 was built in parallel as a shorter-range medium bomber using almost the same Tu-85 fuselage sections, tail and several other parts, but with a shorter length and smaller wing with a then-unique installation of two extremely large turbojets at the roots, recessed into the sides of the fuselage. Crew accommodation, defensive armament and auxiliary systems were all derived from the Tu-4, the Soviet derivative of the B-29, but the bogie landing gears were new, and folded backwards into fairings projecting aft of the wing in a way that was to become a Tupolev trademark.

The Tu-88 was far ahead of its nevertheless excellent Ilyushin rival, and it was ordered into production with the service designation Tu-16 in October 1953. The basic bomber had the heavy defensive armament of seven 23mm guns, and carrying a heavy load of nuclear or conventional bombs was a formidable aircraft, giving the Soviet Union a powerful long-range striking capability it had not really possessed since the days of the Tupolev TB-3 in the 1930s. Altogether 2,000 were built, the last probably being delivered by 1962. Early in production the 8700kg (19,180lb) AM-3 engines in the initial batch were replaced by the slightly more powerful AM-3M (RD-3M), and many aircraft were equipped for flight refuelling by a curious method in which the hose links the wingtips of tanker and receiver. A derived aircraft was the Tu-104 civil transport, built in large numbers from 1956.

In 1958 licence arrangements were concluded with China, but after the break between the two countries work was slow and it was not until 1968 that the H-6 model began to come off the line at the factory at Xian, which is also supplying spares to Egypt. By late 1982 about 120 H-6s had been delivered, all apparently conventional bombers.

This basic model, called Badger-A in the West, has in the Soviet Union largely been rebuilt into later models, although nine were supplied unaltered to Iraq. Badger-B was a missile carrier with a 'Kennel' AS-1 hung under each wing; this was supplied to Indonesia, with missiles, but is now no longer used. Badger-C, first seen with the -B type in 1961, carried the large 'Kipper' AS-2 anti-ship missile under the fuselage, and had a new nose filled by a giant surveillance radar.

Badger-D was the first of the long-serving special reconnaissance versions, in this case with the surveillance radar of -C plus a row of ventral radomes and an enlarged radar blister under the nose. Badger-E is the -A rebuilt as a reconnaissance aircraft with a pallet housing up to eight cameras and other gear in the bomb bay. The -F variant is an -E with deep wing pylons carrying Elint pods.

A rebuilt -B with wing pylons for 'Kelt' AS-5 rocket missiles, Badger-G has often been seen since 1977 with one of the long-range precision-guided 'Kingfish' AS-6 missiles on the left pylon. Some have a Kingfish under each wing. G-modified, first seen in 1981, has special Kingfish equipment and a powerful new radar. Badger-H is an EW (electronic warfare) platform, with a bomb bay packed with chaff dispensers to jam hostile radars, and much new equipment. A more advanced ECM (electronic countermeasures) aircraft, Badger-J has powerful jammers and a canoe radar under the fuselage. Another electronic recon version is the -K, with new sensing devices.

Today the VVS-DA (air force long-range aviation) has about 300 -A bombers, 40 tankers, 90 ECM platforms and 15 reconnaissance versions. The AV-MF has 275 -G and -G-mod, 70 tankers and 40 for Elint and ECM.

COUNTRY OF ORIGIN Soviet Union.

CREW **Most:** 6, **C/D:** believed 5.

TOTAL PRODUCED About 2,000.

DIMENSIONS Wingspan 32·93m (108ft 0½in); length, **A and most other versions:** 34·8m (114ft 2in), **C/D:** about 36·9m (121ft); wing area 164·65m² (1,772ft²).

WEIGHTS Empty, **A:** 37200kg (82,000lb), **G/H/K:** about 39000kg (86,000lb); maximum loaded 72000kg (158,730lb).

ENGINES Two 9500kg (20,950lb) Mikulin RD-3M turbojets.

MAXIMUM SPEED Typical, at 6km (19,685ft) and above: 992km/h (616mph).

SERVICE CEILING 12·3km (40,350ft).

RANGE **A**, max bombload: 4800km (3,000 miles), **A**, max fuel: 5760km (3,579 miles), later versions, typical: 6000km (3,730 miles).

MILITARY LOAD **A:** three turrets with automatic radar-directed gunlaying, each with two NR-23 cannon (23mm); in most versions a seventh NR-23 fixed to fire ahead; weapon bay 6·5m (21ft) long in **A** and **B** and most **G** (not G-mod) for up to 9000kg (19,850lb) of bombs or other stores; **B:** formerly carried two Kennel missiles, **C:** formerly carried one Kipper missile, **G:** two Kelt missiles or one (sometimes two) Kingfish, **G-mod:** one or two Kingfish. **Other variants:** no offensive load.

USERS China, Egypt, Indonesia (inactive), Libya, Soviet Union.

0   4m

Tupolev Tu-16
Badger-G Mod

Almost all Tu-16 Badger aircraft seen in the West have been unpainted except for national insignia and occasional black numbers and other stencils. The subject of these illustrations is one of the so-called Badger-G Mod type, equipped to carry two AS-6 'Kingfish' long-range cruise missiles and with an unknown device mounted ahead of the nose. This particular aircraft was photographed by the Swedish air force, for whom several Soviet aircraft have deliberately posed since 1981. The nose equipment (which the artist has interpreted from an indistinct photograph) is larger than the inverted-T arrangement seen on Badger-G bombers of the Egyptian air force which carry the earlier AS-5 'Kelt' under each wing. It has been assumed the device is connected with establishing the missile on course and perhaps transmitting to it updated information on the position of a moving target. So far as is known all Tu-16s were built during the 1950s, and most have been converted or updated several times. Numerous versions are carriers of long-range missiles, and it is believed that with an effort the bomber can climb to an altitude at which the radio horizon is beyond the range of the missile(s) carried. Thus it can 'see' further than the missile can fly. AS-6 range at low altitude is given as 220km (135 miles), rising to at least 400km (186 miles) at high altitude (say 27·4km, 90,000ft). The large ventral radar of Badger-G Mod ought to be able to lock on to large ship targets at such a range, the missile flying on mid-course guidance until its own active terminal (radar or IR) guidance is activated. The AS-6 wing pylons are also fitted to another variant, Badger-C Mod, which formerly carried the turbojet AS-2 'Kipper' missile under the fuselage.

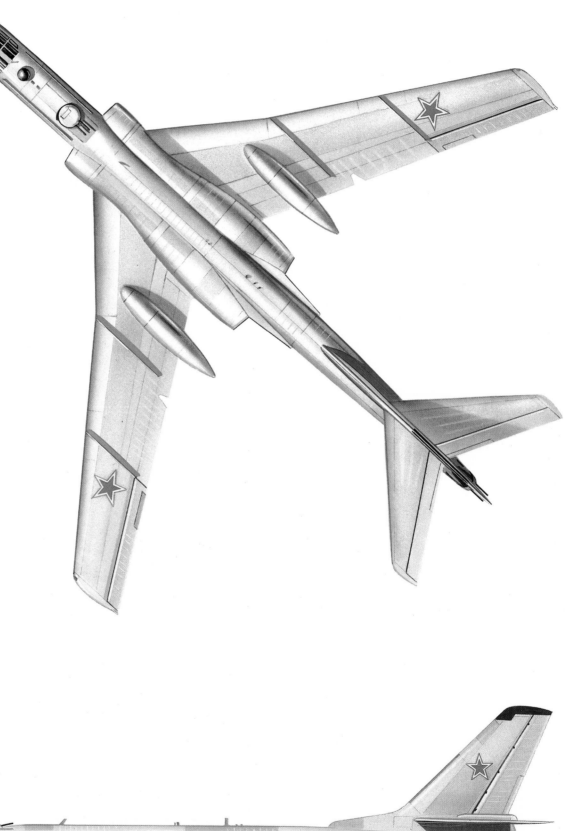

Tupolev Tu-16

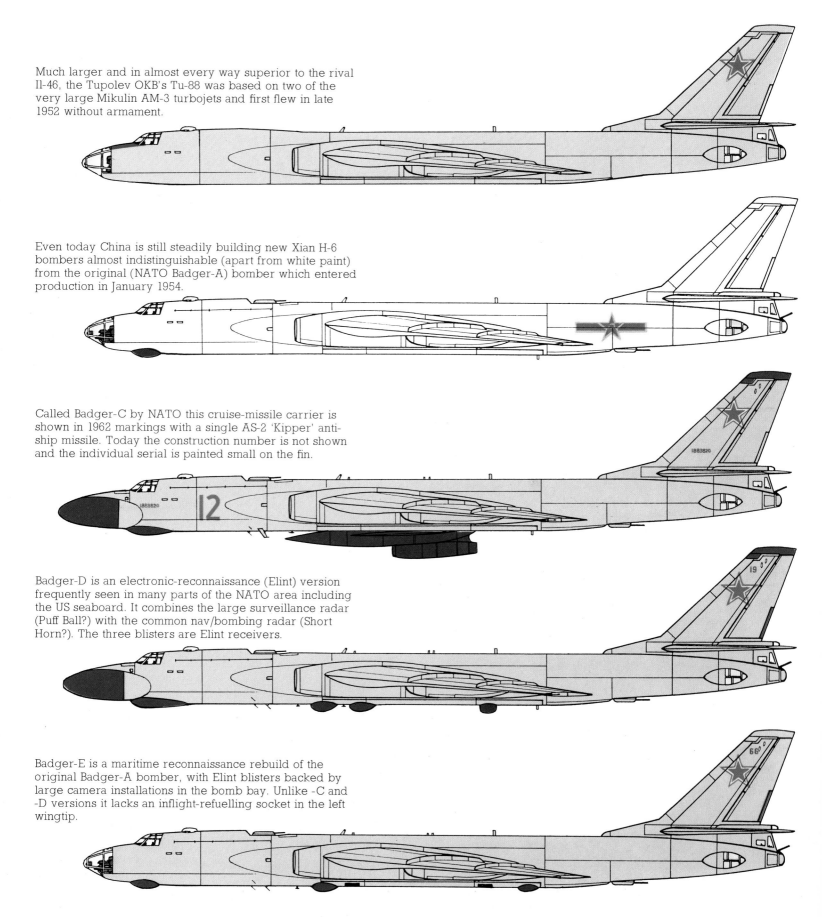

Much larger and in almost every way superior to the rival Il-46, the Tupolev OKB's Tu-88 was based on two of the very large Mikulin AM-3 turbojets and first flew in late 1952 without armament.

Even today China is still steadily building new Xian H-6 bombers almost indistinguishable (apart from white paint) from the original (NATO Badger-A) bomber which entered production in January 1954.

Called Badger-C by NATO this cruise-missile carrier is shown in 1962 markings with a single AS-2 'Kipper' anti-ship missile. Today the construction number is not shown and the individual serial is painted small on the fin.

Badger-D is an electronic-reconnaissance (Elint) version frequently seen in many parts of the NATO area including the US seaboard. It combines the large surveillance radar (Puff Ball?) with the common nav/bombing radar (Short Horn?). The three blisters are Elint receivers.

Badger-E is a maritime reconnaissance rebuild of the original Badger-A bomber, with Elint blisters backed by large camera installations in the bomb bay. Unlike -C and -D versions it lacks an inflight-refuelling socket in the left wingtip.

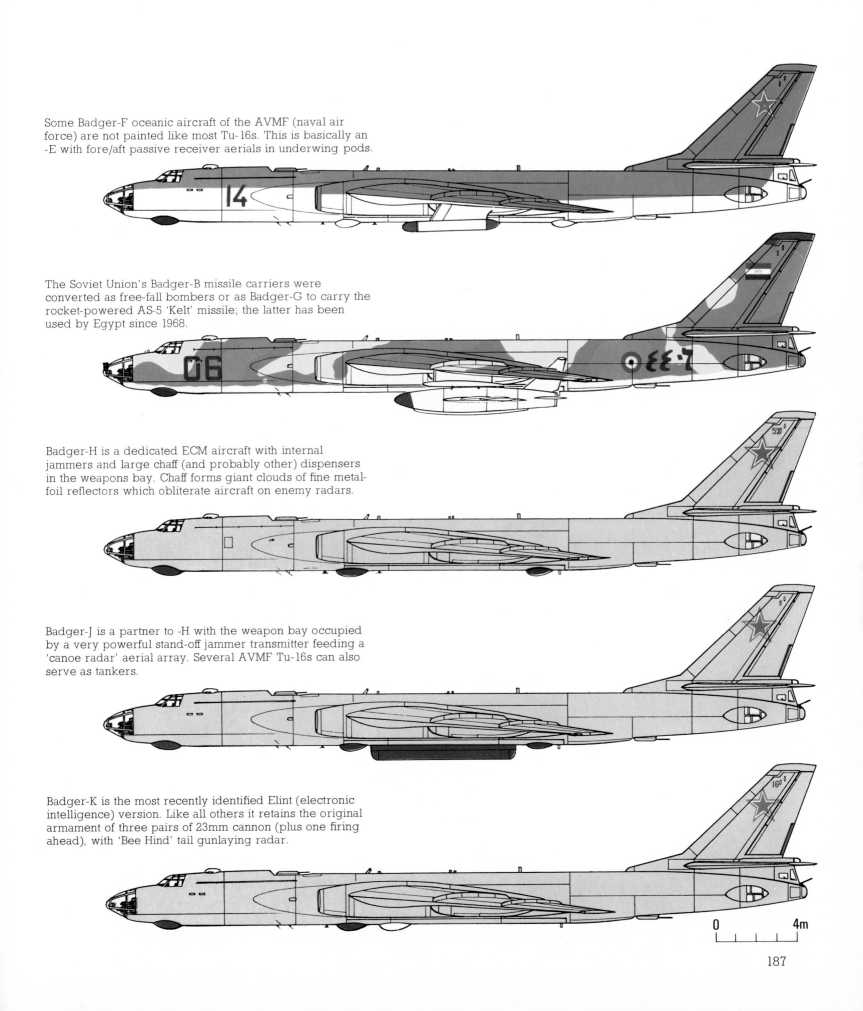

Some Badger-F oceanic aircraft of the AVMF (naval air force) are not painted like most Tu-16s. This is basically an -E with fore/aft passive receiver aerials in underwing pods.

The Soviet Union's Badger-B missile carriers were converted as free-fall bombers or as Badger-G to carry the rocket-powered AS-5 'Kelt' missile; the latter has been used by Egypt since 1968.

Badger-H is a dedicated ECM aircraft with internal jammers and large chaff (and probably other) dispensers in the weapons bay. Chaff forms giant clouds of fine metal-foil reflectors which obliterate aircraft on enemy radars.

Badger-J is a partner to -H with the weapon bay occupied by a very powerful stand-off jammer transmitter feeding a 'canoe radar' aerial array. Several AVMF Tu-16s can also serve as tankers.

Badger-K is the most recently identified Elint (electronic intelligence) version. Like all others it retains the original armament of three pairs of 23mm cannon (plus one firing ahead), with 'Bee Hind' tail gunlaying radar.

0   4m

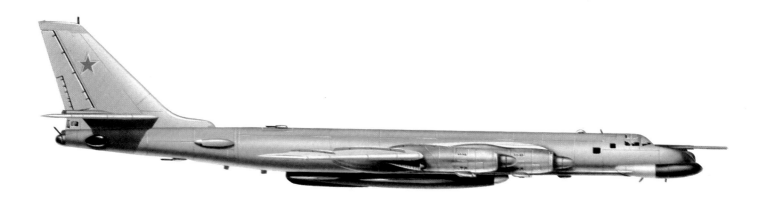

Tupolev's monster turboprop strategic bomber remains a unique achievement, essentially combining jet speed with propeller fuel-economy. The subject on these pages is one of the rarer versions, called Bear-C by NATO and first identified in 1964. A long-range anti-ship aircraft, it has extensive navigation, surveillance and electronic-warfare systems, including the very powerful 'Crown Drum' search radar in the chin position (one of seven different radars identified aboard aircraft of the Bear family). Under the belly is recessed an AS-3 'Kangaroo' cruise missile, the largest missile ever routinely carried by any aircraft. Developed by the MiG bureau, this missile has a nose like a MiG-21, and when carried by the Bear this is faired over to reduce drag. The white fairing is jettisoned after release of the missile. The three twin-23mm gun turrets are retained, and a flight-refuelling probe is fitted. There is an electronic blister on each side of the rear fuselage but none on the tips of the tailplane. All the aircraft of this sub-type in service are believed to be conversions from the original bombers built more than 20 years ago. Continuing low-rate production is almost certainly confined to the enlarged and heavier Tu-142 Bear-F ASW version.

Tupolev Tu-142
Bear-C

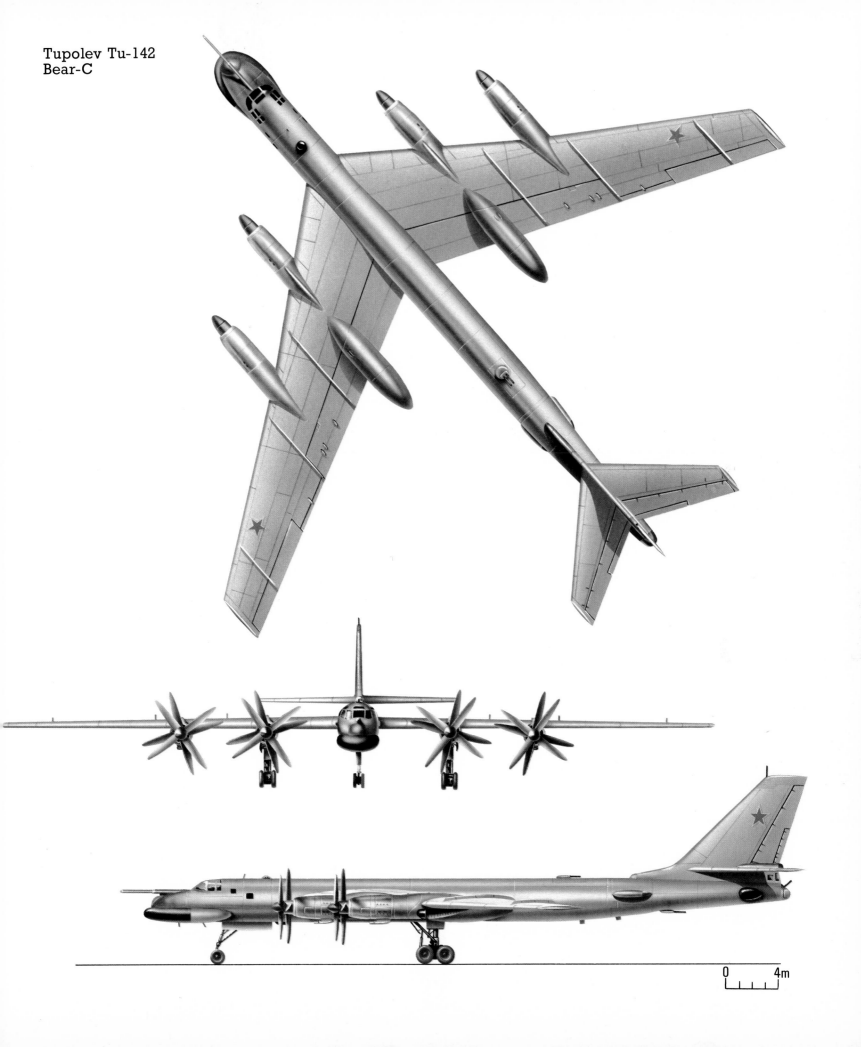

0   4m

Tupolev Tu-20/-114/-126/-142

Given the OKB (design bureau) number of Tu-116, the Tu-114D was virtually a Tu-95 converted into a long-range transport. No 7802 was one of two operated by the Soviet VVS (air force); there was also at least one civil example, No 76462. It had a 24-seat cabin in the rear fuselage.

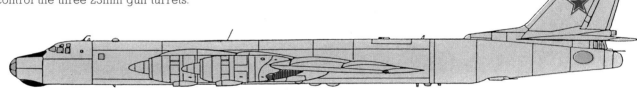

In its day the Tu-114 was the biggest aircraft in the world. Combining Tu-95 aerodynamics and propulsion with a gigantic pressurized fuselage, it had a crew of 10 to 15 and seats for up to 220, at a time when 120 was exceptional. Regular services began in April 1961 after prolonged delays.

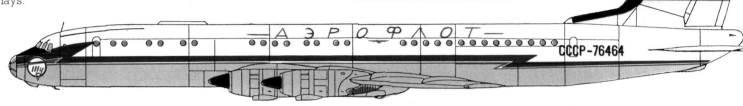

Called Bear-A by NATO, the original bomber was given the VVS designation Tu-20. It differed little from the prototype of 1954 apart from having full mission avionics, including 'Short Horn' bombing radar and 'Bee Hind' tail armament radar to control the three 23mm gun turrets.

Bear-B was first seen in 1961 and introduced the enormous AS-3 'Kangaroo' cruise missile (sometimes replaced by AS-4 'Kitchen') with associated 'Crown Drum' targeting radar ·with the main aerial in a 'duckbill' radome. There are many variations; most were fitted in 1962 with flight-refuelling probes. Bear-C (see p. 188/9) has a blister on both sides of the rear fuselage (as shown) instead of just on the right side.

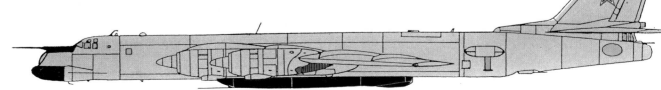

Bear-D is a maritime reconnaissance, missile targeting and Elint (electronic intelligence) version, first seen in 1967. Most retain the three defensive turrets, but other payload is devoted to at least 27 major avionic items including two large downlook radars. Passive receiver pods are on the tips of the tailplane, and on the example illustrated a large avionic compartment replaces the tail turret. About 50 serve with the AVMF.

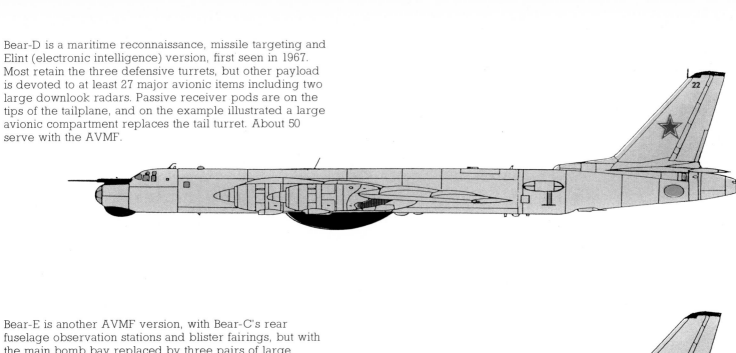

Bear-E is another AVMF version, with Bear-C's rear fuselage observation stations and blister fairings, but with the main bomb bay replaced by three pairs of large optical cameras and other reconnaissance (and usually Elint) gear.

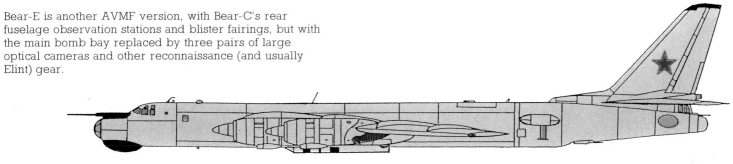

Bear-F, designated Tu-142 by the OKB, is a totally new and largely redesigned version for ASW missions with the AVMF, and still in low-rate production in the 1970s. Weight is substantially increased, the stretched fuselage is rearranged for ASW sensors and weapons, and the upper and lower defensive turrets are removed. At least 30 are in oceanic service.

First seen in 1968 the Tu-126, called Moss by NATO, is an interim airborne warning and control platform of which at least ten were produced by rebuilding the ex-Aeroflot Tu-114s. An early US assessment claimed that the surveillance radar was 'ineffective over land'; certainly the 32 propeller blades would cause severe interference.

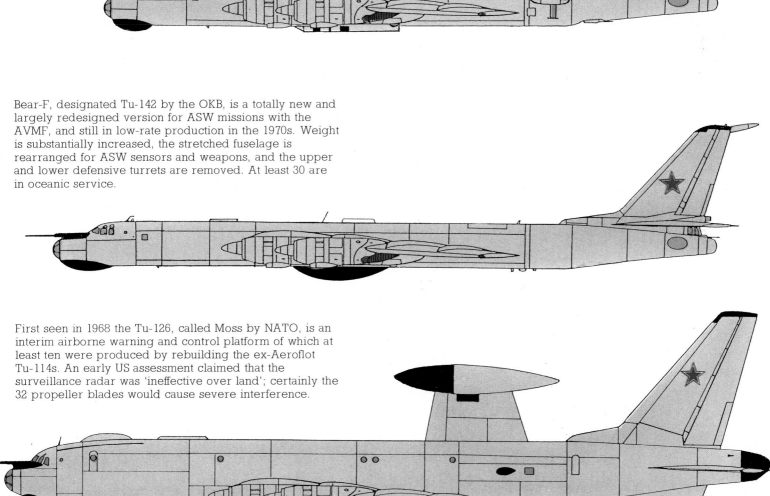

0   4m

Tupolev Tu-20/-142

At the Soviet Aviation Day flypast in July 1955 the highlight was the appearance of a gigantic new bomber, which dwarfed the seven MiG-17s that escorted it. Amazingly, it had a 35° swept wing and tail, but had propellers. Initial assessments soon indicated not only a speed close to that of jets but also a radius of action exceeding that of any other military aircraft. Called 'Bear' by NATO, it caused such consternation in the Pentagon that hundreds of extra B-52s were built at a frantic pace.

What nobody then expected was that 30 years later newly built aircraft of this family would still be throbbing across the globe, in a host of sub-variants mostly unconnected with bombing, although deeply concerned with the Soviet Union's strategic power as a whole. From the same basic design stemmed the civil Tu-114D (almost a direct conversion of the same airframe for pioneer ultra-long airline flights); the Tu-114 high-capacity passenger liner (biggest in the world until the Boeing 747 'Jumbo' of 1969); the Tu-126 surveillance/control platform; and an updated ASW (anti-submarine warfare) variant designated Tu-142. Many of these aircraft, except the -142, are rebuilds of airframes already tired from years of hard service. Certainly, Soviet designers have little to learn about how to make large structures that can go on flying longer than the service careers of the men who fly them.

This is the more remarkable in view of the demanding nature of the original requirement combining jet speed and height with extremely long range. This called for an enormous, long-span wing which posed a great challenge. Fuel is carried from tip to tip, the leading edge has thermal anti-icing, and movable surfaces include large area-increasing flaps and upper-surface spoilers. The slender fuselage, on the other hand, was almost the same as the preceding straight-wing Tu-85, the ultimate development of the series of bombers derived from the American B-29. The enormous turboprop engine was created by a team of captured German engineers in the late 1940s, and drove 5·6m (18ft 4in) eight-blade contra-rotating propellers whose tips moved faster than sound. From its earliest days this propulsion system set world records for speed and load over long distances.

The aircraft seen in 1955 was the Tu-95 prototype. The production bomber, with VVS (air force) designation Tu-20, entered the inventory of the DA (long-range aviation) in 1956 with free-fall bombs. Recently survivors have been rebuilt and, surprisingly, been re-designated Tu-95 to accord with the design bureau number. The Bear-A model was followed by Bear-B with a colossal Kangaroo AS-3 missile recessed under the belly, with initial guidance by a 'Crown Drum' nose radar. Some -Bs have been converted to launch supersonic Kitchen AS-4 missiles. Others were turned into Bear-Cs with a flight-refuelling probe and a range of sensors and electronics for maritime patrol.

By 1967 British and US airspace was being investigated by Bear-D, a largely new model for the AV-MF (naval aviation). This has a glazed nose, large chin radar, even bigger belly radar and extensive sensors and EW (electronic warfare) equipment, plus a probe. Bear-E is a straightforward camera-equipped reconnaissance conversion of Bear-A. Bear-F, the new Tu-142 for the AV-MF, has a longer forward fuselage, a rear fuselage devoted to sonobuoys and other stores and many other changes. It has only the tail turret for defence.

In 1982 the DA had about 113 A/B versions; the AV-MF used 80, of which about 40 were Bear-Ds and 40 -Fs. In addition the VVS deploys at least ten Tu-126 airborne warning and control aircraft rebuilt from Tu-114 transports. These have the large circular-section fuselage reskinned without many windows, and housing a mass of electronics including the main radar served by the 11m (36ft) rotodome mounted on a pylon above the fuselage. There are many other sensors and a total crew of at least 12, the mission being surveillance of airspace and the direction of defending interceptors or friendly attack aircraft.

COUNTRY OF ORIGIN Soviet Union.

CREW **Most:** 7, **Bear-B**, some derived sub-types: 6, **Tu-126:** 12.

TOTAL PRODUCED Approximately 300.

DIMENSIONS Wingspan, except 126: 51·1m (167ft 8in), **126:** 51·2m (168ft 0in); length, **most:** 47·5m (155ft 10in), **F:** 49·5m (162ft 5in), **Tu-126:** 55·2m (181ft 1in); wing area 311·1m² (3,349ft²).

WEIGHTS (estimated) Empty, typical of all: 75000kg (165,000lb), maximum loaded, except F: 170000kg (375,000lb), **F:** 188000kg (414,500lb).

ENGINES Four 14,795hp Kuznetsov NK-12MV turboprops.

MAXIMUM SPEED **Most:** 870km/h (540mph), **F:** 805km/h (500mph), **126:** 850km/h (528mph).

SERVICE CEILING **Most:** 13·4km (44,000ft), **F:** 12·5km (41,000ft).

RANGE **Most**, including 126: 12550km (7,800 miles), **F:** 17500km (10,900 miles) or 12550km (7,800 miles) with maximum weapon load.

MILITARY LOAD **Most:** three defensive turrets each armed with two NR-23 (23mm) cannon, **F:** one (tail) turret only, **126:** no armament; **A:** normal internal bombload of 11500kg (25,350lb), **B:** one Kangaroo stand-off missile, later replaced by one Kitchen AS-4 missile, **C/D/E:** no offensive armament, **F:** various ASW weapons (details unknown).

USER Soviet Union.

Tupolev Tu-22/-22M

The story of the Tu-22 and -22M again illustrates the Soviet capacity for never shirking the problems of offering military competition, never giving up and, after many years of effort, at the end of the day coming out on top through sheer staying power. The original aircraft was planned in 1954 to compete with the USAF's B-58 supersonic bomber, an aircraft right on the limit of available technology. The prototype, with Tupolev OKB (design bureau) number Tu-105, flew in late 1958 or early 1959, and fell well short of the B-58 in most respects: it had only about 60 per cent of the Mach 2 speed and 8250km (5,125-mile) range of the American aircraft. Western analysts who studied ten pre-production Tu-22s at a 1961 fly-past thought the range was 2250km (1,400 miles), which if correct would have made the aircraft virtually useless.

Moreover, in the early 1960s bombers were on the one hand having to fight for funds against ballistic missiles, which appeared to be surer nuclear delivery systems, and on the other were fast becoming vulnerable to defensive SAMs (surface-to-air missiles) which made the ability to fly faster or higher pointless. But for many tasks, such as missions that might be recalled, or attacks on ships and other moving targets as well as all forms of reconnaissance, there was no alternative to the manned platform. Some 250 Tu-22s were thus built from 1964 to '69 in four versions, known in the West only by their NATO names:

Blinder-A is the baseline bomber, with an extremely large fuselage with a nose radar, pressure cabin for crew of three in tandem, capacious fuel tanks, weapons bay with double-fold doors, engines above the rear fuselage on each side of the fin spars, a single radar-directed tail gun, and bogie landing gears folding backwards into Tu-style pods. Blinder-B carries a stand-off missile, and has a larger radar, flight-refuelling probe and, in one form, a very large group of reconnaissance sensors instead of the missile or bombs. The naval version, -C, is for multi-sensor reconnaissance and EW (electronic warfare), and -D is a trainer with a superimposed instructor cockpit. In late 1982 about 125 -Bs (plus 12 for reconnaissance) and 40 -Cs were in use, plus about 40 trainers, as well as small numbers with Iraq (-A) and Libya (-B/-D). Aircraft of the two latter air forces have seen action.

Development of a variable-geometry scheme applicable to existing aircraft in the mid-1960s was clearly of great benefit to the Tu-22, and the Tu-22M probably flew in about 1968. Only the outer wing panels were pivoted, and major parts of the aircraft remained unchanged. About 20 of this type were built in the early 1970s, although reports claim that they entered DA (long-range aviation) service. But the Tupolev designers continued to develop the aircraft and by 1974 had produced a very much heavier and more powerful version with new engines fed by very large lateral inlet ducts and with the landing gears retracting inwards to be housed in the fuselage.

NATO called the original -22M Backfire-A and the developed version Backfire-B. The VVS designation of -B has been guessed in the West as either Tu-26 or Tu-30. Radar and satellite study of flight testing revealed impressive performances, one -B taking on fuel from an M-4 tanker and then remaining on test for a further ten hours. Features include a pressure cabin for a crew of four, seated two by two unlike the Tu-22; a weapon bay for many kinds of bombs, and options of wing pylons or racks under the engine inlet ducts for missiles or free-fall bombs; and an unrivalled array of electronic devices for navigation, weapon delivery and safe penetration of hostile airspace.

Since 1979 pilots of these fine aircraft, in both the DA and the AV-MF, have gone out of their way to bring their machines alongside Western photographic aircraft. Backfire has figured in SALT (arms limitation) talks, although the Soviet Union insists it is not intended as a direct threat to the USA. Production at some 42 aircraft per year had by 1983 built up to a force of some 230 Backfires in service.

COUNTRY OF ORIGIN Soviet Union.

CREW **22:** 3, **22M:** 4.

TOTAL PRODUCED **22:** about 250, **22M:** 230-plus by 1983.

DIMENSIONS Wingspan, **22:** 27·7m (90ft 10½in), **22M** at 20° sweep: 34·45m (113ft 0in), at max 55°: 26·21m (86ft 0in); length, **22:** 40·53m (132ft 11½in), **22M:** 40·23m (132ft 0in); wing area (estimated), **22:** 145m² (1,550ft²), **22M:** 168m² (1,808ft²).

WEIGHTS (estimated) empty, **22:** 39000kg (86,000lb), **22M:** 48000kg (105,800lb); maximum loaded, **22:** 84000kg (185,000lb), **22M:** 122500kg (270,000lb).

ENGINES **22:** two augmented turbojets, believed to be 14000kg (31,000lb) Koliesov VD-7 or 13000kg (28,660lb) Soloviev D-15; **22M:** two augmented turbofans, believed 20000kg (44,090lb) Kuznetsov NK-144.

MAXIMUM SPEED (both clean, high altitude): **22:** 1480km/h (920mph, Mach 1·4), **22M:** 2125km/h (1,320mph, Mach 2).

SERVICE CEILING **22:** 18km (59,000ft), **22M:** 19km (62,350ft).

RANGE Clean, high-altitude **22:** 6500km (4,050 miles), **22M:** 8050km (5,000 miles).

MILITARY LOAD **22:** one NS-23 tail gun, internal bay for (**A**) about 10000kg (22,000lb) of bombs, (**B**) one Kitchen AS-4 supersonic missile recessed into bay, (**C**) none, (**D**) practice bombs; **22M:** twin 23mm guns in radar-directed tail turret, internal bay for up to 12000kg (26,455lb) of nuclear or conventional bombs, plus external racks under inlet ducts for 10000kg (22,050lb) of free-fall bombs or wing pylons for one or two Kitchen AS-4 or Kingfish AS-6 stand-off missiles.

USERS **22:** Iraq, Libya, Soviet Union, **22M:** Soviet Union.

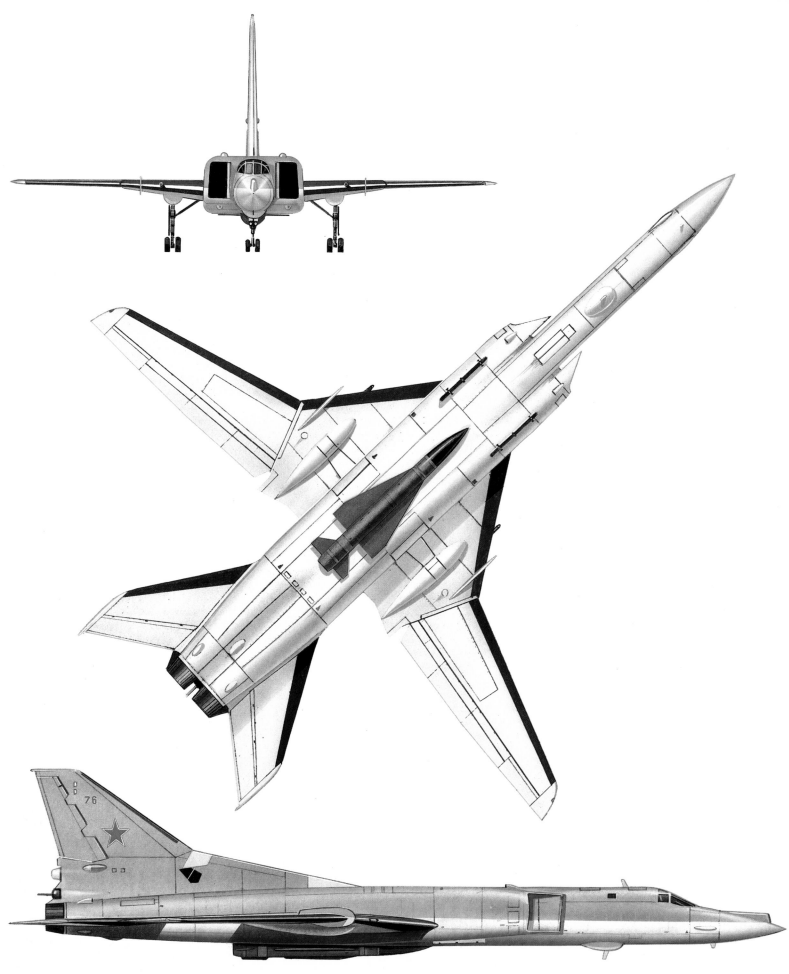

Tupolev Tu-22M
(Backfire B)

Believed to have the Soviet
designation Tu-22M, despite the
separation by two generations of
development from the Tu-22, the
long-range strike and multi-role
reconnaissance platform, known to
NATO as Backfire-B, is a powerful
and capable aircraft with no
counterpart in the West. Deliveries
from the Kazan factory appear to
be divided approximately 50/50
between the ADD (long-range
aviation) and AV-MF (naval
aviation). Most of the examples
intercepted by Western fighters
have been from the AV-MF and
they have shown numerous (mostly
minor) differences. For example,
this aircraft, tail number 76, has the
blunt main tail radome (used
among other things by the aerial of
the gunlaying radar) which may
have higher drag than the long
pointed variety. An AS-4 'Kitchen'
attack missile is recessed under
the centreline (precluding carriage
of weapons internally, although the
weapon bay may be occupied by
fuel) and the large racks under the
inlet ducts are not loaded.
Different views show the probe fitted
and removed (as it was in 1979–81)
and outer wings at minimum and
maximum sweep angles. The AS-6
'Kingfish' missile is expected
eventually to be carried by this
aircraft, probably on wing pylons
as it is on the subsonic Tu-16
Badger. Landing-gear geometry in
this drawing is speculative.

0   4m

Tupolev Tu-22/-22M/Blackjack

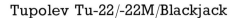

The basic production aircraft in the Tu-22 family is the free-fall bomber called Blinder-A by NATO. This example from the VVS (Soviet air forces) is unpainted and is fitted with the retractable inflight-refuelling probe. The small number in use are believed to serve with the DA (Long-Range Aviation).

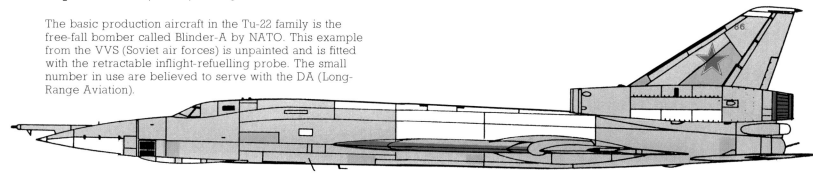

Blinder-B is a variant modified to carry the supersonic long-range missile known to NATO as AS-4 'Kitchen'. The missile is carried half-recessed inside the weapon bay, whose double-fold doors incorporate removable portions to leave a cut-out shaped to fit the missile. Strike cameras are housed in the landing-gear fairings. FR probe is white.

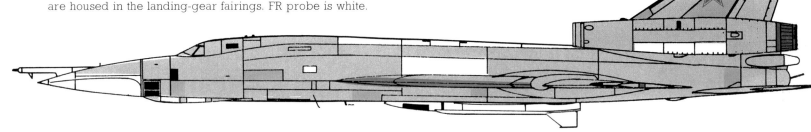

This Blinder-C reconnaissance aircraft is one of about 60 delivered in 1968-70 to the Soviet AVMF (naval air force), of which some 40 still serve in this role, the rest being apparently modified for various EW (electronic warfare) duties. Ten dark and three light rectangular panels along the underside denote the locations of optical cameras and other sensors.

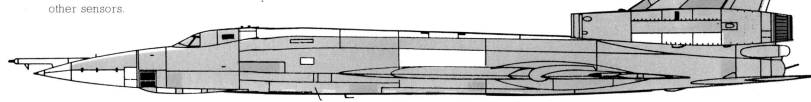

In 1973 a force of 12 Blinder-A bombers was supplied to the air force of Iraq, which at that time was receiving massive Soviet arms supplies. It has no probe and probably lacks some avionic items which the Soviet Union regards as technically sensitive, but several of these powerful aircraft participated in the war with Iran.

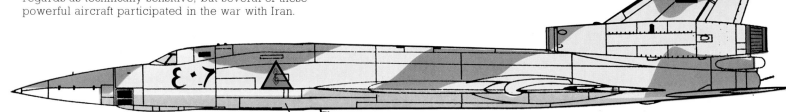

196

According to published records the Libyan Arab
Republic's air force received 20 Blinder-B missile-carriers,
but this particular aircraft is outwardly a Blinder-A with a
smaller main mapping/bombing radar (Blinder-B radar is
bulged hamster-cheek style). Probes were removed.

In the Blinder-D dual-pilot version the instructor occupies
an additional pilot cockpit which replaces the rearmost of
the three cockpits in other models. The new cockpit is at a
higher level and like the original pilot station has an
upward-ejection seat (the other seats in regular bomber
versions eject downwards).

This Backfire-B of the AVMF (naval air force) has made
several missions in the neighbourhood of Swedish
airspace, showing off its external bomb racks and blunt tail
radar (an alternative rear-facing radome is streamlined).
The probe is shown removed.

Highly provisional, and drawn to a smaller scale, this
drawing completes the current family of Tupolev strategic
jets by showing the enormous and extremely long-ranged
swing-wing bomber first dubbed Ram-P and now named
Blackjack by NATO. Larger than the B-1, this aircraft has
been in flight test since 1981, and is expected to become
operational at about the same time as the B-1 in 1985–6.

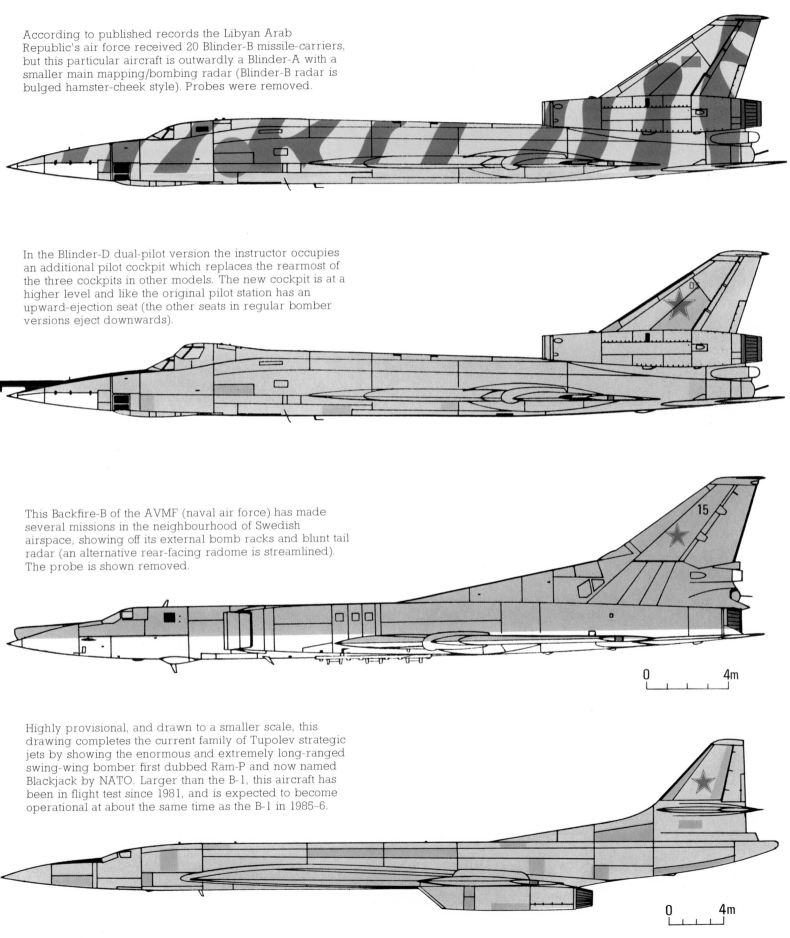

0   4m

0   4m

Vought A-7K
Corsair II

This aircraft was the first A-7K two-seater to be assigned to the Air National Guard; the recipient unit was the 162nd Tactical Fighter Training Group, Arizona ANG, based at Tucson. This unit has since carried out conversion training for the other 13 ANG Corsair squadrons. It has 16 of these dual-control machines, the other squadrons being scheduled eventually to receive two A-7Ks each for on-base refresher training and checks. The A-7K is a fully operational aircraft, despite the additional cockpit, and this example is shown with 1136-litre (250 gal, 300 US gal) tanks, fuselage pylons under the wing roots each rated at 227kg (500lb), and outer wing pylons carrying Maverick missiles and triple Mk 82 bombs. Note the Pave Penny laser receiver under the nose and the anti-collision beacon above the dorsal refuelling receptacle, compatible with the boom of a KC-135 or KC-10A.

0   4m

Vought A-7 Corsair

Outwardly almost indistinguishable from later Corsairs, the first of the three A-7A prototypes (BuAer 152580) made its first flight on 27 September 1965. It is depicted completely clean, but with the instrumentation boom.

This aircraft was the fifth of the 199 production A-7As for the US Navy. Early aircraft all went to various test and training programmes, carrying assorted weapons and tanks, and doing catapult and deck trials. This Corsair went to the Pacific Missile Test Center.

Aircraft BuAer 154390 was the 30th of the 196 A-7Bs, similar to the first model except for a slight uprating of the TF30 engine. It was used in Vietnam by VA-155 'The Silver Foxes', at the time embarked aboard USS *Roosevelt* as an element of CVW-19.

This aircraft, BuAer 156770, was one of the first 67 bought as A-7Es but retaining the TF30 engine and thus designated A-7C. New features included an M61 multi-barrel gun and ventral doppler blister. Unit: VX-5 'The Vampires' at China Lake, California.

The TA-7Cs are all rebuilds, from 24 A-7Bs and 36 A-7Cs, all retaining the original engine, but fitted with the complete A-7E nav/attack avionics. This example, BuAer 154531, was operated by VA-122 'The Flying Eagles', in the Pacific Fleet with home base NAS Lemoore, California.

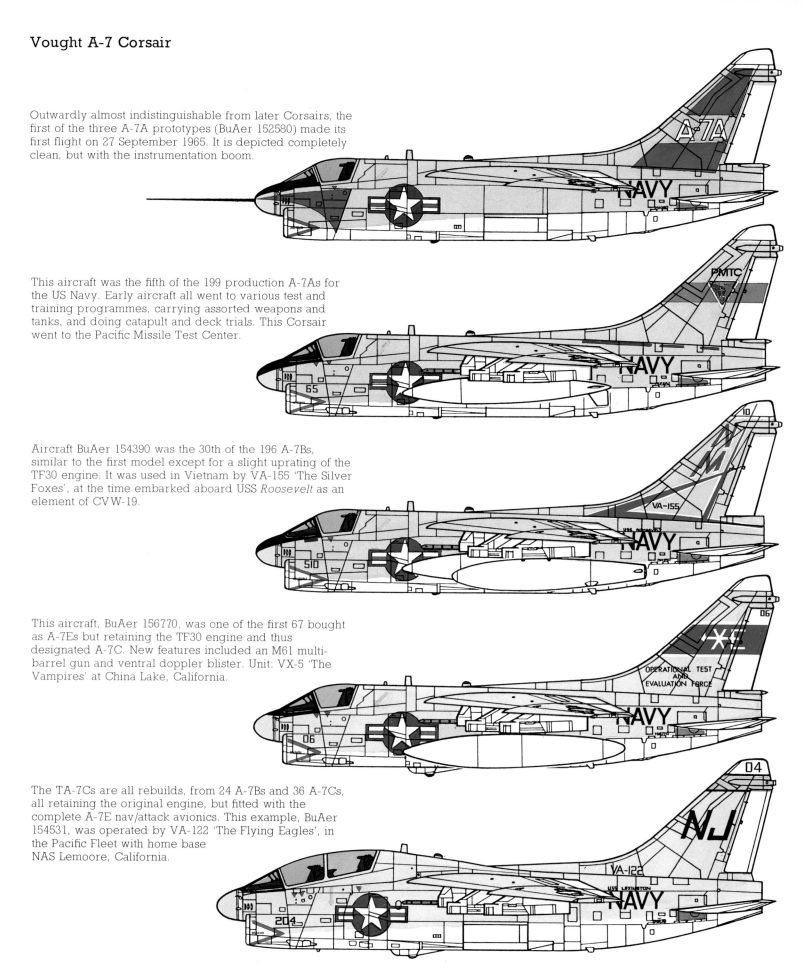

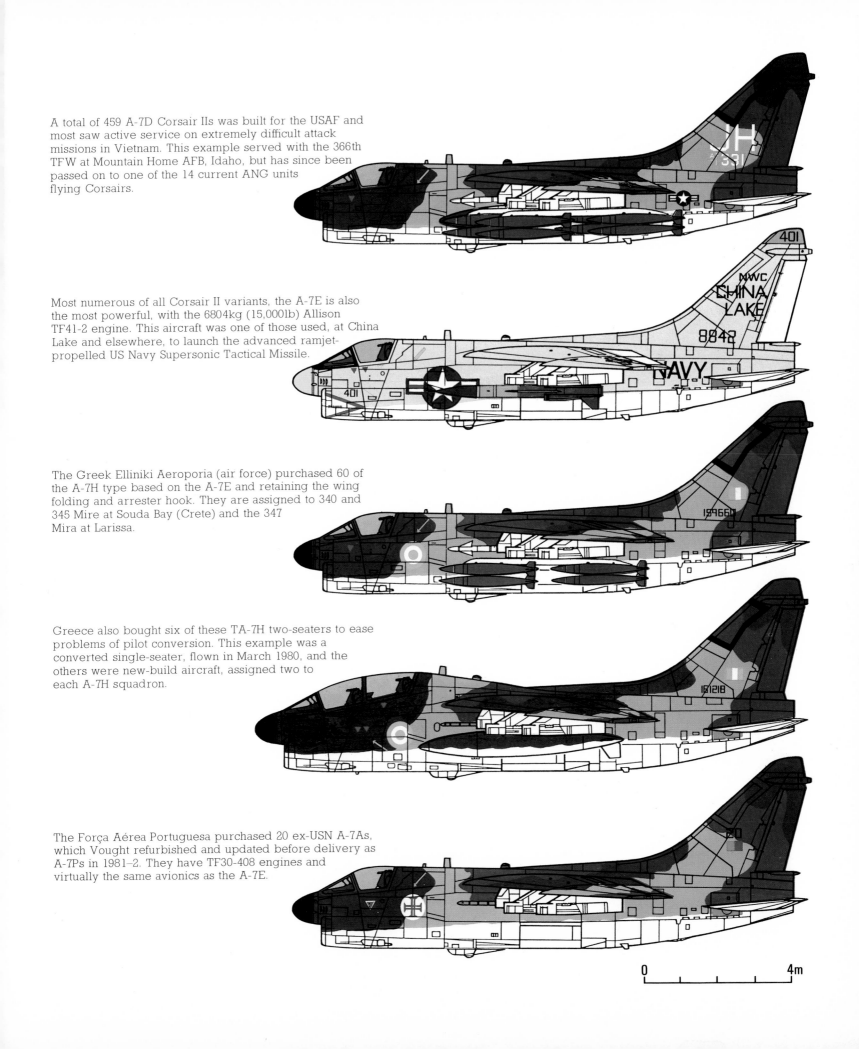

A total of 459 A-7D Corsair IIs was built for the USAF and most saw active service on extremely difficult attack missions in Vietnam. This example served with the 366th TFW at Mountain Home AFB, Idaho, but has since been passed on to one of the 14 current ANG units flying Corsairs.

Most numerous of all Corsair II variants, the A-7E is also the most powerful, with the 6804kg (15,000lb) Allison TF41-2 engine. This aircraft was one of those used, at China Lake and elsewhere, to launch the advanced ramjet-propelled US Navy Supersonic Tactical Missile.

The Greek Elliniki Aeroporia (air force) purchased 60 of the A-7H type based on the A-7E and retaining the wing folding and arrester hook. They are assigned to 340 and 345 Mire at Souda Bay (Crete) and the 347 Mira at Larissa.

Greece also bought six of these TA-7H two-seaters to ease problems of pilot conversion. This example was a converted single-seater, flown in March 1980, and the others were new-build aircraft, assigned two to each A-7H squadron.

The Força Aérea Portuguesa purchased 20 ex-USN A-7As, which Vought refurbished and updated before delivery as A-7Ps in 1981–2. They have TF30-408 engines and virtually the same avionics as the A-7E.

0   4m

Vought A-7 Corsair II

In the late 1950s the Vought F-8 Crusader was the best fighter operating from the decks of carriers, with speed in one version as high as Mach 2. Its builders extended the production run to 1,259 aircraft, many of which were subsequently remanufactured at a price not far short of the cost new; but who would have guessed that Vought would then establish a second programme, for 1,550, by redesigning the F-8 to cut its speed by more than half!

When it studied a replacement for the A-4 Skyhawk attack aircraft in 1960 the US Navy automatically called for supersonic speed, but by early 1963 it had learned better and instead it asked for heavy bombload, long range and a low price. On 11 February 1964 Vought (then called LTV Aerospace) was named winner with the A-7, which the Navy said would 'provide more strike capability per dollar than any other aircraft either in the inventory or on the drawing board'. It looked like an F-8 that had run into a brick wall, and was soon called the SLUF by its pilots, for 'short little ugly fella'.

Its wing was deeper than the thin supersonic wing of the F-8, making it lighter and able to hold more fuel; and it did not need to be pivoted for variable-incidence in the unique style of the F-8. The ailerons were moved outboard, spoilers added and the leading edge hinged to form droop flaps from root to tip. The large augmented turbojet was replaced by an unaugmented turbofan, and the tall but stumpy fuselage was covered in panels giving instant access to the navigation and weapon-delivery avionics. Not least, six deep pylons were bolted under the wing, and two on the sides of the fuselage, able to carry a design bombload of 9072kg (20,000lb).

The first A-7A flew on 27 September 1965, and delivery to Navy squadrons began on 14 October 1966. A year later Corsairs were in action in Vietnam, and the last of 199 of the A model was delivered in early 1968. By May 1969 Vought had delivered a further 196 of the B version, with a more powerful engine. So useful were they that the Corsair was adopted by the USAF; and

fitting a British-derived engine, the Allison/Rolls-Royce TF41, offered numerous advantages. In addition, the USAF's A-7D had a new gun and a more advanced navigation and weapon-aiming system which greatly enhanced its ability to hit point targets at night or in bad weather. Vought built 459 of the D type. They had a brilliant career with TAC (Tactical Air Command), seeing much SE Asia combat, and today equip 14 Air National Guard squadrons.

The last important version was the Navy A-7E, which kept all the new features of the D plus a more powerful TF41 and a folding flight-refuelling probe instead of the D's boom receptacle. The first 67 Es had the TF30 engine, and 36 were rebuilt as TA-7C dual trainers, as well as 24 Bs. The main run of A-7Es continued to No 596 in March 1981 and the force still equipped 26 Navy squadrons in late 1982. The Navy has updated 91 Es by an FLIR (forward-looking infra-red) pod, its image projected on the British Marconi HUD to improve night attack capability.

In 1975 deliveries began of 60 A-7H Corsairs to the Greek air force, based on the E and retaining folding wings. This customer also bought five TA-7Hs, similar to the TA-7C but without an FR probe. Portugal bought 20 refurbished As designated A-7P, with avionics virtually up to E standard.

While prospects exist for further export sales of refurbished A-7s, the run of new aircraft was extended by the adoption of a two-seat model for the Air National Guard. This final version, which resulted from the success of the TA-7C in the Navy, was originally to be the TA-7D, because it is basically a two-seat D. Its actual designation of A-7K reflects its new features and its retention of full combat capability. The dorsal fin is extended forwards to form a fairing over the large boom receptacle. Like some Ds, the K carries a Pave Penny laser marked-target receiver pod under the nose. The ANG is to receive 42 of these versatile two-seaters, deliveries of which began in 1981. The latest proposed advanced A-7 version is the A-7X with twin F404 engines.

COUNTRY OF ORIGIN USA.

CREW **Most:** 1, **TA-7C, TA-7H** and **A-7K:** 2.

TOTAL PRODUCED About 1,550.

DIMENSIONS Wingspan 11·8m (38ft 9in); length, **most:** 14·06m (46ft 1½in), **TA/K:** 14·92m (48ft 11½in); wing area 34·83m² (375ft²).

WEIGHTS Empty, **A:** 7214kg (15,904lb), **D:** 8951kg (19,733lb), **E:** 8592kg (18,942lb); maximum loaded, **A:** 17237kg (38,000lb), **D/E:** 19051kg (42,000lb).

ENGINE One unaugmented turbofan, **A:** 5150kg (11,350lb) Pratt & Whitney TF30-P-6, **B:** 5534kg (12,200lb) TF30-P-8, **P, TA-7C:** 6078kg (13,400lb) TF30-P-408, **D, K:** 6464kg (14,250lb) Allison TF41-A-1, **E:** 6804kg (15,000lb) TF41-A-2, **H:** 6804kg (15,000lb) TF41-A-400.

MAXIMUM SPEED Clean, sea level, **A, D:** 1091km/h (678mph), **E:** 1115km/h (693mph).

SERVICE CEILING Typical 13·1km (43,000ft).

RANGE With four drop tanks, **A:** 6600km (4,100 miles), **D:** 4899km (3,044 miles), **E:** 4604km (2861 miles).

MILITARY LOAD **A/B:** two 20mm Colt Mk 12 guns, two fuselage side pylons for AIM-9 Sidewinder AAMs (air-to-air missiles), four wing pylons each rated at 1588kg (3,500lb) and each plumbed for drop tank of 1136 litres (250 gal, 300 US gal) size plus two wing pylons each rated at 1134kg (2,500lb); **all other versions:** as above but 20mm guns replaced by one 20mm M61A-1 with 500 or 1,000 rounds.

USERS Greece, Portugal, USA (AF, ANG, Navy).

Yakovlev Yak-25/-28

Aleksandr S. Yakovlev had a 50-year active career in what used to be the perilous Soviet environment in which designers occasionally 'disappeared'. Today the situation is better, and for 20 years he has been the dean of his country's designers, called in to comment on every major programme.

His own designs embrace sports aircraft, trainers, fighters, helicopters, large jetliners and jet vertical-lift machines. His largest post-1945 family comprises a diverse group of twin-jets which all stemmed from the Yak-25 night and all-weather fighter produced in answer to a Kremlin request of 18 November 1951. Winning over the rival La-200B and MiG I-320(R), it boldly opted for a new configuration—something Russians try to avoid—with twin jets slung under a mid-mounted swept wing notable for its complete absence of taper, a swept tail with high tailplane, and tandem landing gears, almost all the weight being supported by the rear unit just behind the aircraft's centre of gravity. Small outrigger wheels were extended below the wingtips, the whole arrangement being just like today's Harrier. The enormous radar, called Scan Three by NATO, filled the bulky nose, and the pilot and observer sat in tandem ejection seats. Armament comprised two massive NS-37 guns under the fuselage, plus a retractable box of rockets.

More than a thousand Yak-25s were built; NATO called the type Flashlight. The -25R was a reconnaissance version, the -25U a dual trainer, and a single-seater known as the RV had a long-span unswept wing for ultra-high-altitude reconnaissance in the style of the U-2. Many Yak-25s withdrawn from PVO (air defence forces) units in the 1960s were converted as pilotless targets.

From this original family the Yak OKB (design collective) developed many later types known by Western code-names Flashlight-C and -D, Mangrove, Brewer, Firebar and Maestro; confusingly, the true designations have never been discovered. Flashlight-C introduced the first aerodynamic improvement with an extended-chord wing centre section with acute leading-edge sweep, and, later, the extended-chord outer wings of -D which were also stretched beyond the tip gears. By 1956 R-11 engines were fitted in lengthened nacelles.

By 1958 major development had led to the new Yak-28 family (Brewer bomber/recon models and Firebar interceptors). These are larger and heavier, have further aerodynamic improvements to take advantage of the augmented (afterburning) engines, and almost completely new airframes with the wing raised nearer the top of the fuselage and tandem twin-wheel main landing gears spaced far apart under the front and rear fuselage.

One reason for the raising of the wing was to allow for a large internal bay, used in Brewer versions for bombs, reconnaissance cameras and other sensors or for various jammers and sensors in EW (electronic warfare) models. Almost all Brewer versions have a glazed nose for the navigator, observer, recon-systems operator or EW officer, with the pilot in a single-seat fighter-type cockpit behind. Brewer-A/B/C attack versions have one or two 30mm guns submerged in the forward fuselage, and almost always a mapping and bombing radar ahead of the bomb bay. Brewer-D is a multi-sensor recon version still widely used, and Brewer-E a family of EW aircraft. The Yak-28U (Maestro) trainer has stepped pupil and instructor cockpits with hinged canopies, and is one of various versions with shorter engine inlets, with more prominent centrebodies.

The Yak-28P (Firebar) interceptors are becoming obsolescent, but in 1982 about 300 were still in use. This was the successor to the original Yak-25, with the new airframe, fuel instead of a weapons bay, tandem cockpits further forward than in any Brewer, powerful Skip Spin radar (in later aircraft faired under an extremely pointed radome) and armament of two Anab missiles, one guided by radar and the other with IR (infra red) homing. Some -28Ps can also carry two Atoll close-range missiles, and all have tail-warning radar.

COUNTRY OF ORIGIN Soviet Union.

CREW Except RV: 2, **RV:** 1.

TOTAL PRODUCED **Yak-25:** about 2,000, **Yak-28:** about 2,000.

DIMENSIONS Wingspan, **25:** 12·34m (40ft 5¾in), **RV:** about 21·5m (70ft 6in), **28P:** 12·95m (42ft 6in); length, **25:** 16·65m (54ft 7½in), **RV:** about 15·5m (51ft 0in), **28P:** 21·65m (71ft 0½in); wing area, **25:** about 36m² (334ft²), **28P:** about 37·6m² (405ft²).

WEIGHTS (estimated) Empty, **25:** 9850kg (21,715lb), **28P:** 12250kg (27,000lb); maximum loaded, **25:** 14000kg (30,900lb), **28P:** 20000kg (44,100lb).

ENGINES **25:** two 3600kg (7936lb) Tumanskii (ex-Mikulin) RD-9B augmented turbojets; **RV:** two 2700kg (5,952lb) RD-9 unaugmented turbojets; **28P and most Brewers:** two 5950kg (13,120lb) R-11 augmented turbojets.

MAXIMUM SPEED **25:** 1015km/h (631mph) at low altitude, falling to 956km/h (594mph) at high altitude; **RV:** about 800km/h (500mph); **28P:** 1180km/h (733mph, Mach 1·1) at high altitude.

SERVICE CEILING **25:** 14km (45,900ft), **RV:** 21km (69,000ft), **28P:** 16·75km (55,000ft).

RANGE **25:** about 2000km (1,240 miles), **RV:** about 3200km (2,000 miles), **28P:** 2575km (1,600 miles).

MILITARY LOAD **25:** two NS-37 guns, plus provision for box of unknown number of 55mm rockets; **RV:** none; **28P:** one IR Anab and one radar Anab plus provision for two Advanced Atoll or Aphid close-range missiles.

USER Soviet Union.

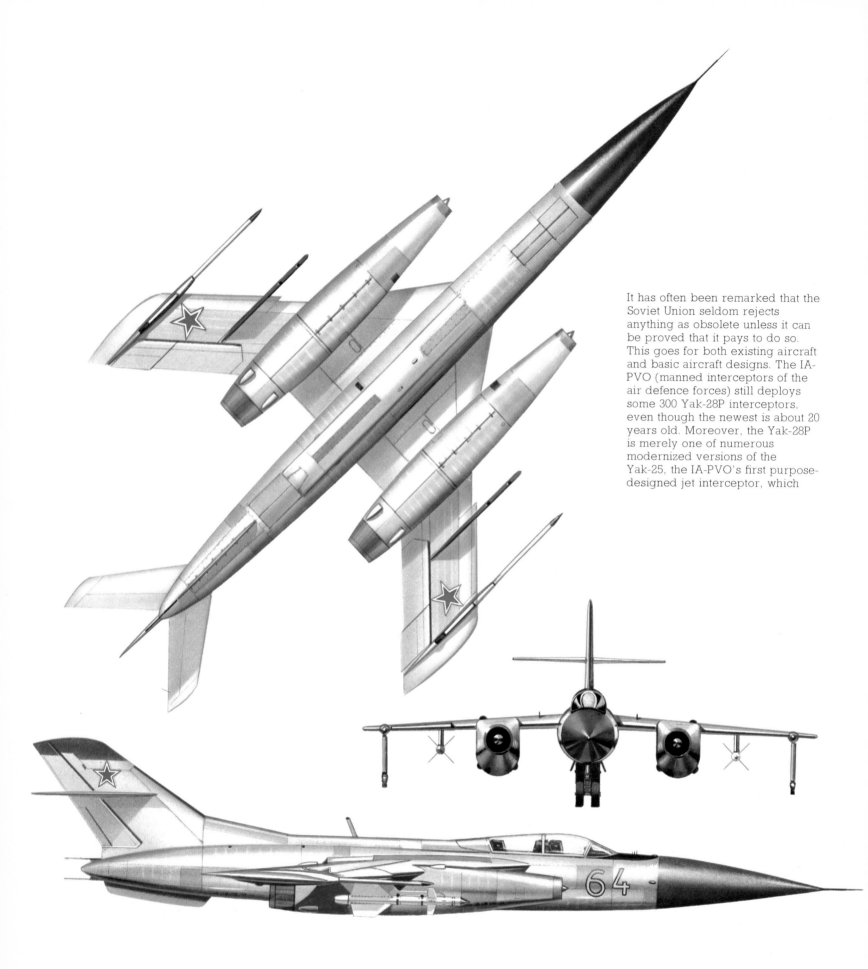

It has often been remarked that the Soviet Union seldom rejects anything as obsolete unless it can be proved that it pays to do so. This goes for both existing aircraft and basic aircraft designs. The IA-PVO (manned interceptors of the air defence forces) still deploys some 300 Yak-28P interceptors, even though the newest is about 20 years old. Moreover, the Yak-28P is merely one of numerous modernized versions of the Yak-25, the IA-PVO's first purpose-designed jet interceptor, which

Yakovlev
Yak-28P

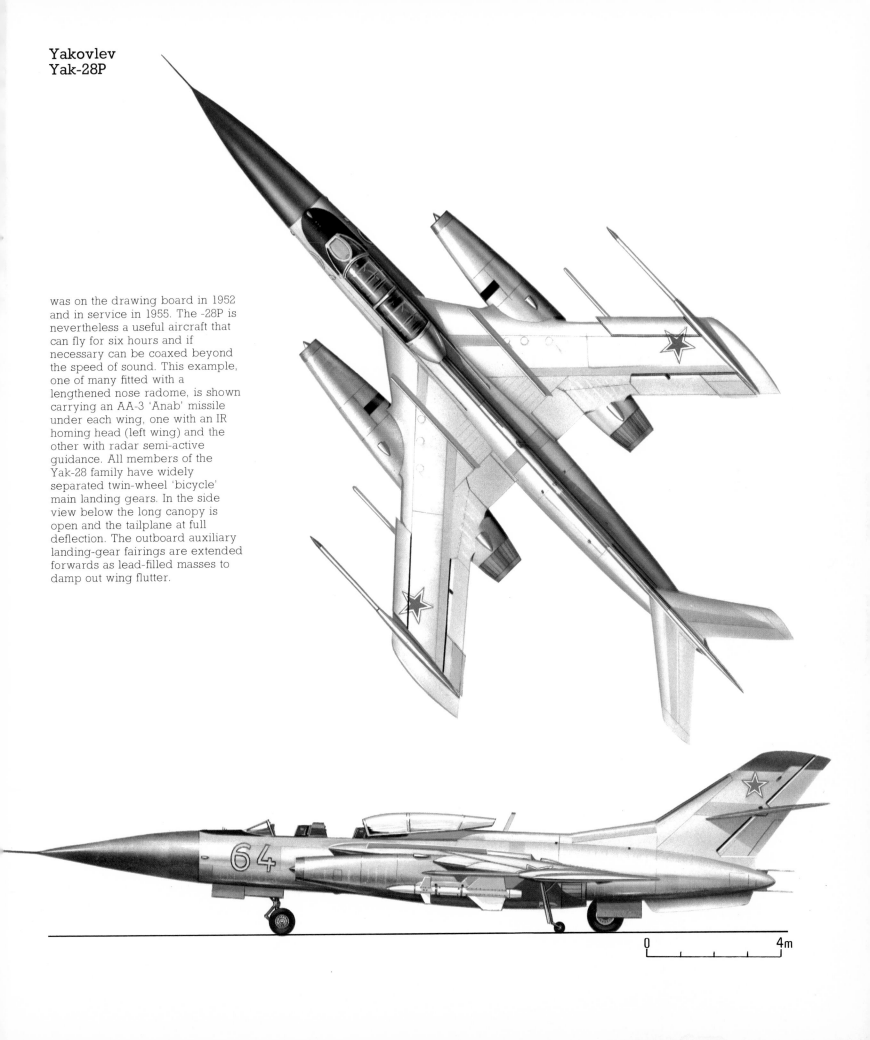

was on the drawing board in 1952 and in service in 1955. The -28P is nevertheless a useful aircraft that can fly for six hours and if necessary can be coaxed beyond the speed of sound. This example, one of many fitted with a lengthened nose radome, is shown carrying an AA-3 'Anab' missile under each wing, one with an IR homing head (left wing) and the other with radar semi-active guidance. All members of the Yak-28 family have widely separated twin-wheel 'bicycle' main landing gears. In the side view below the long canopy is open and the tailplane at full deflection. The outboard auxiliary landing-gear fairings are extended forwards as lead-filled masses to damp out wing flutter.

0   4m

Yak-25/-28

This Yak-25 was almost certainly retained by the Yakovlev OKB for trials and development; the production interceptors did not have the red wings and fuselage trim. This aircraft was originally fitted with the two heavy 37mm guns that formed the basic armament under the fuselage.

Believed to be designated Yak-25RV (RV could stand for 'record height' or for 'high-altitude reconnaissance' in Russian), this development had unswept wings of over 21·25m (70ft) span, as well as a single-seat cockpit and many other changes. One of several -25RVs, it was the first of this family to fly with more powerful R-11 engines.

Code-named Brewer-A by NATO, and possibly a Yak-26, this tactical attack aircraft was one of the first production models of the second generation with augmented R-11 engines and redesigned airframe. The navigator sat in the nose compartment and had equipment for visual bombing. A 30mm gun was fitted on the right side of the fuselage.

Brewer-B differed chiefly in having a mapping and blind-bombing radar immediately aft of the nose landing gear. The aft-facing rod aerials at the tail have usually been considered in NATO to be rear-warning radar.

Brewer-C was the first production member of the family with a new long-chord wing with a dogtooth, underwing tanks for greater operational radius, and uprated (probably R-11F) engines with longer inlet ducts.

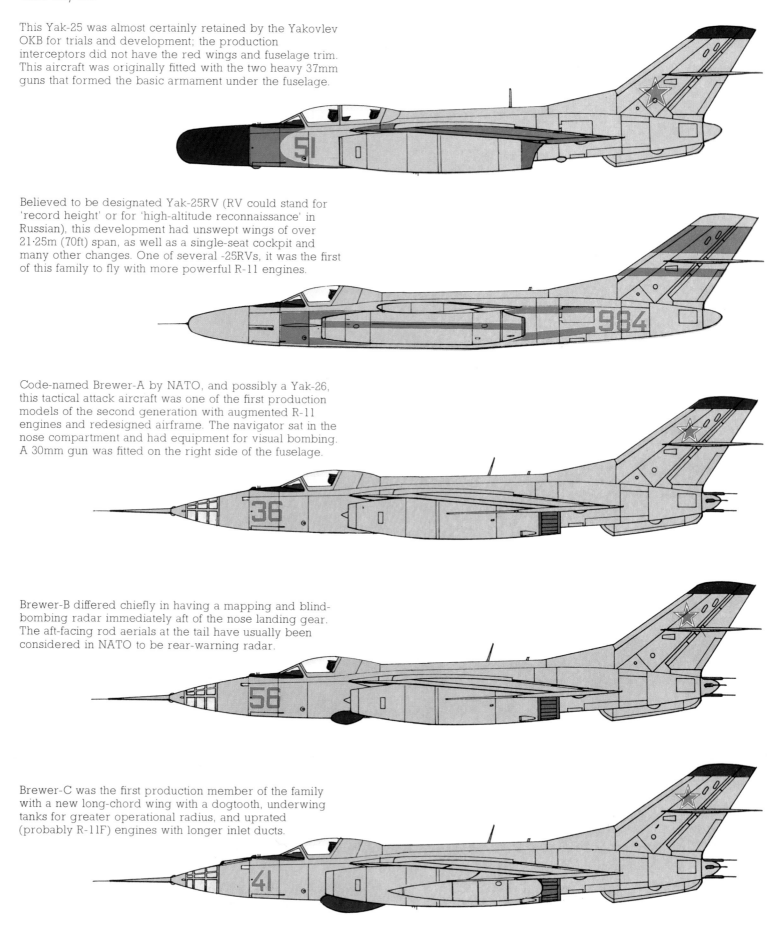

Brewer-D, like its predecessor undoubtedly a member of the Yak-28 family, is a dedicated reconnaissance aircraft with a large camera and IR linescan pallet carried in the former bomb bay (and hidden here by the engine nacelle). About 200 are believed to remain in service.

Brewer-E is an EW (electronic-warfare) aircraft, of which about 40 are believed to be used as active jammers and probably about the same number in other EW roles. Most have an unglazed nose, although the second crew member is still seated in the forward compartment. A large jammer pod occupies the weapon bay, and dispenser pods are carried under the outer wings.

The Yak-28U dual trainer has the low-rated engines, fed by short nacelles with prominently visible inlet bullets. The pupil's canopy cannot slide and so is hinged to open to the right. All armament is usually removed.

The first production Yak-28P interceptors had this radome, shorter and less pointed than the type now in use, although there is no evidence the radar itself has changed and the AA-3 'Anab' missiles remain the same. This aircraft is painted in what is believed to be a nuclear-radiation reflective finish.

0   4m

Cap badge, Marshals and Generals,
Soviet air force

Star applied to fin of Soviet aircraft

Pilot's sleeve patch,
Soviet air force

Glossary

AAM Air-to-air missile.
AB Airbase, military airfield.
AEW Airborne early warning.
AFB US Air Force base.
afterburner Jetpipe for turbojet in which extra fuel can be burned, giving temporary extra thrust.
AIM Air intercept missile.
ALCM Air-launched cruise missile.
AMI Aeronautica Militare Italiano.
Amraam Advanced medium-range AAM.
ANG Air National Guard, US state-by-state part-time air force.
anti-flutter body Heavy mass added to wingtip or tail to damp out flutter.
ASM Air-to-surface missile.
ASW Anti-submarine warfare.
augmentor Afterburner for turbofan in which extra fuel is burned in both fan air and hot core gas; hence 'augmented'.
avionics Aviation electronics: radio, radar, navaids, landing aids, air-data systems, autopilot, fire-control, weapon delivery and many others.
AV-MF Soviet naval air force.
blind Pilot has no external attitude reference, e.g. in cloud.
canard General term for tail-first, usually meaning horizontal auxiliary surface (fixed or movable) is ahead of wing.
canoe radar Has radome shaped like a canoe.
CAP Combat air patrol.
CCV Control-configured vehicle, aircraft aero-dynamically shaped and with masses so distributed as to have maximum manoeuvrability.
centrebody Streamlined shape, often a forward-facing cone or half-cone, to generate oblique shockwaves and improve flow into engine inlet at supersonic speeds.
chaff Small strips of aluminium foil sized to wavelengths of enemy radars and released in billions to generate false targets, obliterating whole radar display.
chord Distance across wing from leading edge to trailing edge, measured parallel to axis of fuselage.
Co-In Counter-insurgent.
collision-course Interception technique in which, instead of traditional stern-chase, defending aircraft aims direct for calculated future position of target.
core Basic gas turbine (compressor, combustor and turbines) of a turbofan; generates all power of engine, but fan (not part of core) generates most of thrust.
CVW Code for a US Navy carrier air wing made up of squadrons required for different missions.
DA Soviet long-range (bomber) force.
dedicated For that purpose only.
differential Describes tailplanes (tailerons) or spoilers that can be driven in opposite directions, e.g. left up and right down, to act as roll control.
DLI Deck-launched intercept.
dogtooth Sudden discontinuity, or abrupt kink, in leading edge to generate strong vortex improving upper-surface flow.
doppler Radar that measures changes in frequency of its waves reflected from target, e.g. to measure true speed of aircraft over Earth's surface or to pick out moving target against background.
dorsal Along upper surface of fuselage.
drogue Device towed behind aircraft and shaped to avoid unwanted oscillations, especially one fitted to free end of inflight-refuelling hose.
drop tank External fuel tank which when empty can be jettisoned.
ECM Electronic countermeasures.
ehp Equivalent horsepower, measure of power for turboprop that takes into account shaft power to propeller and also useful thrust from exhaust gas.
Elint Electronic intelligence, finding out about hostile radios, radars and other emitters.
emitter Device emitting electromagnetic signals.
ESM Electronic surveillance (or, in UK, support) measures.
EW Electronic warfare, which includes ECM, Elint, ESM and other activities.
EWSM Early-warning support measures.
FA Frontal aviation, Soviet tactical air forces.
FAC Forward air control, airborne observer who directs attack aircraft on to hidden and localized (so-called point) targets on ground.
Fast Fuel and sensor, tactical.
fence Fixed strip across upper surface of wing to force airflow to move directly across chord instead of (because of strong pressure gradient) flowing outwards towards tips.
fin Fixed vertical tail surface, called stabilizer in America.
first pass Flying at full throttle at treetop height directly across a point target, without having to stop and search for it.
flaperon Movable wing trailing-edge surface combining functions of flap (increase lift and, when necessary, drag) and aileron (provide roll control).
flare Formerly, device dropped to illuminate ground at night; today, intense source of IR (heat) ejected from attacking aircraft to draw away missiles.
FLIR Forward-looking infra-red; sensor for providing IR picture of terrain ahead.
flutter Potentially dangerous vibration of any part of aircraft caused by aerodynamic forces.
fly-by-wire Flight-control system in which commands are transmitted as electrical signals.
glove Fixed inner portion of swing wing.
hardpoint Place on aircraft strengthened for attachment of pylon.
HARM High-speed anti-radiation missile.
high-authority System with great power to control itself and/or the aircraft, implying extremely high reliability.
hi-lo-hi Flight profile of mission in which first part is flown hi (high altitude, typically higher than 11km, 36,000ft) for fuel economy; attack is flown lo (low-level, which depending on air force may be 300m/1,000ft or as low as 60m/200ft) to avoid being shot down; and return to base is again hi.
Hotas Hands on throttle and stick, objective being for pilot to have every control normally needed during a mission mounted on either engine throttle or top of control column.
HUD Head-up display, optical/avionic device, projecting numerical information, target and navigation symbols, gunfire and weapon-delivery information and possibly many other items on transparent screen ahead of pilot, all focused at infinity.
IFF Identification friend or foe, automatic avionic device which when interrogated by friendly aircraft or ground station instantly gives correct response; failure to do so brands target as hostile.
inertial Using accelerations imparted to vehicle, from the moment it begins to move from its parking spot, to determine its exact position at any subsequent moment.
IR Infra-red radiation (heat).
jammer High-power device for obliterating all useful radio or radar transmissions on particular wavelength(s).
Labs Low-altitude bombing system, specifically a system for tossing a nuclear bomb high to give aircraft time to escape.
Lantirn Low-altitude navigation targeting IR for night.
LEX Leading-edge extension, a large strake added ahead of inner leading edge to generate powerful vortex and increase aircraft manoeuvrability.
Linescan Sensor resembling TV but working on IR wavelength which builds up detailed line-by-line picture of ground beneath.
Mach number Aircraft speed expressed as decimal fraction of local speed of sound; Mach 1 is 1225km/h (761mph) in warm air at sea level but only 1062km/h (660mph) in cold air at high altitude.
MAD Magnetic-anomaly detector, finds submerged submarines by detecting small changes in strength/direction of local terrestrial magnetic field.
marked target Ground target illuminated by friendly laser, aimed by troops or by cooperating aircraft, on to which smart weapon will home.
MR Maritime reconnaissance.
multi-mode radar One capable of being used for navigation, attack on surface targets, interception of hostile aircraft, avoiding surface obstructions and possibly other tasks, as distinct from one that, for example, may be good for navigation but unable to see a hostile aircraft.
NAS US naval air station.
N/AW Night/adverse weather.
OAS Offensive avionics system, powerful emitting/jamming/decoy system to enable bomber to navigate, find target, deliver bombs and defeat hostile defence systems.
OKB Experimental design bureau (Soviet Union).
pitot boom Forward-pointing probe carrying apertures that sense local atmospheric pressure and also pitot (ram) pressure generated in forward-facing inlet, difference giving a measure of airspeed.
pitot inlet Any plain hole, without a centrebody or other device to improve airflow.
pod Streamlined container for load carried externally.
point target One of small dimensions, such as bridge, tank or radar, which with conventional weapons demands great delivery accuracy.
probe Rigid tube pointing directly ahead, e.g. to carry pitot instrumentation, or forming self-sealing fuel inlet pipe to engage in drogue on tanker's hose.
PVO Soviet air-defence forces.
pylon Streamlined connector between aircraft and something carried externally, e.g. engine, radar, bomb or tank.
radome Electrically transparent streamlined fairing over radar aerial system.
ram inlet Forward-facing inlet designed to generate highest possible pressure and maximum airflow in duct downstream; ram pressure results from bringing molecules of air to low velocity relative to aircraft, converting kinetic energy to pressure energy.
recon Reconnaissance, using cameras, radars, IR and TV to obtain information on hostile activities.
RPV Remotely piloted vehicle, small aircraft controlled by pilot not flying in it.
SAC Strategic Air Command, part of USAF.
SAM Surface-to-air missile.
shock Shockwave, generated when air encounters solid body moving at over Mach 1; at Mach 1 wave is almost perpendicular but it leans back at increasing angle as Mach number increases. Hence shock body, solid body whose function is to generate shockwave at particular location.
shp Shaft horsepower.
signature Characteristic features of emission from radar or any other emitter denoted by wavelength(s), pulse repetition frequency, modulation and other variables which can identify the emitter, just as fingerprint can identify a human.
SLAR Side-looking airborne radar, a reconnaissance sensor.
smart Precision-guided by laser (rarely, by other means).
sonobuoy Packaged device dipped or dropped into ocean to detect submarine; passive buoy listens for target noises, active buoy emits intense ultrasonic signals and listens for reflections.
spoiler Surface hinged above upper surface of wing to cause increased drag and reduced lift; used differentially can provide roll control.
SRAM Short-range attack missile.
stealth Technology that attempts to reduce all signatures of aircraft so close to zero that detection from a distance is extremely difficult, especially when bomber has its own clever avionic systems to cause masking or confusion.
STOL Short take-off and landing.
STOVL Short take-off, vertical landing (Harrier mission).
strake Usually narrow forward extension from root of wing, or fence-like strip along fuselage, to improve airflow.
supercirculation Internal system in aircraft for sucking and/or blowing through slits or porous areas to increase lift or reduce drag; simplest form is blown flap, in which high-pressure air is ejected at about speed of sound across upper surface of depressed wing flaps.
swing wing Variable-sweep wing.
synthetic-aperture radar Advanced form of radar which by phasing its emissions in time creates same effect as signals emitted from radar of colossal physical dimensions.
Tacco Tactical co-ordinator.
taileron Differential tailplane, able to act as ailerons.
tailplane Horizontal tail, formerly fixed but in modern combat aircraft usually a powered primary control surface, called horizontal stabilizer in North America.
Tarps Tactical aircraft recon-pod system.
TFS, TFW USAF Tactical Fighter Squadron or Wing.
TRAM Target-recognition attack multisensor.
turbofan Turbojet with greatly enlarged low-pressure compressor (or fan) generating large flow of air of which part goes through core and rest is expelled as cool jet; more efficient than turbojet.
turbojet Simplest gas turbine, comprising compressor, combustor and turbine, with simple jetpipe giving thrust.
USS United States Ship.
variable-geometry Capable of changing its shape; usually means variable-sweep.
variable-incidence Wing whose incidence (angular setting on the fuselage) can be controlled by the pilot, usually to tilt fuselage nose-down for landing instead of having to land at steep nose-up attitude with poor view ahead.
variable inlet Engine inlet whose shape, area and profile can vary (usually automatically) according to engine power and flight Mach number and altitude.
variable-sweep Capable of having wing sweepback angle controlled by the pilot, or by automatic system, to match shape of aircraft to low speed (minimum sweep) or high supersonic speed (maximum sweep).
ventral On underside of fuselage.
VFR Visual flight rules, i.e. good daytime weather.
Viff Vectoring (of Pegasus engine nozzles) in forward flight, to enhance manoeuvrability.
VTOL Vertical take-off and landing.
VVS Soviet air forces.
zero/zero Capable of being safely used at zero height and zero speed (most older ejection seats could be used safely only with aircraft above a lower speed limit, and often only above a lower limit of altitude).